AIRPOWER
AND THE
NORMANDY CAMPAIGN

AIRPOWER
AND THE
NORMANDY CAMPAIGN

EDITED BY
MIKE BECHTHOLD

Naval Institute Press
Annapolis, Maryland

Naval Institute Press
291 Wood Road
Annapolis, MD 21402

© 2025 by the U.S. Naval Institute
All rights reserved. No part of this book may be reproduced or utilized in any form or by any means, electronic or mechanical, including photocopying and recording, or by any information storage and retrieval system, without permission in writing from the publisher.

Library of Congress Cataloging-in-Publication Data

Names: Bechthold, Michael, editor
Title: Airpower and the Normandy Campaign / edited by Mike Bechthold.
Description: Annapolis, MD : Naval Institute Press, [2025] | Includes
  bibliographical references and index.
Identifiers: LCCN 2025012111 (print) | LCCN 2025012112 (ebook) | ISBN
  9781682478271 hardcover | ISBN 9781682478288 ebook
Subjects: LCSH: World War, 1939-1945—Campaigns—France—Normandy | World
  War, 1939-1945—Aerial operations | World War, 1939-1945—Regimental
  histories | Normandy (France)—History, Military—20th century | Air
  warfare—History—20th century | Air power
Classification: LCC D756.5.N6 .A35 2025 (print) | LCC D756.5.N6 (ebook)
LC record available at https://lccn.loc.gov/2025012111
LC ebook record available at https://lccn.loc.gov/2025012112

♾ Print editions meet the requirements of ANSI/NISO z39.48-1992 (Permanence of Paper). Printed in the United States of America.

9 8 7 6 5 4 3 2 1

Maps and figures created by Mike Bechthold.

CONTENTS

List of Illustrations — vii

Acknowledgments — xi

Introduction — 1
Mike Bechthold

PART 1. PREPARATIONS FOR THE CAMPAIGN

1. The Air War for Normandy, 1944: How to Apply Airpower for Victory — 19
   S. Mike Pavelec

2. The Transportation Plan: A Reassessment — 37
   Stephen Moore

3. Derailing the Wehrmacht?: The Debate and Implementation of the Transportation Plan — 62
   Sebastian Cox

4. All Roads Lead to Normandy, Not Berlin: Leadership's Self-Imposed Challenges on U.S. Bomber Crews' Combat Motivation — 82
   Heather Venable

5. Blinding the Enemy: The Radar War before D-Day — 105
   Matthew Bone

PART 2. THE NORMANDY CAMPAIGN

6. Air Control from the Sea: Tactical Air Command and Control during Operation Neptune — *Christopher Finn* — 133

7. The French Connection: Civilians under the Bombs for the First Forty-Eight Hours — *Stephen A. Bourque* — 156

8. Airpower in a Set-Piece Attack: U.S. Ninth Air Force and the Capture of Cherbourg, 22–30 June 1944 — *Mike Bechthold* — 178

9. The Blunted Harpoon: Luftwaffe Antishipping Operations off Normandy, June–August 1944 — *Russell A. Hart* — 203

10. The Allied Tactical Airpower System in Normandy — *Paul Johnston* — 234

11. The Air Support Rollercoaster: Canadian Soldiers' Morale in Normandy — *Alexander Fitzgerald-Black* — 261

12. Airpower Lessons Learned and Mislearned: A Comparative Analysis of Heavy Bomber Support in Operations Cobra and Queen — *Christopher M. Rein* — 284

13. One Nation, Many Headlines: The Royal Australian Air Force Contribution to the Normandy Campaign as Portrayed by Contemporary Print Media — *Adam Lunney* — 306

Concluding Thoughts — *Mike Bechthold* — 328

Contributors — 335

Index — 341

ILLUSTRATIONS

FIGURES

6-1	Plan of Operations Flat aboard HMS *Largs*	142
6-2	Fighter Direction Tender Configuration	145
6-3	*FDT 217*, Labeled	145
6-4	Eastern Task Force Communications Links	146
10-1	Impromptu Request Procedure with Standard Tentacle	249
10-2	Impromptu Request Procedure with FCP or VCP	250

MAPS

1-1	Normandy	16
2-1	Major Railway Targets in the Transportation Plan (Strategic Air Forces Only)	43
2-2	Reichsbahn Survey of Rail Transport Attacks	54
5-1	German Radar Sites	117
6-1	Normandy Fighter Patrol Areas	138
8-1	Cherbourg	187
11-1	Normandy: The Canadian Sector	266
11-2	The Shambles	278
11-3	The Chase	279
12-1	Bomb Plot, Operation Cobra, 25 July 1944	288
12-2	Marking Devices, Operation Queen	296
12-3	Bomb Plots, Operation Queen, Eschweiler	299

PHOTOGRAPHS

1-1	Air Chief Marshal Sir Arthur Harris and Major General Ira Eaker	23
1-2	B-26 Marauder over Normandy beaches	31
2-1	Blainville marshaling yard	48
2-2	Attack on the Châlons-sur-Marne marshaling yard	49
3-1	Meeting of the Supreme Command	64
3-2	Trappes marshaling yard	73
4-1	B-24 Liberator crew	86
4-2	B-17 Flying Fortress crew	90
5-1	Giant Würzburg radar	107
5-2	Wasserman (Chimney) radar	109
5-3	King George VI inspects a Hawker Typhoon Mark Ib	115
6-1	Task force heading to Omaha Beach, 6 June 1944	141
7-1	Lisieux after the Allied bombardment, June 1944	157
7-2	Argentan marshaling yard	168
7-3	French boys watching Allied convoy, 28 July 1944	173
8-1	Generalleutnant Karl-Wilhelm von Schlieben and Lieutenant General J. Lawton Collins, 27 June 1944	182
8-2	Lieutenant General Lewis Brereton and General Elwood R. Quesada, 8 June 1944	184
8-3	Douglas A-20 over Cherbourg Peninsula, 22 June 1944	191
9-1	Mulberry harbor off Omaha Beach	206
9-2	Mistel Ju 88 carrying an Fw 190	223
10-1	U.S. air support party	244
10-2	Visual control post in Normandy	246
10-3	P-47 Thunderbolt flying armored column cover	247
11-1	Canadian troops watch Operation Totalize bombing	272
11-2	Ammunition truck burning during Canadian advance, 8 August 1944	273
12-1	U.S. soldiers dig out fellow soldiers, 25 July 1944	289
12-2	Aerial-recognition panels mark Allied front lines, 16 November 1944	297

12-3	B-26 Marauder over Weisweiler	300
13-1	Duke of Gloucester, 9 March 1944	309
13-2	French children show interest in RAAF Spitfire, July 1944	319
14-1	Bombing raid on Saint-Lô, 7 June 1944	330
14-2	Bulldozers clear the roads through Saint-Lô, July 1944	331

TABLES

0-1	Sorties Flown by Allied Air Forces, 1 April–5 June 1944	3
0-2	Sorties Flown by Allied Air Forces, 6 June–31 August 1944	4
0-3	Aircrew and Aircraft Lost by Allied Air Forces, 1 April–31 August 1944	4
2-1	Strategic Transportation Plan Targets	42
2-2	Summary of Efforts against Railway Targets	51
2-3	Tons of Bombs Dropped, March–June 1944	52
2-4	Attacks with over 100 Civilian Fatalities	56
4-1	Percentage of Pilots Willing to Return to European Theater	84
5-1	Probability of Physical Destruction of Enemy Radar Stations by Heavy and Medium Bombers	111
5-2	Probability of Physical Destruction of Enemy Radar Stations by Fighter-Bombers (Bombs)	113
5-3	Probability of Physical Destruction of Enemy Radar Stations by Fighter-Bombers (Rockets)	113
9-1	Luftwaffe Bomber Forces in Western Europe, 1 June 1944	205
9-2	Luftwaffe Bomber Unit Reinforcements, June–August 1944	208
10-1	Categories of Air Support	237
10-2	Light and Medium Bombers	239
10-3	Fighter-Bombers	240

ACKNOWLEDGMENTS

The question of air support in Normandy has long been at the heart of my academic career. Starting with my undergraduate thesis on operational research in Second Tactical Air Force and continuing with my master's thesis on the Ninth Air Force in Normandy, the topic has been of great interest. And not just to me. Over the last few decades, much has been published on airpower in World War II and Normandy in particular. Historians have greatly enriched our understanding of the topic. Normandy has also been a favorite topic for campaign studies. These books always discuss the air force but often in a secondary or supporting role. I remain surprised that to date there is no single-volume study of airpower in Normandy in all its guises—tactical, strategic, reconnaissance, naval, etc. This current volume is not that, but rather an attempt to return our discussion of airpower to the forefront of our understanding of the Normandy Campaign.

It seems counterintuitive for this book on airpower to be published by the Naval Institute Press, but their History of Military Aviation Series, ably directed by series editor Paul J. Springer, has quietly become one of the best airpower lists in the field.

Thank you to Adam Kane, the press director, for taking a chance on this project. Adam was the acquisitions editor for my first monograph, and it has been a pleasure working with him again on this project. His team, including Senior Acquisitions Editor Padraic (Pat) Carlin, Production Editor Brennan Knight, and the rest of the Naval Institute Press crew, has gone above and beyond to make this book a reality. I also have high praise for independent editor Kevin Brock, who had the unenviable task of bringing unity and structure to the words of a disparate collection of writers. This book is undoubtedly better due to his hard work.

Over the last two decades, the Royal Canadian Air Force Heritage Fund has provided essential funding for air force–related history and heritage projects. This fund supported the creation of maps and diagrams for this volume and for that I am grateful.

Finally, a very special thank you to all the contributors in this volume. Having edited several previous collections, I know well that the task of an editor can be thankless and managing the contributors like herding cats. I'm pleased to say that this collection of authors has (mostly) defied those stereotypes. They have met deadlines and responded promptly to all queries to make this project a success. All have given freely of their time to produce first-class academic studies of the air war in Normandy. The contributors come from different nations and are at different career stages—full-time, part-time, and retired academics, graduate students, serving and retired military officers, and independent researchers—but all are experts at the top of their field. We are fortunate to benefit from their extensive knowledge.

We hope you learn something about airpower in Normandy from the chapters in this study but more importantly, we hope this book spurs you to further research, writing, and publishing on this important topic.

Mike Bechthold
February 2025

INTRODUCTION

Mike Bechthold

Airpower was central to the Allied victory in Normandy. On D-Day—6 June 1944—nearly 12,000 Allied aircraft supported the invasion. Fighters swept the Luftwaffe from the sky; heavy, medium, and fighter-bombers struck targets on the beaches and beyond; reconnaissance aircraft ranged over the countryside to seek invaluable intelligence; maritime patrol aircraft screened the fleet from attacks by U-boats and surface craft; and transports ferried airborne troops to battle and later resupplied them. The air battle was not finite like the amphibious assault. Spatially, the Allies flew sorties from Holland to Brittany and over the English Channel, North Sea, and Bay of Biscay. Temporally, missions to support the invasion began months earlier, as the air forces worked to gather intelligence, destroy the Luftwaffe, and degrade the ability of the enemy to discover and react to the invasion. Activities peaked on 6 June, but airpower continued to play a central role throughout the Normandy Campaign.

There can be no doubt that Allied airpower was essential to victory in Normandy. Air Chief Marshal Arthur Tedder, one of the foremost commanders of the Royal Air Force (RAF) during World War II, stated in his memoirs that the use of airpower in Normandy "meant the difference to us between a precarious foothold and a swift advance. By this, I do not mean to say that air-power had won the battle alone; but I was at the time, and I remain, confident that without the exercise of air-power . . . victory could not have been won."[1] Noted British military historian John Terraine considered the Battle of Normandy "an outstanding triumph of air power." He argued that airpower "paved the way into Europe; . . . covered the landings and made it impossible for the Germans to concentrate against them; . . . maintained interdiction, and pressure on the enemy when the 'master plan' failed; [and] . . . completed the overwhelming victory."[2] American historian Thomas A. Hughes, the biographer of U.S. Air Force (USAF) general Elwood "Pete" Quesada, concurred, stating that airpower "played a crucial and perhaps decisive role" in the liberation of western France.[3]

There are critics of the value of airpower in Normandy. Max Hastings, whose opinion must often be taken with a grain of salt, is perhaps the most critical when he states: "It has become an historical cliché of the Normandy campaign to assert that Allied airpower was decisive in making victory possible. This is a half truth."[4] While conceding that the achievement of air superiority by destroying the Luftwaffe in the skies over Germany was essential, he maintained that the air forces inflicted little significant damage to the German army in the field, provided meagre support to the Allied armies on the battlefield, and did little to slow the enemy reinforcements sent to Normandy.[5] Hastings had obviously never been a part of a fleet under sustained aerial attack; air superiority over the English Channel was essential. He then almost immediately contradicts himself by concluding his section "Limits of Air Power" by stating, "The execution of the Transportation Plan was central to ensuring that the invasion forces won the battle of the build-up."[6] Given everything that had happened from Taranto to Pearl Harbor to the South China Sea to Malta, it is impossible to see how Operation Overlord could have been launched if all those troops, ships, and materiel were seriously threatened by hostile airpower. If the question is in doubt, look no further than Hitler's *planned* Operation

Sea Lion in 1940. If airpower had done nothing more than protect the Allied invasion fleet, it would have been considered a successful mission.

Terry Copp adds more nuance to his criticism of the air forces when he states that they "waged a separate war against the enemy's air force, lines of communication and targets of opportunity . . . and were overwhelmingly successful at winning the campaign they chose to fight, but it was not the same battle the army was waging."[7] This, however, is a very army-centric view of the battlespace. Many soldiers considered that if they could not see aircraft operating over their heads, then the air forces were not doing anything useful. During Operation Battleaxe in 1941, the RAF reacted to army criticisms of their support in the Western Desert of Egypt and Libya by providing the ground forces with the exact type of aerial support they requested—it cost them the battle.[8] The role of the army in the Normandy victory cannot be forgotten or overstated, as it ultimately took high-intensity combat and boots on the ground to inflict half a million casualties and destroy two German armies in seventy-six days of fighting.

Perhaps the fairest evaluation of airpower's contribution in Normandy can be found in the British official history, which states that with "the ubiquitous and effective manner in which both tactical and strategic air forces filled their

Table 0-1 • Sorties Flown by Allied Air Forces, 1 April–5 June 1944

Command	Approx. number of sorties	Approx. tonnage of bombs dropped
Second Tactical Air Force	28,600	7,000
Air Defence of Great Britain	18,600	
RAF Bomber Command	24,600	87,200
RAF Coastal Command	5,000	–
U.S. Eighth Air Force—VIII Bomber Command	37,800	69,900
U.S. Eighth Air Force—VIII Fighter Command	31,800	600
U.S. Ninth Air Force	53,800	30,700
Totals	200,200	195,400

Source: Adapted from L. F. Ellis, Victory in the West, vol. 1, The Battle of Normandy (London: HMSO, 1962), 109.

momentous role in preparatory operations, in the landings and throughout the subsequent fighting . . . it is no more possible to assess separately their contribution to Overlord than it is to value the parts played in combined operations by each of the three Services."[9] In the eight to ten weeks before the invasion, the Allied air forces flew over 200,000 sorties in support of the coming operations.[10]

While the pace of operations was high before the invasion, it intensified as the air forces supported the armies in France. Between 6 June and 31 August 1944, the British Commonwealth and U.S. air forces flew an additional 480,000 sorties.[11]

Table 0-2 • Sorties Flown by Allied Air Forces, 6 June–31 August 1944

Command	Number of sorties	
Second Tactical Air Force and Air Defence of Great Britain	151,370	
RAF Bomber Command	54,687	224,889
RAF Coastal Command	18,832	
U.S. Eighth Air Force	133,146	255,428
U.S. Ninth Air Force	122,282	
Total		480,317

Source: Adapted from L. F. Ellis, *Victory in the West*, vol. 1, *The Battle of Normandy* (London: HMSO, 1962), 487.

Table 0-3 • Aircrew and Aircraft Lost by Allied Air Forces, 1 April–31 August 1944

Command	Aircrew killed or missing		Aircraft lost	
1 April–5 June 1944				
Allied Air Forces	12,000 (approx.)		2,000 (approx.)	
6 June–31 August 1944				
Second Tactical Air Force and Air Defence of Great Britain	1,035		829	
RAF Bomber Command	6,761	8,178	983	2,036
RAF Coastal Command	382		224	
U.S. Eighth Air Force	7,167	8,536	1,168	2,065
U.S. Ninth Air Force	1,369		897	
Total (June–August)	16,714		4,101	
Grand Total (April–August)	28,714 (aprrox.)		6,101 (aprrox.)	

Source: Adapted from L. F. Ellis, *Victory in the West*, vol. 1, *The Battle of Normandy* (London: HMSO, 1962), 488.

Even though the Luftwaffe was largely destroyed, the cost of the air campaign was heavy. In the period before the invasion, the Allied air forces lost some 12,000 aircrew and over 2,000 aircraft. The butcher's bill remained high once the invasion started, with another 16,700 aircrew killed or missing and 4,100 aircraft destroyed.

In many ways, airpower in the spring and summer of 1944 remains understudied. It is a topic that features widely in the extensive literature on the Normandy Campaign, but there are few works that focus directly on the role played by the Allied air forces in driving the Nazis out of France. The official histories are a good place to start, but beyond that there are few monographs on the topic.

There are numerous reasons for this. Perhaps the best understanding for it is in an article by Sebastian H. Lukasik in the Air University's online journal *Wild Blue Yonder*.[12] Lukasik argues that the view of the U.S. Army Air Force (USAAF) of being first and foremost a strategic weapon led it to consider the tactical experience in Normandy irrelevant in the realms of lessons learned and institutional memory. This became entrenched in the postwar world as the now-independent USAF adopted a nuclear mission. Even the service's Tactical Air Command, "the direct organizational descendant of the tactical air commands" employed in Normandy, became a "junior SAC [Strategic Air Command]," with a focus on the delivery of tactical nuclear weapons rather than the provision of close air support for ground forces.[13]

This shift in focus was evident even among USAF commanders who were intimately involved in the provision of tactical air support in Normandy as they changed gears in the postwar atomic era. Lukasik uses Brigadier General James Ferguson as an example of this trend. In 1953, less than a decade after Normandy, Ferguson told an audience at the Air War College that "in light of new forms of military technology, close air support of the sort that allowed Allied forces to break out of Normandy and advance toward Paris was no longer relevant."[14] His opinion mattered. The general served in Normandy as the assistant chief of staff of Quesada's 9th Fighter Command, and shortly after D-Day, he was deployed to France to serve as a forward air controller directing fighter aircraft in close air support missions. Later in Korea, he served as the vice commander of Fifth Air Force, the tactical air force supporting the U.S. Eighth Army on the peninsula.[15]

According to Lukasik, the pendulum began to swing back toward a focus on tactical aviation in the 1970s and 1980s, as fighter pilots began to replace the bomber generals and the costs of ignoring close air support and battlefield interdiction in Korea and Vietnam became apparent. As the concept of "AirLand Battle" guided American war planning and the services embraced a culture of jointness (even if this was a shotgun wedding due to the passing of the Goldwater-Nichol Act rather than an act of true love), planners turned to the Normandy air campaign to help guide their current practices.[16]

As the USAF found itself once again committed to close air support missions in Iraq and Afghanistan, it was clear that the air force had fully embraced its role on the battlefield. Lukasik provides an example from 2009 that clearly demonstrates this change: "During its tour in Afghanistan in 2009, the 335th Fighter Squadron, a unit of F-15E fighters tasked with flying CAS [close air support] missions, displayed a sign in its headquarters at Bagram airbase that proclaimed: 'The mission is an eighteen-year-old with a rifle, everything else is secondary.' This sentiment would not have been out of place in any of the units that Quesada commanded in Normandy seven decades earlier in support of Omar Bradley's infantry.[17] It must be noted, however, that close air support was the only offensive air mission possible in Afghanistan. There were no supply lines to interdict and no enemy air force to defeat.

But there were still challenges. During the same period, the Canadian Armed Forces held a workshop on air-land integration, which brought together historians and current practitioners to discuss the issues in both its historical and current forms. One discussion between Canadian Army and Air Command officers who had recently returned from Afghanistan made it clear the two services were not on the same page.[18] Their debate on the roles and responsibilities involved in the provision of close air support was not significantly different from early discussions between soldiers and airmen on the Western Front in 1918, in North Africa in 1941, in Normandy in 1944, in South Korea in 1951, in South Vietnam in the late 1960s and early 1970s, and in Iraq, Afghanistan, and the Suwalki Gap more recently.[19] At the heart of the debate, both then and now, was the question of the best use of air resources. Soldiers value close air support that they can see and often look at airpower no different than artillery. Air forces understand the importance of providing direct support to the ground forces, but they also have missions farther afield aimed at isolating the combat area and attacking targets outside the traditional battlefield. In Normandy the air force flew interdiction and armed-reconnaissance missions. Today, this is referred to as battlefield air interdiction. The tension between air and ground perspectives on the use of airpower may be found throughout this volume.

While the USAF as an institution has a renewed appreciation for the importance of airpower in Normandy, historians have been slow to follow. In the last three decades, no academic monographs have been published on that aspect of the campaign. Thomas Hughes, Ian Gooderson, David Spires, Christopher M. Rein, and Ben Kite have produced excellent studies that include a significant focus on airpower in the summer of 1944, but each cast a much wider net than Normandy.[20] Benjamin Franklin Cooling and R. Cargill Hall's three *Case Studies* volumes produced by the U.S. Office of Air Force History each contain excellent chapters covering air operations in Normandy.[21] Two books by Stephen A. Bourque deserve special mention here. In 2018 he published a study that focused on how the Allied bombing campaign affected French civilians. He followed this up with a short monograph looking at the failure of Allied heavy bombing on D-Day. Both works provide a model on the type of innovative research that brings to light aspects of the air campaign that had previously been overlooked and/or misunderstood.[22] And there has been a plethora of recent books that examine the commanders who shaped air operations in World War II in general and Normandy in particular.[23]

What is missing from the historiography is a comprehensive history of the Normandy air campaign (and, indeed, the entire Northwest European theater) similar to the excellent studies produced by Christopher M. Rein, Alexander Fitzgerald-Black, and Robert S. Ehlers Jr. on airpower in the North African, Sicilian, and Mediterranean Campaigns.[24]

The current volume intends to fill some of the gaping holes that exist in our understanding of airpower and the Normandy Campaign. It will not be the last word, but rather hopes to invigorate debate on the topic and spur additional research and writing. Several key questions are addressed in the chapters that follow:

- What role did airpower play in the lead, up to the invasion? How effective was it?
- How effective was this support in helping ground operations?
- What influence did higher command and interservice rivalries have on the provision air support in Normandy?
- How did airpower affect French civilians?
- What role did the German Luftwaffe play?
- How well did the three services work together? How did their relations change and evolve during the campaign?

This collection presents new and innovative scholarship, drawing on the work of experienced airpower historians along with emerging scholars, to present new and nuanced appraisals of the role of airpower in the Normandy Campaign. It is international in scope and looks at the air campaign through the lens of various national perspectives: British, American, Canadian, Australian, and German. A key design of the book is its multidomain approach (to co-opt a modern term), which explores the roles and interplay of the three services as a central tenet. As such, the following chapters are written from a purple or joint perspective, not air force light blue, army green, or navy dark blue.

The book is divided into two sections that essentially correspond to the periods before and after D-Day. The Transportation Plan was the preparatory air campaign designed to impede the German response to the landings in Normandy. It was a controversial strategy at the time and divided leaders into those who supported the use of heavy bombers in a tactical role and those who considered that the strategic air campaign against Germany offered the clearest path to victory and must not be interrupted for any reason. The intervening eighty years have done little to settle the debate. This is clearly represented herein by three chapters that directly address this topic. Mike Pavelec looks at the Transportation Plan through the lens of General Dwight D. Eisenhower. He argues that while the decisions for employment of airpower in the leadup to D-Day were rational, logical, and militarily sound, divisions arose on the best way to employ the air resources. Pavelec considers an analysis of Eisenhower's decision in favor of the Transportation

Plan as an instructive historical case of the most appropriate and effective use of airpower given the existing circumstances.

Stephen Moore examines the politics behind the Transportation Plan. Based on the differing national historiographic assessments of the operation, Moore considers the various national, political, and technical challenges as well as personality conflicts to better understand the twisted road taken to achieve its ultimate implementation. Sebastian Cox traces the implementation of the Transportation Plan by exploring the arguments around the plan as well and the wider air command-and-control arrangements for Overlord. At the core of his chapter is a look at the monumental struggle within the Allied high command between the "Bomber Barons," along with elements in the Air Ministry and War Office, who rejected a diversion from their strategic bombing offensive and favored a purely tactical pre-D-Day plan, and those in the Allied Expeditionary Air Force (AEAF) and Supreme Headquarters Allied Expeditionary Force (SHAEF) who favored using the powerful strategic bombers to disrupt German communications in France and Belgium to render more-direct assistance to Overlord.

Heather Venable examines the issue of combat motivation as it relates to U.S. bomber crews in 1944. She argues that commanders like Gen Carl Spaatz, who accepted his commanders' view that crews had uniformly high levels of morale, were out of touch and did not understand or admit that their morale was far more precarious than commonly thought. His obsession with using strategic bombardment as the way to end the war with Germany, thereby making Normandy unnecessary, made him dangerously out of touch with his men.

The final chapter in part 1, written by Matt Bone, looks at the RAF role in blinding the Germans by attacking their coastal radar installations. The task, which appears to be a simple operation, was complicated by limitations in the ability of fighter-bombers and their weapons, the hardness of the targets, and the heavy defenses surrounding the sites. As one veteran Typhoon pilot observed, "These radar installations were, without doubt, the most formidable targets and getting at them was like fighting your way into a hornet's nest."[25]

Part 2 turns to an in-depth examination of air operations commencing with the Normandy landings in June 1944. Two of the chapters examine the workings of the air support systems. Christopher Finn details the development of an effective air command and control (C2) network at sea leading up to Operation Neptune. He then discusses the C2 system in place during the invasion and analyzes how well it functioned during the transition from its UK-based headquarters to one located in France. Paul Johnston provides a much-needed examination of how the Allied system of air support worked in Normandy. He details the differences and similarities in the RAF and USAAF systems as well and the mechanisms by which ground forces requested air support.

Uniquely in this collection, Russell Hart examines the air war from the enemy's perspective. His chapter considers Luftwaffe antishipping operations in Normandy with the intent to inflict significant damage on the Allied invasion fleet. Despite herculean efforts, the Luftwaffe sank few warships or transports. Hart demonstrates that aerial minelaying was the most effective aspect of the Luftwaffe's operations, while their overall efforts were limited by materiel shortages, inexperienced crews, and its inability to overcome the Allies' air superiority, which shattered the Luftwaffe's maritime strike force.

Three case studies focus on specific operations in Normandy. Stephen Bourque follows up his masterful work *Beyond the Beach* to look at the Allies' bombing program during the first forty-eight hours of the landings as it affected French civilians. He demonstrates that as predicted, the bombing made little difference to the course of tactical operations or the German military's defensive performance. Yet its effect on the civilian population and infrastructure was profound, collectively resulting in history's most significant incident of friendly collateral damage. In one of the great unnamed operations of the Normandy Campaign, Mike Bechthold examines the extensive air operation conducted on 22 June 1944 to support the U.S. Army's drive on the port of Cherbourg. A USAAF analysis immediately after the war labeled this attack "one of the few significant misapplications of tactical air power in the entire career of Ninth Air Force."[26] A close examination of the battle, however, reveals it to be an effective, if not decisive, milestone in the development of the Allies' system of tactical air support. Christopher Rein uses a comparative lens to examine the successes and failures of U.S. heavy bombers in Operation Cobra in Normandy in July 1944 and Operation Queen in Germany only four months later. Rein shows that even contemporaries took some of the wrong lessons from airpower's successes in Normandy, and the use of heavy bombers in support of ground forces, while potentially decisive, depended heavily on factors that are often beyond the USAAF's control.

The final theme examined in this collection is the way that air support was received by the Allies. Alexander Fitzgerald-Black examines Canadian army war diaries to better understand how air support affected soldiers' morale. He discovered that the clear skies and one-sided dogfights in June gave the soldiers of 3rd Canadian Infantry Division a great deal of confidence. In contrast, later air support failures—including the friendly-fire incidents of Operations Totalize and Tractable—depressed Canadian troops to the point that some feared the Allied air forces more than the Luftwaffe. The changing peaks and valleys of Canadian soldiers' morale lead Fitzgerald-Black to christen this effect "the air support rollercoaster." In a similar vein, Adam Lunney looks at the Royal Australian Air Force's (RAAF) participation in Normandy through its coverage in period newspapers. Unlike the other Allied nations fighting in Normandy, Australians faced questions about why they were fighting in France when the Japanese Empire presented a direct threat to their nation. Lunney surveys newspapers to understand how the contributions of RAAF aircrew and ground crew were portrayed in the contemporary press and examines how well those stories reflected reality. His comments on the propagandized nature of those articles, which show what was overstated, what was understated, and what was left unsaid, provide us with a better understanding of how the Australian home front viewed their air force's participation in the Normandy fighting.

During World War II, the Allies struggled at times to create a tactical-airpower system that could effectively support the army in the field. Hollywood would have you believe that aircraft could appear at a critical moment and save the day. In *Saving Private Ryan* (1998), an American P-51 fighter-bomber appears out of the blue just as a German attack threatens to overrun the beleaguered survivors of Captain Miller's rescue party. With immaculate timing and pinpoint precision, the pilot assesses the situation and without hesitation (or terminal guidance) attacks the German Tiger tank as it crosses the bridge within yards of the captain. The aircraft destroys the tank without any collateral damage and halts the German advance. Airpower once again saves the day! Questions of target acquisition, air–ground liaison, bomb lines, weapons accuracy, and myriad other details need not be considered in this movie version of tactical air support. Though Hollywood makes the timely destruction of German tanks seem simple, it was actually a complex, expensive, and difficult task. The Allies worked hard throughout the war to improve air operations in support of the army. By Normandy, they had created an effective, but not perfect, system. They made great advances in aircraft, technology, tactics, and perhaps most importantly, personal relations, which could make or break the provision of effective and timely support at the tactical, operational, and strategic levels of war. Taken together, the chapters in this collection explore these issues in some detail and expand our understanding of airpower's true role in the decisive Allied victory in Normandy.

NOTES

1. Arthur Tedder, *With Prejudice: The War Memoirs of Marshal of the Royal Air Force Lord Tedder, GCB* (London: Cassell, 1966), 585.
2. John Terraine, *The Right of the Line: The Royal Air Force in the European War, 1939–1945* (London: Hodder and Stoughton, 1985), 662.
3. Thomas A. Hughes, "Normandy: A Modern Air Campaign?" *Air and Space Power Journal* 17, no. 4 (Winter 2003): 28.
4. Max Hastings, *Overlord: D-Day, June 6, 1944* (New York: Simon and Schuster, 1984), 266.
5. Hastings, *Overlord*, 266–68. The only exception to his first point were Operations Cobra and Goodwood, where the heavy bombing attacks inflicted significant, if not decisive, damage on the Germans.
6. Hastings, *Overlord*, 276.
7. Terry Copp, *Fields of Fire: The Canadians in Normandy* (Toronto: University of Toronto Press, 2003), 259–60.
8. Mike Bechthold, *Flying to Victory: Raymond Collishaw and the Western Desert Campaign, 1940–1941* (Norman: University of Oklahoma Press, 2017), chap. 8.
9. 1962), 487.
10. Ellis, *Victory in the West*, 1:109.
11. Ellis, *Victory in the West*, 1:487.
12. Sebastian H. Lukasik, "Drawing a Straight Line?: The Normandy Campaign and U.S. Air Force Culture since the Second World War," *Wild Blue Yonder*, 29

December 2022, https://www.airuniversity.af.edu/Wild-Blue-Yonder/Articles/Article-Display/Article/3234748/drawing-a-straight-line-the-normandy-campaign-and-us-air-force-culture-since-th/.

13. Lukasik, "Drawing a Straight Line?" David Spires has made a similar argument. See David N. Spires, *Air Power for Patton's Army: The XIX Tactical Air Command in the Second World War* (Washington, DC: Air Force History and Museums Program, 2002), 315.
14. Lukasik, "Drawing a Straight Line?" Lukasik has paraphrased Ferguson's message.
15. Richard H. Kohn and Joseph P. Harahan, eds., *Air Superiority in World War II and Korea: An Interview with Gen. James Ferguson, Gen. Robert M. Lee, Gen. William Momyer, and Lt. Gen. Elwood R. Quesada* (Washington, DC: Office of Air Force History, 1983), 2–3.
16. Lukasik, "Drawing a Straight Line?"
17. Lukasik, "Drawing a Straight Line?"
18. Air Command was the official name of Canada's air force between 1975 and 2011. On 16 August 2011, the service's historic name, Royal Canadian Air Force, was reinstated.
19. Observation by Mike Bechthold, participant-presenter at the 2011 Air-Land Integration Workshop, Canadian Forces Aerospace Warfare Centre, Trenton, Ontario, 8–9 March 2011.
20. Thomas Alexander Hughes, *Overlord: General Pete Quesada and the Triumph of Tactical Air Power in World War II* (New York: Free Press, 1995); Ian Gooderson, *Air Power at the Battlefront: Allied Close Air Support in Europe 1943–45* (London: Frank Cass, 1998); Spires, *Air Power for Patton's Army*; Christopher M. Rein, *Forging the Ninth Army–XXIX TAC Team: The Development, Training, and Application of American Air-Ground Doctrine in World War II* (Fort Leavenworth, KS: Army University Press, 2019), Ben Kite, *Through Adversity: Britain and the Commonwealth's War in the Air, 1939–45*, vol. 1 (Warwick, UK: Helion, 2019); Ben Kite, *Undaunted: Britain and the Commonwealth's War in the Air, 1939–45*, vol. 2 (Warwick, UK: Helion, 2021).
21. W. A. Jacobs, "The Battle for France 1944," in *Case Studies in the Development of Close Air Support*, edited by B. F. Cooling (Washington, DC: Office of Air Force History, 1990); Jacobs, "Operation Overlord," in *Case Studies in the Achievement of Air Superiority*, edited by B. F. Cooling (Washington, DC: Air Force History and Museums Program, 1994); Jacobs, "The British Strategic Air Offensive against Germany in World War II," in *Case Studies in Strategic Bombardment*, edited by R. Cargill Hall (Washington, DC: Air Force History and Museums Program, 1998); Stephen L. McFarland and Wesley Phillips

Newton, "The American Strategic Air Offensive against Germany in World War II," ibid.
22. Stephen Alan Bourque, *Beyond the Beach: The Allied War against France* (Annapolis, MD: Naval Institute Press, 2018); Bourque, *D-Day: The Deadly Failure of Allied Heavy Bombing on June 6* (New York: Osprey, 2022).
23. Hughes, *Overlord*; Richard G. Davis, *Carl A. Spaatz and the Air War in Europe* (Washington, DC: Center for Air Force History, 1993); Vincent Orange, *Coningham: A Biography of Air Marshal Sir Arthur Coningham* (London: Methuen, 1990); Vincent Orange, *Tedder: Quietly in Command* (London: Routledge, 2004); Vincent Orange, *Churchill and His Airmen: Relationships, Intrigue, and Policy-Making, 1914–1945* (London: Grub Street, 2013); Brian D. Laslie, *Architect of Air Power: General Laurence S. Kuter and the Birth of the US Air Force* (Lawrence: University Press of Kansas, 2017); David R. Mets, *Master of Airpower: General Carl A. Spaatz* (Washington, DC: Presidio, 1997).
24. Christopher M. Rein, *The North African Air Campaign: U.S. Army Air Forces from El Alamein to Salerno* (Lawrence: University Press of Kansas, 2012); Alexander Fitzgerald-Black, *Eagles over Husky: The Allied Air Campaign in the Sicilian Campaign, 14 May to 17 August 1943* (Warwick, UK: Helion, 2019); Robert S. Ehlers Jr., *The Mediterranean Air War: Airpower and Allied Victory in World War II* (Lawrence: University Press of Kansas, 2015).
25. Desmond Scott, *Typhoon Pilot* (London: Leo Cooper, 1982), 101.
26. *Condensed Analysis of the Ninth Air Force in the European Theater of Operations* (1946; repr., Washington, DC: Office of Air Force History, 1984, 23.

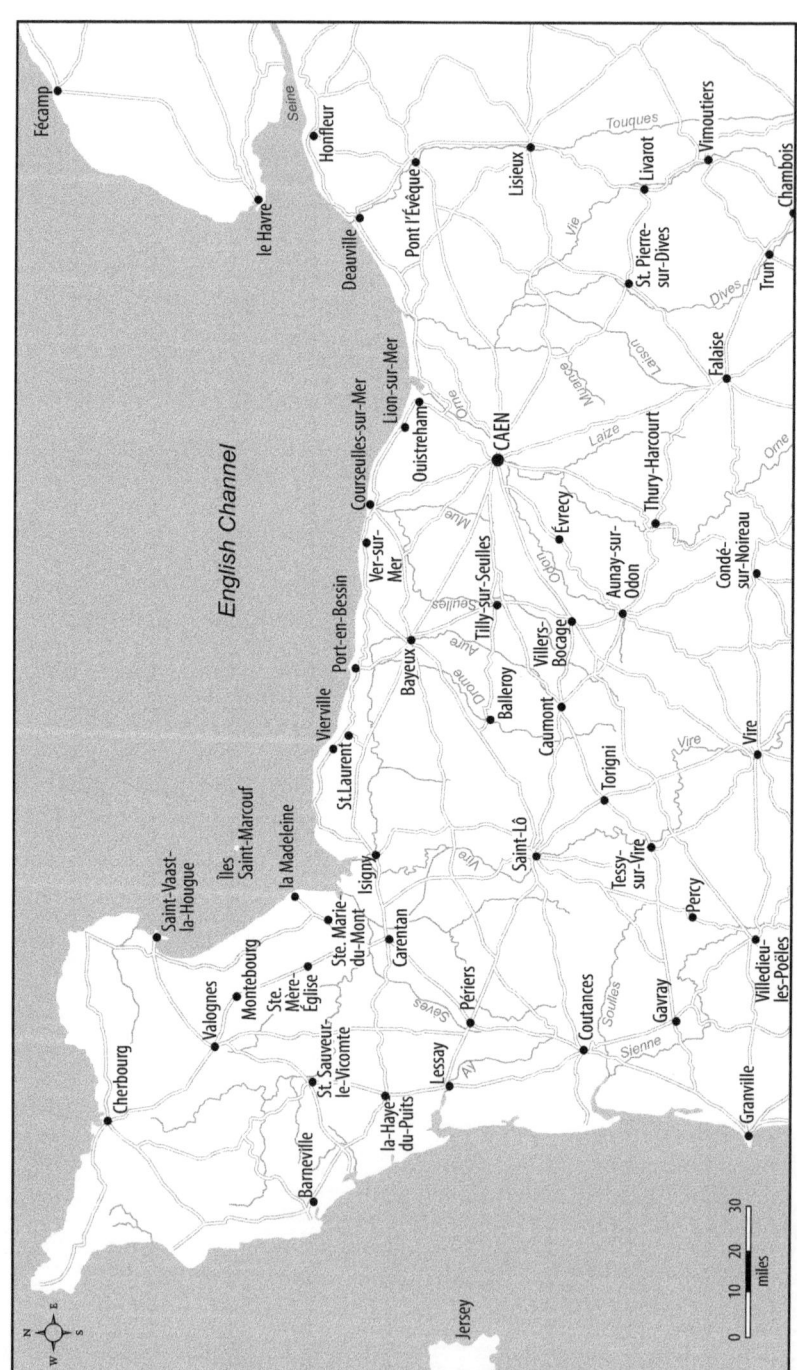

Map 1-1 • Normandy

PART 1

PREPARATIONS FOR THE CAMPAIGN

1

The Air War for Normandy, 1944

How to Apply Airpower for Victory

S. Mike Pavelec

By 1944, the Allies thought they had figured out how airpower should be employed. After the abortive attempts in the Great War, the interwar period saw tremendous evolution of the aerial weapon as well as complementary theory. Into the fifth year of the war in Europe (the third for the United States), Allied airmen became entrenched in their ideas of how their weapon systems could be used to decisively defeat the Germans.[1] In the preparation for Operation Overlord, airpower practitioners differed on their ideas about how to employ the air weapon. Each of the commanders had different ideas about how to apply airpower for the best effect. Ultimately, General Dwight Eisenhower, the supreme Allied commander in Europe, had to decide from among the differing theories and applications of these resources and oversee the planning and execution of the air campaign in preparation for the invasion.

At the conclusion of the Great War, technology still preceded theory, and practice was exploited at the command level. Colonel Billy Mitchell, the air commander of the American Expeditionary Forces, massed airpower for the Saint-Mihiel offensive in September 1918. Pulling together over 1,600 aircraft, he focused on air superiority to overwhelm the Germans at the point of attack.[2] Using borrowed British and French aircraft, with a number of American pilots finally in combat, he attempted to gain air superiority, bomb German supply lines—with British bombers at night—and interdict the Germans at the point of attack, all while maintaining surveillance capabilities to gather information. The aerial interdiction operations were a success; Mitchell's airmen literally saw the Germans retreating after the massive, combined air-land campaign.[3] The British continued their aerial operations over the front, but Major General Hugh Trenchard, as general officer commanding, directed the operations of the newly formed Independent Bombing Force (IBF), tasked with attacking Germany itself, as best he saw fit. Due to technological limitations—the technology of the time limited the bombers' range—Trenchard focused on targets in the German industrial centers of the Ruhr. Hoping to disrupt the production cycle by bombing the workers and ideally the enemy's factories, the IBF concentrated on a "strategic" aerial campaign against German industry.[4]

As the war wound down, airmen—practitioners and theorists—returned home to reflect on their wartime exploits and try to come to some consensus about the importance of airpower in the Great War. Some were more successful than others. In Italy Giulio Douhet led the Central Aeronautic Bureau after some trouble with insubordination, including jail time from a court-martial, ending the war as an air commander. After the war he penned *Command of the Air*, then retired.[5] Unfortunately for the rest of the world, his tome was written in Italian; the first English translation appeared only by 1942. The influence of the Italian continues to today, but it is unclear the influence he had in his own time.[6] Regardless, Douhet wrote that an overwhelming air attack with a fleet of five hundred "battleplanes" could bomb an enemy capital with explosives, incendiaries, and chemical weapons, causing social unrest and forcing capitulation of the hostile government. His ideas, seemingly farfetched today, were based on the social revolutions at the end of the Great War in Germany and Russia; Douhet was trying to figure out a way to apply airpower for maximum effect against a vulnerable civilian population.

In Britain, Trenchard was named chief of the Air Staff (CAS) for the newly formed Royal Air Force (RAF) and exerted direct and significant influence on the evolution of British airpower theory and acquisitions even amid demobilization after the war.[7] He concluded, based heavily on the secret survey of operations completed after the war, that bombing German industry was not only a good idea but also an effective tool of airpower in war. In Trenchard's own estimation, the destruction of material was good, but the disruption to the average German worker was even more important, citing his personal opinion that it was a 20:1 ratio of morale to physical effect.[8] Furthermore, as the CAS, his judgment went unquestioned in British military-academic circles, and he was able to emphasize the morale effects of "strategic" bombing into the postwar years, which in turn influenced government investment, procurement and acquisitions, and doctrine. The British began to believe that strategic bombing was the key for the future application of airpower by the fledgling RAF. This is not to say that Trenchard was incorrect in his assumption about the importance of morale bombing, which is inherently difficult to measure. The importance of the statement is that the RAF focused on the potential of airpower based on difficult metrics. The RAF focused heavily on bombing capabilities in exercises and procurement while still expanding other missions to prove its importance. Thus, although there was an emphasis on bombing and developing large, long-range platforms to do so, the RAF also added coastal defense, air policing, and other missions to its tool kit.

In the United States, Mitchell theorized that airpower would be the decisive tool for future conflict. In his writing, considering the political milieu, he argued for an offensive defense to protect an isolationist United States from enemy seaborne attack. He hypothesized that aircraft, cheaper and easier to construct than a surface fleet, could protect American coastlines from enemy fleets.[9] His mixed forces of aircraft (bomber, observation, and pursuit) could be employed as an offensive defense to maximize American national security objectives. He got into trouble when he accused the U.S. Navy and

U.S. Army of misusing airpower and faced a court-martial in 1925. But even in his trial, he was given a platform for several days to argue his case for airpower.[10] Although he was convicted of insubordination, Mitchell was put on half pay, effectively forcing him to retire, which he did. But a number of young majors spoke on his behalf, including Henry H. "Hap" Arnold and Carl Spaatz, prominent names in later Army Air Corps circles. Even though Mitchell was gone from the services, his ideas lived on at the Air Corps Tactical School. The school at Maxwell Field in Alabama worked on the problem of how to apply airpower for greatest strategic effect. What emerged was the idea of the industrial web theory of strategic bombing, employing high-altitude daylight precision bombing.[11] The American emphasis was on bombing the enemy's ability to fight by destroying weapons and disrupting production. Unlike the British emphasis on morale, the American target was measurable and definitive. U.S. commercial manufacturing fed into the idea in that Boeing, Consolidated, Lockheed, and Douglas were already building long-range, reliable, heavy-lift platforms for commerce—business, mail, and passengers—to ply the vast distances across the United States. These designs would translate well into bomber aircraft when the time came.

Thus, at the start of the war—1939 for the British and 1941 for the Americans—theory and doctrine were hand in hand with technology; both the British and the Americans had inventories and capabilities designed to test their national theories of airpower application. The British began in earnest with probing attacks into occupied France and Belgium as well as bombing missions against close German cities like Bremen and Wilhelmshaven, targeting German shipping and shipbuilding, as well as a return to the Ruhr to disrupt German industry and production. By 1940, at the height of the German attacks on London in the Battle of Britain, RAF Bomber Command targeted Berlin, finally within reach of its heavy aircraft. The British shifted tactics early, transitioning to night bombing to reduce losses faced during daylight to German fighter defenses. The strategy was the same—destroy the German will to fight—but the doctrine changed to decrease losses.[12] This presented problems: night flying was inherently more dangerous and made finding targets difficult. But RAF Bomber Command, under Air Chief Marshal Arthur Harris, was determined to bomb the Germans into submission.[13]

Photo 1-1 • Air Chief Marshal Sir Arthur Harris, commander of RAF Bomber Command, and Major General Ira Eaker, commander of U.S. Air Forces in Europe until January 1944, were key advocates of using heavy bombers to attack Germany rather than to support the army. *U.S. Air Force Photo 79569AC*

Harris' area-bombing "de-housing" campaign intended to disrupt German industry, but the emphasis was actually on German morale.[14] The Americans had a different idea, but in practice it seemed very similar.

After the U.S. entry into the war, in early 1942 the emphasis became the destruction of the German war economy and measurable effects to destroy the enemy's ability to fight, regardless of their will. The psychological damage was important but less obvious; the Americans decided to focus on results.

A pair of documents outlined their ideas and focus, Air War Plans Division-1 and Air War Plans Division-42.[15] Both documents—the first written before American entry and the other after—outlined production and procurement and offered ideas on the implementation of strategic bombing against Germany. The overarching idea was that the Americans would employ heavy bombers during the day and strike German industry with precision. B-17s and B-24s with Norden bombsights would target aviation-industry and petroleum targets to degrade German military capabilities. Obviously, civilian workers would suffer and die, but the emphasis was on German industry. Each half of the Allied air offensive thus targeted enemy industrial output, but they each had different ideas about what the effects would be.

In 1943 the Allies drew up the "Bomber Offensive from the United Kingdom" plan during the Casablanca Conference (January–February 1943). Together RAF Bomber Command and the U.S. Army Air Forces (USAAF) focused on

> The progressive destruction and dislocation of the German military, industrial, and economic systems and the undermining of the morale of the German people to a point where their capacity for armed resistance is fatally weakened. Every opportunity to be taken to attack Germany by day to destroy objectives that are unsuitable for night attack, to sustain continuous pressure on German morale, to impose heavy losses on German day fighter force and to conserve German fighter force away from the Russian and Mediterranean theaters of war.[16]

This was the plan for the second front requested by the Soviets, at least until the western Allies could establish an actual ground campaign in Europe.

The Combined Bomber Offensive (CBO) as implemented included American bombers operating by day and British bombers at night in a semicoordinated campaign against German industry and morale. The priority was the destruction of German aviation to establish Allied air superiority. Once that was achieved, according to the plan, everything else would fall into place. If the Allies could secure air superiority, they would be free to roam and bomb at will. Thus, while the British targeted German industrial cities at night, the Americans focused on the aircraft industry and bottlenecks during the day.

The results were lackluster. Initially, the British had trouble finding cities in darkness and could not break German morale. The Americans found the factories but paid dearly for deep penetration raids into Germany, especially in the two Schweinfurt–Regensburg attacks. And German output actually increased. The war of attrition in the air did not have the intended results.

Harris, at RAF Bomber Command, wanted to go after Berlin. To him, the symbolic and actual nerve center for the Third Reich was the heart and mind of the German war effort. According to interwar theory, destruction of the enemy capital would have the effect of destroying the command-and-control structures as well as leading to popular unrest due to attacks on the enemy's civilian population.[17] But the British were not able to prove that strategic bombing was having the intended effects; the Germans continued to resist.

Likewise, Spaatz and Ira Eaker, commanding the U.S. strategic air forces, faced difficulties in achieving American objectives. Losses were too high, and results were fleeting. The Americans improved accuracy with different tactics like self-defending bomber boxes and increasing the numbers of escort fighters—as well as the technological evolution of longer-range escorts with drop tanks—but German defenses improved as well. The "solution" to countering German production continued to evade the CBO planners.

In August 1943 Winston Churchill, Franklin Roosevelt, and their military planners gathered in Quebec for the Quadrant Conference. The leaders decided on several topics, including the atomic-bomb project, the ongoing Pacific War, and the invasion of the European continent, which was given the name Operation Overlord. If the Germans could not be brought to heel with airpower alone, then the western Allies would invade with a substantial ground force.[18] The CBO would continue, but differing plans for the application of airpower were investigated and considered. The question remained how to best apply airpower for maximum strategic effect, with the new variable of a cross-channel invasion set for late spring 1944.

By early 1944, each of the Allied air commanders had differing views on how to best apply airpower for an ultimate decision over Germany. At RAF Bomber Command, Harris argued that the best use of his British "heavies" was to continue to bomb German cities by night.[19] He had led Bomber Command since 1942 and fully embraced Douhet's theories of airpower.[20]

Bomber Command was forced to adopt striking German cities for several reasons, mostly technological. At the beginning of the war, British bombers had difficulty surviving missions in the face of strong German daytime fighter opposition, with most not even reaching their targets. So, Bomber Command resorted to nighttime attacks. Unfortunately for the British, early on they could not find anything smaller than cities and adopted "area bombing" as their operational mission. "Bomber" Harris argued that his planes were simply "de-housing" German workers and not attacking civilians directly, but in the end the plan was to burn cities, kill workers, and disrupt production, focusing on the will of the Germans to continue the war. Even as technology and accuracy improved, according to Harris, the best use of RAF Bomber Command was the continued destruction of German cities at night.

On the American side, Lieutenant General Carl Spaatz, commander of the U.S. Army Strategic Air Forces in Europe, echoed Harris' ideas.[21] Spaatz was concerned that any deviation from Operation Pointblank, the bombing of German aircraft factories, would diminish the Allied effort to achieve and maintain air superiority. Since the start of the air campaign, his bombers had focused their wrath on German aircraft factories, hitting with "precision" attacks during the day. American bombers had begun to effectively disrupt German aircraft industry at the source, crippling enemy air defenses by destroying industrial targets. Spaatz's operational concept was that the U.S. Eighth Air Force, flying from England, could destroy Germany's aircraft industry, thus preventing the Nazis from fielding any aircraft in defense of the Reich. He, too, was against any operational plan that diminished the Pointblank efforts. In his mind U.S. bombing should focus on the means available to the enemy.

In addition to the heavy bombers, Eisenhower also had at his disposal fleets of transport aircraft, specifically the Douglas C-47 Skytrain (Dakota in RAF service); gliders; and tactical fighters, light and medium bombers, and high-speed reconnaissance aircraft. Ike gathered a planning staff to consider the best use of all the air assets for a successful invasion of the Continent. As compared to the Pacific theater, he had a directive from Roosevelt as well as Churchill to get Allied forces ashore in France. This political consideration, to keep the Soviets in the war and open a second front, was made at the highest levels and had to be implemented by Ike and the Allied forces; they could no longer simply apply airpower alone to the German problem. Thus, Eisenhower focused on how to get troops safely ashore on the Continent while using airpower to its best abilities for success.

There were any number of ways the airpower weapon could be employed. Harris and Spaatz could continue to ravage German industry and workers with their long-range heavy bombers. This would, in theory, destroy German materials and morale and prevent them from staging any countermeasures, at least in the air. Ike could use the bombers to destroy German oil production, denying the enemy the fuel required to move equipment to Normandy, but the Germans had known reserves of fuel for aircraft, tanks, and trucks as well as stockpiles of coal for trains. Ike could target the proposed landing beaches, but that would give up surprise and create problems once the Allied troops landed. And the German defenses there were virtually bombproof, reinforced by millions of cubic meters of concrete in preparation for an Allied attack all along the coast. One attractive solution was to dismantle the transportation network in northern France in order to prevent additional reserves from providing strength to the eventual counterattack. But that raised further concerns; the Allies would have to bomb French railway cities, roads, and bridges to destroy the German's ability to reinforce.[22]

In February 1944, planners presented the Initial Joint Plan for aerial operations in support of Operation Overlord.[23] In it Air Chief Marshal Sir Trafford Leigh-Mallory, commander of the Allied Expeditionary Air Force, outlined his ideas on how the air weapon could be used in preparation for the planned invasion. According to the plan, the RAF and USAAF would order that "the bombing offensive against the Reich was implicitly subordinated to preliminary air activities in support of the invasion."[24]

The proposal met with immediate pushback from Spaatz and Harris. On 15 February 1944, in a meeting attended by Leigh-Mallory, Spaatz, and Harris, the American reiterated his desires to continue bombing German industry, stating that the Transportation Plan was at "cross purposes with his directives."[25] Spaatz wanted to continue Pointblank attacks to disrupt the German aircraft industry. Harris concurred, stating his RAF bombers should "intensify its attacks on German cities."[26] Leigh-Mallory, who outranked both, "made it clear that he intended for the strategic air forces to begin the rail center bombings under his own direction by 1 March 1944."[27] Spaatz went outside the chain of command and complained to General Hap Arnold in Washington that the Pointblank directive was in jeopardy. Arnold commented to Ike: "The transportation plan might have tragic consequences if it were implemented too early.... [A] premature shift of heavy bomber effort from strategic targets in Germany to rail centers in France and Belgium might result in a battle for air supremacy over the beachhead on D-Day."[28] Eisenhower demurred and delayed Leigh-Mallory's directive for a month.

Fortunately for the Allies and Spaatz, American emerging technology combined with a renewed offensive that assuaged Spaatz's fears about German capabilities. Operation Argument (Big Week), 20–25 February 1944, was an all-out day-and-night effort to destroy German counter-air capabilities once and for all. For the first time, Eighth Air Force and RAF Bomber Command, flying from England, and Fifteenth Air Force, flying from bases in Italy, were able to mount thousand-bomber raids aimed at the German aircraft industry. New technology in the form of long-range drop tanks gave escort fighters additional fuel and extended range to fight in the skies over Germany. North American P-51 Mustangs and Republic P-47 Thunderbolts ranged ahead of the bomber streams to shoot down intercepting fighters. American fighters ravaged the Germans in the air while the bombers destroyed German aircraft manufacturing on the ground. In that single week over one hundred Luftwaffe pilots were killed in the aerial battles over Germany, fatally crippling Nazi air defenses in the West.[29] Spaatz had his air-superiority victory just in time to switch to Ike's Transportation Plan in mid-April.

But even in success, Spaatz argued that the bombers be used in a strategic role to support Overlord. On 5 March, on the heels of the successful Big Week, he was still insistent on this vision. He submitted his "Plan for the Completion of the Combined Bomber Offensive" to Eisenhower, outlining his intent to bomb the German oil and rubber industries.[30] Spaatz argued that he could knock out this production so that the enemy would run out of reserves in six months. He continued—with extensive documentation—that the Transportation Plan required more assets than envisioned and would not have the predicted effects in time.[31] Spaatz argued for a fifteen-day campaign by Eighth Air Force and a ten-day campaign by Fifteenth Air Force to crush German oil and rubber production. His emphasis was definitively away from French and Belgian targets, in part to preserve the fragile alliance with the Free French. Only after these strategic campaigns were completed, he argued, would he be willing to release the bombers for the proposed interdiction campaign against French transportation.[32] Spaatz maintained that bombing the transportation network—an estimated five hundred targets—would not reduce the Germans' ability to reinforce, citing the need for only fifty trains a day for effectiveness. Arnold leaned toward Spaatz's opinions but deferred to Eisenhower.[33] Spaatz argued that the Luftwaffe would not defend French rail yards, but they would defend their country's oil industry, meaning a continuing depletion of Luftwaffe men and material if the latter was attacked with vigor.

With all the information in front of him and with all the political, strategic, operational, and technological variables under consideration, Ike decided on the Transportation Plan. In his estimation it offered the best chance of immediate success for establishing a foothold on the Continent. But even as he decided, Prime Minister Churchill and the British War Cabinet argued once again against bombing targets in occupied France, citing unnecessary civilian casualties.[34] When Ike threatened to "go home, unless he commanded the [RAF] air forces [for the Transportation Plan and] during the invasion," Churchill acquiesced, giving him the authority.[35] At midnight on 13–14 April 1944, Eisenhower assumed control of all air assets for the prosecution of the air plan for Operation Overlord.[36]

Air Operations for Operation Overlord

Once decided, the Transportation Plan was put into action. In the leadup to D-Day (6 June), the British and Americans launched 18,500 sorties and dropped 68,000 tons of bombs on French and Belgian rail networks in order to hamper German movement.[37] The bombers focused on 114 rail centers specifically, with the Fifteenth Air Force adding 3,000 tons of bombs against fourteen targets in the south. Medium bombers, having better accuracy, targeted bridges. Tactical fighter-bombers sought out moving targets, including trucks and locomotives as well as specific tracks and rail facilities.

"Chattanooga Day" (21 May 1944) kicked off a series of 2,700 sorties flown against transportation targets leading up to D-Day a few weeks later.[38] A weekly comparison is informative: bombers dropped 12,000 tons of bombs the first week of April, climbing to 19,000 tons the week before D-Day.[39] These efforts severely reduced rail traffic to the region. In January 1944 there were 45,000 rail cars loaded and moving; by June there were fewer than 6,000. And "military" freight cars suffered most, reduced to only 3,000 by 6 June.[40] There were still more than Spaatz had predicted, but enemy rail traffic was severely reduced by Allied air operations. With the reduction in rolling stock, destroyed locomotives, and damaged rail lines, the Germans could not move men and equipment to the front at the speed of rail; they had to devise alternate ways to get defenders to the front lines.

As D-Day approached, Eisenhower mustered all the available air assets for the impending invasion. All aircraft were put on high alert and prepared for the big day. Just after midnight on 6 June, the invasion plan was enacted. Ike commanded a massive armada; in addition to the invasion force and the ships, he had over 11,000 aircraft for the operation. Over 2,300 transports and gliders began the assault in the nighttime darkness. C-47s carrying 20,000 paratroopers, with some transports towing either Horsa or Waco gliders, crossed the channel to deliver their soldiers. Enemy fire and cloud obscured the landing sites, and most went off course. The exception was the excellent piloting that landed five Horsas right on target and allowed British glider-borne infantry to capture the Bénouville (Pegasus) and Ranville (Horsa) bridges.

In advance of the seaborne landings, heavy bombers dropped their ordnance behind enemy lines to soften up the defenses while medium bombers attacked closer to the front. Fighters and fighter-bombers roamed the skies looking for Luftwaffe defenders, which rarely appeared, and attacked targets of opportunity on the ground. In all, the Allies launched over 16,000 sorties on D-Day, many pilots flying more than one flight over the beachhead. The Luftwaffe mounted a paltry defense, only capable of somewhere between 150 and 200 sorties in total, with only a handful of warplanes getting close to the invasion beaches. Allied forces enjoyed complete local air supremacy for D-Day.

Photo 1-2 • A B-26 Marauder medium bomber of the U.S. Ninth Air Force passes over the Normandy beaches as it returns from a mission on 6 June 1944. *U.S. Air Force Photo 51988AC*

The Outcome

The Allies gained a foothold in France with the successful invasion landings on D-Day. Largely due to the benefits of airpower, the operation was a success. But it was the preparation and leadup that was arguably more important than the day itself. The air cover over the beaches was important, to say nothing of the three divisions of paratroopers dropped behind enemy lines, but it was the bombing campaign before the invasion that significantly influenced the outcome of that eventful day, specifically Eisenhower's decision to go forward with the Transportation Plan. Strategic bombing in a vacuum may have crippled the Germans eventually (or led to better European results for the Soviets), but when putting troops into harm's way, Ike needed to isolate the battlespace. It was not enough to bomb German aircraft industry or oil; the Allies had to prevent the Germans from being able to repel the invasion forces. That came in two distinct but interrelated stages: the defeat of the Luftwaffe over the Continent and isolating the Normandy bridgehead.

With constant and effective air cover, the Allies landed 160,000 troops in the first day, and 2.5 million men at arms by the end of August. Fighter aircraft flew from temporary fields set up on the bluffs above Omaha Beach on D+2. Without Luftwaffe air cover and under constant Allied air harassment, the Germans were forced to move by foot and at night: "Of the 28 divisions for which information is available, 14 travelled the entire distance to the front by road. Eleven divisions travelled by rail to points approximately 150 miles from the battle area, where they were forced to detrain and proceed by road."[41] But this also acknowledges the efforts of the heavies before the invasion; the Allies had wrecked the transportation network prior to the invasion, which prevented the Germans from using it in the first place.

Unfortunately, the Transportation Plan did have serious consequences for the French in the target zones. Stephen Bourque has outlined the effects on the French civilians in occupied France in the leadup to and immediately after the invasion. Although President Roosevelt's and General Arnold's estimate of 10,000 civilians killed was too low and Churchill's estimate of 150,000 was too high, tragically, 60,000 French citizens lost their lives to Allied bombing in preparation for D-Day. The ethics and morals of bombing an occupied country is a topic for another project.

Eisenhower seemed justified in his reallocation of resources for the invasion of the Continent. With consideration for the political, strategic, and operational details, he committed to isolating the battlefield in order to mount a successful amphibious invasion with the minimum number of losses. Fortune favored the Allies; Spaatz broke the back of the Luftwaffe with superior technology just before transitioning to the Transportation Plan. German mistakes facilitated Allied successes as well. But in the final analysis, Eisenhower chose correctly; his Transportation Plan was in fact more judicious and reasoned than Harris' area bombing or Spaatz's oil campaign in the short term. When those commanders returned to their preferred bombing campaigns after Eisenhower was done with their air fleets, they continued, at a furious pace, with the systematic destruction of German industry and cities. This, in addition to the land campaign by the Allies in the West and the Soviets in the East, led eventually to the German surrender in May 1945.

Hindsight

These decisions are the fulcrum of history. But it is also imperative that we use history to judge the present. In airpower circles in the twenty-first century, we still talk about the "correct" (appropriate) use of airpower for "victory." In the classroom I ask aviators (as well as planners, diplomats, and others) what the best use of airpower is to achieve strategic results. Every case is different, but there are similarities. The first is understanding the nature of the conflict, as argued by Carl von Clausewitz. The next is adhering to (and demanding) coherent political guidance. Then in the application phase, there is consideration for whether the "will" or the "means" is more important. Even in the aftermath of World War II, analysts were not convinced that morale (will) could be influenced by bombing: "The results reported ... have established the relationship between bomb tonnage and willingness to surrender. It was pointed out there, however, that morale did not fall off in proportion to the tonnage of bombs dropped and that very heavy raids yielded diminishing returns."[42] Theorists need to revisit Douhet and his disciple Air Chief Marshal Harris. But that does not mean that destroying means works either—see the example of U.S. efforts in Vietnam. We, like Eisenhower, will have to determine how airpower can be *best* employed to achieve strategic outcomes. Ike chose well.

NOTES

1. This chapter focuses specifically on the European theater of operations and the air war against Germany. Japan is another story altogether.
2. Rebecca Grant, "The Dawn of American Airpower at St. Mihiel," *Air & Space Forces Magazine*, 27 July 2018, https://www.airforcemag.com/article/the-dawn-of-american-airpower-at-st-mihiel/.
3. Grant, "Dawn of American Airpower."
4. Andrew Boyle, *Trenchard: Man of Vision* (London, UK: Collins, 1962), chap. 11, esp. 288 (formation of IBF), 306 (outlining operations). See also Russell Miller, *Boom: The Life of Viscount Trenchard, Father of the Royal Air Force* (London, UK: Weidenfeld and Nicholson, 2016), chap. 14, esp. 213–28 (formation and operations of the Independent Force).
5. Giulio Douhet, *Command of the Air*, translated by Dino Ferrari (Maxwell AFB, AL: Air University Press, 2019).

6. *Command of the Air* was translated into French in 1936 and English in 1941. Dr. Peter Dye, in conversation and correspondence with me, suggests that Douhet was discussed widely in British and American circles "in the 1930s," but I am hard pressed to find concrete connections. The earliest English edition I have found is from 1942 in the Air University Archives, Maxwell Air Force Base, Alabama. In the 1983 translation of *Command of the Air*, Richard H. Kohn and Joseph P. Harahan (ix) suggest that there was a translation at the Air Corps Tactical School as early as 1923. Suffice it to say that after the Great War, there were several theorists discussing and contemplating the importance and effectiveness of airpower. What is less clear is their influence (especially Douhet) in the English-speaking world.
7. Boyle, *Trenchard*, 328–31.
8. Trenchard Collection, RAF Museum, London. See specifically files AC71/19 (Correspondence), as well as the Trenchard notes in developing his ideas, specifically in MFC 76/1/21 (microfiche), fiche 2, 5, 6, 7, 8. The notes culminate in the transcript of a speech to the RAF Staff College, where he outlines his ideas on the future of the RAF, the role of bombing, and his emphasis on the psychological ("moral[e]") component of strategic bombing.
9. Billy Mitchell, *Winged Defense* (repr., Auburn, AL: Fire Ant, 2009), esp. 56–76.
10. John T. Correll, "The Billy Mitchell Court-Martial," *Air Force Times*, 1 August 2012, https://www.airforcemag.com/article/0812mitchell/. See also the 1955 film *The Court Martial of Billy Mitchell*.
11. Harold Winton, "The Air Corps Tactical School and the School of Advanced Air and Space Studies" in *Educating Air Forces: Global Perspectives on Airpower Learning*, edited by Randall Wakelam and David Varey (Lexington: University Press of Kentucky, 2020), esp. 154–58.
12. Richard Overy, *The Bombers and the Bombed* (New York: Penguin Books, 2013), chap. 1, esp. 75–82.
13. "Victory, speedy and complete, awaits the side which first employs air power as it should be employed." Secret Document, 17 June 1942 (revised 20 August 1942), H.11, Harris Papers, RAF Museum (London) Archives. See also Secret Notes on Roles and Work of Bomber Command, 8 July 1942, H.14, ibid.
14. Harris to the Political Warfare Executive, "Psychological aspects of bombing policy during the spring and summer," 14 April 1942, H.4B, Harris Papers, RAF Museum (London) Archive. This document outlines the operational plan of Bomber Command for the upcoming year.
15. Tami Davis Biddle, *Rhetoric and Reality in Air Warfare: The Evolution of British and American Ideas about Strategic Bombing, 1914–1945* (Princeton, NJ: Princeton University Press, 2002), chap. 4, esp. 207–8, 210–11.

16. Arthur T. Harris, *Despatch on War Operations: 23rd February 1942 to 8th May 1945*, edited by Sebastian Cox (London: Routledge, 1995), 196.
17. This is according to the theories posited by Trenchard and Douhet and as operationalized by Harris during the war. See Biddle, *Rhetoric and Reality in Air Warfare*.
18. Joint Staff, "The Quadrant Conference: August 1943," Papers and Minutes of Meetings, https://www.jcs.mil/Portals/36/Documents/History/WWII/Quadrant3.pdf.
19. Wesley Craven and James Cate, *The Army Air Forces in World War II*, vol. 3, *Europe: Argument to V-E Day, January 1944 to May 1945* (Chicago: University of Chicago Press, 1951) 75.
20. As outlined in Douhet, *Command of the Air*, which focuses on the aerial bombing of civilian populations.
21. Craven and Cate, *Army Air Forces in World War II*, 3:74–55.
22. Craven and Cate, 3:72–73. See also Stephen A. Bourque, *Beyond the Beach: The Allied War against France* (Annapolis, MD: Naval Institute Press, 2018).
23. Craven and Cate, *Army Air Forces in World War II*, 3:71–72. For additional information, see R. Cargill Hall, *Case Studies in Strategic Bombardment* (Washington DC: Office of Air Force History, 1998); Benjamin Cooling, *Case Studies in the Development of Close Air Support* (Washington, DC: Office of Air Force History, 1990); Charles Webster and Noble Frankland, *The Strategic Air Offensive against Germany, 1939–1945*, vol. 3, *Victory* (London: HMSO, 1961); Arthur Harris, *Bomber Offensive* (Barnsley, UK: Frontline Books, 2015); David Mets, *Master of Airpower: General Carl A. Spaatz* (Novato, CA: Presidio, 1998): Michael S. Sherry, *The Rise of American Air Power: The Creation of Armageddon* (New Haven, CT: Yale University Press, 1987); Richard Overy, *The Bombers and the Bombed: Allied Air War Over Europe 1940–1945* (New York: Penguin, 2013); Biddle, *Rhetoric and Reality*; and Phillips Payson O'Brien, *How the War Was Won: Air-Sea Power and Allied Victory in World War II* (Cambridge: Cambridge University Press, 2015), among others. This is just a small sampling of the many excellent books on the air war over Germany.
24. Initial Joint Plan, NEPTUNE, 1 February 1944, paragraphs 23, 28, quoted in Craven and Cate, *Army Air Forces in World War II*, 3:72.
25. Craven and Cate, *Army Air Forces in World War II*, 3:74.
26. Craven and Cate, *Army Air Forces in World War II*, 3:75.
27. Craven and Cate, *Army Air Forces in World War II*, 3:75.
28. Craven and Cate, *Army Air Forces in World War II*, 3:75.
29. James Holland, *Big Week: The Biggest Air Battle of World War II* (New York: Atlantic Monthly Press, 2018).

30. Craven and Cate, *Army Air Forces in World War II*, 3:76.
31. Craven and Cate, *Army Air Forces in World War II*, 3:76.
32. Craven and Cate, *Army Air Forces in World War II*, 3:77.
33. Craven and Cate, *Army Air Forces in World War II*, 3:77–78.
34. Craven and Cate, *Army Air Forces in World War II*, 3:78–79.
35. Craven and Cate, *Army Air Forces in World War II*, 3:80.
36. Craven and Cate, *Army Air Forces in World War II*, 3:81.
37. U.S. Strategic Bombing Survey (USSBS), vol. 64a, "The Impact of the Allied Effort on German Logistics," 40.
38. USSBS, 64a:42.
39. USSBS, vol. 64a, chap. 2, annex 4, exhibit 2-A, following 62.
40. USSBS, vol. 64a, chap. 2, exhibit 1, 80.
41. USSBS, 64a:45.
42. USSBS, 64b:2.

2

The Transportation Plan
A Reassessment

Stephen Moore

Despite the critical role it played in the success of the Normandy landings, the Transportation Plan tends to be overlooked or trivialized when analyzing the campaign.[1] Contemporary perception of the Transportation Plan misunderstood its strategic nature, and proposers wasted valuable time convincing interested parties that it was critical to the Neptune phase of the campaign, as it would canalize rail traffic and facilitate tactical interdiction, diverting enemy reinforcements onto roads. Many objections were raised by the strategic bomber commanders over the perceived "misuse" of their forces.

The operational advances made by the strategic air forces are generally overlooked in the historiography and rarely analyzed to explain their effectiveness. Indeed, the published official British account of the air offensive against Germany lacks details about the Transportation Plan because it was not part of the Combined Bomber Offensive (CBO) and would be covered in a separate volume on air support for Overlord.[2] As the latter book devotes only eight pages to the campaign, fewer than Sir Charles Webster and Noble Frankland allotted in their CBO study, and the other British "official history" is similarly sparse, this gap in the historiography still hinders the proper understanding of these operations.[3]

The shortage of secondary literature means that this review relies on British and American primary sources, Royal Air Force (RAF) Air Historical Branch narratives, and U.S. Army Air Forces (USAAF) historical studies alongside the corresponding official histories, with a comparatively small amount of subsequent evaluation. Although accounts by writers Stephen Darlow and Lionel Lacey-Johnson document the Transportation Plan, they combine it with the Pointblank offensive rather than treat it as a distinct, separate campaign.[4] Claudia Baldoli and Andrew Knapp highlight the casualties caused in France and Italy by Allied bombing, but while they examine the campaigns against railway targets in both countries, these again merge into the general narrative of other bombing operations.[5] The operational history of the Transportation Plan by Stephen Bourque reflects his uncertainty of what the campaign was designed to achieve—at one point he notes that it never had a code name.[6]

So, since 2019, I have examined why the British and Commonwealth chronology of "the plan" differs from the American narrative, addressed here while documenting the operational level of the campaign. Although some interaction with the decision-making process is inevitable, these disputes will only be acknowledged where they influenced operations. Yet the focus is on the operations of the heavy bombers of RAF Bomber Command and U.S. Eighth Army Air Force—not including the interdiction operations by the single- and twin-engine aircraft of the Allied Expeditionary Air Force (AEAF)—against railway targets before Overlord, with the goal of prompting further research on this aspect of Overlord operations.

Preliminary Planning for Overlord

Once the United States entered the war, the pressure to open a second front in Europe grew steadily. By the end of 1943, all of the Allied commanders were confirmed, with General Dwight D. Eisenhower as supreme commander, Air Chief Marshal Sir Arthur Tedder as his deputy, and Lieutenant

General Carl Spaatz to command the U.S. Strategic Air Forces in Europe (USSTAF). Tedder and Spaatz had served under Ike in the Mediterranean.[7] Air Chief Marshal Sir Trafford Leigh-Mallory was appointed commander in chief, Allied Expeditionary Air Force (AEAF), but there were already doubts about this choice due to his behavior during the Battle of Britain and the "leaning forward into France" fighter offensive of 1941–42.[8] The USAAF official history describes his responsibilities and authority as "troublesome," and the AEAF "never lost its reputation of being a British-dominated organization, a factor which diminished its effectiveness and later caused it to be bypassed in many important matters."[9]

The Allies needed to disguise the location of the main invasion landings and delay the arrival of enemy reinforcements to the beachhead. The Fortitude operation convinced the Germans that a fictional army was poised to land in the Pas de Calais and influenced the possible deployment of their reserves against the Normandy landings for weeks.[10] In order to delay the arrival of reinforcements, the aim was to create a "railway desert" within 150 miles of Caen without giving any indication that Normandy was the area chosen for the landings.[11]

Development of the Transportation Plan

When Tedder was appointed as deputy supreme commander, he brought his scientific advisor Solly Zuckerman with him to join the Overlord planning team.[12] Zuckerman had devised a plan to disrupt rail traffic during the Italian Campaign, identifying multiple nodes as essential target sets by strategic bombing.[13] The USAAF official history proposes that the "authors" of the Transportation Plan might "have been several civilian specialists in the Air Ministry, namely Solly Zuckerman and E. D. Brant" or "possibly it was Air Chief Marshal Tedder."[14] While Zuckerman reviewed the initial plan, the Air Historical Branch narrative clearly states that Brant produced the target list.[15]

The first meeting of the AEAF Bombing Committee took place on 10 January 1944, with the civilian expertise being provided by various railway specialists as well as Zuckerman.[16] By 1 February, the initial plan was finalized, and the list of principal railway centers identified. But the AEAF, although tasked with air support of the invasion, did not possess sufficient resources to fulfil its commitments. Leigh-Mallory had direct command of the RAF's Second Tactical Air Force and Air Defence of Great Britain together with the U.S. Ninth Air Force, with only tactical fighters and light bombers under his control; British and American heavy bombers remained outside of his authority.[17] By accepting that the best way of destroying railway communications was by attacking maintenance and repair centers, Leigh-Mallory "showed his hand" and guaranteed strong opposition.[18]

Delays to the Plan by Opposition from the Commanders

A summary of service opposition to the Transportation Plan helps contextualize the effects at the operational level. The toxic presence of Leigh-Mallory caused twofold opposition—of many toward him personally and of the bomber commanders toward the plan itself. When he expressed reluctance to go down in posterity as the man who killed thousands of Frenchmen, Air Chief Marshal Sir Arthur Harris characteristically questioned whether he would go down in posterity at all.[19] This reinforces the observation that Leigh-Mallory's appointment was not one of the better decisions of the war.[20]

Both Harris and Spaatz anticipated the involvement of their forces in pre-Overlord operations by the end of 1943 and were determined to resist diversion of their heavy bombers away from their "proper" use. Harris argued in January 1944 that his force was unsuitable for the precision targeting required. The Air Historical Branch narrative concedes that Harris was "almost entirely wrong in his assumptions," that "he spoilt his case by exaggeration and overstatement," and that he demonstrated "an unwelcome rigidity of mind and unsympathetic attitude to the invasion project."[21] While discussing the initial plan, Spaatz argued that it disregarded his previous Pointblank directive, and Harris contrasted the targeted railway systems in France and Belgium with those previously attacked in Italy.[22] The different operational priorities of Bomber Command and Eighth Air Force between February and April 1944 jeopardized the completion of the Transportation Plan before the invasion began.

The underlying problems of Bomber Command limited Harris' opposition to the redeployment of his aircraft. The Battle of Berlin had severely damaged British bomber squadrons during the winter of 1943, as Harris stubbornly attacked the German capital even while losses increased. The Air Historical Branch narrative attributes this to a reorganization of Luftwaffe night defenses that made the attack on a single objective untenable, but long journeys across Germany gave night fighters multiple occasions to intercept attacking bombers, on both the outward and return legs, regardless of the number of targets. Once the factors of appalling winter weather and concentrated flak defenses were added, no one should have been surprised when aircraft losses against Berlin climbed. Harris had to withdraw Stirling- and Merlin-engine Halifax squadrons from deep-penetration raids, so losses to his more capable Lancaster squadrons increased, taking the force to the brink with a disastrous raid on Nuremberg.[23]

Despite his disdain for "panacea targets," Harris' obsession with Berlin shows that this was such a panacea target for him.[24] The unexpected firestorm that devastated Hamburg had surprised him, and he became convinced that he could do the same to Berlin. Unfortunately, Berlin was too big, and its modern construction refused to produce a catastrophic conflagration. While Bomber Command drew the wrong conclusions from deep-penetration-raid losses, it led No. 5 Group to experiment with an integrated Pathfinder element to exploit the low-level marking technique developed by No. 617 Squadron. This technique allowed the execution of a main-force attack separate from the rest of Bomber Command. The initial operations of No. 5 Group required testing in occupied territories; regardless, 27 percent of the main-force heavy bombers were unsuitable for longer-range operations.[25] Harris was outmaneuvered when the Operational Research Section admitted that most of the rail centers could be attacked using Oboe.[26] Oboe was introduced in 1943 as a radar-guided blind-bombing aid to control a single aircraft, which was directed to the target by radio-pulse transmissions from a station. A second ground station then transmitted a bomb-release signal so that the markers or bombs fell on the target, providing accuracy within 100 yards.[27]

On 2 March Leigh-Mallory submitted a list of seventy-five targets in France and northern Belgium to the Air Ministry for clearance, with fifty-eight assigned to the heavy bombers (see table 2-1).[28] Planners estimated that the bombing effort required to collapse the French railway system "was well within the capacity of the available bomb lift between March and May," Ideally, operations against transportation targets should start in March to avoid "a general congestion of commitments" as the invasion date approached.[29]

Air Chief Marshal Sir Charles Portal, chief of the Air Staff, who suspected that Harris' "operational appreciations were coloured by his strategic views," proposed a "special directive" to Bomber Command at the beginning of March for experimental attacks to establish whether heavy bombers could hit small aircraft factories, repair depots, and rail centers at night.[30] As the major drawback with Oboe was a limited range of 250 miles for many aircraft, this was not an issue for targets in France.[31]

Despite objecting, Harris agreed to attack the railway center at Trappes on the night of 6–7 March. This successful raid put it out of action for a month, and eight attacks on other rail centers followed throughout the rest

Table 2-1 • Strategic Transportation Plan Targets

	RAF Bomber Command		U.S. Eighth Air Force	
Occupied Territories	Amiens/Longeau	Montzen	Belfort	Mulhouseîle Napoléon
	Angers	Orléans-les-Aubrais	Blainville-sur-l'Eau	Mulhouse/Main Station
	Aulnoye	Ottignes	Brussels/Midi	Mulhouse/Nord
	Boulogne-sur-Mer	Paris–Juvisy	Brussels/Schaerbeek	Nancy
	Courtrai	Paris–La Chappelle	Châlons-sur-Marne	Reims
	Ghent/Meulebeke	Paris–Noisy-le-Sec	Chaumont	Sarreguemines
	Hasselt	Paris–Trappes	Épinal	Strasbourg/Hausbergen
	Laon	Paris–Vaires	Liège/Guillemines	Thionville
	Le Mans	Paris–Villneneuve St. Georges	Liège/Kinkempois	Troyes
	Lens	Rouen/Sotteville	Liège/Renory	
	Lille/Délivrance	Saumur	Luxembourg	
	Lille/Fives	Somain	Metz	
	Louvain	St. Ghislain		
	Malines	St. Pierre-des-Corps		
	Mantes/Gassicourt	Tergnier		
	Miramas	Tours		
Germany	Aachen/Hauptbahnhof		Enrang	
	Aachen/Rothe Erde		Konz	
	Aachen West			
	Brunswick marshaling yard			

Source: Adapted from Lionel Lacey-Johnson, *Point Blank and Beyond* (1991; repr., Shrewsbury, UK: Airlife, 2002), 253–54.

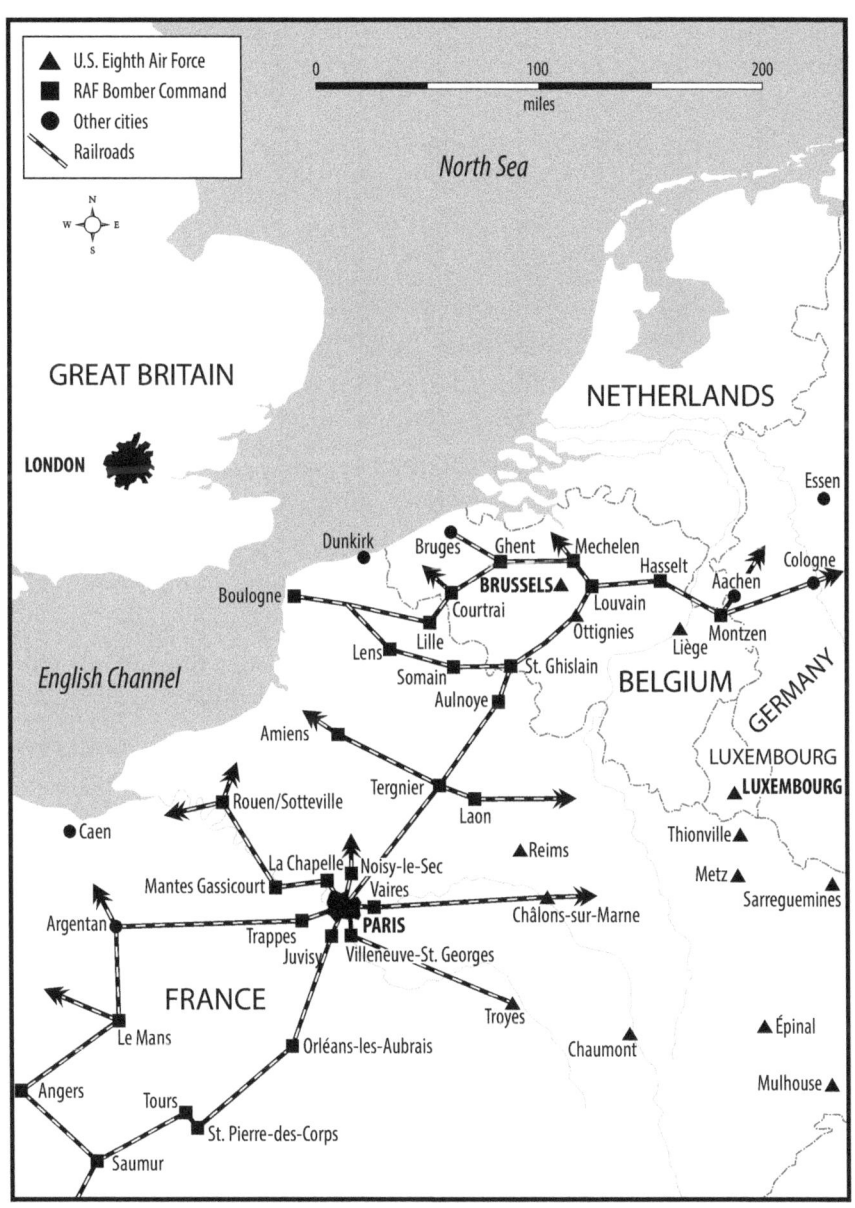

Map 2-1 • Major Railway Targets in the Transportation Plan (Strategic Air Forces Only)

of March.[32] The USAAF official history acknowledges this as the start of Bomber Command attacks in connection with the Transportation Plan.[33] French factories were also bombed using the new No. 5 Group low-level marking technique, which increased accuracy and reduced civilian casualties.[34] These successes weakened Harris' previous arguments and undermined his continued resistance.[35] For the first time since 1942, Bomber Command revised its target-marking methods, enabling each bomber group to develop marking and bombing techniques to suit specific operational needs so that "a great tactical diversification grew up in Bomber Command."[36] Harris subsequently admitted, "At this stage of the war we now had the benefit of several different techniques, developed by different Groups, which were suitable for a variety of targets or conditions of weather."[37]

While Harris was unable to avoid the bombing of transportation targets, the circumstances of the U.S. Eighth Air Force gave General Spaatz a far stronger position. After serious losses in the autumn of 1943, the American deep-penetration raids resumed in February 1944 once the provision of external fuel tanks for escort fighters increased the operational radius of the P-51 Mustang to 850 miles, denying the Luftwaffe the opportunity to attack an unescorted American bomber formation. By attacking Pointblank targets vital to the aircraft industry, defending fighters were compelled to intercept the bombers, leading to "the decisive American victory which followed" during the "Big Week" series of airstrikes.[38] Spaatz therefore argued that attacking transportation targets would threaten his offensive against German aircraft production and prevent the attainment of air supremacy. Eisenhower was equally concerned about control of the skies and delayed the decision for a month, in which time Spaatz won a "momentous victory" that "guaranteed Allied air supremacy for the rest of the war."[39] The USAAF official history notes, "Somehow Air Chief Marshal Harris was won over to the transportation plan," and he opposed the USSTAF recommendation of oil as an objective as a "panacea" target. Tedder's assessment was more forensic: not enough damage to fuel capabilities would be caused before D-Day, but using all air forces together could dislocate railway infrastructure to disrupt rail movements before the landings.[40]

As Bomber Command operations continued, the arguments and counterarguments "were going around in circles and still no decision had been reached on the question of the employment of heavy bombers in preparation for the assault."[41] Portal was the coordinating agent for strategic bomber forces, so he called a conference on 25 March to finalize the integration of the strategic air forces into the Overlord command chain.[42] The Transportation Plan was "accepted, if a trifle unwillingly," after Eisenhower insisted that "he was convinced that apart from the attacks on German aircraft targets, the bombing of rail centers was the only reasonable chance of the air force making an important contribution during the early vital weeks of Overlord."[43] Harris was concerned that Bomber Command might be unable to complete their part of the program due to limitations of Oboe coverage during moon periods, target-marking difficulties, and bad weather. Portal was more concerned about whether the U.S. Eighth Air Force could complete its share of missions in time, as this had not yet been worked out.[44] Tedder assumed responsibility for the plan as part of supervising all air operations for Overlord. This suited Harris and Spaatz, as it removed from direct command Leigh-Mallory, whose last executive action was to forward the next list of twenty-nine priority targets in France and Belgium; subsequent lists were the responsibility of Tedder as deputy supreme commander.[45]

Although Harris described the Transportation Plan as "devised by a civilian professor whose peacetime forte is the study of the sexual aberrations of the higher apes," he trusted Tedder not to abandon strategic bombing "in favour of slogan or panacea warfare."[46] The tone of Leigh-Mallory's dispatch indicated his dissatisfaction with this final resolution of the argument.[47] On 29 March Portal informed the Chiefs of Staff Committee that the Transportation Plan had been agreed between himself and Eisenhower, so operations to progress the plan "should be pressed on without delay." Since certain targets required political authorization, Portal needed to refer them to the War Cabinet for clearance.[48] With three months required to collapse the rail infrastructure, almost a month was already gone. The opposition from the commanders had ended, but they had spent far too much time arguing about their own authority and independence. Now Portal's obligation to refer the plan to the British War Cabinet threatened to block or delay operations so that the rail-network disruption would not be completed before the invasion began.

Starting with Trappes on 6–7 March, Bomber Command had attacked seven rail centers in nine raids as primary objectives. A total of 1,314 aircraft had dropped 6,873 tons of bombs, or 26.4 percent of the tonnage for March.[49] All of these targets were blind marked using Oboe, with the majority of the raiders being Merlin-engine Halifaxes that Harris could not use against German targets.[50] Although classed as successful, both Le Mans and Amiens had to be quickly rebombed, while the attacks on Laon and Aulnoye failed to disrupt rail movements there.[51] Further operational adjustments now awaited political approval, so Portal requested clearance for three further rail targets in France.[52]

Delays to Operations by Opposition from the Politicians

When the War Cabinet Defence Committee met on 5 April, some expressed concerns about the hostility that heavy casualties would cause in France, and they deferred a decision. The proposed attacks "had given rise to considerable differences of opinion" but could continue "experimentally against those rail centres where there was no great risk of inflicting heavy civilian casualties."[53]

This cabinet prevarication continued at subsequent meetings, as Portal struggled to maintain operations to support the plan. Bomber Command therefore continued limited attacks and, by the night of 10–11 April, had completed fifteen Oboe-marked raids on eleven rail centers, involving 2,513 heavy bomber sorties.[54] Two of the 10–11 April operations were follow-up raids on Laon and Aulnoye after the unsuccessful initial attacks.[55] The second Laon raid was equally ineffective, but at Aulnoye two aircraft acting as master bombers released red target indicators after assessing the accuracy of the Oboe markers, leading to an effective attack on the target.[56] This was the first example of the "controlled Oboe" technique, which "introduced the more complex and accurate methods" used in the later transportation attacks.[57] That same night No. 5 Group "made a highly successful attack" on the marshaling yards at Tours using the "visual ground marking technique" developed during precision raids against small targets concurrent to the rail-center attacks throughout March.⁵⁸ This method was pioneered by No. 617 Squadron, specifically its commander, Group Captain Leonard Cheshire, who employed a dive-bombing technique to accurately place markers onto an aiming point illuminated by flares dropped using Oboe or H2S assistance, utilizing the gunsight at "1,000 feet or less" (in some cases, significantly less) to achieve the necessary accuracy.⁵⁹ The entire operation was then controlled by the master bomber via radio telephone in a Mosquito flying low enough to observe the aiming point, backing up the most accurately placed markers, before directing the operation of the main bombing force.⁶⁰ With this, the USAAF official history concedes, "Bomber Command heavies were proving that expertly led night formations could approximate the operations of daylight attackers in effectiveness."⁶¹ These methods contributed to what the British official history describes as the "remarkable advances in the techniques of night precision bombing" during this period.⁶²

At a meeting on 15 April, Tedder announced to Harris, Spaatz, and their staff officers that Supreme Headquarters Allied Expeditionary Force (SHAEF) had assumed command of the strategic bombing forces and would direct all operations associated with Pointblank and Overlord.⁶³ By 18 April, all targets were approved apart from the Paris-area locations of Batignolles and Le Bourget.⁶⁴ By this point, a third of the target list had already been attacked, with civilian casualties lower than expected. Concern was expressed on 19 April that American forces should take an equal share of transportation bombing "in the execution of the plan if it was adopted" (despite Bomber Command already having attacked for over five weeks).⁶⁵

At the Defence Committee meeting on 26 April, Portal reported that Bomber Command had struck nine railway targets in the previous week, dropping 7,880 tons of bombs. In comparison, the AEAF had carried out nineteen attacks on twelve targets using 740 tons. The British had bombed over 30 percent of their transportation target list, while the U.S. Eighth Air Force was yet to start on theirs.⁶⁶ The USAAF official history acknowledges the first Eighth Air Force "missions under the transportation program" began on 27 April, bombing Blainville-sur-l'Eau (343 tons) and Châlons-sur-Marne (230 tons), while Bomber Command "was piling up a notable

Photo 2-1 • According to the USAAF official history, Eighth Air Force carried out its first attacks in support of the Transportation Plan on 27 April 1944 against Blainville-sur-l'Eau (near Nancy) and Châlons-sur-Marne (east of Paris). This photo, taken in the immediate aftermath of the raids, shows significant damage to the Blainville marshaling yard. *U.S. Air Force Photo 51571AC*

series of victories in wiping out rail centers," dropping 33,000 tons on such targets by the end of April.[67] As the American contribution began, cabinet pressure forced Eisenhower to suspend twenty-seven targets "located in thickly populated areas" on 29 April.[68] Prime Minister Winston Churchill urged him to exclude targets where the estimated casualties would exceed 100 civilians, but Eisenhower had committed to the plan and rejected any alternatives. This harassment came to an end at the next Defence Committee meeting on 3 May, when Churchill made the ridiculous decision to endorse the plan, provided casualties were kept below 10,000 civilians. Tedder knew that this was impossible to estimate, let alone guarantee, but he was forced to agree in order to continue operations.[69]

Photo 2-2 • As Eighth Air Force B-24 Liberators leave the target area, a huge explosion sends smoke and flames high into the sky as a result of the attack on the marshaling yards at Châlons-sur-Marne. *U.S. Air Force Photo 51217AC*

Continuation and Results of the Transportation Plan

In a special meeting on 3 May to discuss the continuation of the Transportation Plan, Tedder highlighted that USSTAF targets had not been attacked and traffic was flowing freely along those routes. He was "anxious" that these should be "attacked without further delay," but the USSTAF representative "suggested that the transportation plan had been suspended." Tedder "emphasised" that Eisenhower had expressly ordered that "it had not."[70] The U.S. Eighth Air Force dropped 573 tons on 27 April and on 1 May "carried out its first major mission against rail centers," sending 328 bombers to drop 1,000 tons on five separate targets.[71] On 5 May Eisenhower removed the restrictions on the Transportation Plan, although whether this included the 10,000-fatality limit is unclear—Churchill continued to harass Tedder about bombing deaths well into July.[72]

The USAAF official history documents the difficulties in assessing railway bombing. By the end of April, only French and Belgian traffic was affected—German troop and supply trains were still running "without serious delay." This was undermined by the admission that the campaign "was a long-term program" and that less than half of the required tonnage had been dropped. On 30 April Leigh-Mallory urged an acceleration of effort, particularly for the Eighth Air Force "to begin its full participation."[73] A revised list of objectives was issued, attacking targets with the lowest estimated civilian casualties first and leaving heavier-populated areas for as close to the invasion as possible.[74] In mid-May the Transportation Plan was nearing completion apart from the contribution of the USSTAF, which "still had the bulk of their tonnage to deliver." By D-Day, Eighth Air Force had severely damaged all the twenty-three targets allocated to it, dropping 13,000 tons with a "devastating effect."[75] During the same period, Bomber Command made another thirty-two attacks, bombing targets that included Trappes and Tergnier for a second or third time after repairs had been completed.[76]

While USSTAF attacks used established methods, Bomber Command continued "the further development of night precision bombing techniques."[77] RAF raids in May used variations of controlled Oboe, or the No. 5 Group marking techniques, "with a considerable increase in accuracy."[78] Offset marking was developed, where initial indicators were followed up by red-spot fires dropped by the master bomber, backed up by further aircraft canceling inaccurate markers with another color. As markers were often obscured by smoke and dust from bombing, spot fires were deliberately planted 300–400 yards from the actual aiming point. Specially selected crews in the formation made "complicated mathematical calculations" in "somewhat inconvenient circumstances" to provide an average wind speed and direction, adjusted with a calculated "false vector," which was transmitted to the main bombing force, so that bombs aimed at the offset markers would hit the hidden target.[79] Some operations also used a variation of the No. 5 Group technique, "Musical Newhaven," dropping target indicators instead of spot fires when the standard method could not be used.[80] All methods used a master bomber to direct the attack, giving better results than blind Oboe marking but still less effective than the No. 5 Group technique.[81]

As the destruction of rail facilities continued, the effect on military traffic increased by the end of May. "A growing paralysis was gradually creeping over the railway network of the Region Nord," as intensified attacks isolated Normandy while creating "the impression that the Pas de Calais was the threatened area."[82] Table 2-2 shows that fifty-one of eighty targets were so heavily damaged that no further attacks were required (Category A), twenty-five severely damaged but required further attacks (Category B), and only four so little damaged that they required further early attention (Category C).

Table 2-2 • Summary of Efforts against Railway Targets

	AEAF	U.S. Eighth Air Force	Bomber Command	Totals
Number of Targets	20	26	39	85
Total Sorties	8,736	4,462	8,751	21,949
Tonnage Dropped	10,125	11,648	44,744	66,517
Category A	14	15	22	51
Category B	2	8	15	25
Category C	2	0	2	4

Sources: Air Historical Branch, Air Ministry, *The Liberation of North West Europe* (UK National Archives, 1952), 1:174 –75; *The Liberation of North West Europe* 3:27.

Without heavy bombers, the Transportation Plan could not have been completed, especially when some targets were found unsuitable for AEAF aircraft. The "lion's share" of the targets were attacked by Bomber Command, and their initial allocation of targets was increased by ten.[83] The American contribution to the effort only became significant in May, and even at this stage, the U.S. Eighth Air Force expended more tonnage on aviation targets, and 10,000 combined tons was still being dropped on towns, mostly to prevent fighters relocating closer to the invasion zone. The transportation tonnage dropped by Bomber Command was twice that of the USSTAF, as shown in table 2-3. While the British increased their contribution to include targets unsuitable for the AEAF, it is unlikely that USSTAF would have been able to compensate if Bomber Command had been unable to fulfill its share of the plan.[84]

By 21 May, most of the trains still running were of military importance. Restrictions on attacks against engines and rolling stock were then removed, and tactical interdiction by fighters began on a huge scale, with the AEAF

Table 2-3 • Tons of Bombs Dropped, March–June 1944

TARGET CATEGORY	RAF Bomber Command 7 March–6 June 1944		U.S. Eighth Air Force 17 April–6 June 1944	
	Tonnage	% of Total Effort	Tonnage	% of Total Effort
All Aircraft Targets	7,788	6.73	24,125	34.09
Dock and Ports	29	0.02	70	0.10
Military Installations	17,038	14.72	1,446	2.04
Long-Range Weapons	1,842	1.59	9,239	13.06
All Oil Targets	—	—	3,834	5.42
All Industrial Targets	4,154	3.59	1,924	2.72
Towns	40,533	35.01	11,588	16.38
All Transportation Targets	44,356	38.31	18,532	26.19
Miscellaneous	31	.03	—	—
Total Tonnage	115,771	100.00	70,758	100.00

Source: "The Strategic Air War against Germany, 1939–1945: Report of British Bombing Survey Unit," 1949, tables 7, 8, Ike Skelton Combined Arms Research Library, Call no. N20639.7, https://cgsc.contentdm.oclc.org/digital/collection/p4013coll8/id/4323/.

destroying 157 locomotives and damaging 82 by D-Day.[85] Movement by rail was now slow, difficult, and dangerous.[86] The overall volume of traffic began to fall in the middle of March 1944 and, by the beginning of July, was only 20 percent of January levels.[87] The results were "impressive and immediate," with freedom of movement removed throughout most of France and Belgium, making a decisive counterattack "impossible to the enemy." Movement of reinforcements and supplies at night put "enormous demands" on vehicle and fuel resources, choking roads with unintended volumes of traffic.[88] This was what the Transportation Plan had been designed to do: canalizing rail traffic onto lines to facilitate tactical interdiction and forcing enemy reinforcements onto roads. The network was never completely interrupted, but rebombing after repairs kept the disruption level high, although certain targets were excluded due to concerns about civilian casualties; Tedder noted that Le Bourget was never attacked for this reason, so it "provided throughout [the campaign] the main leak for military movement to Normandy."[89] Unlike other invasion operations, the Transportation Plan had no code name, which has hindered its subsequent understanding. The USAAF official history notes that Spaatz and the USSTAF considered attacks on rail centers less important than "bridge-breaking and line-cutting," as did U.S. embassy railway experts, the U.S. Strategic Bombing Survey, and the president of the French railway system.[90] This error does not recognize that these efforts "constituted merely the strategic phase of the whole plan for delaying the movement of enemy reserves."[91] Without the initial reduction of the rail infrastructure by strategic bombers, the subsequent tactical-interdiction campaign would not have been possible, let alone successful.

German Reactions to Bombing and Civilian Casualties

A German Reichsluftfahrtministerium (Ministry of Aviation) report on 3 June 1944 states, "The raids carried out in recent weeks have caused the breakdown of all main lines." Even moving "only the most vital military traffic," the "large strategic movement of German troops by rail is practically impossible at the present time." The report concluded that the Allies intended to completely wreck the rail network and conceded that they were succeeding, so much that the Reichsbahn (German rail service) was contemplating abandoning further repair work. Map 2-2 shows the targets attacked by the Allied air forces, mostly to the north and east of Paris, away from the actual Normandy invasion area.[92]

This map, however, does not convey the difficulties the Germans experienced in reaching the Normandy battlefield. The 1st SS Panzer Division left Belgium on 17 June and did not reach Caen until 4 July after a seventeen-day journey of 270 rail miles and 140 road miles. This trip would have previously taken three days. The bombing of marshaling yards caused delays of a week; the rail centers of Paris were so devastated that the division had to take to the road and arrived in Normandy short of fuel and low on morale.[93] This is a typical example of the difficulties facing German reinforcements. By the time these units arrived, their combat fuel reserve was gone, little replacement fuel arrived by train, and tired men were thrown into combat in small packets without unit integrity.

Churchill continued to harass Tedder about casualties, culminating in a blunt memorandum on 7 July asking, "How many Frenchmen did you kill?" Tedder replied that there were "varying estimates" of French casualties but no "reliable figure," noting that "casualties [from transportation bombing] were being dwarfed" by those in the "Normandy towns and villages" now that ground fighting was taking place.[94] Zuckerman estimated civilian casualties at 10,000 killed and wounded, perhaps influenced by the Defence Committee endorsement.[95] One modern estimate counts 12,000 French dead from the Transportation Plan, and Stephen Bourque highlights that "perhaps 10,000 Belgians perished" in these attacks—civilians who are generally overlooked.[96]

At least seven Bomber Command attacks caused more than 100 civilian fatalities, as shown in table 2-4. Over 400 civilians were killed in each of Lille, Ghent, and Noisy-Le-Sec (Paris). At Noisy, 464 were killed, and the damage to this depot was so severe that it was not fully repaired until six years after the war. Improvements to target-marking techniques and aircraft operating at lower altitudes made night bombing possible without incurring unacceptable political consequences. At the same time, there was widespread resentment toward the Americans because of indiscriminate high-altitude attacks, such as one at Mantes-Gassicourt on 29 May that killed 200 civilians.[97] The strategic bomber campaign in support of the Transportation Plan

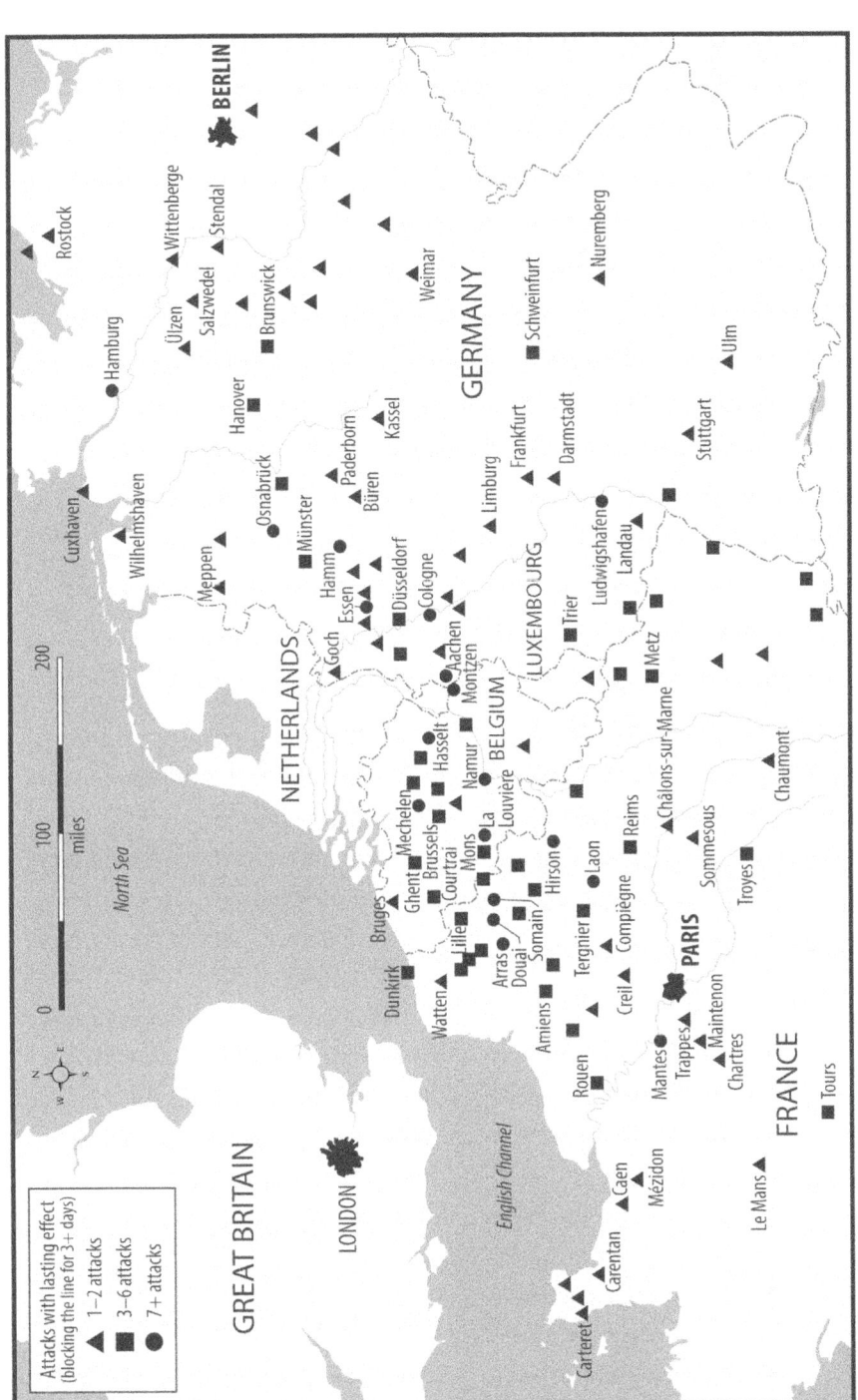

Map 2-2 • Reichsbahn Survey of Rail Transport Attacks

Table 2-4 • Attacks with over 100 Civilian Fatalities

Date	Target	Civilian Fatalities
26–27 March	Courtrai	252
9–10 April	Lille	456
10–11 April	Ghent	428
18–19 April	Paris–Noisy-le-Sec	464
1–2 May	Malines	171
12–13 May	Louvain	160
28–29 May	Angers	252

Source: Martin Middlebrook and Chris Everitt, *The Bomber Command War Diaries* (London: Penguin, 1990), 486, 492–93, 495, 503, 510, 516.

ended on 2 June, where it began, when Bomber Command attacked Trappes for the third and last time.[98]

Conclusion

The Transportation Plan was intended to delay the arrival of enemy reinforcements to the Normandy beachheads. This provoked opposition by the air commanders and by the British government despite authority having already been given to Eisenhower. The commanders' opposition to Leigh-Mallory was resolved by strategic requirements being routed through Tedder, while the operational objections faded away following successful experimental attacks during March 1944.

The historiography of this campaign has been conflated by including rail targets that were not part of the Transportation Plan in the results. The Transportation Plan had no code name, which has distorted the overall effectiveness of the attacks on the transport nodes, which overloaded the capacity of the railway network. The contemporary misunderstanding of the strategic nature of the effort has continued in the historiography, which generally considers the Transportation Plan as either part of Pointblank or wider Overlord operations, diluting its strategic component to insignificance. The different perceptions of the Transportation Plan on either side of the Atlantic are reflected in the relevant official histories and restricted military narratives and historical studies. While USAAF sources acknowledge that Bomber Command attacks on transportation targets began in March, they do not consider the Transportation Plan started until Eisenhower assumed command of the strategic air forces on 15 April, despite targets on "the list" being bombed for six weeks.

The different circumstances and operational priorities of Bomber Command and the U.S. Eighth Air Force jeopardized the completion of the Transportation Plan before the invasion began. Bomber Command had revised its target-marking methods, leading to increased accuracy and reduced civilian casualties. While Harris was unable to avoid the bombing of transportation targets, Spaatz was in a far stronger position. Harris was concerned that Bomber Command might be unable to complete their part of the program due to operational limitations, but the real issue was whether the Eighth Air Force could complete their share of the plan in time. The British cabinet was uncomfortable with civilian-casualty estimates and the strategic merits of the plan, so a limited target list was authorized on a weekly basis until the plan was approved. While USSTAF attacks used established methods, Bomber Command continued developing night precision-bombing techniques, and RAF raids in May used variations of controlled Oboe, or the No. 5 Group marking techniques.

As the destruction of rail facilities continued, the disruption on military traffic increased by the end of May. This was what the Transportation Plan had been designed to do: canalizing rail traffic onto limited lines to facilitate tactical interdiction and forcing enemy reinforcements onto the roads. The volume of traffic started to fall in the middle of March 1944 and, by the beginning of July, was at 20 percent of January levels, with around 12,000 civilians killed, as even "accurate" bombing during World War II spread outside of the intended target area.

NOTES

1. This chapter is based on a presentation from the Normandy 75 Conference held at Portsmouth University in June 2019 and conversations following it. These highlighted a divergence of understanding between British and Commonwealth historians and their American counterparts of what the Transportation Plan was and when it took place. During the conference, Mike Pavelec identified

the start for the Transportation Plan as 15 April 1944. When challenged about that date, as RAF operations had begun in early March, the argument was that April was when strategic bombing forces came under SHAEF control, but this remains unconvincing.
2. Sebastian Cox, "The Historiography of Bomber Command," Exploring the Frontiers of Air Power Research, University of Birmingham Centre for War Studies Workshop, 8 September 2011.
3. L. F. Ellis, *Victory in the West*, vol. 1, *The Battle of Normandy* (London: HMSO, 1962), 97–101, 110–12; Hilary St. George Saunders, *Royal Air Force, 1939–1945*, vol. 3 (London: HMSO, 1954), 87–89. The airpower section in Ellis was undoubtably written by Sir James Robb. Its eleven pages on Normandy compare to the twenty-four within Sir Charles Webster and Noble Frankland, *The Strategic Air Offensive against Germany* (subsequently *SAOAG*), vol. 3, *Victory* (London: HMSO, 1961), 22–39, 151–56.
4. Stephen Darlow, *D-Day Bombers: The Veterans' Story* (London: Grub Street, 2004), 51; Lionel Lacey-Johnson, *Point Blank and Beyond* (1991; repr., Shrewsbury, UK: Airlife, 2002), 48.
5. Claudia Baldoli and Andrew Knapp, *Forgotten Blitzes: France and Italy under Allied Air Attack, 1940–1945* (London: Continuum, 2012), 2–3.
6. Stephen Alan Bourque, *Beyond the Beach: The Allied Air War against France* (Annapolis, MD: Naval Institute Press, 2018), 151. During a "lively" exchange following the presentation of my paper at Portsmouth, Bourque insisted that there was never a Transportation Plan, although he conceded that transportation targets were bombed, again highlighting the divergence of understanding between the two groups of historians.
7. Arthur B. Ferguson, "Winter Bombing," in *The Army Air Forces in World War II*, edited by Wesley Frank Craven and James Lea Cate, vol. 3, *Europe: Argument to V-E Day* (Chicago: University of Chicago, 1951), 6.
8. John Terraine, *The Right of the Line: The Royal Air Force in the European War, 1939–1945* (London: Hodder and Stoughton, 1985), 204, 609.
9. Ferguson, "Winter Bombing," 5–6.
10. Peter Caddick-Adams, *Sand and Steel: A New History of D-Day* (London: Arrow, 2020), 297–98.
11. Lacey-Johnson, *Point Blank and Beyond*, 46.
12. Solly Zuckerman, *From Apes to Warlords* (London: Hamish Hamilton, 1978), 214.
13. Zuckerman, *From Apes to Warlords*, 133.
14. Arthur B. Ferguson, "Plan for Overlord," in Craven and Cate, *Army Air Forces in World War II*, 3:73.

15. Air Historical Branch, Air Ministry [hereafter AHB], *The Liberation of North West Europe* (UK National Archives, 1952), 1:142–43.
16. "The RAF in the Bombing Offensive against Germany," vol. 6, "The Final Phase, March 1944–May 1945," 1955, UK National Archives (TNA) AIR 41/56, 8.
17. Webster and Frankland, *SAOAG*, 3:15.
18. Saunders, *Royal Air Force*, 3:85–86.
19. Henry Probert, *Bomber Harris: His Life and Times* (London: Greenhill, 2001), 291.
20. Terraine, *Right of the Line*, 609.
21. "Bombing Offensive against Germany," 6:4–6.
22. AHB, *The Liberation of North West Europe*, 1:146.
23. Roy Irons, *The Relentless Offensive: War and Bomber Command, 1939–1945* (Barnsley: Pen and Sword, 2009), 222.
24. Arthur Harris, *Bomber Offensive* (London: Collins, 1947), 220.
25. "Bombing Offensive against Germany," 6:270.
26. "Bombing Offensive against Germany," 6:10, 34.
27. "Air Publication 1093D, vol. 1: Introductory Survey of Radar, Part 2," 1947, UK National Archives (TNA) AIR 10/2288, chap. 5, secs. 4–8.
28. AHB, *The Liberation of North West Europe*, 1:148.
29. "Bombing Offensive against Germany," 6:9.
30. Webster and Frankland, *SAOAG*, 3:27.
31. "Air Publication 1093D, vol. 1," chap. 5, sec. 7.
32. Saunders, *Royal Air Force*, 3:87.
33. Arthur B. Ferguson, "Pre-invasion Operations," in Craven and Cate, *Army Air Forces in World War II*, 3:151.
34. Harris, *Bomber Offensive*, 199.
35. "Bombing Offensive against Germany," 6:5.
36. Webster and Frankland, *SAOAG*, 3:130.
37. Harris, *Bomber Offensive*, 202–3.
38. Webster and Frankland, *SAOAG*, 3:131–32.
39. Ferguson, "Plan for Overlord," 75.
40. Ferguson, "Plan for Overlord," 77.
41. "Bombing Offensive against Germany," 6:14.
42. Ferguson, "Winter Bombing," 6.
43. AHB, *The Liberation of North West Europe*, 1:154.
44. "Bombing Offensive against Germany," 6:15–16.
45. AHB, *The Liberation of North West Europe*, 1:155.
46. Probert, *Bomber Harris*, 291–292.

47. Trafford Leigh-Mallory, "Air Operations by the Allied Expeditionary Air Force in N.W. Europe," *London Gazette*, 31 December 1946, 4th supp., 2 January 1947, 38.
48. AHB, *The Liberation of North West Europe*, 1:155–56.
49. Joe L. Norris, "The Combined Bombing Offensive," USAF Historical Study 122 (1947), USAF Historical Research Agency, Maxwell AFB, AL, 162.
50. Webster and Frankland, *SAOAG*, 3:151.
51. Martin Middlebrook and Chris Everitt, *The Bomber Command War Diaries* (London: Penguin, 1990), 479–86.
52. AHB, *The Liberation of North West Europe*, 1:156.
53. AHB, *The Liberation of North West Europe*, 1:158–59.
54. "Bombing Offensive against Germany," 6:38; Webster and Frankland, *SAOAG*, 3:151. Uncharacteristically, the official history only identifies fourteen raids.
55. Middlebrook and Everitt, *Bomber Command War Diaries*, 493.
56. "Bombing Offensive against Germany," 6:39.
57. Webster and Frankland, *SAOAG*, 3:151.
58. "Bombing Offensive against Germany," 6:41.
59. Webster and Frankland, *SAOAG*, 3:153; "Bombing Offensive against Germany," 6:35.
60. Webster and Frankland, *SAOAG*, 3:153.
61. Ferguson, "Pre-invasion Operations," 152.
62. Webster and Frankland, *SAOAG*, 3:151.
63. AHB, *The Liberation of North West Europe*, 1:161–62.
64. "Strategic and Tactical Direction of Air Forces: Transportation Targets Committee, 18 April 1944," UK National Archives (TNA) AIR 37/1012.
65. AHB, *The Liberation of North West Europe*, 1:162–63.
66. "Liberation of North West Europe," 1:163.
67. Ferguson, "Pre-invasion Operations," 153.
68. "Air Support of 'Overlord' during the Preparatory Period, 29 April 1944," UK National Archives (TNA) AIR 37/1012.
69. AHB, *The Liberation of North West Europe*, 1:165–70.
70. AHB, *The Liberation of North West Europe*, 1:167.
71. Ferguson, "Pre-invasion Operations," 155.
72. "Bombing Offensive against Germany," 6:42.
73. Ferguson, "Pre-invasion Operations," 153–54.
74. "Bombing Offensive against Germany," 6:42.
75. Ferguson, "Pre-invasion Operations," 154–55.
76. "Bombing Offensive against Germany," 6:42.
77. Webster and Frankland, *SAOAG*, 3:154.

78. "Bombing Offensive against Germany," 6:42.
79. Webster and Frankland, *SAOAG*, 3:154–56. As Noble Frankland had served as a navigator in Bomber Command, his professional opinion on the navigation requirements of these operations is significant.
80. "Bombing Offensive against Germany," 6:41.
81. Webster and Frankland, *SAOAG*, 3:158.
82. AHB, *The Liberation of North West Europe*, 3:26–27.
83. Ferguson, "Pre-invasion Operations," 152.
84. AHB, *The Liberation of North West Europe*, vol. 3, apps. 18, 19.
85. Leigh-Mallory, "Air Operations by the Allied Expeditionary Air Force," 45.
86. AHB, *The Liberation of North West Europe*, 3:28.
87. "The Strategic Air War against Germany 1939–1945: Report of British Bombing Survey Unit," 1949, UK National Archives (TNA) AIR 10/3866, 116.
88. "Bombing Offensive against Germany," 6:28.
89. Arthur Tedder, *With Prejudice: The War Memoirs of Marshal of the Royal Air Force Lord Tedder, GCB* (London: Cassell, 1966), 541.
90. Ferguson, "Pre-invasion Operations," 161.
91. AHB, *w*, 1:177.
92. "Translations from Captured Enemy Documents, vol. IX: Luftwaffe Operations Staff/Intelligence No. 2512/44, Air Operations against the German Rail Transport System during March, April and May 1944," 1940–45, UK National Archives (TNA) AIR 20/7708, 1–2.
93. Lacey-Johnson, *Point Blank and Beyond*, 200.
94. "Copy of encl. 52A, file DSC/TS. 100, part 5, 10 and 13 July 1944," UK National Archives (TNA) AIR 37/1012.
95. Zuckerman, *From Apes to Warlords*, 252.
96. Lacey-Johnson, *Point Blank and Beyond*, 165; Bourque, *Beyond the Beach*, 161.
97. Baldoli and Knapp, *Forgotten Blitzes*, 198; Bourque, *Beyond the Beach*, 199.
98. Middlebrook and Everitt, *Bomber Command War Diaries*, 518.

3

Derailing the Wehrmacht?
The Debate and Implementation of the Transportation Plan

Sebastian Cox

Shortly before Christmas 1943, Air Chief Marshal Sir Charles Portal, chief of the Air Staff, wrote to Air Chief Marshal Sir Arthur Harris, air officer commanding in chief Bomber Command, telling him that the Royal Air Force (RAF) was, "for good or ill," committed to Overlord. Portal requested Harris to meet Air Marshal Sir Trafford Leigh-Mallory, commander in chief, Allied Expeditionary Air Force (AEAF), to consider the division between the continued bombing of Germany, the "rupture of enemy communications," and direct support of the assault.[1] In response Harris claimed that his command was incapable of anything but area bombing of German cities, which he maintained should remain his focus.[2]

These were the opening moves in what was to become a monumental struggle within the Allied high command between, on the one side, the commanders of the strategic bomber forces, the "Bomber Barons"—Harris and Lieutenant General Carl Spaatz, commander of the U.S. Strategic

Air Forces in Europe (USSTAF)—and on the other side Air Chief Marshal Sir Arthur Tedder, deputy supreme commander, Supreme Headquarters Allied Expeditionary Force (SHAEF); Leigh-Mallory; and Professor "Solly" Zuckerman, Tedder's scientific advisor. The Barons favored continuing their strategic air offensive against targets in Germany under the so-called Pointblank Directive, while Tedder and Leigh-Mallory favored using the powerful strategic bombers to disrupt German communications in France and Belgium to render more-direct assistance to Overlord. The scales in the debate that followed were apparently heavily weighted in favor of the Barons, as they had the support of a panoply of backers: to whit, the Directorate of Bomber Operations (DBOps), the assistant chief of Air Staff (Intelligence) (ACAS[I]), and the Air Ministry Intelligence organization (AI); the powerful Enemy Objectives Unit (EOU) within the U.S. Embassy in London; the Joint Intelligence Committee (JIC); the Ministry of Economic Warfare (MEW); British Army officers in 21 Army Group; and the Directorate of Transportation in the British War Office as well as the staffs of the USSSTAF, U.S. Eighth Air Force, and Bomber Command. Tedder and AEAF, however, had the important benefit of support from railway experts within the British Railway Research Service (RRS). Standing above these protagonists, and ultimately the arbiters in the strategic debate, were Portal and General Dwight Eisenhower, supreme commander, SHAEF.

The AEAF set up the Bombing Committee in January, under the chairmanship of Air Commodore E. J. Kingston-McCloughry, to review the potential for using strategic bombers in support of Overlord. Zuckerman, as its scientific advisor, looked at extant COSSAC (chief of staff to supreme Allied commander) bombing plans and quickly concluded they were too narrowly focused in time and area and too dependent on a window of good weather. Heavily influenced by Zuckerman and assisted by E. D. Brant and Charles Sherrington of the RRS, the committee produced successive and ever broader strategically focused draft plans. It is important to note that Zuckerman's influence in recharacterizing the plan as "strategic" and recommending implementation "forthwith" was a significant change of emphasis that did not entirely align with the views of the air staff or indeed COSSAC planners. COSSAC and the air staff in November 1943 had assumed the "diversion" of heavy bombers to Overlord from Pointblank would start with a preliminary phase commencing just two weeks prior to D-Day. COSSAC had listed attacks on the transport system as *fifth* on its list of priorities, whereas it listed continuing attacks on Germany as the second priority in order to keep fighters in Germany and the Low Countries.[3] Portal's early reaction to the question of the correct priority for the heavy bombers was to try to reach the "optimum" compromise between the pro-Germany and

Photo 3-1 • Meeting of the Supreme Command, Allied Expeditionary Force, London, 1 February 1944. Front row (*left to right*): Air Chief Marshal Sir Arthur Tedder, deputy supreme commander; General Dwight Eisenhower, supreme commander; General Sir Bernard Montgomery, commander, 21st Army Group. Back row (*left to right*): Lieutenant General Omar Bradley, commander, U.S. 1st Army; Admiral Sir Bertram Ramsay, Allied naval commander in chief; Air Chief Marshal Sir Trafford Leigh-Mallory, Allied air commander in chief; Lieutenant General Walter Bedell Smith, chief of staff to Eisenhower. *IWM TR 1631*

pro-communications schools. He suspected the "truth" lay somewhere in between the two extremes and instructed his staff to examine the issue.[4]

Meanwhile, the existing draft plan was approved at the sixth meeting of the AEAF Bombing Committee chaired by Leigh-Mallory on 24 January 1944, which included senior soldiers from SHAEF. Both before and during the meeting, there was some skepticism among the soldiers that the plan would be effective, as some thought the first reinforcing divisions would come by road and others that the Germans had empty troop trains already prepared and would prioritize available locomotives to move them. The USSTAF representative, Colonel Richard Hughes, stated that the "remaining" Pointblank targets would only absorb some 20 percent of the Eighth Air Force prior to D-Day and that "alternative targets would be welcomed."[5] This was presumably the origin of Leigh-Mallory's suggestion to Portal that the Eighth Air Force might take on German rail targets as alternatives for Pointblank attacks and that, he gathered, Spaatz would be happy to do so.[6]

A fundamental problem for the AEAF advocates of the Transportation Plan was the fact that Leigh-Mallory had no command authority over the strategic air forces. Whatever plans he made required either voluntary cooperation by the strategic commanders or orders to them from the Combined Chiefs of Staff (CCS). The overall command arrangements for the air side of Overlord in the first three months of 1944, unlike those of the land and naval forces, remained to be settled and were the subject of intense debate heavily influenced by the swirling interaction of national political interests, personal ambition and personality clashes, and fundamental strategic disagreements. Leigh-Mallory therefore had to utilize persuasion, not direction, until such time as the command issue was settled. By early February, AEAF had produced a revised plan that Leigh-Mallory circulated to Harris and Spaatz and invited them to a meeting on 15 February, attended also by Tedder. The deep-rooted objections of Spaatz and Harris to the proposal rapidly became clear. Leigh-Mallory would already have been aware of Harris' view, but his letter to Portal of late January suggests that he may initially have believed Spaatz to be less hostile. Leaving aside the merits or otherwise of the plan, a key underlying issue was a fundamental disagreement concerning the attainment of air superiority to facilitate Overlord. Spaatz believed it was crucial to obtain it *before* the invasion was launched, whereas Leigh-Mallory believed it would be achieved through a climactic air battle sparked by the invasion itself.

The revised AEAF plan under discussion now incorporated a direct assault on the forty-nine Luftwaffe airfields within 130 miles of the beachhead, absorbing 20,000 short tons of bombs, and allocated 45,000 short tons to rail targets in France, Belgium, and Germany. Yet while it characterized Pointblank as "an indispensable ingredient of Overlord," it allocated it just 12,000 short tons. Moreover, the statement regarding Pointblank was followed by the assertion that "air supremacy cannot be assured until the joining of the *decisive* [emphasis added] air battle which will mark the opening of the Overlord assault."[7] Leigh-Mallory compounded that error in Spaatz's eyes when opening the meeting by stressing "in particular" the need to disorganize the French and Belgian railways "before Overlord is launched." Spaatz's immediate rejoinder was to point out that the outline plan appeared to ignore his current directive, which had been reaffirmed in a signal just two days previously; that he did not believe the decisive battle would coincide with the invasion; that many of the targets selected would fail to provoke the Luftwaffe into offering combat; and that he remained to be convinced of its overall soundness.[8] Harris agreed with Spaatz and questioned whether the Italian and Franco–Belgian railway systems, Zuckerman's previous study of attacks that underpinned the plan, were comparable in size and stated that the proposal postulated unrealistic optimal figures for Oboe accuracy. Tedder spoke little but concluded the meeting by stating that the portions postulating rail paralysis "should be reconsidered." The meeting minutes concluded with apparent agreement that the representatives from Bomber Command and Eighth Air Force would cooperate with AEAF staff "to work out final details and assessing the effort and accuracy."[9]

The Transportation Plan assumed that the strategic air forces would start attacking these targets from 1 March 1944, and when Spaatz asked Leigh-Mallory early in the meeting when it was assumed those units would come under the AEAF commander's control, he was told that date.[10] Herein lies a key issue underlying the whole debate regarding the plan, namely the command and control of the heavy bombers. The American had little regard for Leigh-Mallory, as Tedder made plain to Portal when he wrote, "Spaatz has made it abundantly clear that he will not accept orders or even co-ordination from Leigh-Mallory."¹¹ Spaatz had told Eisenhower the day before the meeting that he had "no confidence in Leigh-Mallory's ability" and viewed "with alarm" any proposal to put the heavy bombers under him.¹² Leigh-Mallory's assertion that he would be placed in command over Spaatz in just two weeks' time would have gone down badly and done nothing to persuade the latter to compromise his views.¹³ Tedder's letter was in reply to one from Portal in which the CAS said he had met with Spaatz on 18 February, and the latter had suggested the committee producing the Overlord bombing plan (presumably the AEAF Bombing Committee) should be formalized.¹⁴ Portal would have been aware that the new directive, which Spaatz had referred to at the 15 February meeting, had specified that the primary objective of the bombers remained the Luftwaffe and referred to Overlord *fifth* in the list of priorities, even then only specifying that "preparation and readiness . . . should be maintained without detriment to the Combined Bomber offensive."¹⁵ He also wrote that he understood the Bombing Committee now included representatives from USSTAF, Bomber Command, and the Air Ministry. While that had implicitly been the conclusion of the 15 February meeting, there is no evidence that the AEAF committee ever met formally afterward.¹⁶

Given Spaatz's views, it seems almost certain that his motive in suggesting that the committee be formalized under the CCS with wider representation, including the strategic air forces, was to change it from an agent of AEAF to one in which parties opposed to the Transportation Plan would be dominant. Given that the CCS had just approved this new directive and that he knew General Henry "Hap" Arnold, chief of the USAAF in Washington, would back him and not Leigh-Mallory, Spaatz had every reason to believe he was on firm ground. It is important to bear in mind that in mid-February, when these various discussions took place, the Americans were far from achieving the air superiority specified in the Pointblank directive. The concerted weeklong attack by the USSTAF, pitting the U.S. bombers against the German aircraft industry and the fighters against the Luftwaffe fighter arm, known as "Big Week," began only on 19 February.¹⁷

In his letter of 18 February, Portal asked Tedder for his views on the Spaatz proposal to appoint a CCS committee to make recommendations.

The CAS indicated his recognition not only that Eisenhower had a major stake in deciding pre-Overlord bombing strategy but also that Pointblank and pre-Overlord bombing had to be "blended" until the heavy bombers came directly under Ike's direction. Portal was clearly not blind to the ulterior motives behind Spaatz's proposal even before he received Tedder's blunt assessment regarding Spaatz and Leigh-Mallory. He thus penned a short second letter to Tedder the same day, enclosing a "cockshy" draft of a CCS directive that attempted a delicate balancing act between the competing requirements. The proposed directive would have placed a requirement on the strategic forces to undertake attacks on communications prescribed by Eisenhower in parallel with Pointblank. Yet it also stated that the allocation between the two would be the responsibility of the bomber commanders, subject to weather, and that progress would be reviewed fortnightly by Portal and Eisenhower, who would then issue directions on behalf of the CCS as to relative priorities. In a postscript to his first letter, Portal wrote that the directive, if adopted, "might make the 'formalisation'(!) of the Cttee unnecessary."[18] We should note the use of the exclamation mark. By the time Spaatz made his suggestion regarding the committee at his 18 February meeting with the CAS, he had already sought to prepare the ground to prevent the Transportation Plan's adoption. Indeed, he made his move even before the meeting on the fifteenth. Colonel Hughes' deputy at USSTAF intelligence wrote to Hughes on 10 February stating that if the strategic air forces were opposed to the plan, they would have to provide some form of alternative proposal to put before Eisenhower. He concluded by recommending that "a quick and decisive effort be made to prevent the Strategic Air Forces being engulfed [sic] in the Zuckerman program." Two days later Spaatz directed USSTAF planners to prepare an alternative plan.[19] Unsurprisingly, they concluded, "Axis European transportation cannot be recommended as a target system for strategic attack."[20]

In his "personal and confidential" reply to Portal's letters, Tedder, in addition to his remarks above about the Spaatz–Leigh-Mallory relationship, indicated that he thought unified command of the air forces essential, no committee could produce a unified plan, and thus far the AEAF Committee had only served to show that the bomber commanders "are determined not to play." He recognized that Portal could order Harris to cooperate and believed he himself could "bring Spaatz to heel" but was concerned that the British chiefs of staff and particularly the prime minister would not allow Bomber Command to come under unified control, nor would the Americans ever accept a situation where they were under Tedder but Bomber Command was not.[21] Shortly thereafter the prime minister himself weighed in on the issue and confirmed Tedder's anxiety as well founded. Winston Churchill minuted Portal on 29 February and made clear that he believed Tedder should have overall control of Overlord air forces and be empowered to issue orders to Harris and Spaatz regarding forces assigned "permanently or temporarily" to Overlord, yet he was opposed to handing over Bomber Command "as a whole" to Eisenhower or Tedder.[22] The previous evening Churchill had met with Ike, and it is clear that his minute to the CAS was a result of this. In recounting the meeting Eisenhower told Tedder that the prime minister was himself "disturbed" at the thought of Leigh-Mallory being given command of the strategic bombers. Eisenhower replied that he was still seeking an agreed way forward and asked Churchill to avoid intervening at that stage. The general urged Tedder to press forward with planning conferences to get agreement, "otherwise the PM will be in this thing with both feet." As soon became plain, the prime minister's feet would indeed affect the issue, but not until later in the day.[23]

Meanwhile, given the unsatisfactory outcome of the 15 February meeting and in reaction perhaps to Spaatz's and Harris' comments regarding the soundness and feasibility of the plan, Leigh-Mallory set up a further meeting ten days later at his headquarters. In addition to E. D. Brant and Captain C. E. Sherrington from the RRS, he invited four senior railway executives who were members of the Railway Executive Committee (REC), the body through which the government ran the UK railway system during the war. Leigh-Mallory instructed a staff officer, Group Captain Lucas, to invite the Air Ministry to send a representative to the meeting as well. From this point onward, both the depth of opposition to the plan and the lengths to which its opponents were prepared to go to undermine it became clear. Lucas telephoned the director of Bomber Operations, Air Commodore Sidney Bufton, whose instantaneous hostility was obvious: he told Lucas that the Air Ministry (that is, Bufton) would prefer a meeting at a "lower level" without Leigh-Mallory, that it should be held at the Air Ministry rather than at AEAF headquarters, and that he would "prefer that their 'team' came along as a body... as 'We don't want our people tampered with.'"[24] Bufton followed up this extraordinary response, effectively challenging the AEAF commander's right to call a meeting, by consulting with Oliver Lawrence of MEW and then circulating his own paper to the REC. This started by outlining a number of assumptions, including that the Germans had sufficient locomotives and rolling stock available elsewhere to move into the affected area, so shortages would not be "a limiting factor on the movement of... reinforcements." The other "assumptions" were similarly phrased, and paragraph five of the paper stated that the chairman (effectively Leigh-Mallory) should ask the railway representatives a series of nine questions with the answers conditioned "in every case" by Bufton's prior assumptions.[25] This, too, was an extraordinary demand to make of the chair of a meeting, especially one who was his superior by three ranks and was not even in his chain of command. Aside from its basic impropriety, it implied "that AEAF were deliberately framing the meeting so that false deductions would be made from the answers of the railway experts."[26] Furthermore, having told Lucas he would like Squadron Leader W. S. Wigglesworth from Air Intelligence 3e (AI3e) plus a MEW representative and the Air Ministry scientific advisor to attend, Bufton subsequently appeared at the AEAF meeting with a phalanx of "uninvited" guests, including Lawrence of MEW; the Air Ministry scientific advisor, Sir George Thompson; Wigglesworth; three members of the EOU; Major General Frederick Anderson and Colonel Richard Hughes from USSTAF; and Air Vice-Marshal Robert Oxland from Bomber Command, along with his own deputy, Wing Commander Gordon Morley. Of course, not one of these uninvited attendees was a supporter of the AEAF plan. In addition, Major General "Freddie" de Guingand and Brigadier Edgar Williams from 21 Army Group and Major General Charles Napier of SHAEF's Transportation Branch were present.

A heated three-and-a-half-hour discussion followed in which extensive argument revolved around the questions of whether the AEAF plan to disrupt the rail system would reduce capacity sufficiently to affect German military traffic and whether bridge attacks and blocking lines to the lodgment area on or shortly before D-Day was the better option. In general, the railway experts were in favor of attacking the railway servicing system over a period of months and believed it could be crippled. The non-AEAF airmen proposed both blocking and bridge attacks or a combination but only in the immediate preinvasion period. There was also discussion of the overall German stock of locomotives, which was put at 50,000 by Lawrence (a figure challenged by the rail experts), and what proportion could or would be transferred by the Germans to the Franco-Belgian region to replenish losses from the bombing attacks. Those opposed to the Transportation Plan doubted whether sufficient time or bombing capacity was available to hit all the targets, especially factoring in the weather, enemy repair capability, and the potential need for repeat attacks, arguments that could equally well apply to their alternative short-term tactical plan. They also asserted that servicing could be done at facilities elsewhere. De Guingand stated that immediate reserves would come by road, but that any delay, even a single day, might prove vital. Neither side was convinced by the other's arguments, and the meeting reached no very positive conclusions. In a personal record of the meeting separate from the official verbatim minutes, Zuckerman pointed out that the opponents of the plan focused on critiquing various elements without appreciating that it proposed an attack on the system as a whole, employing his favorite analogy of attacking the human body where doctors could repair damage to one organ but not multiple failing parts simultaneously. He was particularly critical of the contributions at the meeting by Morley, Bufton's deputy.[27]

On the day following the meeting, Major General Napier wrote to AEAF. He warned against either over- or underestimating the effects of railway-center attacks but concluded that heavy strikes from D-90 to D-15 would not prevent enemy movement completely. Still, it would hamper the efficiency of the system and military movements and cause economic problems since the Germans could only stop commercial traffic for a short period. Napier was explicit that attacks during the "operational phase [the short pre-D-Day attacks] would achieve nothing if there had been no previous attrition." This letter indicates that some officers in important positions in SHAEF were already in support of the Transportation Plan, and it certainly appears to have given Zuckerman encouragement.[28] Wigglesworth of AI3e also sent a letter to the AEAF planners after the meeting clearly intended to support the Air Staff view by quoting results of bridge attacks from the Italian Campaign.[29] Moreover, those opposed to the plan did not limit themselves to providing supportive material for alternative approaches. On 26 February Deputy CAS (DCAS) Air Marshal Sir Norman Bottomley, who had not been present, reported to Portal that the meeting had "agreed that the execution of the plan could have little or no effect on the movement of strategic reserves to the battle area": a statement that would have come as a considerable surprise to the AEAF representatives and railway experts present at the meeting. The DCAS, citing discussions he held after the meeting with Bufton, Thompson, and USSTAF's Major General Anderson, also stated that Leigh-Mallory had "confused" the issue by indicating he was looking at it over six to nine months post-D-Day, a considerable exaggeration. Bottomley's wholly inaccurate representation of the meeting's conclusions is another indication of the lengths that those opposed to the plan were prepared to go to undermine it. His minute also proposed forming a committee to address the issue but with AEAF outnumbered by Air Staff, Bomber Command, and USSTAF representatives. In his response Portal noted that Bottomley's statement regarding reserves "was a considerable admission," which it would indeed have been had it been true. Portal still inclined toward establishing a committee, possibly because he felt it would be the best method to achieve a compromise with Spaatz, who had first suggested it.[30]

On the same day, CAS Portal also minuted DCAS Bottomley separately that a "profitable programme" was needed for Bomber Command in the "moon period" from then until Overlord. He mentioned "disruption of communications in France," though the principal focus of this minute was French industry.[31] Portal followed this with a second minute that was to prove of crucial importance in the application of the Transportation Plan. He suggested to Bottomley that a special directive should be issued to Bomber Command ordering attacks on specific targets in France to ascertain the actual capability of the heavy bombers in night attacks of precise targets in occupied territory.[32] Six days later the directive was issued, and Bomber Command subsequently attacked the specified targets over the following month, starting with the raid on Trappes on 6 March (see chapter 2).

Photo 3-2 • "Chewed and twisted by RAF interdiction attacks," states the original U.S. Army Air Forces caption, "Trappes marshalling yards in Paris, France could not be used by the enemy to rush reinforcements north after the Normandy landings." Trappes was successfully hit by 267 aircraft from RAF Bomber Command on the night of 6–7 March 1944. Air Chief Marshal Tedder used this example to convince others of the viability of the Transportation Plan. *U.S. Air Force Photo 57353AC*

Given the behavior of Bufton both before and during the meeting, it is little surprise that when Leigh-Mallory subsequently met with Bottomley on 28 February, he asked that Bufton should no longer have any association with AEAF's Overlord planning. In response, Bottomley interviewed Bufton and wrote the same day apologizing for the air commodore's behavior in circulating his questionnaire and especially paragraph five. The DCAS claimed that the DBOps's only motive was "to see a sound plan was arrived at . . . rather than any wish to thwart your wishes," which whether Bottomley believed it or not was demonstrably untrue, as subsequent events would show. He asked Leigh-Mallory to reconsider his request; Bufton remained a major influence in the process.³³

Meanwhile, the two opposing camps prepared detailed plans. On 3 March the AEAF produced a revised plan that proposed a prolonged assault on the enemy rail system, with both a strategic and a tactical phase. It rejected a purely tactical assault as too reliant on weather and instead proposed two alternative strategic plans, one concentrating on seventy-four targets in France and Belgium and six in Germany, while the second numbered seventy-six targets, with thirty-two of those in Germany.³⁴ USSTAF completed its proposal on 5 March. Revealingly entitled "Plan for the Completion of the Combined Bomber Offensive," it rejected Axis transportation as a target system because there were too many targets (they specified five hundred!), and it would require nine months before its effects would be felt. Instead, they recommended attacks on Axis oil production, specifically fourteen synthetic plants and thirteen refineries.³⁵ With this so-called Oil Plan, opponents of the Transportation Plan now had a concrete proposal around which they rapidly coalesced. At Bufton's request a committee was assembled to review both plans. This group comprised Wigglesworth of AI3e, Lawrence from MEW, Charles Kindleberger of EOU, and Lieutenant Colonel Ewing from the War Office Transportation Directorate. All these organizations had previously expressed doubts about the plan, and unsurprisingly they concluded that it was unlikely to succeed. The panel assessed that the Germans would require only sixty-four trains per day to maintain *and* reinforce their forces in France and Belgium, and this represented just 10 percent of the system's capacity and 1 percent of the locomotives based on the overall German rail system. Bizarrely, the committee examined AEAF's plan on the basis that it required attacking 140–150 rail centers, whereas the proposal in front of them listed only 73 such sites; members claimed this was because Air Intelligence 3c(1) had provided the target list but did not explain why they believed Air Intelligence and not the AEAF plan itself. The committee appears to have examined an early draft of the plan but no draft listed 150 targets.³⁶ The USSTAF plan was analyzed by Air Commodore Grant of Air Intelligence and Lawrence of MEW, both organizations opposed to AEAF's plan, and they concluded it was the best option for employing the strategic bombers.³⁷ The ACAS(I), in passing these conclusions back to Bufton, stated that he supported their assessment and believed the USSTAF plan was "far more likely to bring about the conditions in Germany which we aim to bring about."[38]

On 11 March Tedder met with Bottomley, the three assistant chiefs of Air Staff, Bufton, and Air Intelligence, along with Air Vice-Marshal Philip Wigglesworth of AEAF.[39] There was no meeting of the minds. In reporting back to Portal, Bottomley was clearly influenced by both the committee report and the consensus Air Staff view and repeated almost verbatim their negative views on the Transportation Plan. Tedder demanded that the JIC review the plan before deciding on its implementation. Meanwhile, he wrote a fiercely critical minute to Portal regarding the committee report and the USSTAF Oil Plan, stating correctly that neither paper had reviewed the rail plan impartially nor had Zuckerman or the RRS been consulted. He pointed out that the criticisms in both ascribed objects and methods formed no part of the actual plan and also that the committee paper was illogical in arguing for a short-term tactical plan while rejecting a strategic plan on the grounds it could have no effect for months.[40] In his reply Portal said he was studying all the papers he could on Overlord but had reached no conclusion, even provisionally. He did, however, challenge Tedder over his point regarding the logicality of the short-term tactical, long-term strategic issue, to which the latter responded with the perfectly reasonable argument that the tactical and strategic were complementary—he could not understand if the strategic was judged not to show results for months, how the tactical could show results in days, the more so if the rail traffic had not already been canalized by strategic action.[41]

If Tedder expected that the JIC would be more objective in its assessment of the plan, he was to be disappointed. Their report of 18 March concluded that the enemy's consumption for all their air, naval, and ground forces in France and Belgium daily was approximately 300 tons per division, requiring some 30 trains. They further calculated the number of trains required for reinforcing divisions, casualty evacuation, and necessary economic traffic and concluded that in the five weeks after D-Day, the highest number of trains required would be 123, falling subsequently to 62, but that if need be, the Germans could operate on 80 trains per day or possibly less "without gravely imperilling" their opposition to Overlord.[42] Tedder reacted in a minute written to Portal on 22 March dissecting the JIC report. He pointed out that, apart from Charles Sherrington, the JIC "consultants are the same people" who produced the earlier report: the Air Ministry representative on the JIC was ACAS(I) and the MEW representative, C. G. Vickers, deferred to that officer on rail capacity. Tedder enclosed with his response a note that Sherrington had produced regarding the earlier committee report. Sherrington pointed out that "it was a new theory of war" that divisions engaged in combat required less supplies than inactive divisions, noting that during the Great War, active divisions required 1,000–1,500 tons per day and that 400 tons was the equivalent of just seven Tiger tanks. Sherrington noted the original report's misquoting of the plan both concerning the figure of 141–150 targets to be attacked, which again had never featured, and in suggesting that the plan stated that 800–1,000 locomotives could be transferred from the eastern front. The proposal actually stated that even if transferred, the locomotives were unlikely to be of value in western Europe.[43] It seems clear that both the committee and the JIC reports were guilty of "situating the appreciation."

Even before he received Tedder's note, Portal had told the Chiefs of Staff on 19 March of his intention to hold a meeting to assess whether the Transportation Plan "can achieve what is expected of it and should be adopted."[44] In the interim both sides in the debate produced commentaries—on one side, analyses of the plan itself, and on the other, criticisms of it. Zuckerman pointed out that the critics assessed the plan in relation to the offensive against Germany, whereas it was aimed at the situation in France; had unrealistic assumptions on the numbers of trains needed for supply and reinforcement; assumed the plan aimed at halting, not disrupting, traffic; and in proposing a short period of tactical disruption took no account of the myriad tasks already assigned to the overstretched air forces.[45] Major General Donald McMullen, War Office director of transportation, wrote to Leigh-Mallory stating that the large capacity of the rail system and the small percentage (so he judged) required for military movement meant it "unlikely that the movement of enemy forces to and in France could be very seriously delayed."[46] Lawrence of MEW and Air Commodore George Grant of Air Intelligence analyzed the USSTAF proposal and concluded that it was the "best plan available" to prepare for a successful Overlord, produce Rankin conditions in Germany (Operation Rankin was the plan for the rapid reoccupation of Europe in the event of a precipitate German collapse) and assist the Russians. The postwar Air Historical Branch Narrative comments that Lawrence and Grant appeared "more occupied with the possibility of Rankin occurring rather than Operation Overlord."[47]

Both Tedder and Spaatz prepared papers setting out their respective positions, while other interested parties also offered their two cents' worth. Spaatz argued for the attack of twenty-seven oil targets, which he stated produced 80 percent of Germany's synthetic production and 60 percent of its refined capacity. He quoted the JIC paper in arguing that the rail capacity was so large and German "essential traffic so small" that transportation attacks would not affect the early battle or prevent reinforcement.[48] Tedder pointed out vis-à-vis the Oil Plan that of the seventeen targets in Germany, nine involved deep-penetration raids and five were in the Ruhr, where smoke and flak made precise attack problematic. He also stated that attacking oil could not produce an effect quickly enough to assist Overlord. Tedder further argued that neither the AEAF nor Bomber Command could play a significant part in the Oil Plan, whereas the Transportation Plan concentrated all available airpower on one target system, maximizing its effect.[49] Field Marshal Alan Brooke, the chief of the Imperial General Staff, also wrote to CAS Portal and, clearly influenced by his Transportation Directorate and the JIC, believed that transportation attacks would have "virtually negligible" effect on German reinforcements prior to D-Day, and although some delay would result post-D-Day, it would be a matter of "days rather than weeks," admitting that this "might well be worth achieving."[50] Among the blizzard of paper arriving on Portal's desk the day before the meeting was an Air Intelligence assessment of Luftwaffe strength and a further minute from Bufton, which again argued that the bomber forces could not affect a sufficient proportion of the Axis transport system in the time available to influence Overlord and that oil could and should be attacked. He sought to reverse Tedder's argument by stating that the railways being a "common denominator of the whole enemy war effort is a clear indication of its unsuitability as a vital target," though the actual plan only targeted part of the system. Bottomley, perhaps aware by now that Bufton's views were far from balanced, disagreed and accepted Tedder's argument that transportation could be hit by all three air forces, whereas oil could not, and that rail strikes would have some effect from the outset and by D-Day the effects would be "great." He was clearly influenced by the successful attacks on Trappes and elsewhere as well as by Ultra evidence that day of German transport problems in Italy.[51]

The next day, Saturday, 25 March 1944, the major protagonists assembled: Portal and Eisenhower; Tedder and Leigh-Mallory; Spaatz and Anderson; Bufton, Bottomley, and ACAS(I) Air Vice-Marshal Francis F. Inglis; Major Generals John Kennedy and McMullen; and Lawrence from MEW. Tedder introduced his plan, stressing the intent to disrupt and canalize traffic, thus ensuring the success of the ensuing tactical phase and slowing the enemy buildup. Portal spoke next and stated that all agreed the Transportation Plan would have a most serious effect on efficiency (which may have caused American eyebrows to raise), but the question was whether the reduced traffic was still sufficient for German needs in Normandy. Eisenhower spoke in support of Tedder, stressing the criticality of the early weeks of Overlord and the proposal's link with the tactical plan, concluding that in default of any alternative, he believed it should be adopted. Kennedy favored the tactical plan and denigrated the civilian rail experts, comparing them unfavorably with his Transportation Directorate. Spaatz then spoke in favor of the Oil Plan on both strategic and tactical grounds. The decisive intervention came, ironically, from Lawrence of MEW, who had consistently opposed the AEAF plan. When the CAS asked whether the results of the Oil Plan would be felt "early enough," Lawrence stated it would be some four or five months after implementation before results would be felt. Portal responded that this showed "conclusively that the oil plan would not help Overlord in the first few critical weeks." Eisenhower agreed, and the die was cast. The meeting accepted that Tedder would produce a directive to implement the Transportation Plan.[52]

In all the convoluted, often devious, arguments and machinations, the critical individual was Deputy Supreme Commander Tedder, who made few early interventions, allowing Leigh-Mallory and Zuckerman to absorb much of the opponents' heat, but instead engaged constantly with Portal and

Eisenhower, the key decisionmakers. But even once adopted by SHAEF, the Transportation Plan had still to overcome formidable opposition from the politicians, led by the prime minister, who was supported by his own scientific advisor, Professor Frederick Lindemann, and a majority of the War Cabinet.

NOTES

1. Portal to Harris, 23 December 1943, Folder 10, Papers of Sir Charles Portal, Christchurch Oxford [hereinafter PP].
2. Harris to Portal, 27 December 1943, UK National Archives [hereinafter TNA] AIR 8/1187; Harris, untitled paper, 13 January 1944, TNA AIR 14/734.
3. Letter and note, COSSAC RAF Branch to DBOps, 2 November 1944; and minute, DCAS to PS/CAS, 4 November 1944, TNA AIR 8/1187.
4. Minute, CAS to ACAS(P), 5 January 1944, TNA AIR 8/1187.
5. "Minutes of Sixth Meeting of AEAF Bombing Committee," 24 January 1944; and comment by Colonel Melville, Plans Section (unspecified, possibly 21 Army Group), 21 January 1944, in Air Historical Branch [hereinafter AHB] Narrative, *The Liberation of North West Europe*, vol. 1, Appendix VI/78.
6. Leigh-Mallory to Portal, 29 January 1944, TNA AIR 37/513.
7. AHB, *The Liberation of North West Europe*, vol. 1, Appendix VI/87.c.
8. The directive is reproduced in Sir Charles Webster and Noble Frankland, *The Strategic Air Offensive against Germany*, vol. 4, *Annexes and Appendices* (London: HMSO, 1962), app. 8, xxxvi. For original, see Air Ministry Directives, vol. VI (January–August 1944), TNA AIR 14/780.
9. AHB, *The Liberation of North West Europe*, vol. 1, Appendix VI/86.
10. AHB, *The Liberation of North West Europe*, vol. 1, Appendix VI/86.
11. Tedder to Portal, 22 February 1944, TNA AIR 37/1011.
12. Quoted in Richard G. Davis, *Carl A. Spaatz and the Air War in Europe* (Washington, DC: Center for Air Force History, 1993), 332.
13. AHB, *The Liberation of North West Europe*, vol. 1, Appendix VI/86.
14. Portal to Tedder, 18 February 1944, TNA AIR 37/1011.
15. See note 8.
16. Portal to Tedder, 18 February 1944, TNA AIR 37/1011; AEAF Bombing Committee—Minutes of Meetings, n.d., TNA AIR 37/512.
17. See Davis, *Carl A. Spaatz,* chap. 10 passim.
18. Portal to Tedder, 18 February 1944, TNA AIR 37/1011.
19. Lt. Col. Weicker to Col. Hughes, 10 February 1944, quoted in Gordon A. Harrison, *Cross Channel Attack* (Washington, DC: U.S. Army Center of Military History, 1951), 219.

20. USSTAF Plan for the Completion of the Combined Bomber Offensive, 5 March 1944, TNA AIR 37/1025.
21. Tedder to Portal, 22 February 1944, TNA AIR 37/1011.
22. Churchill Minute M.194/4 to CAS, 29 February 1944, TNA AIR 37/1011.
23. Memo, Eisenhower to Tedder, 29 February 1944, TNA AIR 37/1011.
24. AHB, *The Liberation of North West Europe*, vol. 1, Appendix VI/89A.
25. AHB, *The Liberation of North West Europe*, vol. 1, Appendix VI/90.
26. "AEAF Notes on the Planning and Preparation for Invasion of NW France, by Flight Officer Lady E Freeman," TNA AIR 37/1213, 416.
27. There are at least three records of the meeting: a verbatim set of minutes, AHB, *The Liberation of North West Europe*, vol. 1, Appendix VI/88; a summary, ibid.; and personal account by Zuckerman, 27 February 1944, TNA AIR 37/1041.
28. Maj. Gen. Napier to AVM H. E. Wigglesworth, 26 February 1944, TNA AIR 37/513. Zuckerman quotes Napier's letter in his memoir; see Solly Zuckerman, *From Apes to Warlords: An Autobiography* (London: Collins, 1988), 241.
29. Wigglesworth [AI3e] to Kingston-McCloughry, 28 February 1944, TNA AIR 37/513.
30. DCAS Minute to CAS, 26 February 1944, and handwritten comment by CAS, 27 February 1944, TNA AIR 20/3223.
31. Minute, CAS to DCAS, 27 February 1944, TNA AIR 2/4477.
32. Sir Charles Webster and Noble Frankland, *The Strategic Air Offensive against Germany*, vol. 3, *Victory* (London: HMSO, 1962), 27.
33. Bottomley to Leigh-Mallory, 28 February 1944, TNA AIR 37/733.
34. AHB, *The Liberation of North West Europe*, vol. 1, Appendix VI/92.
35. USSTAF Plan for the Completion of the Combined Bomber Offensive, 5 March 1944.
36. AHB, *The Liberation of North West Europe*, vol. 1, Appendix VI/97.
37. AHB, *The Liberation of North West Europe*, vol. 1, Appendix VI/105.
38. Minute, AVM Inglis, ACAS(I), to DBOps, 10 March 1944, in AHB, *The Liberation of North West Europe*, vol. 1, Appendix VI/97.
39. AVM Philip Wigglesworth should not be confused with his relative, Squadron Leader W. S. Wigglesworth. The former was a senior air staff officer in AEAF and was in favor of the Transportation Plan. W. S. Wigglesworth was an intelligence officer in AI3e in the Air Ministry and, although initially in favor, later opposed the plan.
40. Minute, DCAS to CAS, 12 March 1944; and note, Tedder to CAS, 13 March 1944, TNA AIR 8/1188.
41. Portal to Tedder, 14 March 1944; and Tedder to Portal, 15 March 1944, TNA AIR 8/1188.

42. JIC (44)106(O) (Final), 18 March 1944, in AHB, *The Liberation of North West Europe*, vol. 1, Appendix VI/101.
43. Loose minute, Tedder to Portal, 22 March 1944; and Sherrington to Kingston-McCloughry (with notes), 15 March 1944, in AHB, *The Liberation of North West Europe*, vol. 1, Appendix VI/101.
44. CAS Memorandum for COS, 19 March 1944, TNA CAB 80/81/83.
45. Zuckerman, "Observations on Comments by ACAS(I) to DBOps on the AEAF Plan for the Preparatory Bombing of Railway Centres," n.d.; and "Detailed Comments on [USSTAF] Part 2—Target Potentialities of Axis European Transport—March 1944," n.d., in AHB, *The Liberation of North West Europe*, vol. 1, Appendix VI/98.
46. Letter and Memo (extract), McMullen to Leigh-Mallory, 19 March 1944, TNA AIR 37/1011. The memo is reproduced in full in AHB, *The Liberation of North West Europe*, vol. 1, Appendix VI/100.
47. AHB, *The Liberation of North West Europe*, vol. 1, Appendix VI/105; AHB, *The Liberation of North West Europe*, vol. 1, Appendix VI/152.
48. Note, Spaatz, "Employment of Strategic Air Forces in Support of Overlord," 24 March 1944, TNA AIR 37/1011.
49. Note, Spaatz, "Employment of Strategic Air Forces in Support of Overlord," 24 March 1944; note, Tedder, "Employment of Allied Air Forces in Support of Overlord," 24 March 1944, TNA AIR 37/1011.
50. Letter and memo, Brooke to Portal, 24 March 1944, TNA AIR 37/1011.
51. DDI3 Paper, "German Air Force Strength," 24 March 1944; and minute, Bottomley to Portal, 25 March 1944, TNA AIR 20/838; Minute Bottomley to Portal, 24 March 1944, TNA AIR 8/1188.
52. Minutes of meeting, 25 March 1944, TNA AIR 37/1011.

4

All Roads Lead to Normandy, Not Berlin
Leadership's Self-Imposed Challenges on U.S. Bomber Crews' Combat Motivation

Heather Venable

Perhaps one of the most rhetorically gifted speakers ever, Winston Churchill dubbed bomber crews the "masters of the air" in 1944 after they had begun to gain air superiority against German fighters. But bomber crews themselves tended to take a far different view.[1] Some measure of air superiority did little to reduce the terror they faced over Germany, given the significant ground–air defenses they faced. These air defenses caused fear and even a sense of hopelessness, as a bomber could not return fire at antiaircraft guns on the ground like they could fighter aircraft in the skies.[2] One medical officer who interviewed 205 aircrew members who had completed a duty found that one-third of them had wanted to ask to be grounded out of "fear" but managed somehow to keep going.[3] Unlike Churchill, they realized they were anything but the masters of the air.

Churchill's view dominates, though, because the stories of the bomber crews have too often been seen through the words of the leaders rather than the led. This tendency to fail to appreciate the morale of these crews can be seen as far back as Wesley Craven and James Cate's classic seven-volume history, *The Army Air Forces in World War II*, the third volume of which purports to provide a glimpse into airmen's motivation prior to the Normandy invasion: "Preparations reached all the way into the smaller air units.... *Morale was undoubtedly high, conspicuously so*, and tension was great.... [T]he historic importance of the events about to unfold was everywhere sensed [emphasis added]."[4]

This depiction suggests a kind of unified, strong, and cohesive motivation—a dedication to doing anything necessary to support the long-awaited landing. Yet one notices a contradiction. The author makes assumptions about morale being "undoubtedly high" only next to describe a kind of visible morale. In other words, one assumed crew members must be highly motivated, thus they were.

The highest-ranking officer of the U.S. Army Air Forces (USAAF) in Europe made a similarly cursory acceptance of high morale on 1 June 1944. In his diary, Lieutenant General Carl Spaatz, commanding officer of U.S. Strategic Air Forces (USSTAF), described his division commanders' high morale and accepted their claims that their crews maintained similarly high spirits.[5] Spaatz's seeming refusal to dig deeper might indicate that he really did not want to press his commanders, for he knew the precarious state of his bomber crews' morale. His obsession with using strategic bombardment as *the* way to end the war with Germany, thus making Operation Overlord unnecessary, made him out of touch with his troops and unable to take simple steps to improve their morale.

Scholars have not adequately assessed the state of bomber crews' morale in World War II because of a romanticized haze that surrounds their epic contributions.[6] For example, Mark Wells' *Courage in Air Warfare*—one of the only monographs on bomber crews—verges on American exceptionalism. He claims American crews better endured the Combined Bomber Offensive and suffered far less psychological casualties as opposed to the Royal Air Force.[7] Being astounded at what bomber crews endured is understandable, but it should not be the primary lens for exploring the experiences of Eighth Air Force crew members. By celebrating the seeming resilience of American bombing crews, Wells does not adequately stress the toll it took on the men. In December 1944 two Medical Corps officers interviewed 100 airmen who had successfully completed thirty combat missions. They found that almost half had developed "moderate" or "severe" anxiety. One-fifth of these airmen suffered so much from this that it interfered with their ability to fulfill their flying duties.[8] Conducted during the war, this survey did not even begin to explore the enduring ramifications of these crew members of their combat for the rest of their lives, if they survived their next tour of duty.

Even before the medical officers conducted this survey at the end of 1944, the worrying state of combat morale can be seen in a survey distributed to 350 bomber pilots just before D-Day and to 650 fighter pilots after D-Day. Although the results are not entirely analogous because of timing differences, the bomber crews' negativity about their experience is striking. Asked if they would consider returning to the European theater after thirty days of rest, only 10 percent of bomber pilots said yes. By contrast, 29 percent of fighter pilots expressed their willingness to return (see table 4-1).[9] Nearly a quarter of all bomber pilots conceded they would consider another theater after thirty days of rest, but fighter pilots again outweighed bomber pilots, with 42 percent far more enthusiastically answering yes. Asked if they would choose combat flying if they could do it all over again, 85 percent of fighter pilots affirmed their decision. Just over 52 percent of bomber pilots, however, were "pretty sure" they would make the same choice. Similarly, 27 percent of bomber pilots said they would not choose to do combat flying again, and 18

Table 4-1 • U.S. Pilots Willing to Return to the European Theater of Operations after 30 Days' Rest Stateside

	Bomber Pilots	Fighter Pilots
Yes	10%	29%
Undecided	15%	42%
No	75%	29%

Source: Headquarters, European Theater of Operations, "Survey of Fighter Pilots in the Eighth Air Force: A Comparison with Heavy Bomber Pilots," 7 August 1944, File 141.28, Air Force Historical Research Agency, Maxwell AFB, AL.

percent were unsure. By contrast, less than 5 percent of fighter pilots would change their minds.[10]

In contemplating bomber crew morale on the eve of the Normandy invasion, it is important to consider the power of hindsight. In the late spring of 1944, the consequences of the air campaign on the Luftwaffe were not yet clear to bomber crews. The effect on their own morale of the substantial air superiority that had been achieved would change their perspective, but at the time of D-Day, these Americans still doubted how sizeable of a dent they had made in the Luftwaffe. The increased pace of operations in April and May also exhausted the men. Even those crews who had served in the difficult year of 1943 did not notice much of an improvement in terms of the ease of their missions prior to Normandy.[11]

High-ranking USAAF officers began to take notice and were increasingly worried about the state of morale in the spring and summer of 1944. As Chief of Air Staff Lieutenant General Barney M. Giles explained to Spaatz regarding some of his pilots who had returned to the United States in May for a short recuperation period, "The fighter pilots seemed full of go, worried badly for fear they would miss the big show. Your bomber people seemed more quiet and infinitely more tired. A few of the bomber people said they didn't want to go back."[12] Morale problems ran deeper than Giles acknowledged.

Bomber crews struggled to retain their combat motivation even in support of such a seminal and long-awaited military operation as Normandy, and senior leadership failed to draw explicit connections that might have made the crews' sacrifices over Germany seem more worthwhile. These leaders, particularly Lieutenant General Spaatz, had invested intellectually so heavily in strategic bombing that they suffered from cognitive dissonance, which can be understood as the process of selecting self-affirming pieces of information while omitting competing evidence.[13]

This cognitive dissonance impeded leaders from connecting to their men to make a compelling case for why bomber crews should repeatedly risk their lives.[14] Failing to convey a compelling narrative reflected leaders' fixation with strategic bombing as the optimal way of using airpower in war, no matter the context or cost.[15] Yet many crew members resisted the idea of hitting civilian targets, viewing missions to Berlin as particularly problematic.[16] Ironically,

Photo 4-1 • An Eighth Air Force B-24 Liberator crew is shown just after landing in England following a mission over Germany. The stress, strain, and exhaustion are evident on the mens' faces as they debrief before being released. *U.S. Air Force Photo 53495AC*

though, these raids proved to be crucial in the battle for air superiority prior to Normandy, providing critical, albeit indirect, ground support. But senior leaders rarely conveyed that message. As a result, a fundamental disconnect occurred, with some aircrews inclined to emphasize the futility of their work, while the "Bomber Barons" focused on demonstrating the utility of strategic bombing as the best way of winning the war. As a result, bomber crews lost faith with the Eighth Air Force even as senior leaders worked desperately to concoct compelling narratives.

In addition to cognitive dissonance, some messaging so often fell flat because officers did not understand the complexity of maintaining their crews' morale. For some, ensuring strong morale required nothing more than the rigorous selection of crew members in the United States.[17] As Vanda Wilcox rightly points out, however, motivation is never "static."[18] Military historian John Lynn also provides a useful model of motivation in his study of the Revolutionary-era French army. He divides motivation into three stages: initial, sustaining, and combat.[19] Initial motivation describes a military member's feelings about service, whether it be as a volunteer or a draftee. The bomber crews consisted solely of volunteers. Although all airmen volunteered to be part of the USAAF, a number ended up being "voluntold" as to their role within the crews themselves. Many navigators and bombardiers, for example, had dreamt of being pilots, only to have those hopes squashed. While the USAAF had plenty of pilot recruits, they had far fewer men wanting to be navigators and bombardiers. The army in part recruited excessive numbers of potential pilots to fill other essential positions as well since every two of five selectees washed out.[20] Early on, a very high initial motivation could fall dramatically, being intermixed with feelings of bitterness and disappointment as to one's ultimate role in an aircrew.[21]

Thus, initial motivation could change greatly during Lynn's second phase, the sustaining period. Sustaining motivation begins in training and continues to be a factor when airmen are not in combat, allowing them to endure the boredom and routine of service. These frequent periods of rest could be challenging, especially after difficult missions. As Staff Sergeant Earl Williamson Jr. recorded in his diary after completing his first mission, his "temporary eagerness vanished after reporting to base."[22] Staff Sergeant Thomas Hansbury, an experienced tail gunner in the 322nd Squadron, found his second tour easier than his first. Yet he still experienced significant challenges. After their thirteenth mission, Hansbury was held back on guard duty while his crew flew a mission to Oschersleben, Germany. After enemy flak hit and destroyed his crew's airplane, he struggled to adjust while suffering from survivor's guilt. Hansbury desperately hoped for immediate assignment to another mission as a coping mechanism so he could "forget" about what had happened to his friends, obsessively penning twenty-two letters to occupy his mind. He also "had a few beers . . . [but] it didn't work. Only a mission will do the trick, I hope."[23] Diversions, including trips to London, could help pass the time; still, the waiting game proved challenging to the sustainment of motivation, as did preparing for a mission only to have it canceled.

Despite great variations in motivation among individual airmen, fighter pilots generally maintained higher morale than bomber crews. Their drive came from several important sources. The defensive responsibility to protect bomber crews greatly motivated fighter pilots.[24] Similarly, providing direct ground support to assist their fellow Americans resulted in an immediate mental payoff in contrast to the bomber crews' more anonymous destruction of targets or indirect forms of aiding ground forces. As one fighter pilot explained, he had no objection to "strafing the enemy 'because it helps the American soldier out,'" and it angered him to see "Forts [B-17 Flying Fortresses] go down, as fellows in the bombers seem so g— d— helpless."[25] Fighter pilots had a clear sense of purpose that proved instrumental in and out of combat.

Thus, fighter pilots exemplify how sustaining motivation and combat motivation—Lynn's last category—can overlap. Combat motivation refers to—unsurprisingly—how individuals react in short-lived spurts of battle, generally characterized by an intense focus on simple survival. Steps could be taken to improve combat morale for aircrews, such as ensuring that the men received enough sleep. While a full examination of each of Lynn's phases as they relate to USAAF airmen is impossible, it is useful to consider one aspect of service that sustained bomber crews. Surveys comparing airmen's motivation to infantry and more elite troops like paratroopers showed that they prided themselves in serving in the USAAF. Similarly, 77 percent of airmen either believed or convinced themselves that they were making an "important" contribution to the war.[26] Indeed, the belief in the worth of one's contributions critically sustained them, given how much risk their efforts entailed. What exactly the average airman thought he was contributing, however, is difficult to tease out, as simple survival dominated their thoughts. For the most part, they had little investment in the strategic bombardment's decisive success, unlike their leaders who had created high-altitude daylight precision-bombardment doctrine and now sought to implement it.

Yet that doctrine had avoided targeting civilian morale, as airmen preferred as well. A survey of 3,000 bomber crew members conducted in the week before the landing at Normandy showed similar doubts, highlighting frustration with attacks on cities. Some particularly balked at raids against Berlin, which had begun in March 1944. They believed these missions served publicity purposes more than military ones, arguing that the destruction of a city could not break the enemy's will.²⁷ One airman even argued that it made "the [German] people more bitter toward us."²⁸ Some scholars have suggested that it is unhelpful to apply what they consider to be the ethical standards of today to the past in critiquing city bombing.²⁹ But the doubts some airmen had at the time regarding the morality of aspects of the Combined Bomber Offensive suggest that their ethics did not differ dramatically from twenty-first-century Western attitudes regarding avoiding targeting civilians.

Many airmen surveyed also expressed little antipathy toward their opponents and lacked a clear sense of why the Germans were fighting. Multiple medical officers attested to the fact that most American airmen did not hate the Germans, thus significantly reducing target attractiveness and making killing more difficult, especially given the likelihood of injuring civilians.³⁰ Of a group of 150 airmen who had completed tours in heavy bombers, only 29 percent felt "personal hate" toward the Germans.³¹ A different study conducted by medical officers arrived at a starker conclusion in their key findings, stating that when "marked hostility toward the enemy was expressed it was invariably a projection of the individual's deep, repressed aggressive drives."³² In other words, these researchers saw this hate not as an enabler of successful combat, but more as a reflection of a troubled civilian background. In this light it is perhaps understandable why a study of gunners—constituting a better educated group in comparison to the civilian population at large—found even they had little sense of why they were fighting. After completing their gunnery training in the United States, only 44 percent understood U.S. participation in the war, and these airmen had volunteered specifically to be gunners.³³ But as many acknowledged later, they sometimes made decisions about how they would serve in the USAAF largely on a whim, without giving serious thought to the ramifications of their decisions. While a general sense of service animated young American men against the Japanese after Pearl Harbor, it did not translate neatly into hate for the Germans or a deep-seated understanding of why they were fighting in Europe.³⁴ As First Lieutenant Norman Retchin, a B-17 pilot, described after his first combat mission: "It's a damn strange feeling, flying over enemy country for the first time. There are people in the air [and] on the ground whose sole purpose is to kill you, [and] you don't even know them. At least

Photo 4-2 • Technical Sergeant Nicholas D. Schoenberger is congratulated by his pilot, Lieutenant Donald E. Jones, after completing his thirtieth mission over Nazi-occupied Europe, 27 March 1944. Schoenberger, a B-17 Flying Fortress radio operator, was the first member of his bomb group to complete his tour. *U.S. Air Force Photo 65675AC*

we could be properly introduced [and] know each other long enough to work up some sort of mutual distaste."[35]

Prior to his first mission, Retchin spent weeks firing himself up to kill Germans. After his first combat mission, however, he wrestled more with the threat of being killed himself than of killing others. Added to that was the anonymity of a deadly process in which he had little active animosity.

Airmen wanted to know that their efforts contributed to the war effort, and they also preferred to hit clearly defined military objectives.[36] One anonymous crew member, for example, described his strategic bombing missions as being akin to "killing sheep."[37] It also helped when officers informed them of the purpose their mission served. One, for example, described the bombing of an aircraft target as paying immediate dividends by explaining that the crews sought to hit the part of a factory from "whence the planes 'went out the door.'"[38] It could be difficult at times, however, to measure what the bombers had accomplished in hitting factories, especially through overcast skies.[39] Providing more direct support to the ground campaign—such as striking railroad stations used to transport enemy troops—was more eagerly desired after the Normandy invasion. Those officers responsible for canvassing bomber crews, however, rarely hit upon this solution.[40] Instead, they repeatedly asked the men the extent to which participating in strategic bombing increased their morale, albeit never seemingly determining if crews understood that mission similarly to officers in higher headquarters. Surveyors presented this as the first point of information in one report's "main findings."[41]

Just as fighter pilots sustained their combat motivation through a deep sense of supporting bomber pilots, so, too, might bomber crews have come to understand how their missions targeting Berlin and German oil factories enabled the Normandy landing, as these targets best provoked German fighter resistance.[42] Lieutenant General Spaatz expressed these views in private correspondence, writing to General Henry "Hap" Arnold, commanding general of the USAAF, in May 1944 about how he picked targets that he "anticipated will force the [Luftwaffe] into the air against us."[43]

In public communications, though, Spaatz focused on strategic bombardment. In the spring of 1944, he began devoting "special attention" to publishing articles in service magazines popular with airmen, particularly *Yank* and *Stars and Stripes*.[44] But these pieces highlighted the precise issues that airmen found so disquieting. An April *Yank* article, for example, gleefully celebrated the massive destruction wreaked upon Germany, describing not only how countless "German factories still smoke, but from ruins, not production," but also how entire "sections of Nazi cities—cities now in name only—are junk heaps. Germany's civilians trek from shattered homes by the millions, searching for refuge from bombs." Even as the Allies were "poised in England to invade the Continent," *Yank* appeared to celebrate civilian casualties, explaining that Berlin was receiving "43,000 tons" of TNT, with one pound being "enough to kill several persons."[45]

Airmen also wanted a definitive goal of combat missions to work toward, but USAAF policies became less precise in enabling crews to track their progress in March 1944. Previously, heavy bomber crews had a tangible goal of completing twenty-five missions to work toward, but that number now increased to thirty even as leaders insisted that it should not be relied upon as a kind of "virtual contract." Personnel were told to consider thirty sorties as the "lower limits which crews should reach." They could also expect to return to Europe after thirty days of rest, thus shattering the men's understanding that those who had survived a thirty-mission tour would be done with combat.[46]

While leaders like Major General James H. Doolittle suggested that USAAF leadership in Washington, DC, initiated these changes, it seems more likely that Lieutenant Generals Ira C. Eaker and Spaatz convinced General Arnold to approve the change in policy.[47] Spaatz remained focused on the fleeting opportunity to win the war with airpower alone to preempt the Normandy landings.[48]

Doolittle sought to motivate his crews by referring to decreased casualty rates, but unsurprisingly, his efforts fell short.[49] In a series of memos released in March 1944, he optimistically pointed out that he and his commanders all agreed that "after a short period of leave," many crew members "would be willing and able" to return to combat.[50] One memo sought to reassure crews that "conditions [would] change once the German and Japanese air forces pass[ed] their peak."[51] Yet the June survey revealed that only 13 percent of those surveyed would willingly serve in Europe again, with this feeling intensifying for those who had more than twenty missions compared to less experienced crew members.[52]

As the pace of operations increased in the spring of 1944, Eaker and Spaatz reacted by trying to reduce some aircrews' stateside recovery times from one month to three weeks.[53] The situation simultaneously became more complicated because, if one relieved aircrews from combat, then surely one had to provide something similar for those fighting on the ground. Thus, Lieutenant General Jacob L. Devers, the senior U.S. Army commander in the North African theater of operations, became involved, understandably insisting that the relief of crews also necessitated similar rest for "front line ground units." Yet he did not acknowledge the need to recover from the psychological toll of combat. Rather, to him, returning to the United States should be an "earned privilege gained by killing the enemy."[54]

Meanwhile, in a stunning blow to airmen's morale, the Royal Air Force announced in April that German fighter strength had increased by 300 aircraft over the last five months. In considering how to keep this statement from affecting his crews' morale, Spaatz confided to his diary, the "great tribute to the Eighth Air Force is that they have sustained the greatest losses of any other Air Force operating during this War, and have survived. Our crews must be made to know and believe that these losses have been worthwhile."[55] His words reveal a general disconnected from his men. Spaatz did not stress the enormous burden suffered by thousands of men and the price they paid; rather, he celebrated that the Eighth Air Force had suffered more losses than any other numbered air force. He then referred to the primacy of the organization's survival over the loss of men's lives. He also chose not to wrestle with why such losses were "worthwhile" or how he might connect with men who just wanted to complete their tours and get back home, men who had little hatred toward their enemy or even much sense of why they were fighting.[56]

Concerns with morale intensified over the course of April. A few days after visiting various bases, Spaatz learned that many airmen believed that they were not receiving the "true story." Subsequently committing himself to providing the crews with facts, he believed that his "most important job just now" had become "keeping up morale of these boys who are doing the fighting."[57] With this goal in mind, Spaatz and his public-affairs officers produced a detailed four-page press release. Reflecting the general's antipathy for the planned Normandy invasion, the press release depicted the ongoing air battle against Germany not as the precursor to the Normandy landing, but rather as the "preliminary step toward unleashing the full bomb lift of both air forces against the Reich."[58] In the same vein he concluded by asserting that aircrews had "thwarted" the "expansion of the major arm of the German force," which would lead directly to "complete victory over the Axis powers." Spaatz's press release—he proudly included a copy with a letter to General Arnold—reflected his solution to the pressing problem of crew morale: give them a history lesson. In effect, he wrote a conference paper on the history of the Combined Bomber Offensive. After reading the proposed text of the release, a colonel tried to explain to the general that his crews doubted everything in print anyway.[59]

Throughout April, Spaatz continued to balk against the entire idea of Overlord. He wrote, but did not send, a letter to Arnold that highlighted that his bombers only had the responsibility of supporting Overlord's "*initial success* [emphasis in original]."[60] Two days later in a conference with another USAAF general, Spaatz described Overlord's purpose as being to "seize and hold advanced air bases." Thus, he argued, the invasion need not proceed because his bombers already could hit any required target in Germany.[61] A worried Arnold, who wanted to see a decisive strategic-bombardment campaign as much as Spaatz, wrote a few weeks later to rein him in, urging the lieutenant general to keep "tactical requirements foremost in [his] mind," to include providing constant support of the ground forces and localized air superiority in Normandy.[62] Spaatz's antipathy toward the entire operation continued after D-Day. Writing in his diary a week after the landing, he characterized army officers as cowardly: the "only thing necessary to move forward is sufficient guts on the part of the ground commanders."[63]

As Spaatz resisted using strategic bombers to support D-Day, other indications of morale problems continued emerging. Senior leaders reacted by examining other causes for low morale rather than acknowledging the conditions faced by the crews. High-ranking members of the Eighth Air Force sent a handful of communications on this topic in the summer of 1944. Lieutenant General Spaatz, for example, urged the promotion of all wing commanders to brigadier general purportedly because the "combat crews of the organizations concerned feel that the work of their organization . . . is not recognized when their commander is not given the rank called for."[64] A follow-up message cited the significant casualties of aircrews in the previous month—the loss of 5,168 men—to "urgently" call for their wing commanders' promotions.[65] Using the loss of life in such a transactional way truly highlights the disconnect between the leadership and the rank and file.

The mission of "strategic bombardment" overrode all. After reports surfaced that airmen might be landing in Sweden and Switzerland to escape the war, Major General F. L. Anderson, deputy commanding general for operations, USSTAF, expressed his deep faith in what strategic bombardment had achieved.[66] No one in the entire world, he exclaimed, should have higher morale than the "U.S. Strategic Air Forces" because of its utmost efficiency in having "caused the greatest damage to the enemy." Echoing Spaatz's comments about the Eighth Air Force, Anderson similarly suggested airmen bask in how their organization had "overcome terrific losses and odds."[67] One might not be surprised if the crew members flying these missions did not connect with his vision. Nor did Anderson show much interest in understanding the airmen themselves; instead, he wanted to investigate them solely to determine how to improve the selection process of future crew members. This approach enabled him to divorce himself from any desire to improve the morale of airmen currently serving in Europe. By contrast, medical officers a month later ironically recommended implementing policies to address some of these now-interned airmen's greatest grievances, including providing more certainty regarding how many missions they needed to fly before getting a rest period and not flying more than three days of missions in a row.[68] They also recognized the importance of highlighting strategic bombing as supporting the ground forces for improving morale, recommending that an "even greater emphasis than in the past should be put upon the need of our ground troops for the aid given by heavy bombers in cutting off the flow of German war materials."[69]

Lieutenant General Spaatz took a slightly less defensive approach in response to the reports than Major General Anderson, but concerns with strategic bombardment also informed his response. Like Anderson, he reminded General Arnold how "effectively" airpower had been applied against Germany over the previous months. He then insisted that only a senior officer "thoroughly versed in the significance of air operations" should interrogate the internees. Although Spaatz acknowledged that some interns might have suffered "psychological damage," he preoccupied himself primarily with ensuring that someone with operational experience and high rank question the crews.[70] For him, the significance of air operations centered on strategic bombardment first and foremost. In replying to Spaatz, Arnold instead stressed the necessity of identifying and returning crews "near the breaking point" to the United States.[71] Similarly, Doolittle—identified by name in the report as causing morale problems—even admitted that "some justification" existed for the men's complaints, which should be addressed.[72] In concerning themselves with factors affecting the crews' sustaining and combat motivation, these leaders sought to balance requirements to defeat Germany with the psychological health of their airmen. By June 1944, for example, Arnold hoped to at least give every crew an "even chance at surviving" their tours.[73]

Meanwhile, though, the first batch of 300 crew members had returned to the United States. At a 1 July 1944 conference, Colonel Lloyd P. Hopwood of the Military Personnel Division expressed his concern at the "serious troubles" with the crews, insisting they should not return to combat. Hopwood's finding was not surprising, as flight surgeons had already identified "all of your bomb crews" as having been "relieved from operational flying by the flight surgeons" prior to their leave.[74] Of that number, sixty-five officers had been in Europe for more than one year, some without any leave whatsoever. Continued discussions turned up other "definite irregularities" that suggested leaders had neglected crew morale. One urgent message sent to the Twelfth Air Force, for example, cited cases of crew members flying more than fifty missions without being rewarded with an "air medal or other decoration of any kind."[75]

From his interviews, Hopwood concluded that the leave program had been a waste, as these men would not "be much good" in theater. The colonel worried so much about the crew members' psychological health that he advised Lieutenant General Eaker to prepare positive public relations in case word leaked out of the men's morale, wondering what to expect from the continued arrival of veteran crew members returning home for a short rest.

In responding to Hopwood's comments, Eaker showed some sympathy for his crews, but he continued to support an indeterminate number of missions for them based on the existing situation in Europe. He believed that the psychological condition of the first batch of crew members demonstrated the "urgent need for a sound program for return of crews for rest" to prevent them being "broken in body and spirit."[76] Eaker further stressed that the USAAF had not shown "enough sympathy in the past for the real need for sending men home."[77] Yet he cautioned that this first batch of airmen on leave might contain "malingerers and shirkers" who must be identified.[78] In a contradictory telegram to General Arnold and Lieutenant General Giles sent the next day, Eaker brought up the subject again and reaffirmed how he had "obviously picked for first relief those in gravest need of relief first."[79]

It is difficult to reconcile his emphasis on his own selections with how he questioned the crews' motives, seeking to hunt down any who might have abused his own process.

Meanwhile, concerns about the number of bomber crews landing in neutral countries like Sweden and Switzerland continued to trouble USAAF officers in Washington, DC, toward the end of July 1944, even as officers in Europe pushed back at any suggestions of problems with morale. An especially pointed message from General Arnold, for example, highlighted the "accumulating" evidence regarding the "appreciable number" of aircraft seeking to avoid continuing services. Arnold enjoined Lieutenant Generals Spaatz and Eaker to "aggressively" focus themselves on releasing aircrews before "war weariness provokes an uncontrollable urge to grasp release."[80]

Unsurprisingly, perhaps, Spaatz and Major General Anderson continued to push back at any suggestion of depressed crew morale. Indeed, they argued that spirits remained "high" and urged maintaining this condition, asking Arnold to take action "on the promotion to Brigadier Generals of the list previously submitted." Strikingly, their most strongly worded recommendation concerned not the crews themselves, but the promotion of those who oversaw them, which would improve the status of USAAF officers in relation to other services. While Spaatz defended his airmen's morale and valor, he proposed no solution to improving their living or working conditions except to promote high-ranking officers.[81]

The failure of leaders in Europe to provide adequate attention to their aircrews' psychological struggles continued through the early fall. In September 1944 a memo disseminated by one USAAF leader in the Mediterranean explained that all crew members authorized to return to the United States would receive a "thorough physical examination" to determine each individual's suitability to return to combat. Only those "unquestionably physically and mentally fit" would be returned. Notably, however, the memo only referenced a *physical* examination to determine both physical *and* mental fitness.[82] USAAF leaders in Europe had yet to come to terms with the extreme psychological challenges of combat.

They were, however, dedicated to promoting a more centrally organized form of airpower to improve the USAAF's status. In the spring of 1944, some USAAF officers in Washington, DC, pushed back at Spaatz's expressed determination to unify all American tactical and strategic airpower under his control. Anderson simultaneously and unsurprisingly pursued similar ideas, determined to get the USAAF to approve organizational changes to enable the "prestige which comes from mass grouping under unity of command."[83] Opposed officers included Major General Lawrence Kuter, who importantly had attended the Air Corps Tactical School, where ideas of strategic bombardment reigned and were applied to the development of Air War Plan 1, which informed the USAAF submission to the War Department on how to wage a strategic air campaign against Germany. Kuter had even commanded a bombardment wing in England. He believed in strategic airpower yet also appreciated what tactical airpower could accomplish.[84] As such, he criticized Spaatz's proposal, considering his ideas to be "dangerous" because they allowed strategic air forces to use tactical air forces in support of independent missions against the German homeland at the expense of missions needed to support Allied ground forces. Kuter, worried about "[Lieutenant] General Spaatz's concept that bombing alone can win or nearly win the war," sought to prevent aircraft from being stripped from tactical missions to support strategic bombardment.[85]

Even if leaders showed little understanding of their crews' experiences, their thinking about airpower's contributions to the war effort slowly evolved in light of the ongoing ground campaign through France toward Germany in the fall of 1944. Now that ground operations clearly could not be avoided, Spaatz increasingly came to terms with the fact that airpower would not win the war by itself. By October, when he viewed the ground war to have stagnated, he prepared plans for what he called Operation Hurricane. In keeping somewhat with earlier ideas, he envisioned using concentrated strategic and tactical airpower against the Ruhr area of Germany, although he now more cleverly argued that these attacks would be "tied in closely with the present scheme of maneuver of the ground forces." He purportedly hoped that the next "significant break-through" on the ground should result in German defeat.[86] While his opinion could epitomize misplaced optimism, it seems that Spaatz had reconciled himself to the fact that airpower would not win the war singlehandedly or be able to claim the victory alone.

Cognitive dissonance greatly affected leaders' ability to connect with and comprehend the morale of their bomber crews, who listened to the bombast of bomber generals before flying to Berlin, only to wonder how they were winning the war by doing so. While the aircrews generally and bomber pilots specifically entered the war with significant amounts of initial motivation, they found it difficult to sustain that motivation, even on the eve of the greatest amphibious invasion the world has ever seen.

NOTES

1. Quoted in Donald L. Miller, *Masters of the Air: America's Bomber Boys Who Fought the Air War against Nazi Germany* (New York: Simon & Schuster, 2006), ix.
2. Headquarters, European Theater of Operations, "Survey of Fighter Pilots in the Eighth Air Force: A Comparison with Heavy Bomber Pilots," 7 August 1944, File 141-28, Air Force Historical Research Agency, Maxwell AFB, AL [hereafter AFHRA]. Nine percent found their combat missions to be less difficult compared to when they started, whereas 23 percent found them more difficult, and the rest found them to be of similar difficulty.
3. Capt. Howard B. Burchell, "Interviews with 205 Air Crew Returnees: Tentative Findings," AFHRA, 520-742-8.
4. Wesley Frank Craven and James Lea Cate, *Argument to V-E Day*, vol. 3 of *The Army Air Forces in World War II* (1951; repr., Washington, DC: Office of Air Force History, 1983), Kindle, Loc 3613.
5. Lt. Gen. Carl Spaatz Diary, 2 June 1944, Box 15, Carl Spaatz Papers, Library of Congress (LOC).
6. John McManus, *Deadly Sky: The American Combat Airman in World War II* (New York: NAL Caliber, 2016), 1.
7. Mark Wells, *Courage in Air Warfare: The Allied Aircrew Experience in the Second World War* (London: Frank Cass, 1995).
8. Maj. Douglas B. Bond and Maj. Howard B. Burchell, "A Study of 100 Successful Airmen with Particular Respect to Their Motivation and Resistance to Combat Stress," December 1944, AFHRA 520-7411-1, 13–14. An earlier study concluded that 98 percent of men developed "operational fatigue," of whom one-third suffered "severely." Maj. Donald W. Hastings, Capt. David G. Wright, and Capt. Bernard C. Glueck, *Psychiatric Experiences of the 8th Air Force: First Year of Combat (July 4, 1942–July 4, 1943)* (New York: Josiah Macy Jr. Foundation, 1945), 135.
9. Headquarters, European Theater of Operations, "Survey."

10. Headquarters, European Theater of Operations, "Survey."
11. "Main Findings from Survey of Heavy Bomber Crews," AFHRA 520-742-8, iii.
12. Lt. Gen. Barney Giles to Lt. Gen. Carl Spaatz, 23 May 1944, Box 15, Spaatz Papers, LOC.
13. Tami Davis Biddle, *Rhetoric and Reality in Air Warfare: The Evolution of British and American Ideas about Strategic Bombing, 1914–1945* (Princeton, NJ: Princeton University Press, 2002), 4.
14. Interview with Col. Benjamin O. Davis, 19 December 1944, Special Interviews, 3 October 1944–8 March 1945, AFHRA 142-05-12, 1–2.
15. Biddle, *Rhetoric and Reality*, 4–6.
16. Research Branch, Special Service Division, "Survey of Combat Crews in Heavy Bombardment Groups in ETO: Preliminary Report," 8, Spaatz Papers, LOC; Miller, *Masters of the Air*, 277–78.
17. Maj. Gen. F. L. Anderson, attachment to Chas E. Rayens to Military Attache, American Embassy, London, Eng., "Air Force Morale," 8 June 1944, Box 91, Spaatz Papers, LOC.
18. Vanda Wilcox, *Morale and the Italian Army during the First World War* (New York: Cambridge University Press, 2016), 6.
19. John A. Lynn, *The Bayonets of the Republic: Motivation and Tactics in the Army of Revolutionary France, 1791–94* (Boulder, CO: Westview, 1996), 35.
20. Wesley Frank Craven and James Lea Cate, *Men and Planes*, vol. 6 of *The Army Air Forces in World War II* (1955; repr., Washington, DC: Office of Air Force History, 1983), xxxiv; "The Military Experiences of Walter Neuwirth," World War II—Prisoners of War—Stalag Luft I, accessed 5 March 2024, http://www.merkki.com/neuwirthwalter.htm.
21. Craven and Cate, *Men and Planes*, 585.
22. Earl G. Williamson Jr., "My Lucky Thirty," 30 January 1944, 91st Bombardment Group, www.91stbombgroup.com/airmen_diaries/diary_earl_williamson.pdf.
23. Thomas J. Hansbury, "My 2nd Tour of Duty," 2 July 1944, 91st Bombardment Group, http://www.91stbombgroup.com/airmen_diaries/diary_thomas_hansbury2.pdf.
24. Bond and Burchell, "100 Successful Airmen."
25. Bond and Burchell, "100 Successful Airmen."
26. Research Branch, Special Service Division, "Survey of Heavy Bombardment Groups in ETO," Table A, 26, Spaatz Papers, LOC.
27. Research Branch, Special Service Division, "Survey of Heavy Bombardment Groups in ETO," 8.
28. Research Branch, Special Service Division, "Survey of Heavy Bombardment Groups in ETO," 11. For some German civilians' sentiments, see Kevin T. Hall,

Terror Flyers: The Lynching of American Airmen in Nazi Germany (Bloomington: Indiana University Press, 2021).

29. Robin Neillands, *The Bomber War: The Allied Air Offensive against Nazi Germany* (Woodstock, NY: Overlook Books, 2003), 4.
30. Maj. David G. Wright, *Notes on Men and Groups under Stress of Combat: For the Use of Flight Surgeons in Operational Units* (New York: Josiah Macy Jr. Foundation, 1945), 12; Bond and Burchell, "100 Successful Airmen"; Capt. Howard B. Burchell, "Interviews with 205 Air Crew Returnees: Tentative Findings," AFHRA, 520-742-8.
31. Hastings, Wright, and Glueck, *Psychiatric Experiences of the 8th Air Force*, 135.
32. Bond and Burchell, "100 Successful Airmen."
33. USAAF Aviation Psychology Program Research, Report 11, AFHRA, File 141-28-11, 268, 284–85; Bond and Burchell, "100 Successful Airmen."
34. See, for example, James Holland, *Big Week: The Biggest Air Battle of World War II* (New York: Atlantic Monthly Press, 2018), 147; and Tom Faulkner, *Flying with the Fifteenth Air Force: A B-24 Pilot's Missions from Italy during World War II*, edited by David L. Snead (Denton: University of North Texas Press, 2018), 33.
35. First Lt. Norman Retchin, "An Airman's Diary: 1st Lt Norman Retchin," 16 April 1943, 91st Bombardment Group, www.91stbombgroup.com/airmen_diaries/diary_norman_retchin.pdf.
36. See, for example, J. W. Smallwood, *Tomlin's Crew: A Bombardier's Story* (Manhattan, KS: Sunflower University Press, 1992), 142.
37. Research Branch, Special Services Division, "Preliminary Report: Survey of Combat Crews in Heavy Bombardment Groups in ETO," June 1944, AFHRA, File 520-742-8, 1–3.
38. Smallwood, *Tomlin's Crew*, 147. For an especially informed airman whose squadron must have taken special care in explaining the progress of the air war to crews, see Williamson, "My Lucky Thirty," esp. 6, 28 March 1944.
39. Smallwood, *Tomlin's Crew*, 141.
40. For this approach almost as an aside, see Col. O. N. Solbert, Memorandum to Commanding General, USSTAF, 11 July 1944, AFHRA, File 520-742-8. But even supporting ground troops was not a simple solution, with crews concerned their bombs might strike too close to their own men. Smallwood, *Tomlin's Crew*, 135.
41. While studies indicate conditions like anonymity and the number of airmen included, they do not define "strategic bombing" or how varying understandings of this term might shape airmen's responses. Research Branch, Special Service Division, "Preliminary Report: Survey of Combat Crews in Heavy Bombardment Groups," 1–3.

42. Spaatz Diary, 19 April 1944, Box 14, Spaatz Papers, LOC.
43. Lt. Gen. Carl Spaatz to Gen. H. H. Arnold, 10 May 1944, AFHRA 519-1612-3.
44. Lt. Gen. Carl Spaatz to Gen. H. H. Arnold, 5 May 1944, Box 15, Spaatz Papers, LOC; statement, General Spaatz to Public Relations Officers, 8 April 1944, ibid. The issue became even more pressing on 12 April, when the Royal Air Force briefed that in April the Germans had 300 more fighters than in November 1943. Spaatz worried such a statement could cause a "very serious morale problem." See Lt. Gen. Carl Spaatz to Air Chief Marshal Sir Charles F. A. Portal, 13 April 1944, ibid.
45. "Pre-Invasion Bombs," *Yank,* 14 April 1944, http://www.unz.com/print/Yank-1944apr14-00010/.
46. Maj. Gen. J. H. Doolittle, "Policy on Relief of Combat Crews," 4 March 1944; Spaatz to Arnold, Ref. U60369, 1 April 1944; and Headquarters Eighth Air Force, Policy on Relief of Combat Crews, 4 March 1944, AFHRA 622-1621.
47. Eaker to Spaatz, Outgoing Message, 7 April 1944, AFHRA 622-1621; Doolittle to Commanding General, 8th Fighter Command, "Relief of Combat Crew Personnel," 4 March 1944, ibid.
48. Maj. Gen. L. S. Kuter, "Memorandum for the Chief of the Air Staff," 11 May 1944, AFHRA 145-81-155.
49. Doolittle to Commanding General, 8th Fighter Command, "Relief of Combat Crew Personnel," 4 March 1944.
50. Headquarters, Eighth Air Force, Policy on Relief of Combat Crews, 4 March 1944, AFHRA 622-1621.
51. Doolittle to Commanding General, 8th Fighter Command, "Relief of Combat Crew Personnel," 4 March 1944.
52. Report E-56, "Attitudes of Heavy Bomber Crews toward Combat Flying," AFHRA File 141.28.
53. Lt. Gen. Ira C. Eaker to CG Na TOUSA, M-14332, 15 April 1944, AFHRA 622-1621.
54. Lt. Gen. Jacob L. Devers, AFHQ Message Form 2277, April 1944, AFHRA 622-1621. Also see Headquarters, Mediterranean Allied Air Forces, Message General 2166, 15 April 1944, ibid.
55. Lt. Gen. Carl Spaatz to Sir Charles Portal, 13 April 1944; and C. Portal to Spaatz, 14 April 1944, AFHRA 519-1612.
56. Lt. Gen. Carl Spaatz to Gen. H. H. Arnold, 5 May 1944, Box 15, Spaatz Papers, LOC.
57. Spaatz Diary, 19 April 1944, Box 14, Spaatz Papers, LOC.
58. Lt. Gen. Carl Spaatz, Progress in the Air War, 20 April 1944, Box 14, Spaatz Papers, LOC.

59. Spaatz Diary, 20 April 1944, Box 14, Spaatz Papers, LOC.
60. Lt. Gen. Carl Spaatz to Gen. H. H. Arnold, 8 April 1944, Box 14, Spaatz Papers, LOC.
61. Notes taken during a conference between General Spaatz and General Vandenberg, 10 April 1944, Box 15, Spaatz Papers, LOC,.
62. Gen. H. H. Arnold to Lt. Gen. Carl Spaatz, 24 April 1944, Box 14, Spaatz Papers, LOC.
63. Lt. Gen. Carl Spaatz, Daily Journal, 15 and 17 June 1944, Box 14, Spaatz Papers, LOC.
64. "To Arnold for Spatz [sic]," 29 July 1944, AFHRA 622-1621-2, September 1944–April 1945; Lt. Gen. Ira C. Eaker to Lt. Gen. Barney M. Giles, August 31, 1944, AFHRA 622-1621-2, April 1944–February 1945.
65. Message, Devers and Eaker to Marshall and Arnold, Ref. F 91034, AFHRA 622-1621-2, April 1944–February 1945.
66. Charles F. Sturgeon, "From High School into the Frying Pan," 20 June 1944, 91st Bombardment Group, www.91stbombgroup.com/airmen_diaries/diary_charles_sturgeon.pdf.
67. Maj. Gen. F. L. Anderson, attachment to Chas E. Rayens to Military Attache, American Embassy, London, Eng., "Air Force Morale," 8 June 1944, Box 91, Spaatz Papers, LOC.
68. William Corcoran to Colonel Rayens, 23 May 1944, Box 91, Spaatz Papers, LOC.
69. Col. O. N. Solbert, Memorandum, USSTAF, 11 July 1944, Box 91, Spaatz Papers, LOC; Thomas J. Hansbury, "My 2nd Tour of Duty," 16 November 1944, 91st Bombardment Group, http://www.91stbombgroup.com/airmen_diaries/diaries.html. Some bomber crews wanted to support the infantry, but even this support could not be provided easily. One crewmember expressed his angst at being asked at times to support soldiers because their bombs might do more hurt than good. Smallwood, *Tomlin's Crew*, 135. One young B-24 pilot had been told that his mission was "supposed to have helped the ground forces." He planned to peruse *Stars and Stripes* to see how exactly he had done that. Still, he recognized that his bomber was not "designed" for direct "infantry support missions." Faulkner, *Flying with the Fifteenth Air Force*, 79.
70. Lt. Gen. Carl Spaatz to [Arnold], 13 July 1944, Box 91, Spaatz Papers, LOC.
71. Incoming Message for Spaatz and Eaker, 27 July 1944, Box 91, Spaatz Papers, LOC.
72. Minutes of Commanders' Meeting, 20 July 1944, Box 91, Spaatz Papers, LOC.
73. [Unknown] to Lt. Gen. Ira C. Eaker, 19 June 1944, AFHRA 622-1621.

74. Teletype Conference between General Eaker and General Giles, 1 July 1944, "Leave and Furlough Policy Procedure Combat Crew Personnel," 2, AFHRA 622-1621-2, September 1944–April 1945.
75. Message 24813, "Twelfth Air Force," 15 July 1944, AFHRA 622-1621-2.
76. Teletype Conference between General Eaker and General Giles, 1 July 1944, 2.
77. Teletype Conference between General Eaker and General Giles, 1 July 1944, 5.
78. Teletype Conference between General Eaker and General Giles, 1 July 1944, 6.
79. Eaker for Arnold and Giles, Outgoing Message, M-23210, 2 July 1944, AFHRA 622-1621-2.
80. Arnold to Spaatz and Eaker, WARX 71515, 27 July 1944, AFHRA 622-1621.
81. "To Arnold for Spatz [sic]," 29 July 1944, AFHRA 622-1621-2, September 1944–April 1945.
82. Maj. Gen. I. H. Edwards, "Relief of Combat Crew Personnel," 9 September 1944, AFHRA 622-1621-2.
83. Unidentified letter from Air Staff member, 22 April 1944, AFHRA 145-81-155.
84. Brig. Gen. Laurence S. Kuter, quoted in Report, n.d. [1943–45], AFHRA 505-90-13.
85. Maj. Gen. L. S. Kuter, "Memorandum for the Chief of the Air Staff," 11 May 1944, AFHRA 145-81-155; Col. Joe L. Loutzenheiser, "Air Command in Europe," 6 June 1944, AFHRA 145-81-155.
86. Lt. Gen. Carl Spaatz to Gen. H. H. Arnold, 4 October 1944, AFHRA 145-81-155.

5

Blinding the Enemy
The Radar War before D-Day

Matthew Bone

For six weeks in the spring of 1944, the lead-up to D-Day saw the fighter-bombers of the Second Tactical Air Force (2 TAF) tasked with a plethora of targets. While Noball operations against the V-1 flying-bomb launch sites continued unabated, a new target type was prioritized. Looking north from the six landing beaches in Normandy, eight German radar stations stood guard, watching the sea and sky. These, along with the radar station at Saint Peter Port, Guernsey, would need to be destroyed before Overlord. Yet to ensure secrecy as to the invasion site, every radar station from Holland to Brest would have to be destroyed or blinded.

Over the course of May and early June, 2 TAF's fighter-bombers were given a long target list, with the radar stations firmly at the top. These operations 2 TAF would assign to squadrons equipped with the de Havilland Mosquito, Supermarine Spitfire LF Mk IX, and Hawker Typhoon Mk Ib. The "Radar War" was won at low level and high cost. The pilots of the Allied tactical air forces ensured that the Overlord fleet and its hundreds of thousands of men had the best possible opportunity to succeed on D-Day. They achieved this with the aid of near-overwhelming airpower and the unheralded bravery of the pilots tasked with this deadly essential mission. As Group Captain Desmond Scott, DSO, OBE, DFC, and Bar would remember, "These radar installations were, without doubt, the most formidable targets and getting at them was like fighting your way into a hornet's nest."[1]

Within the Air Ministry, a team under Dr. R. V. Jones, assistant director of intelligence (science), had been monitoring German radar developments throughout the early years of the war. Jones' team would be involved in countering as much of this as possible, but to beat the German stations, they needed to understand them. This led to snatch missions such as Operation Biting on the night of 27–28 February 1942. This famous raid saw a combined airborne and naval effort to pinch the latest German radar equipment stationed on the French coast at Bruneval. The operation, which has since passed into legend, provided vital intelligence into the latest developments of both the Freya and Würzburg radar systems.[2]

Despite the best efforts of Jones and his team, German radar coverage penetrated deep into UK airspace. The reports they compiled showed just how deep. One briefing report, issued on 3 March 1944, detailed the four main types of aircraft-reporting radar and the Seetakt ship-watching radar in use along Hitler's Atlantic Wall.[3]

Würzburg and Freya were the two main radar systems deployed by the Germans. Developed by the Telefunken Company as a gun-laying director, the Würzburg was the world's first radar accurate through clouds and was deployed in two main types. The FuMG 39E operated on a 50-cm wavelength and had a sixteen-mile range, with an accuracy of twenty-seven yards. The larger FuSE 65, known as the Giant Würzburg, was equipped with an eight-yard-diameter antenna and had a range of fifty miles.

The Gema Company developed the Freya, which was an eminently flexible system. Each array was made up of three 2.7-yard by 5.6-yard elements that would transmit, receive, and capture Identification Friend or Foe (IFF) signals. Operating at a 1.2-m wavelength, a tenth of that of the British Chain Home, the Freya could be deployed in multiple configurations for different

Photo 5-1 • The Giant Würzburg was the main gun-laying radar used by the Germans during the war. This example was deployed on the high ground overlooking Arromanches-les-Bains, the site chosen by the Allies for one of their Mulberry harbors. Allied ships and elements of the artificial harbor can be seen in the background of the photograph, taken 22 June 1944. *U.S. Air Force Photo A-72626AC*

effects. The array was mounted in a rotating casement, allowing it 360-degree coverage. It had an average detection range of ninety-three miles but lacked the ability to calculate altitude accurately.

Each night-fighter box utilized a standard combination of a Freya and two Würzburgs. The Freya would direct one of the Würzburgs onto the night fighter, which would then track the bomber and allow the ground controller to vector the night fighter into position for an attack.[4] How Freya was deployed also mattered. Beyond its standard deployment, this radar system was also used in two other applications to give different range visibilities.

The Mammut radar used multiple horizontal Freya arrays and was known as "Hoarding" to Allied planners due to its large rectangular layout, looking like an advertising billboard. Measuring thirty yards wide by ten yards high, the beam was limited to a 100-degree arc but was able to detect a target up to 185 miles away.

The Wasserman radar (Allied codename "Chimney") was a long-range, height-finding system that deployed multiple Freya arrays vertically. This, according to Alfred Price, was the finest early warning radar produced in the Second World War.[5] The Freya arrays were attached to a concrete tower forty-four to fifty-five yards high, around which it could be rotated, raised, and lowered. This gave excellent height, range, and bearing readings on targets up to 175 miles away.

Seetakt was a surface-search and gun-laying radar deployed either on ships of the Kriegsmarine or as part of a shore battery. With a line-of-sight range of around 20 miles, Seetakt, like Würzburg, was well ahead of anything deployed by the Allies until 1942–43. It was a shock to the Royal Navy when L. Brainbridge-Bell of Naval Intelligence was dispatched to Montevideo in South America to look over the scuttled *Graf Spee* and spotted the array on the pocket battleship.[6]

While the identification of all the sites was being carried out, in January 1944 a report entitled "Physical Destruction of Enemy Radar Stations" was compiled and released.[7] At the outset, its author states that the scales of effort "should be treated with caution, since they are based upon meagre accuracy data, although the best available." The resulting report would be based upon an order of magnitude.

Next, the report evaluated each type of possible attack. Commandos would be of use for data gathering near the coast, though an airborne force would possibly be more effective, but the scale of attacks needed prior to Overlord precluded this as practicable. Attacking with naval gunfire was deemed unsuitable due to the nature of naval shells and the lightweight construction of the radar arrays themselves. In addition, direct hits would be required on the casements and T-Huts, where the operators lived and worked. This action

Photo 5-2 • The Wasserman radar, known as "Chimney" by the Allies, was considered the finest long-range height-finding radar employed during World War II. This example was found at the Carneville Luftwaffe Station located east of Cherbourg—la Brasserie. *U.S. Air Force Photo 72643AC*

would be of use on the day of the landings but not before. That left aerial attack, but the report warned that this "is not promising even if methods are selected to fit the peculiarities of each type [of radar array]."[8]

Highlighting the realities of precision attack during the Second World War were the relatively small size of the target area and the radar arrays themselves. For example, the Cap d'Antifer aircraft-reporting station, two kilometers from Bruneval, comprised two sites. The first on the cliffs on the north of the site measured roughly 550 yards by 275 yards at its longest points. At its largest, this would be a target area of around thirty-one acres. Within that space, there was only one Freya and one Giant Würzburg unit.

The report calculated the probability of the effectiveness of aerial attack on radar compounds and the estimated number of sorties for different types of aircraft (see table 5-1). What is striking from this data is the accuracy an Oboe-guided raid could achieve by 1944 and that of a daylight raid by Royal Air Force (RAF) Bomber Command. Oboe, developed by Alec Reeves and Francis Jones at the Telecommunication Research Establishment in 1941, utilized two ground transmitting stations that gave the aircraft a circular trajectory from the station. By sending out audible pulses the pilot could adjust his course to stay on track, and when the signals from the two stations converged, he would know his aircraft was over the target and would drop target indicators, bombs, or both.[9] A raid of fewer than 300 heavy bombers would give a decent chance of damaging a radar site. Yet the report's authors, aware that "the targets are microscopically small," advise that the use of heavy bombers was impractical given the wider strategic needs for their use, limiting their utilization in attacking radar sites.[10] The planner's attention thus turned to fighter-bombers.

The fighter-bomber was the Second World War's bastard child of necessity. With planners focusing on bombers always getting through and some nations dabbling with dedicated dive-bombers, it became clear very early in the war that a tactical interdiction aircraft was required. Given the long lead times needed to develop a dedicated warplane, fighters were adapted to this role. All major fighter types would, at some point in the war, deliver underwing ordnance. On the Allied side by 1944, the frontline fighter-bombers had coalesced into five main types. Within 2 TAF, the Supermarine Spitfire LF

Mk V and Mk IX (the LF designation pointing to a Rolls-Royce Merlin 66 tuned for low-altitude performance), the Hawker Typhoon Mk Ib, and the de Havilland Mosquito were the frontline fighter-bombers. The U.S. Army Air Forces' Ninth Tactical Air Force would field the Republic P-47 Thunderbolt and the Lockheed P-38 Lightning.[11]

Table 5-1 • Probability of Physical Destruction of Enemy Radar Stations by Heavy and Medium Bombers

Aircraft	Bomb Load	Accuracy in yards[a]	Type of Bombing	Sorties to be dispatched for the following chances of destroying one support column		
				12.5%	25%	50%
Lancaster	18 x 500 lbs.	200	Day, Visual Individual	56	119	286
B-17	12 x 500 lbs.	5% within 40,000 sq. yds.[b]	Day, Formation	84	178	429
Lancaster	18 x 500 lbs.	200 / 400[c]	Night, with PFF[d]	71	150	361
Stirling	24 x 500 lbs.	219	Oboe Blind Bombing	10	22	54
B-17	12 x 500 lbs.	219	Oboe Blind Bombing	21	44	107
B-26	8 x 500 lbs.	5% within 40,000 sq. yds.[e]	Day Boxes of 6	126	267	643

Source: Adapted from "Physical Destruction of Enemy Radar Stations," 12 January 1944, Attacks on Enemy Radar Installations, TNA AIR 37/510.

Notes:

a Accuracy based upon circular error probability, which refers to the average distance between a target and the terminal end of an object's path of travel. This anticipated room for error considers the distance of each missed shot from the intended target.

b The B-17 Flying Fortress data was based upon a 5-percent accuracy within 10,000 square yards from available operational data. The 40,000 square yards in the original table may have been a mistake given the footnote to the table.

c Two hundred yards was based on the bombing accuracy of target indicators; 400 yards was for the follow-up bombing.

d Pathfinder Force (PFF).

e The B-26 Marauder data was based upon the Audinghen raid of 25 November 1943, when a 5.25-percent accuracy within 40,000 square yards was achieved.

A fighter-bomber is a flexible weapon system that can deliver a large amount of ordnance onto a relatively small target area with greater accuracy than a heavy or medium bomber. Its inherent speed also means that it can get into and out of trouble quickly. For a target like a radar site that is watching you approach, speed would be of the essence. The planners first considered the standard available bomb load for the fighter-bombers in service, the 500-pound Medium Case (MC) bomb, as outlined in table 5-2.

The Freya radar was protected by a blast wall encompassing it about 1.6 yards from the array's casement. A 500-pound MC bomb would cause a roughly 6.5-yard crater, so to damage the Freya, a bomb would need to land within 7.7 yards of it. Drop two bombs, and the margin for error increases slightly to 13 yards. A Würzburg was unprotected by a wall and mounted on a plinth-like casement. As such, to cause damage, a single bomb would need to land within 12 yards of the apparatus.

Even from a cursory glance, the number of sorties needed for a successful dive-bombing operation appears prohibitive. Cannon and .50-caliber machine-gun fire was expected to also be effective, mostly against Würzburgs, but the two types of attack in the same sortie were not correlated in the report. The new RP-3 rocket with a 60-pound Semi-Armor Piercing (SAP) warhead was an exciting prospect for attacking the Wasserman radars. The number of sorties of RP-armed aircraft to achieve a hit on the vital lower 6.5 yards of its chimney is shown in table 5-3.

This analysis was promising, and the report suggests that a Wasserman ideally would be attacked by a strike package of eight RP Typhoons, each with eight 60-pound SAP RP-3s, and six additional Typhoons flying flak cover. Throughout the report, the emphasis is on the supporting structures, as the three-quarter- to one-and-a-half-inch gauge metal of the arrays themselves would allow bomb or rocket fragments to pass through without noticeable damage and would be relatively straightforward to repair.

The conclusion was not promising. Attacking with any of the available means, the Freya and Mammut sites, due to the nature of their construction, were considered "difficult to damage" and impracticable to be attacked with bombs. Only RP trials could ascertain the effectiveness of rockets, thus a test attack would be needed.

Table 5-2 • Probability of Physical Destruction of Enemy Radar Stations by Fighter-Bombers (Bombs)

Type of Bombing	Number of 500-lb bombs per aircraft	Accuracy in yards[a]	Sorties dispatched to give the following chances of at least one hit on:					
			Freyas or Coast-Watchers			Würzburgs		
			12.5%	25%	50%	12.5%	25%	50%
Dive-Bombing	Single Bomb	396	645	1387	3302	323	694	1653
	2 Bombs	396	298	641	1525	146	314	747
Low Level	Single Bomb	192	151	325	773	76	163	389
	2 Bombs	192	69	148	353	34	73	174
	4 Bombs	192	34	73	174	18	39	18
	6 Bombs	192	23	49	118	12	26	61
	8 Bombs	192	18	39	92	9	19	46

Source: Adapted from "Physical Destruction of Enemy Radar Stations," 12 January 1944, Attacks on Enemy Radar Installations, TNA AIR 37/510.

Note:
[a] Accuracy was based upon circular error probability. The data for this table was based on practice trials conducted by operational pilots at Leysdown Range in Kent, England.

Table 5-3 • Probability of Physical Destruction of Enemy Radar Stations by Fighter-Bombers (Rockets)

	Accuracy in yards[a]	Chances of achieving at least one hit		
		12.5%	25%	50%
Sorties Required	7.7	4	8	15

Source: Adapted from "Physical Destruction of Enemy Radar Stations," 12 January 1944, Attacks on Enemy Radar Installations, TNA AIR 37/510.

Note:
[a] The accuracy (7.7-yard deviation) was based on the early training of RP-armed Typhoons. Interestingly, they added an operational factor of three to this figure.

Attacking radar sites on the coast of occupied Europe was not something that Air Defence of Great Britain (ADGB) and 2 TAF had spent much effort perfecting.[12] The well-placed concern was that harassing the sites would only lead to their reinforcement with additional flak defenses, making them even harder to destroy when the time came. Nonetheless, permission was sought, initially from ADGB's 11 Group and transferred to 2 TAF, to fly a strike against the Wasserman array at Ostend, Belgium. This site was selected as it was not in the invasion target area, had a Wasserman that Jones' team had been monitoring, and was well within the range of the RP Typhoon squadrons based at RAF Manston, Kent.

Transferring officially to 2 TAF on 1 March 1944, No. 198 Squadron was commanded by Squadron Leader "Johnny" Baldwin. Baldwin's remarkable RAF career started with a nineteen-day detention at Uxbridge after a disagreement with the training corporal, who had questioned his parentage. From there, Baldwin would see service as an aircraftsman with the Advanced Air Striking Force in France in 1940 before a period building "extremely crude mines" at RAF Cosford and leading a Bomb Disposal team before he was accepted in pilot training.[13] He completed his course at No. 2 British Flying Training School at Glendale, California, and was posted to No. 609 "West Riding" Squadron, the crack Hawker Typhoon unit in the RAF, as a flight sergeant.

Baldwin soon mastered the Typhoon. An ace within eight months of joining No. 609, he rose from flight sergeant to command of a squadron within a year. Within three months of his appointment to command No. 198 Squadron, the unit had shot down forty-seven enemy aircraft.[14]

Orders for the Ostend strike arrived in mid-March, and reconnaissance sorties were flown on 14 March, which discovered that the Wasserman was in a prone position; the strike would have to wait. On 16 March Baldwin and Flying Officer Jack Williams took off at 0810 hours to have a look at the chimney. Finding it still lowered and the weather unfavorable, they returned to Manston. Baldwin returned with Flight Lieutenant Raymond Lallemant, a Belgian, two hours later, finding the chimney raised and the weather perfect.

At 1240 hours twelve Typhoons from No. 198 Squadron departed Manston. Eight aircraft would fly flak suppression while Baldwin would lead four others to attack the chimney. They crossed the coast at 8,000 feet and appeared

Photo 5-3 • Hawker Typhoons, either launching rocket projectiles or dropping bombs, were one of the main types of aircraft used by the RAF to attack German radar installations along the coast of France. Here, King George VI inspects a Hawker Typhoon Mk Ib (MN454 "HF-S") of No. 183 Squadron prior to the Normandy landings. *IWM CH 13240*

as if they were flying a normal sortie before they broke, with two sections attacking the flak positions and Baldwin's section attacking the chimney. Baldwin and his No. 2, Warrant Officer Donald Mason, scored hits halfway up the chimney and at the base respectively; the rest of the flight missed. With the chimney still standing, they reformed without losses and returned to Manston to refuel and rearm.

No. 198 Squadron was airborne again at 1515 hours and over the target forty-five minutes later. The same section again attacked with their rockets, and again Baldwin scored a hit about a third of the way from the top of the chimney, with his remaining rockets landing 700 yards beyond. Mason and Flight Lieutenant John Niblett, DFC, scored hits on the base of the chimney. As 198 raced for home, the Ostend chimney was still standing.[15] Following this attack, the squadron would rotate through a week of dedicated RP training at Armament Practice Camp Llanbedr, Wales, at the end of March in preparation for what was to come.

R. V. Jones and his team got to work analyzing the gun-camera footage, images from photoreconnaissance flights, and intelligence from the Belgian resistance. They were able to ascertain that while the chimney was still standing, the arrays and the turning mechanism sustained significant damage, which required dismantling the station for repairs, a process that would take weeks to complete.[16] The data gathered suggested that RP Typhoons should aim their attacks halfway up the chimney so that even near misses would cause significant damage. A memo for the Allied Expeditionary Air Force (AEAF) at Norfolk House in London quoted Jones as having "considered the attack most satisfactory"—high praise indeed from him.[17]

Jones' team left no stone unturned in their data gathering. Using photoreconnaissance and the "ping-pong" system, which allowed for the bearing on a radar transmitter to be narrowed down to a quarter of a degree, every radar station on the Channel coast was mapped and its radar sets identified. The report assigned the chimney arrays the highest priority for destruction. Hoarding arrays were next on the list, and the Freyas ranked third. Seetakt was identified as important, but the gun-laying capabilities of the Würzburgs were deemed more dangerous. The destruction of these sites would mean that "no comprehensive picture of the operation would be available in the [enemy's] filter room." Coupled with this, "the removal of all giant and small Würzburgs . . . would render the gunnery ineffective, save as a barrage."[18]

As each radar site within ten miles of the coast between Brest and Calais was identified, the scale of the target list became clear. In total, the Germans had constructed sites containing a total of

- 6 Chimneys
- 6 Hoardings
- 38 Würzburgs
- 7 Coast-Watchers (Seetakts)
- 42 Giant Würzburgs
- and a "large number" of small Würzburgs, with an estimate of at least 1 per flak battery.

From the early reports on the requirements to destroy the different radar types, Jones and his team mapped the vulnerabilities of each and the effort required for a 50-percent success rate. Notably, the two immediate results of the attack were clear in the introduction: "1, Destruction of equipment. 2,

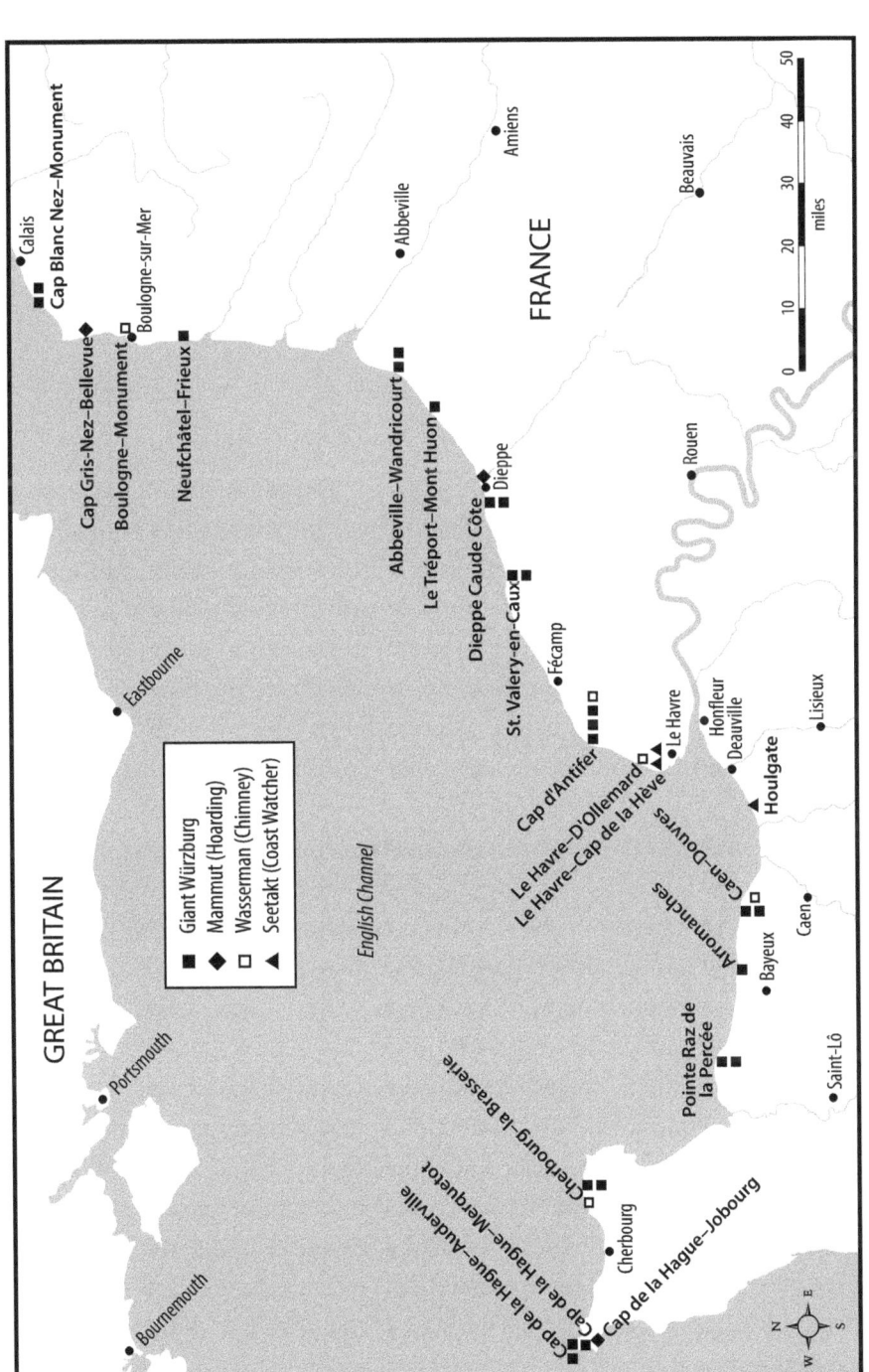

Map 5-1 • German Radar Sites

Killing of skilled operators."[19] The trained soldiers who operated the systems were as important a target as the radar arrays themselves. Several immediate consequences of achieving one or both aims would follow:

- A shortage of components
- Overloading of maintenance services
- Possible diversion of resources into radar production due to the continuing threat of attack
- A shortage of trained personnel
- Replacement of operators accustomed to the locality by fresh operators
- Lowering of skilled operators.[20]

Further testing occurred to understand the effectiveness of the RP against the retaining walls around a Freya emplacement. These found that a 60-pound SAP RP was effective, and when following with a strafing pass with a 20-mm cannon, 50-percent damage was achievable, providing the wall was not too strong. Time and again, the fighter-bomber was seen as the best option available. The summary gave the primary objective as "lowering [the] efficiency of the early warning and interception systems. It is not of itself sufficient to provide elimination of these systems but would form a useful adjunct to jamming."[21]

An estimated one thousand sorties would be required to achieve the aims needed to make Operation Neptune a success. This came from a comparison with the Noball operations, where the V-1 sites were also hard to find. If attacks against radar stations were similar, then a 50-percent increase in the sortie count would be expected. Ultimately, 2 TAF alone would fly over 1,600 sorties against the German radar sites.

Planners with 2 TAF categorized the order of attack for radar sites between Cap Blanc Nez in the Pas de Calais and Cap de la Hague at the tip of the Cotentin Peninsula. The targets would be attacked in five phases, which would see the far flanks of the Normandy landing beaches attacked first while working toward the compounds overlooking the beaches themselves. A total of forty-two individual sites were identified, and with the landings planned for early June, 10 May was set for the start of the offensive. Understanding that the chimneys would take the longest to repair, these would be among the first attacked. Again, the understanding was that while all sites could be repaired, the killing and injuring of their operators would lower their efficiency and effectiveness.

Planning for radar-site attacks took into consideration the inherent inaccuracy of the available munitions. The Circular Error Probability (CEP) calculation was used to show the difficulty of putting munitions into the target area, let alone onto the target itself. RP Typhoons, the rarer type of fighter-bomber, were considered the most accurate, with only a seven-meter CEP. This compares to the bomb-armed Spitfire LF Mk IX and "Bombphoon" Typhoons, which were judged to have a CEP of 396 yards. Yet this is misleading when the reality of using the RP-3 rocket is considered. This weapon was released in a dive, aimed through a lightly modified air-to-air gunsight, and was essentially a cordite-powered firework.

To achieve a relatively high chance of a hit or a damaging near miss, pilots were taught to release their 60-pound SAP rockets in clear air with a 60-degree dive at a height of 4,000 feet and roughly 1,640 yards from the target. For every 153 yards the pilot released his rockets from that ideal firing point, the rockets would drop 15.3 yards short or 15.3 yards long. Other factors also affected accuracy. For every 2 gs of force being pulled, the rockets would deviate by around 30 yards. Every 4 degrees of sideslip used to counteract a crosswind would cause the rocket to deviate by 50 yards. For every 20-mph gust of wind, the rocket would be blown 30 yards off course.[22] All of these calculations were needed from a twenty-something-year-old pilot diving at 500 mph while being shot at. A former U.S. Army AH-64 Apache pilot who reviewed these figures remarked that they were very familiar, as even with the targeting systems in modern helicopters, "some degree of Kentucky windage" was always required to increase the probability of a hit with an unguided rocket.[23]

The high-sortie estimates for the completion of the campaign seem conservative when considering the accuracy on offer by the fighter-bombers. Yet they were the best tool for the job, and from 10 May 1944, 2 TAF's fighter-bombers attacked these radar and the Noball sites daily, weather permitting.

While the phased planning looked first to the flanks, one central site was of prime importance. The radar station at Cap d'Antifer, north of le Havre, would be one of the first targeted. On 11 May No. 609 Squadron attacked, and the results provided an early indication of the difficulty and cost that the campaign would bring. The two sites at Cap d'Antifer were roughly a mile apart. The semaphore station on the cliffs held a Freya and a Giant Würzburg. To the south was a chimney site, and inland to the east was another Freya and Giant Würzburg. Cap d'Antifer's position on the left flank of the landing beaches meant that it was a high-priority target.

On the evening of 10 May, Wing Commander Peter Brooker and No. 609 Squadron's commanding officer, Squadron Leader Johnny Wells, flew a reconnaissance sortie over the target selected for a wing-strength attack the next day. While the Bombphoons of No. 197 Squadron attacked the inland targets, No. 609 went for the clifftop Freya and Giant Würzburg. Cutting inland with the intention of escaping out to sea after their strike, the twelve Typhoons were met with a barrage of 20-mm and 37-mm flak.

Five Typhoons were lost on the mission. The first aircraft hit, MN544, was that of twenty-year-old Flight Lieutenant Robert Wood. His Typhoon burst into flames and collided with that of Flight Sergeant Ken Adam (a future two-time Oscar winner and James Bond set designer) in JP659. Although losing about two and a half feet of his port wing, Adam limped back to RAF Thorney Island, but Wood was killed when his aircraft crashed into a house. Following them into the target was Flying Officer Pierre Léopold Soesman, one of 609's large Belgian contingent, who left Princeton University to join the Royal Canadian Air Force (RCAF). Soesman in MN496 was hit by flak but made it out to sea before bailing out. He failed to inflate his dinghy, and by the time the air-sea rescue (ASR) Walrus seaplane arrived, Soesman had disappeared. No. 609 Squadron's intelligence officer, Frank Zeigler, noted the operation was a "dodgy do."[24] Cap d'Antifer was still operational.

The pattern of operations for May 1944 is clear from the No. 609 Squadron Operations Record Book (ORB). The squadron was flying two to three missions a day at anything from flight (four aircraft) to squadron (twelve aircraft) strength and often in concert with other squadrons. Attacking railway, transport, communications, and Noball targets across northern France was taking a toll. With missions over France resulting in sortie lengths of sixty to seventy-five minutes, the maintenance of the aircraft was critical.

Coupled with this, the Hawker Typhoon was in the middle of a fundamental upgrade program.

Designed in 1937, the Hawker Typhoon was Sydney Camm's follow-up to the Hurricane and fell very much into the same generation as it, the Spitfire, and the German Messerschmitt Me 109. Built with a thick wing and powered by a monstrous 2,200-hp Napier Sabre engine, the Typhoon was very fast, very rugged, and, early in its service, plagued with issues. The hardest to rectify was a structural issue that resulted in the tail separating from the airframe. Several aircraft and their pilots were lost to such failures, including Hawker test pilot Kenneth Seth-Smith. This issue would baffle Hawker, who raced to find the reason for the failures. Reinforcement of the rear transport joint along with the addition of twenty "fish plates," the most visible modification, would see a 20-percent increase in fuselage strength but did not solve the problem.

The survival of one pilot, William "Killy" Kilpatrick, would yield vital clues to the mystery as would the remarkable testing of the Royal Aircraft Establishment at Farnborough. Investigators subjected a Typhoon fuselage to a series of resonance tests in which the harmonics of the fuselage were stressed until destruction. This revealed that a harmonic node could form at 9.3 Hz and 13.2 Hz, which in certain circumstances would cause the tail to separate from the aircraft. The modification to resolve this issue was MOD 353, which involved increasing the inertia and mass-balance weights in the aircraft below the control column and tail respectively, therefore dampening the resonance. In early 1944 this modification, along with the combat-vital bubble canopy and vibration-dampening four-blade propeller, was being rushed out to all units, which saw their aircraft cycle through maintenance units for updating.[25]

The confidence in MOD 353 was so high that the Typhoon's "bad reputation" was finally felt to be behind it until 24 May, when concern about its tail returned. No. 175 Squadron was ordered to attack another cliff-top radar station at Cap de la Hève, northwest of Le Havre. It was the second squadron-strength operation of the day for No. 175 after a wing-strength attack at the radar station at Holgate that morning. The squadron assigned four aircraft to the antiflak role, while the remaining seven aircraft went after the radar installation with RPs. While attacking the Freya, Pilot Officer Stuart Finlayson (RCAF) in Typhoon JR311 fired his rockets and, as he pulled out of the dive, his tail separated midway down the fuselage. Finlayson crashed into the target. His aircraft was not seen to take fire, which raised concerns that the new modification did not work. Actually, in the haste to modify aircraft, JR311 was accidentally missed along with several other Typhoons.[26] This was quickly rectified but showed the unrelenting pressure on all parts of 2 TAF and the Allied air forces to keep up the pressure on the Germans in northern France.

By late May, 2 TAF's efforts were becoming a war of attrition, and the extent of the effort of their crews was brought into sharp relief. On the twenty-fourth, Nos. 198 and 609 Squadrons attacked the Cap de la Hague radar station inland at Jobourg on the Cherbourg Peninsula. No. 609 attacked first, and its pilots had front-row seats for what happened next. No. 198 attacked low, led by Squadron Leader John Niblett, DFC, who had flown on the squadron's Ostend test attack back in March, and the four Typhoons were met with a hail of 37-mm flak. Niblett pressed home his attack and made it through. His number 2 was Flying Officer Hal Freeman (RCAF) in MN410. Freeman was hit by 37-mm flak that, according to a German prisoner of war interrogated later, "practically took his tail off." Despite the damage to his aircraft, Freeman managed to stay on target and fired his rockets into the radar structure. As he pulled up in his damaged Typhoon, it was hit by Flight Sergeant Edward Vallely in JP503, who was attacking next in line, and both men were killed when their aircraft crashed into the site. The attack and the impact of two seven-ton Typhoons on the array meant that twenty-three of the twenty-eight power cables were cut.[27]

On return to RAF Thorney Island, No. 609 Squadron's pilots reported that it would have been a "piece of cake" for Freeman to have aborted his attack and climbed away to bail out.[28] Wing Commander Desmond Scott, the commanding officer of No. 123 Wing, collated the reports and, after receiving the POW testimony, recommended Freeman for the Victoria Cross. Surprisingly, the recommendation was turned down, and Freeman received the lesser honor of Mentioned in Despatches. Scott was disgusted with this change, which occurred despite endorsements from R. V. Jones and Air Marshal Trafford Leigh-Mallory, the AEAF commander.[29]

As June broke, the invisible deception plan was in full swing. No. 100 Group was putting the final touches on its plans under the ever-watchful eye of Jones. While beyond the scope of this chapter, No. 100 Group's Operations Glimmer and Taxable would create the illusion of a "ghost fleet" in the English Channel heading toward Calais, while Operation Mandrel would jam what was left of the radar network along the invasion beaches. For these plans to work, a minimal level of radar coverage would be needed. If too much was left serviceable, then No. 100 Group would not be able to mask the task force steaming south to Normandy.

The second day of June was particularly busy, especially for No. 123 and 136 Wings based at RAF Thorney Island, near Portsmouth, where the invasion fleet was assembling. At 1530 hours Flight Lieutenant Frank "Dutch" Holland led twelve No. 184 Squadron Typhoons to attack the radar station at Barfleur-le-Vicel on the eastern side of the Cotentin Peninsula. Their target was a Seetakt radar, and they were accompanied by two tactical-reconnaissance Mustangs of No. 430 Squadron (RCAF). A recurring theme throughout the Noball and Radar operations and the Normandy Campaign that followed was that of locating the correct targets in the dense Norman countryside. The No. 184 Squadron ORB takes no little delight in the fact that Dutch Holland was not sure that the site they attacked was the right one, especially with two Canadian Mustangs taking pictures of every moment of the attack through their oblique cameras.

The other Thorney Island squadrons would not get off so lightly. Wing Commander Peter Brooker led No. 123 Wing to attack the radar station at Dieppe Caude Côte, behind what had been Green Beach during the Dieppe Raid of 19 August 1942. The Freya radars there had been a target of the South Saskatchewan Regiment raiders, who had radar technician Flight Sergeant Jack Nissenthal embedded with them for the purpose of inspecting and removing items of interest for Jones to examine. On that day in 1942, the South Sasks never got close to the radar site. Now, nearly two years later, the RAF were trying to destroy the complex. The seventeen RP Typhoons split up, with the individual flights either coming in low over the sea or attacking from out of the sun to try and split the flak, the radars being "well covered by heavy and light A.A."[30] No. 198 Squadron's low attack was led again by Squadron Leader John Niblett, DFC. As he approached the coast, his Typhoon (MN192) was hit by "light flak" and burst into flames, crashing into the cliffs that had so held up the South Sasks.[31] In total, sixty-four rockets were fired into the radar station, with hits claimed, but the loss of a squadron leader just before D-Day, one who had been involved in 2 TAF's first Radar War attack, was further proof of the high cost of this effort. Two of the Thorney Island squadrons would fly again that evening, attacking the radar at Cap Gris-Nez, before having a "very well attended" Officer's Mess Dance with all four squadrons as life went on.[32] No. 198 Squadron was ordered to return to Dieppe the next day to finish the job.

One of the key radar sites left till late on in the campaign had the unique distinction of being on British soil. German forces occupied the island of Guernsey on 29 June 1940, which they subsequently heavily fortified. Located above Saint Peter Port is Fort George. Originally built in the late eighteenth century, this bastion fort now housed two Freyas and two Giant Würzburgs. Guernsey's position was outside the main axis of the coming invasion, but the radar and flak at Fort George would be perfectly positioned to pick up and fire upon the over 800 IX Troop Carrier Command aircraft and gliders carrying the U.S. 82nd and 101st Airborne Divisions. The airborne plan had the transports make a left turn just before the Channel Islands on their run into the drop zones in Normandy, so ensuring this radar array was dark was vital. Five squadrons of Typhoons struck Fort George on 27 May and 2 June. These attacks caused much damage, but on 3 June all the radar was still active.

Eight Bombphoons from No. 439 Squadron (RCAF), each armed with two 500-pound bombs, attacked on 3 June. Diving down from 12,000 feet at over 500 mph, the Typhoons encountered heavy flak but dropped their sixteen bombs on the fort and raced out to sea. Only two aircraft were damaged.[33] This attack knocked out both Giant Würzburgs and a Freya, but another Freya remained active. No. 439 Squadron returned to finish the job two days later. They struck again on the morning of the 5 June with eight Typhoons, led by Flight Lieutenant John Saville and armed with instantaneous-fused 500-pound MC bombs. Diving on Fort George from 12,000 feet in an easterly direction to allow the Typhoons to escape out to sea, No. 439's crews saw their bombs land in and around the remaining Freya, knocking it out. They also saw a huge splash in the port a mile from the fort. Assuming a bomb fell long, they formed up but then discovered that Saville was missing. They attempted to raise him on the radio and, when that failed, called in ASR. Racing back to RAF Hurn, four Typhoons were airborne again after thirty-five minutes to assist in the search, which saw the ASR Walrus fly into Saint Peter Port despite heavy flak to try and spot Saville. Their search would prove fruitless, and it would take until 1982 for the Guernsey Nautical Archeology Society to find Saville's Typhoon.[34]

The twenty-four-hour delay to the invasion allowed 2 TAF another day of operations. Losses on 5 June were heavy—a total of eight aircraft and three pilots, including Saville and No. 193's Squadron Leader David Ross, DFC—as Typhoons also attacked the radar at Cap de la Hague and the Spitfires of No. 144 Wing attacked Cap d'Antifer. As No. 257 Squadron returned from their third operation of the day, which included a search for Squadron Leader Ross, they flew over the invasion fleet as it steamed south. Wing Commander Reg Baker ordered radio silence and once on the ground announced to his assembled pilots, "Well, obviously you know tomorrow's D-Day."[35] As the men were briefed, the ground crews applied the now-famous black-and-white identification stripes to the aircraft. Come the morning, 2 TAF would be finally supplying direct support to the ground forces liberating Europe.

As Operation Neptune unfolded on the night of 5–6 June, only 20 percent of the original number of German radar stations had any noticeable emissions across the entire invasion area. Between 0100 hours and 0400 hours, only nine radar stations were operational.[36] In total, across the coast of Northwest Europe, German radar coverage was about 18 percent, and in the invasion area, there was only 4-percent coverage.[37] Leigh-Mallory later reported the operations against German radar: "These results may be summarized as follows: the enemy did not obtain the early warning of our approach that his Radar coverage should have made possible; there is every reason to suppose that Radar controlled gunfire was interfered with; no fighter aircraft hindered our airborne operations; the enemy was confused and his troop movements were delayed."[38]

Radar stations would continue to be attacked over the opening weeks of the Normandy Campaign until ground forces overran the sites. Indeed, during the afternoon of D-Day itself, No. 609 Squadron attacked Cap de la Hève. But the results of these strikes were clear as Allied forces pushed inland, supported by the fighter-bombers of 2 TAF and Ninth Air Force, now retasked to support the armies on French soil. By D+4, the advanced landing grounds in Normandy would see aircraft landing during the day to refuel and rearm before returning to England for the night. By the end of June, the AEAF would be on European soil for good.

The cost of the twenty-six-day Radar War had been high. AEAF aircraft flew 1,668 sorties against the radar sites. The RP Typhoons of 2 TAF flew 694 sorties and fired 4,517 60-pound SAP-armed RP-3 rockets. The Typhoon and Spitfire fighter-bombers contributed another 759 sorties and dropped 1,258 500-pound MC bombs plus a number of 1,000-pound bombs not yet officially authorized for use.[39] During these efforts in May and early June 1944, forty-one Typhoons were shot down, with the loss of twenty-two pilots killed, including two squadron leaders, and three others taken prisoner in all AEAF preparatory attacks before D-Day. An additional fifty-one Spitfires were lost, with ten pilots killed and seven taken prisoner.[40] And yet these losses would be considered low compared to the meatgrinder that the air war over France would become in the following months.[41]

In March 1945 No. 3 Syndicate of the Bombing Analysis Unit carried out a survey of the radar stations along the French coast. Their report investigated whether the campaign had been a success as believed. The unit reviewed the pilots' combat reports using photographic evidence and the testimony of prisoners of war. They found that in the two weeks before 5 June 1944, "17 radar installations (2 Chimneys, 2 Hoardings, 8 Giant Würzburgs, and 5 Freyas) were destroyed or made unserviceable for at least 14 days for the loss of 13 aircraft." The report concluded that, for attacks on radar stations, weight for weight, the RP-3 rocket was found to be four times more effective than bombs. The four main conclusions of the report were:

1. The Policy of direct attack on radar apparatus is supported by the results achieved.
2. The Rocket Projectile is an effective weapon for use against Chimneys and Hoardings. It is not sufficiently accurate for general use against smaller targets.
3. 20 mm cannon fire is effective against exposed and unarmoured cabins. It has a harmful effect also on the morale of the operators.
4. Bombing, when accurate, is very effective against all surface radar targets. Near misses, though doing little damage to radar apparatus, may cut vital power and telephone lines on a crowded site.[42]

R. V. Jones and his boffins had been proved correct. Leigh-Mallory, a commander whose reputation is still much debated, reviewed the Radar War in his dispatch written shortly before his death in an aircraft crash in November 1944:

> These Radar targets were very heavily defended by flak and low-level attacks upon them demanded great skill and daring. Pilots of the R.A.F. Second Tactical Air Force were mainly employed and losses among senior and more experienced pilots were heavy. There is no doubt, however, that these attacks saved the lives of countless soldiers, sailors and airmen on D-Day. . . . The enemy's Radar cover was effectively disrupted and neutralised by air attacks, and in consequence the enemy was virtually "blinded" at the time of the assault.[43]

NOTES

1. Desmond Scott, *Typhoon Pilot* (London: Leo Cooper, 1982), 101.
2. R. V. Jones, *Most Secret War: British Scientific Intelligence, 1939–1945* (London: Hamish Hamilton), 245.
3. AEAF/MS.16700/Int 3/3/44, UK National Archives [hereafter TNA] AIR 37/510.
4. Alfred Price, *Instruments of Darkness: The History of Electronic Warfare, 1939–1945* (London: Greenhill, 2005), 61–69.
5. Price, *Instruments of Darkness*, 71.
6. Price, *Instruments of Darkness*, 77.
7. "Physical Destruction of Enemy Radar Stations," 12 January 1944, Attacks on Enemy Radar Installations, Installations, TNA AIR 37/510.

8. "Physical Destruction of Enemy Radar Stations."
9. Jones, *Most Secret War*, 274–75.
10. "Section II—Methods of Attack and Probabilities of Success," Attacks on Enemy Radar Installations, TNA AIR 37/510.
11. The brunt of operations against the radar sites was born by 2 TAF's Hawker Typhoons, so these operations are the focus here.
12. ADGB was formerly known as Fighter Command; it was renamed after the formation of 2 TAF.
13. James Baldwin, "Johnny's War," *Flypast*, March 2019, https://www.key.aero/article/johnnys-war.
14. Baldwin ended the war as a group captain; was awarded the DSO & bar, DFC & bar, and AFC; and was the leading Typhoon ace with 14½ victories. He disappeared while flying an F-86 Sabre over Korea with the U.S. Air Force in 1952.
15. No. 198 Squadron Summary of Events, March 1944, TNA AIR 27/1170-25; No. 198 Squadron Operations Record Book, March 1944, TNA AIR 27/1170-26; "RP Attack on Radar Chimney, Analysis of Ramrod 651—16th March 1944," Attacks on Enemy Radar Installations, TNA AIR 37/510.
16. Jones, *Most Secret War*, 101–2.
17. AEAF/S 14180/Sigs Plans, 28 March 1944, Attacks on Enemy Radar Installations, TNA AIR 37/510.
18. "Plan for Attack of Enemy Radar, D.D. Science," 24 March 1944, Attacks on Enemy Radar Installations, TNA AIR 37/510.
19. "Plan for Attack of Enemy Radar."
20. "Plan for Attack of Enemy Radar."
21. "Plan for Attack of Enemy Radar."
22. Alfred Price, "The Rocket-Firing Typhoon in Normandy," *Royal Air Force Historical Society Journal* 45 (2009), 109–20.
23. Conversation between the author and Mr. Jonathan Bernstein, January 2022. "Kentucky Windage" is a term in shooting where a correction for wind is made by aiming a firearm to the right or left of the target rather than by an adjustment of the sights.
24. No. 609 Squadron Summary of Events, May 1944, TNA AIR 27/2103-33; No. 609 Squadron Record of Events, May 1944, TNA AIR 27/2103-34.
25. Richard Seth-Smith, "Bad Vibrations: Solving the Hawker Typhoons Structural Problems," *Aviation Historian* 27 (n.d.), 75–86.
26. No. 175 Squadron Summary of Events, May 1944, TNA AIR 27/1111-9; No. 175 Squadron Record of Events, May 1944, TNA AIR 27/1111-10.
27. Scott, *Typhoon Pilot*, 102.

28. George Armour Bell, *To Live among Heroes: A Medical Officer's Dramatic Insight into the Life of 609 (WR) Squadron in NW Europe, 1944–45* (London: Grub Street, 2001), 19.
29. Jones, *Most Secret War*, 412.
30. Rhubarb Operations: Appendix XII—German Coastal Radar Stations in Northern France, April 1944, TNA AIR 40/1668.
31. No. 198 Squadron Summary of Events, June 1944, TNA AIR 27/1170-31.
32. No. 198 Squadron Summary of Events, June 1944.
33. No. 439 Squadron RCAF, Summary of Events, June 1944, TNA AIR 27/1879-8.
34. "The Discovery of Hawker Typhoon 1B, MN210, 439 Sqn RCAF Report," Guernsey Nautical Archeology Society, 1988. Report provided courtesy of Nick Le Huray. See also Nick Le Huray, "Flight Lieutenant John Saville—Typhoon Raids on Guernsey June 1944," *Island Fortress* (blog), 5 June 2023, https://island-fortress.com/2023/06/05/flight-lieutenant-john-saville-typhoon-raids-on-guernsey-june-1944/.
35. Franks, *Typhoon Attack*, 115.
36. Air Chief Marshal Trafford Leigh-Mallory, "Air Operations by the Allied Expeditionary Air Force in N.W. Europe from November 15th 1943 to September 10th 1944," *London Gazette*, 2 January 1947.
37. Air Historical Branch, Air Ministry [hereafter AHB], *The Liberation of North West Europe*, 3:32.
38. Leigh-Mallory, "Air Operations."
39. AHB, *The Liberation of North West Europe*, vol. 3.
40. Christopher Shores and Chris Thomas, *2nd Tactical Air Force*, vol. 1, *Spartan to Normandy, June 1943 to June 1944* (Surrey, UK: Classic, 2004).
41. From 6 June to 25 August 1944, 2 TAF alone lost 264 Hawker Typhoons and 149 pilots killed, the majority to flak, supporting Allied ground forces in France. See Shores and Thomas, *2nd Tactical Air Force*.
42. "Effects on German Radar Stations of Air Attacks Preceding Operation 'Overlord,'" 16 February 1946, B.A.U. Report 45, TNA AIR 37/750.
43. Leigh-Mallory, "Air Operations," 48, 89.

PART 2

THE NORMANDY CAMPAIGN

6

Air Control from the Sea
Tactical Air Command and Control during Operation Neptune

Christopher Finn

Operation Neptune, the start of the liberation of Northwest Europe in the Second World War, was mounted over a distance of 138 miles from shore to shore. With all the air support for the landings coming initially from England and amounting to 13,000 individual aircraft sorties on D-Day alone, delivering effective command and control (C2) of airpower during the assault phase was an enormous challenge. But the planning for Neptune and Overlord, which started as early as 1942, was not conducted in isolation. The 1942 raid on Dieppe—Operation Jubilee—was in part an experiment in the C2 of a joint amphibious operation. This was further developed in the Mediterranean theater in 1943.

Expeditionary air C2 developed in the European theater in 1942 and 1943, and while the planners for the air aspects of Operation Neptune still faced problems in this respect, they arrived at and implemented sea-borne solutions. Of course, problems occurred along with the successes, all with implications in the different conduct of day and night air defense. In the aftermath of the 6 June 1944 landings, solutions employed to deliver continuous C2 of Allied airpower in the transition from bases in England to ones in France were specific to that situation. But sea-based air C2 enjoyed subsequent uses in the final year of the war in Europe. While the ability to control air support assets from headquarters (HQ) ships proved to be of limited value, the ability to control day and night fighters from the fighter direction tenders (FDTs) was of significant value and employed for much longer than envisaged.

Dieppe

The raid on the town of Dieppe on 19 August 1942—Operation Jubilee—was seen by the British chiefs of staff as a "reconnaissance in force" to assess the difficulty of taking a defended port and to gather lessons about tactics and equipment for the future invasion of occupied France.[1]

While the initial main landings at 0523 hours were successful, they soon became bogged down. By 0900 hours, it was clear to the military (i.e., land) force commander, observing from the HQ ship HMS *Calpe*, that the objectives would not be achieved and that extraction was necessary. The evacuation went on from 1106 to 1220 hours, with over a thousand men taken off from the beaches. Of the 6,086 troops involved, 3,623 became casualties (killed, wounded, or missing/captured), 59.5 percent of the total land force.[2] RAF casualties were 13 percent and naval losses 7.2 percent. The Royal Air Force (RAF) and U.S. Army Air Forces (USAAF) flew 2,614 sorties at a cost of 106 aircraft, a loss rate of 4.1 percent.[3] The after-action Air Report assessed that 92 German aircraft were lost, with a further 39 probably destroyed and 140 damaged.[4] German records show the true figures to be 48 destroyed and 24 damaged.[5]

Covering southeast England, No. 11 Group was the obvious formation to control the air operation. Based at RAF Uxbridge in west London, its commander was Air Vice-Marshal Trafford Leigh-Mallory, who had been air officer commanding No. 12 Group during the Battle of Britain. His deputy in HMS *Calpe* was Air Commodore Adrian Cole, Royal Australian Air Force (RAAF).

Key to controlling the air operations over Dieppe were the HQ ship HMS *Calpe* and the standby HQ ship HMS *Fernie*. The naval and military commanders and the air commander's representative were on board *Calpe*, with their deputies aboard *Fernie*. Both ships had VHF radio sets, which enabled the fighter controllers to communicate with the close support fighters (assisting the land forces) and, on changing the channel, to broadcast warnings of enemy activity to the lowest fighter-cover squadron (protecting the naval forces). Neither ship had air-surveillance radar, so this was purely based on visual sightings. The vessels also had a standby set each, and it is likely that, given the need for constant contact with the low-cover squadron and the very positive reports on the effectiveness of the control, one set on each ship was constantly allocated to close support control and one to low-cover control.[6] Because of the collocation of the military and air commanders, close support control was conducted from *Calpe* and fighter-cover control from *Fernie*. Both ships had HF radios to communicate with the tactical-reconnaissance aircraft over the area. These, however, were of minimal use, as the aircraft radios performed poorly. Only *Fernie* had an HF radio and a frequency dedicated to passing air support requests, the "Air Base Wave," via the Royal Navy at Portsmouth to HQ No. 11 Group and receiving acknowledgments back. This was due to the lack of space available on the Hunt-class destroyers that, while their shallow draught made them ideal for operating close inshore, were correspondingly quite small ships. Both HQ vessels were therefore fitted with "police-style radio telephones" over which air support requests were passed from *Calpe* to *Fernie*. Thirty-two additional communication and navigation radio sets were installed in them as well, requiring an additional fifty-six communications personnel to run them.[7]

In submitting his report on the raid to the secretary of state for air, Leigh-Mallory drew the following relevant conclusions in his cover letter:

(iii) That with the present relative strength in aircraft, adequate cover can be provided for an expedition of this nature. . . .

(iv) We gained much valuable information concerning the forward control of aircraft, both as regards Cover Squadrons and Close Support aircraft. Controllers in the two Headquarters Ships were of the greatest assistance to the Fighter Pilots, and this system calls for a wider application in the future.[8]

The need for control of the air was not an identified lesson for the simple reason that it was a stated prerequisite.

The RAF element of the report on communications concludes simply that its signals organization worked well, that a similar but larger organization (HQ ship based) would work well for future operations on a larger scale, and that duplicating signals equipment and command ships would be essential.[9] Control of the close support aircraft was entirely procedural, with HQ No. 11 Group generating sorties in response to requests passed from HMS *Calpe* via HMS *Fernie*. The report noted problems in passing targeting requests from shore to ship and in controlling the number of requests generated by the military commander. Given the space available in the HQ ships, the fact that from midmorning on, the fleet was under increasing enemy attack, and with the steadily increasing confusion as to the state of the land operations, this is not surprising.

The same comments applied to the control of the fighter-cover sorties. In addition, it recognized the value of visual direction and warning of the low-cover squadrons by the fighter controllers on board the HQ ships.[10] The air-force commander concluded his report by stating:

> "This operation showed that such expeditions can be successfully supported and protected by home defence fighters operated by the normal Home Defence Fighter Organisation assisted by forward direction through R/T [radio telegraphy] in ships. This efficient organisation is fully capable of so operating Air Forces to the limit [of] our present fighter range and is bound to be superior to any alternative forward control scheme which could never provide anything like equal facilities."[11]

This statement acknowledged that HQ No. 11 Group could never have conducted this operation without the overarching support of Fighter Command. Having provided the additional resources needed by No. 11 Group, the role of Fighter Command during the operation was to provide what we would now call the recognized air picture. For operations in French airspace, this was supplied by the Chain Home system of long-range, low-frequency radars and by the Chain Home Low system, which had very good medium-altitude, medium-range performance. Dieppe was about seventy miles from the Rye and Polling

Chain Home sites, and the air space above the town from 8,000 to 25,000 feet was in the heart of the performance envelope for the lower main beams of both of those radars. No. 60 Group ran Britain's radar chain; its Operations Record Book for the day records, "Stations in the 11 Gp area provided useful information throughout the Commando Raid at Dieppe, in spite of enemy jamming."[12] One should not, however, overstate the role of radar during Operation Jubilee. Chain Home Low was designed for surveillance and was not a directing radar system. There was no need to direct the fighters to various target areas—the only one was Dieppe, which the landings had created. This obscured the need to provide a future expeditionary air force with the means of directing day and night fighters over an extended front. In fact, planning for an expeditionary radar-based raid reporting system had started in May 1942.[13] In May 1943 the responsibility for this was delegated to the air officer commanding in chief Fighter Command, who was now Air Marshal Leigh-Mallory.

So, what was learned from the air aspects of Operation Jubilee? Leigh-Mallory identified only superficial, overly optimistic, and self-congratulatory lessons. The staff-level observations were somewhat better. The concept of properly equipped HQ ships was accepted, and this concept would be developed in the Mediterranean theater. With the clear assumption, from Leigh-Mallory down, that the "invasion" would have to take place in the Pas de Calais area because of the need for massive shore-based air support, the need for a deployable air-search and fighter-direction capability was, however, roundly ignored.

The Mediterranean

During Operation Corkscrew, the effort to subdue the island of Pantelleria, a floating Filter Room was operational for the first time aboard the HQ Ship HMS *Largs*.[14] While the provision of hostile "tracks" from Filter Rooms ashore (generated from ashore radar sites) allowed the controllers aboard to produce a reasonable picture of the air activity, it was sometimes incomplete. Furthermore, the lack of VHF direction-finding equipment prevented them from identifying and then controlling friendly fighter aircraft.

For Operation Husky, the invasion of Sicily, which commenced on 9 July 1943, the plan was to use the HQ ships for daylight (visual) control of fighters, with radar-equipped ships providing filtered track information.[15] Experiments in Algiers harbor proved that a ground-controlled interception (GCI) station could be successfully mounted on *LST 363*. As a result, for Husky, the plan changed to having three Landing Ship Tanks (LSTs) provide radar coverage for the assault convoys and the landing beaches until shore-based GCI sites could be installed.[16] This provided limited lessons based on use. Firstly, there needed to be better liaison between ashore and afloat GCI units. Secondly, space and interference between radars and army and navy communications meant that GCI units could not be located on the HQ ships. Consequently, recommendations called for the use of specialist air-force fighter-control ships in future amphibious operations. Analysts also identified the need for an air-movement organization.[17]

In November 1943 HQ Allied Expeditionary Air Force (AEAF) formed, with Air Chief Marshal Leigh-Mallory in command, and an integrated signals planning staff was created. It was this staff that took forward the development of FDTs and the HQ ships in the planning for Operation Neptune.[18]

Operation Neptune

The decision to mount Operation Overlord against Normandy rather than the Pas de Calais posed obvious geographic problems for all planners. Map 6-1 illustrates the key issues for signals planners: From RAF Tangmere, low-level VHF coverage extends just over halfway across the Channel, so fighters could not be controlled from England. Furthermore, the Radar Chain could only detect a Heinkel 111–sized target over the invasion beaches if it was above 10,000 feet. The map also shows the position of the three UK FDTs on D-Day and their areas of responsibility.[19]

Additionally, because of the limitations of crystal-controlled radios, there were just 451 discrete VHF frequencies available in total—a spacing of 180 kHz between channels was necessary (today it is 8.33 kHz). Thus, there were 252 frequencies in the whole theater for the RAF, 115 for the USAAF, and 84 for the Fleet Air Arm. Second Tactical Air Force (2 TAF) had just 11 frequencies. Single-engine daylight fighters had just 4 frequencies each, while the larger, twin-engine night fighters were allotted 8 or 12 frequencies.[20]

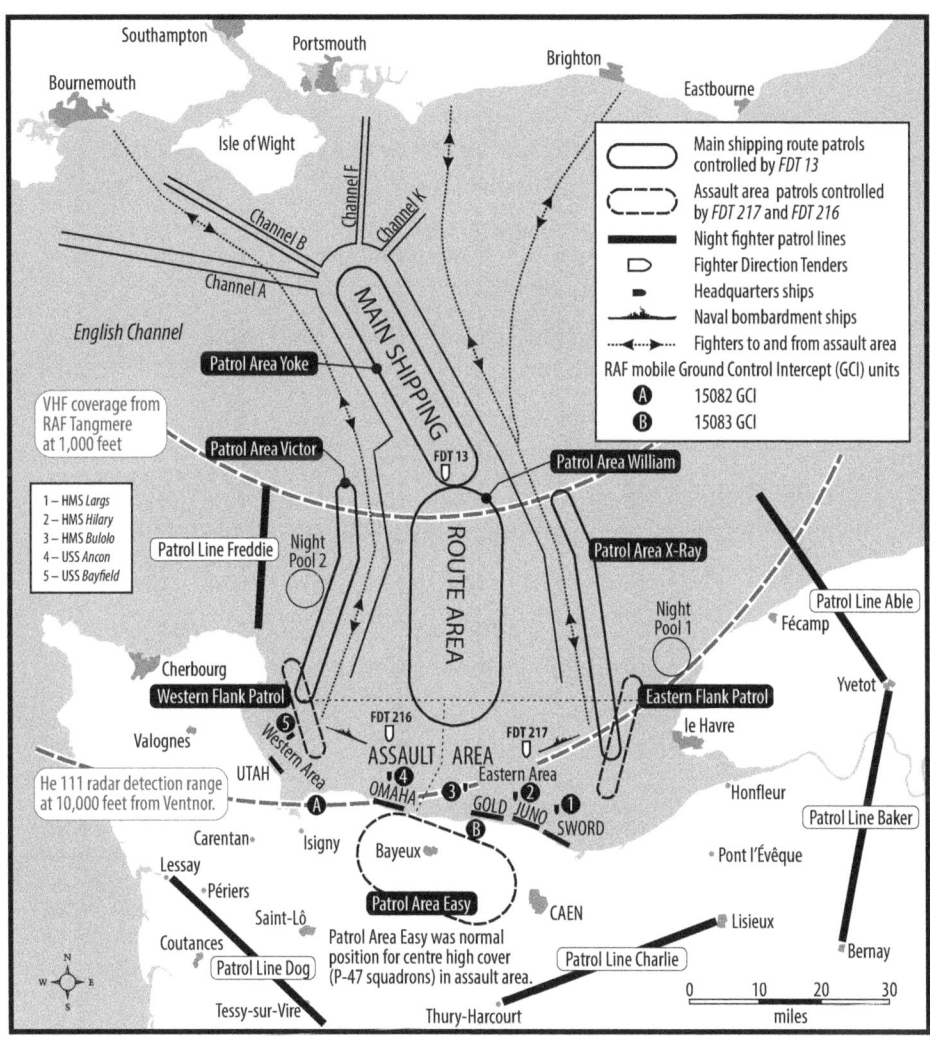

Map 6-1 • Normandy Fighter Patrol Areas

The scale of the C2 problem was enormous. From 2100 hours on 6 June to 2100 hours on 7 June (D+1), a total of 11,844 fighter and bomber sorties were flown in support of Operation Neptune.[21] The heavy bombers of Bomber Command and the U.S. Eighth Air Force flew 2,783 of them, while the Fleet Air Arm flew 150. The AEAF dispatched the majority of total sorties—8,911— broken down in its report into these areas:

> Air support for ground forces—2,544;
> Fighter cover—2,619 (including 2,000 day fighter sorties over the beach-head and shipping areas);
> reconnaissance and air/sea rescue [ASR]—775;
> Fighter escort of transport aircraft and tug/glider aircraft—1,658;
> Bomber escorts—1,465.
> Finally, there were 1,038 Airborne sorties (transport/tug and glider) in this period.[22]

Add approximately 175 Coastal Command sorties, and there were just over 13,000 sorties to manage in the airspace over D+1.

The scope of the AEAF C2 responsibilities in summary were:

Air Defense
Provide raid warnings to the entire force.
Provide daylight fighter cover over the shipping lanes and the beachhead.
Provide night-fighter cover over the shipping lanes and the beachhead.
Coordinate ASR activities by both aircraft and ships.

Air Support
Coordinate preplanned air support.
Task and coordinate immediate (on-call) air support.
Task and coordinate tactical-reconnaissance sorties.
Coordinate the air-spotting sorties that direct naval-gunfire support from the battleships and cruisers.

Once ashore, these functions devolved to the mobile GCI sites, due to be deployed closely behind the assault waves, and to the established air support organization once the AEAF tactical HQ was deployed alongside their land counterparts or had become redundant.

Photo 6-1 • A view of the task force heading to Omaha Beach on 6 June 1944 taken from the headquarters ship USS *Ancon*. Note that many of the vessels tow barrage balloons, designed to ward off low-level air attacks. *(U.S. National Archives 80-G-231247)*

The Headquarters Ships

From west to east, the HQ ships were USS *Bayfield*, Utah Beach; USS *Ancon*, Omaha Beach; HMS *Bulolo*, Gold Beach; HMS *Hilary*, Juno Beach; and HMS *Largs*, Sword Beach. USS *Augusta* served as the naval flagship for the Eastern Task Force and HMS *Scylla* as the naval flagship for the Western Task Force. Figure 6-1 shows the layout of an HQ ship's Operations Flat.[23] The combined operations room, with both the sea-and-land and the sea-and-air plots, was at the aft end. The interception control (or fighter direction post) was for day/visual conditions only but was never needed.[24]

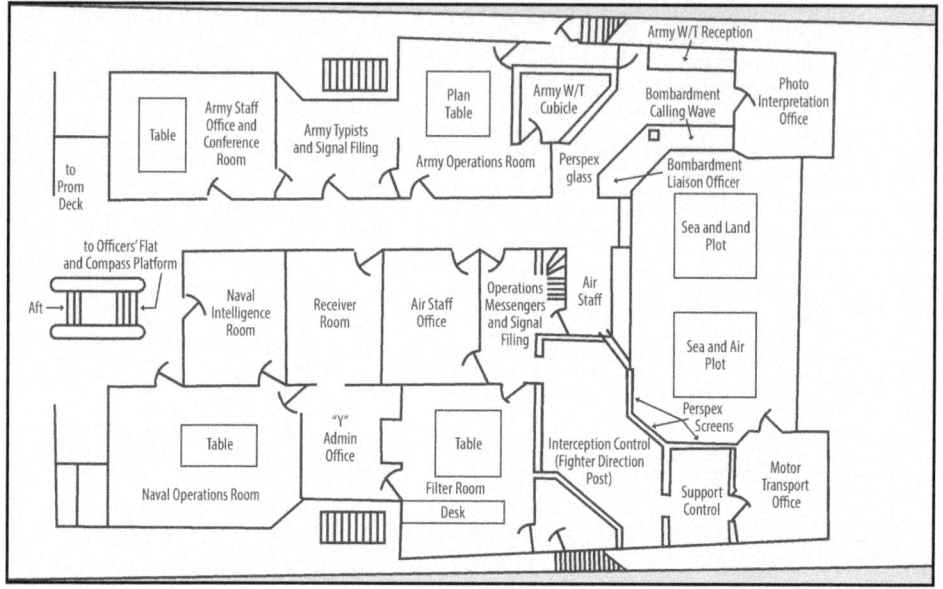

Figure 6-1 • Plan of the Operations Flat aboard HMS *Largs*, the HQ ship for Task Force Sword

Fighter-bomber air support was provided in three ways:

1. Preplanned, either as part of the Joint Fire Plan or once the land forces were ashore for a future operation.
2. By airborne-alert squadrons in the vicinity of the landings.
3. By on-call squadrons at bases in England.[25]

The organization for providing direct air support to the land forces was based on the air support signals unit (ASSU) "tentacles."[26] Each army corps, division, and brigade had its own ASSU with HF radios.

For preplanned air support, composing the majority of air support to Neptune, the ASSU tentacles would pass their requests to 21 Army Group (AG) Main HQ at Portsmouth, with the relevant HQ ships and the 21 AG G (Air) Staff at HQ AEAF (forward) at RAF Uxbridge also receiving the request. The requests would then be collated by 21 AG (Main) and the approved requests passed on to 21 AG G (Air) Staff for action by the colocated combined-control center (CCC). The CCC then tasked the suitable sectors, wings, and squadrons and relayed this to the requesting HQ, the HQ ships, and FDTs. For immediate direct air support during the assault phase only, the ASSUs would pass their request directly to the relevant HQ ship. For on-call air support, they would again route their requests through the HQ ships, with the CCC constantly monitoring the same frequency.[27]

Fighter Direction Tenders

With the established roles and information flows within the UK based GCI sites to work from, the FDT operations layout was more refined than that of HQ ships.

About half of the floor space was taken up with communications equipment. But the heart of the setup was the Filter Room, where the air picture was displayed, and the adjacent Air Control Room, where two fighter controllers worked at large, flat plan-position-indicator (PPI) radar displays. Between the two rooms was a raised dais from which the senior controller could see everything that was happening. Also of note was a large "Y" Office, for the receipt and interpretation of local, immediate signals intelligence based on Luftwaffe transmissions, and the Cypher Office, for receipt of coded signals traffic.

The key daytime staff were a squadron-leader controller (officer in charge), a squadron-leader filter officer, and two flight lieutenants serving as Movements Liaison Section (MLS) officers. At night, when the main controlling task occurred, a squadron-leader senior controller, two flight lieutenants, and three sergeant controllers composed the staff. Two would be on the large PPI displays, known as Skiatrons, controlling (on *FDT 217*) the East and West Pools (night fighters awaiting tasking), with two others controlling the engagements on PPIs in the Radar Room. In *FDT 217* the "Flicker" console (an unsuccessful device to counter the use of "window," or chaff) was used by the spare controller as an extra control position when needed. *FDT 217* was the controlling ship for the whole sector and had on board Air Commodore Cecil Bouchiere, who was Air Marshal Arthur Coningham's senior representative afloat. Coningham commanded both HQ AEAF (forward) and 2 TAF from RAF Uxbridge. It was obvious that the FDTs would provide far more "situational awareness" to the air commander (forward) than the secondhand information available on an HQ ship.

The three FDTs were fitted out in a rush job on the Clyde and underwent sea trials in March 1944.[28] Their air force complement was fourteen officers and 160 airmen each, many of them being from the Royal Canadian Air Force.[29] The FDTs were crewed by eight Royal Navy officers and ninety-two ratings. The front-ramp doors of the vessels were not needed for landing operations, so they were welded shut and armor plating added to provide extra protection against enemy attacks and heavy seas. Without a full load of tanks on board, the flat-bottomed vessels were too light and rolled easily, so pig-iron ballast was added to improve their seakeeping qualities. The FDTs deployed south in April for exercises with No. 12 Group (controlling North Sea airspace from Scotland to the Thames Estuary), whose members were highly praised for their help in the workup.[30] Each ship was configured as shown in figures 6-2 and 6-3.[31]

The operations flat and other offices were separate structures installed on the tank deck, and a platform was built forward for the main GCI radar. With only small access hatches, the RAF crews soon renamed the FDTs "Floating Death Traps."[32] Furthermore, they had to live for extended periods at sea in the cramped quarters designed for short-term occupancy by the tank crews before an amphibious landing.

Each FDT carried key equipment. Starting from the bow, the main GCI radar was a Type 15, which operated on 209 MHz. It was designed to pick up a Heinkel 111–sized target at 103 miles at 20,000 feet but in practice could detect a target at 138 miles and 15,000 feet. This was actually the top half of a Type 7 radar, so it had an identification friend or foe (IFF) interrogator but no height-finding capability.[33] The GCI was mounted on a platform to provide better range against low-level targets. Next aft were the receiver aerial for the Y Service and the direction-finding aerial for the Filter Room. This was the main method by which the filter officer would confirm the identity of a friendly track, especially fighters to be controlled. The Type 11 radar was a backup to the Type 15 and operated at 500 and 600 MHz.[34] This was in the same band as German search radars, and the presumption was it would not

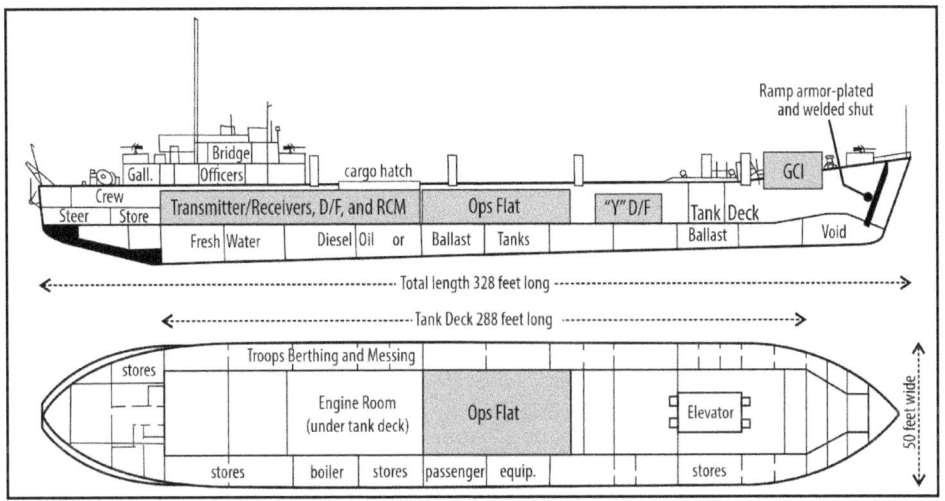

Figure 6-2 • Fighter Direction Tender (FDT) Configuration. Three LSTs were reconfigured to serve as FDTs for the Normandy landings.

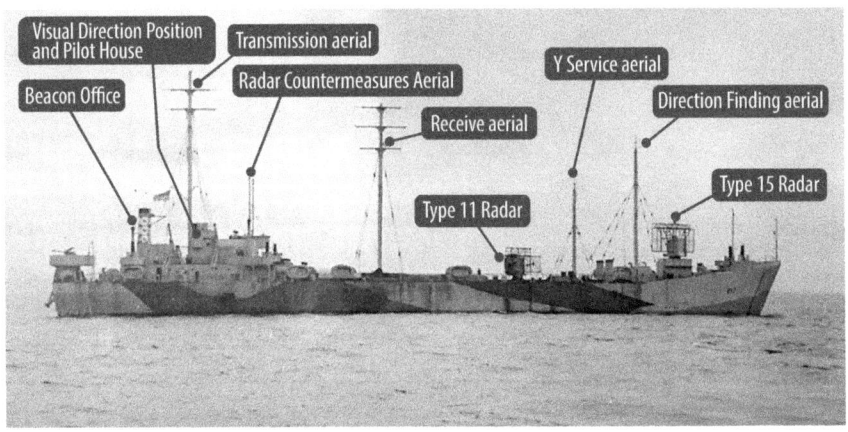

Figure 6-3 • *FDT 217*, Labeled. This image shows *FDT 217* as it was configured for Operation Neptune.

be jammed. In practice, the Type 11 was constantly blotted out by friendly "window" and other radio countermeasures.[35] Then came the transmission and reception aerials and another for radar countermeasures. Finally, each FDT had two radio homing beacons for night fighters.

Unlike the HQ ships, which were national, the FDTs were all Royal Navy ships with the RAF providing the GCI function. This was to mirror the plan for the ashore provision of all the GCI functions by, initially, two RAF GCI units: No. 15082 in the American sector and No. 15083 in the British sector.[36] As shown on map 6-1, *FDT 13* was positioned in the center of the shipping lanes and controlled the airspace overhead. *FDT 216* and *FDT 217* each controlled the American and British sectors respectively. Communications were key to making this arrangement work.

Figure 6-4, derived from descriptions, tables, and diagrams throughout the report by the Wing Commander Air Staff onboard HMS *Bulolo*, shows

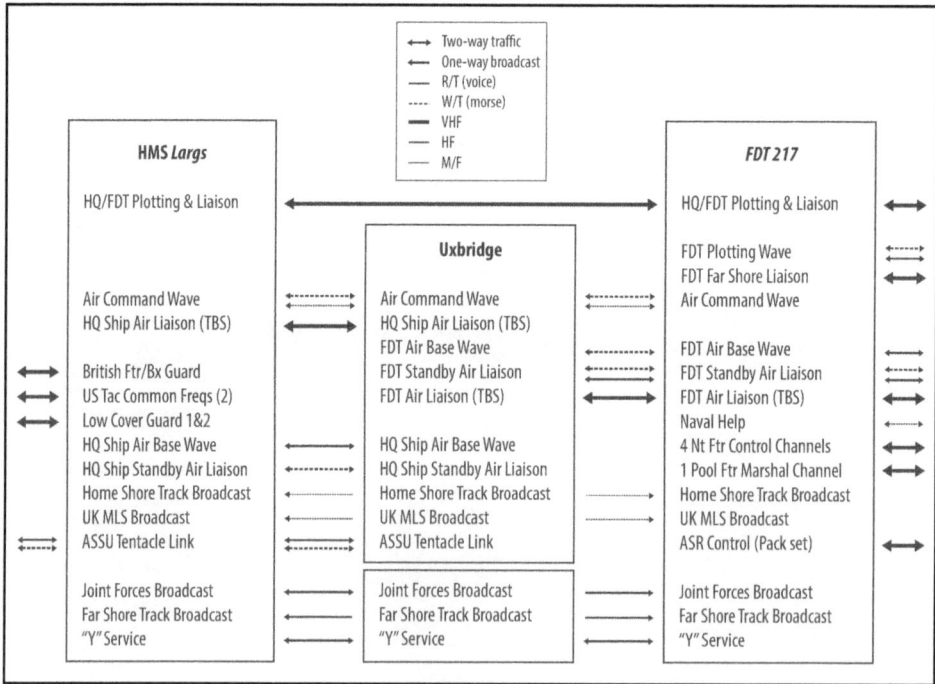

Figure 6-4 • Eastern Task Force Communications Links.

the communications links in the Eastern Task Force between *FDT 217*; one HQ ship, HMS *Largs*; RAF Uxbridge; and general broadcasts from ashore and within the naval force.[37] Thus, the lateral links between *FDT 217* and *Largs* apply equally across the three FDTs and five HQ ships. The following elements are of note:

- There was only one HQ/FDT plotting-and-liaison frequency across the whole fleet.
- Home Shore Track Broadcast was the tracks from the UK air-defense system. The Far Shore Track Broadcast was from the GCI sites once operational in France.
- The UK MLS Broadcast (on aircraft movements) was available to all ships.
- The ASR Control pack set was for coordination of ASR launches and aircraft.
- The five VHF night-fighter control and marshal sets were given over by day to low-cover control.
- TBS refers to a VHF "talk between ships" (and later land units) frequency.

So, how did this work in practice? For air support, the ASSU communications to RAF Uxbridge worked far too well, and there was no need for HQ ships to pass on such requests. Of the 2,554 air support sorties flown on D-Day, nearly all were either immediate, requested through the ASSUs, or preplanned. Very few were available for the HQ ships to task, and as it was, they lacked a clear picture of the land situation to be able to do so effectively.[38] Consequently, the HQ ships' air support functions were not needed. Furthermore, the divisional staffs all went ashore at around H+6, and the loss of the army G (liaison) staffs, who should have remained on board, particularly hampered the ability of the air staff to keep the CCC at RAF Uxbridge updated on the progress of the land battle.[39] The same was true for their role in coordinating tactical reconnaissance.

HMS *Hilary* was the air-raid warning ship for the Eastern Task Force. But it was reliant on a raid warning from *FDT 217* and other broadcast sources. Raid warnings could therefore be patchy, and the lack of control of shipborne antiaircraft fire posed a significant danger to Allied aircraft. A subsequent key recommendation was that, in the future, raid warnings should be the responsibility of the FDTs, given their radar arrays and communications facilities.[40]

Although they had no fighter-control responsibilities, the HQ ships' fighter controllers would pass visual reports of enemy aircraft to the FDTs on the Low Cover Guard 1 frequency. This would also be heard by nearby low-cover fighters and on three occasions resulted in successful, ad-hoc interceptions.[41]

Lastly, HQ ships had a supposedly minor role that turned out to be an extremely important one: coordinating the "spotting pool" aircraft. Twenty-nine capital ships and ninety-five aircraft (seventy-five on D-Day) provided naval-gunfire support to land forces.[42] There were 638 spotting sorties up to D+3, 344 of them on D-Day alone. While each spotter aircraft had a dedicated ship on many occasions, they often failed to make initial contact with them. Consequently, the HQ ships coordinated and reallocated these aircraft to maximize their effectiveness.[43]

With the establishment of air-control facilities ashore, the HQ ships' air C2 functions ceased on D+7, although they continued to fulfill their naval command roles.[44]

The FDTs deployed into position by 0400 hours on D-Day.[45] They observed radar and radio silence until 0725 hours—H-Hour. During daylight hours, 0430 hours to 2330 hours (morning civil twilight minus thirty minutes to evening civil twilight plus thirty minutes), they controlled six Spitfire squadrons (seventy-two aircraft) on low cover, 3,000–5,000 feet over the shipping lanes and beaches. There were also three P-38 squadrons (forty-eight aircraft) on high cover, 8,000–15,000 feet, one each with *FDT 216* and *FDT 217*, on the flanks of the landing area, and the third with *FDT 217*, covering the inshore area. For ASR, there were two further Air Defence of Great Britain Spitfire squadrons and two RAF high-speed launches available per FDT. On D-Day alone these picked up 60 aircrew and 44 soldiers, and over the whole of Operation Neptune, 209 aircrew and 117 airborne troops were recovered by the ASR organization.[46] For the five hours of darkness, No. 85 Group, the 2 TAF Air Defence and Base Group operating from southern England, tasked six squadrons of Mosquito night fighters to operate over the beachhead. These provided two "pools" of eighteen aircraft each, both under the control of *FDT 217*.[47]

At about noon on D-Day, No. 15083 GCI and associated communications units landed without loss or casualty and proceeded to its predetermined operating site near Meuvaines, two kilometers inland of Gold Beach.[48] Sadly, the same was not the case with No. 15082 GCI, which was to provide cover in the American sector.[49] The first attempt to land, at 1130 hours, was aborted due to enemy artillery fire. At 1700 hours a second landing was attempted. Most of the unit's vehicles drowned when they debarked into deeper water than anticipated. Only eight of twenty-seven remained serviceable. All the radar equipment except the Type 15 was lost, and the unit suffered ten men killed, one missing, and thirty-six wounded.

FDT 217 controlled the day and night cover over the Eastern Area and coordinated the cover over the whole area until D+6. At this point it handed over control of the night fighters to No. 15083 GCI, whose reserve equipment was landed on D+1.[50] By D+8, this GCI site had been expanded to become No. 483 Group Control Centre, which then took over the day-fighter role from *FDT 217* as well. With the delay in deploying No. 15082 GCI in the American sector, *FDT 217* was moved to replace *FDT 216* off Omaha Beach near Saint-Laurent, where it remained in operation until D+17. On D+3 No. 15082 GCI was ordered to its preplanned site and began controlling the next day, both GCI sites being coordinated by *FDT 217*.[51] On D+8 *FDT 13* moved from its position in the shipping lanes to an alternate location off Barfleur, where it was replaced on D+11 by *FDT 216*. *FDT 13* and *FDT 217* returned to England at the end of June, leaving *FDT 216* to operate off Le Havre. At 0100 hours on 7 July, *FDT 216* was sunk by a torpedo dropped by a Junkers Ju 88 with the loss of five airmen.[52] Thus ended the month of employment of FDTs of the invasion beaches, a role that was envisaged they would only fulfill for a matter of days, after which shore-based GCI would take over fully.

The FDTs during Operations Neptune and Overlord experienced the following problems:[53]

- Terrain masking and shipping returns made it difficult to control aircraft within twelve miles of the FDTs. The only solution was to move away from the land and shipping, but this then took the FDTs away from the cover of friendly (to them at least, if not their aircraft) antiaircraft fire. The problem was not initially appreciated on HMS *Hilary*, leading to complaints that *FDT 217* was of little help in raid reporting (once a raid had become lost in the confused local radar picture). This was not a perceived problem on the other four HQ ships.[54]

- The Luftwaffe's use of small, low-level raids taking advantage of terrain masking until the last minute.
- The interference of friendly "window" on the Type 15 radar. The Type 11 radar was equally susceptible to this but was not used.
- The unreliability of the Mk IIIG IFF.
- Limited height-finding capabilities.
- Sharing four frequencies between the three FDTs and, later, the two GCI sites ashore.
- The inability to use the single HQ ship/FDT plotting-and-liaison frequency to pass urgent plots due to its being swamped with liaison chat.
- And, above all, the danger poor naval fire discipline posed to the low-cover aircraft.

On the positive side the integration of MLS plots and tactical Y Service interceptions, plus the use of the direction-finding equipment, greatly minimized the effect of the first five factors listed above. The high-level cover of the Type 15 radar proved to be excellent, and the FDTs' beacons were invaluable in marshaling the night fighters.

By day, therefore, the FDTs' task became one of identification and warning. With the sheer number of aircraft present over the shipping lanes and beachhead during the day, it was not possible for the ships to perform a normal GCI function.[55] Consequently, they would take unidentified radar plots and check them first with the information from IFF. But the absence of a confirmed "friendly" response was not confirmation that the track was a hostile one. So, other factors were considered: Was the track behavior indicative of hostile or friendly intent? Did it correspond with a flight notified by the MLS broadcast? Was there evidence of hostile or friendly transmissions detected by the

Y Service operators? Did it correspond to a direction-finder interception of a hostile or friendly transmission? Only after considering these questions would a broadcast be made identifying a hostile, or potentially hostile, track to the covering fighters and the HQ ships. But it was the responsibility of the HQ ships to issue air-raid warnings in their sector.

The issue of "friendly fire" was a contentious one.[56] Naval gunners were not supposed to open fire on aircraft unless fully trained in aircraft recognition, but this was not usually the case. Yet the problem of swift aircraft recognition was exacerbated by low cloud bases that forced aircraft to drop below the supposed 300-foot ceiling and by poor visibility. The placing of Royal Observer Corps personnel on some of the larger ships somewhat reduced the occurrence of friendly fire casualties, but often the naval antiaircraft fire was uncontrolled, with ships opening on any aircraft that came into view, if not into range. To put this into context, in June the AEAF lost 605 aircraft, mostly to enemy antiaircraft fire, yet even this was a loss rate of just 0.7 percent of the 91,477 sorties flown.[57]

At night the FDTs' task was greatly simplified by the reduction in friendly sorties in the beachhead area, although many overnight sorties were mounted from England to interdict German reinforcements. The same track-identification processes were used as by day, but at night the FDTs also controlled the intercept by directing radar-equipped night fighters to the targets.

The achievements of the FDTs during Neptune and Overlord were

- 52 enemy aircraft were destroyed by fighters under FDT direction or control; 24 of these were at night.
- Between D-Day and D+7, 285 night fighters were controlled, 205 of these by *FDT 217*, and 140 radar contacts were made, of which 89 proved to be friendly, while 9 enemy aircraft were destroyed.[58]

Estimates counted between thirty and fifty Luftwaffe sorties per night, mostly in the Eastern Area.

FDT 217 managed and controlled thirty-eight to forty aircraft per night, in addition to controlling the two other FDTs and both land-based GCI sites. By comparison, the equivalent UK based GCI, Happidrome, was able to control between twelve and twenty-four aircraft per night.

With the Fighter Direction Posts (mobile, tactical GCI units) of 2 TAF's Nos. 83 and 84 Groups and the GCI sites of No. 85 Group being deployed during the advance into Holland and Belgium, there was no further need for the FDTs in the northern European theater.[59] *FDT 217* was being fitted out for service in the Far East when the war ended. *FDT 13*, however, sailed for the Mediterranean with an American crew and took part in Operation Dragoon, the landings in southern France on 15 August 1944.[60] Yet the official U.S. Army history makes no mention of Luftwaffe attacks on the landing sites nor of any measures to counter them.[61]

While the FDTs performed well, the HQ ships did not live up to expectations. The ability of the FDTs to control the day fighters during the assault removed one of the HQ ships' main roles. And the ability of the ASSUs to communicate directly with RAF Uxbridge and 21 AG HQ while still in England negated their role of coordinating air support before 2 TAF and 21 AG HQ landed in France. This clearly influenced the decisions to move all the divisional staffs ashore at around H+6 hours and not leave any liaison personnel behind, which further reduced the value of HQ ships.

Yet the HQ ship concept was used one final time in the war in northwest Europe for the amphibious Operation Infatuate, the effort to capture the island of Walcheren as part of the Canadian operation to clear the Scheldt Estuary and open the port of Antwerp. The attack took place on 1 November 1944, with the amphibious-force commander, Captain A. F. Pugsley, Royal Navy, in HMS *Kingsmill* along with the assault-force commander, Brigadier B. W. Leicester, Royal Marines.[62] *Kingsmill* was an American-built Captain-class frigate provided to the Royal Navy under the Lend-Lease program. It was similar in size and draught to the Hunt-class destroyers. The weather was appalling, with a cloud base of 500 feet and visibility of 1,000 meters. But, just as the landing craft were reaching their objective, twelve rocket-armed Typhoons of No. 183 Squadron (2 TAF) called up *Kingsmill* and were given clearance to attack, suppressing German defensive fire at the critical moment.[63]

Conclusion

HQ ships were used several times in World War II, and FDTs were employed in three instances, but Operation Neptune differed from the rest in terms of scale and complexity. HQ ships were an established capability. But the unexpectedly good communications between the land forces and RAF Uxbridge negated their role as a coordination platform for air support operations. Furthermore, without their own air-defense radar suite, they relied on the FTDs for raid warning. The FDTs were a specific solution to a specific problem—that of day and night fighter direction during the biggest Allied amphibious landing of the European war, which occurred outside of land-based GCI cover. Despite limitations of space and equipment and the density of radar responses in the areas of the beaches, they were able to control the numerous fighter sorties, control day ASR operations, control the activities of the GCI sites as they were becoming established ashore, and then gap fill radar coverage over a period of a month. Most importantly, they marshaled and controlled the night fighters, which were essential to protecting the initial buildup of Allied forces from German nighttime bomber attacks, which Allied air supremacy by day had forced the Luftwaffe to employ.

NOTES

1. John Terraine, *The Right of the Line: The Royal Air Force in the European War, 1939–1945* (London: Hodder and Stoughton, 1985), 560.
2. Combined Operations Headquarters, "The Dieppe Raid (Combined Report)," 1943, UK National Archives [hereafter TNA] ADM 234/447, 36.
3. Air Historical Branch [hereafter AHB], "The Air Defence of Great Britain," vol. 5, "The Struggle for Air Supremacy," n.d., 124, RAF College Library, Sleaford, UK.
4. Combined Operations Headquarters, "Dieppe Raid," Annex 7, 164, app. F.
5. AHB 6, "Luftwaffe Losses at Dieppe," 29 November 1946, RAF Dieppe box file, AHB, London.
6. Combined Operations Headquarters, "Dieppe Raid," Annex 10, 177, app. A.
7. Combined Operations Headquarters, "Dieppe Raid," Annex 10, 173.
8. AVM T. Leigh-Mallory to secretary of state for air, "11G/S.500/98/Ops," 5 September 1942, Uxbridge, HQ 11 Gp, RAF Dieppe box file, AHB, London, 3.
9. Combined Operations Headquarters, "Dieppe Raid," Annex 10, 177, app. A.
10. Combined Operations Headquarters, "Dieppe Raid," Annex 10, 177, app. A.
11. Combined Operations Headquarters, "Dieppe Raid," Annex 7, 148.
12. HQ No. 60 Group, F540, 19 August 1942, Operations Record Book, TNA AIR 25/679.

13. "Signals," vol. 4: Radar in Raid Reporting (London: Air Historical Branch, 1950), 407, copy in RAF College Library. https://www.raf.mod.uk/what-we-do/our-history/air-historical-branch/second-world-war-thematic-studies/signals-vol-iv-radar-in-raid-reporting-chapters18-28andappendices/.
14. "Signals," 4:303.
15. "Signals," 4:310.
16. "Signals," 4:311.
17. "Signals," 4:329.
18. "Signals," 4:407.
19. "Operation Neptune: Report on the Role of British Headquarters Ships and Fighter Direction Tenders in the Assault on the Continent of Europe," 1944, app. A, TNA WO 244/12 [hereafter "Report on British HQ Ships and FDTs"].
20. "Signals," vol. 3: Aircraft Radio (London: Air Historical Branch, 1956), 614, copy in RAF College Library, https://www.raf.mod.uk/what-we-do/our-history/air-historical-branch/second-world-war-thematic-studies/signals-vol-iii-aircraft-radio-chapter15-23andappendices/.
21. HQ AEAF, "Report on Air Operations Prior to and in Support of Operation 'Neptune,'" 1944, 36, TNA AIR 37/757.
22. HQ AEAF, "Report on Air Operations in Operation 'Neptune,'" 43, 44.
23. Geoff Slee and Phill Jones, "WW2 Headquarters Ships in [sic]—HQ Ships," Combined Operations, n.d., https://combinedops.com/HEADQUARTERS%20SHIPS.htm (accessed 19 January 2025).
24. "Report on British HQ Ships and FDTs," 6n19.
25. HQ AEAF, "Report on Air Operations in Operation 'Neptune,'" 45.
26. "Report on the Air and Administrative Organization of the 2nd Tactical Air Force" (London: Air Ministry, 1947), 100, TNA AIR 20/7259.
27. "Report on British HQ Ships and FDTs," 5.
28. "Signals," 4:414.
29. Horace R. Macauley, *Ground Controlled Interception Radars in Operation Neptune/Overlord* (n.p., 2000), XI-4, https://marconiradarhistory.pbworks.com/w/file/fetch/157249455/ground controlled interception radars in operation neptune_overlord.pdf.
30. "Report on British HQ Ships and FDTs," i.
31. Office of Naval Intelligence *Allied Landing Craft and Ships*, ONI 226 ([Washington, DC]: Publications and Distribution Branch, Division of Naval Intelligence, 1944), 113, https://www.ibiblio.org/hyperwar/USN/ref/ONI/ONI-226/ONI-226.pdf.
32. Macauley, *Ground Controlled Interception Radars*, XI-14.
33. "Signals," 4:412.

34. "Signals," 4:412.
35. Macauley, *Ground Controlled Interception Radars*, XI-18.
36. "Signals," 4:416.
37. "Report on British HQ Ships and FDTs."
38. "Report on British HQ Ships and FDTs," 5, 6.
39. "Report on British HQ Ships and FDTs," 6.
40. "Report on British HQ Ships and FDTs," 8.
41. "Report on British HQ Ships and FDTs," 6.
42. Seventeen were Spitfire Mk V ERs operated by U.S. Navy pilots who normally flew seaplanes off their respective ships.
43. "Report on British HQ Ships and FDTs," 6.
44. "Report on British HQ Ships and FDTs," 7.
45. All times are in Double British Summertime (GMT +2), as it was the convention to use local time in all operational documents.
46. HQ AEAF, "Report on Air Operations in Operation 'Neptune,'" 77.
47. AHB, *The Liberation of North West Europe*, 3:167.
48. "Signals," 4:424.
49. "Signals," 4:425.
50. HQ AEAF, "Report on Air Operations in Operation 'Neptune,'" 51.
51. "Signals," 4:432.
52. "Signals," 4:431.
53. "Report on British HQ Ships and FDTs," 18–21.
54. "Signals," 4:424.
55. *The Liberation of North West Europe*, 3:69.
56. *The Liberation of North West Europe*, 3:79–80.
57. HQ AEAF, "Report on Air Operations in Operation 'Neptune,'" 64.
58. "Report on British HQ Ships and FDTs," 45.
59. "Signals," 4:449.
60. Macauley, *Ground Controlled Interception Radars*, XI-13.
61. Jeffrey R. Clarke and Robert Ross Smith, *United States Army in World War II, the European Theater of Operations: Riviera to the Rhine* (Washington, DC: Center of Military History, U.S. Army, 1993), chap. 7.
62. Major L. F. Ellis, *Victory in the West*, vol. 2, *The Defeat of Germany* (London, HMSO, 1968), 119.
63. Hilary St. George Saunders, *Royal Air Force, 1939–1945*, vol. 3, *The Fight Is Won* (London: HMSO, 1953), 199.

7

The French Connection

Civilians under the Bombs for the First Forty-Eight Hours

Stephen A. Bourque

It was the evening of 6 June 1944. Thirty-two miles east of Caen is the market town of Lisieux, on the banks of the small Touques River. At eight o'clock that evening, six-year-old J. P. Cordier put on his pajamas and got into bed. Writing forty years after the event, he still remembered his parents discussing the question of leaving their house and escaping the city to avoid the possible Allied bombs. Everyone knew the Normandy landings were underway, and airplanes had dropped leaflets telling residents to get away from the city. But his mother was pregnant, and his father decided it was better for them to stay put in the safest part of the house. When they heard the bombers approaching their city, the parents, according to their practiced routine, moved the family into their makeshift shelter. It was on the ground floor, under the staircase, in the center of the house, and seemed to offer the best protection. Suddenly, bombs began exploding outside. One destroyed the house's back wall, knocking young J. P. unconscious. Forty years later

Photo 7-1 • The city center of Lisieux after the Allied bombings of June 1944. At least forty residents were killed by Allied airpower on the night of 6 June 1944. On the left may be seen the ruins of Saint-Jacques Church. *Public domain*

he recalled briefly waking up and calling out for water. He remembered his mother answering him. Then he again passed out and remained so for several hours. His neighbor, he found out later, had pulled him from the debris and brought him across the street to an undamaged house. Seminary students, supporting the city's rescue group, carried him to the local hospital. He remembered deliriously arguing with the nurses cutting his new socks off his bloody feet. When he finally awoke, he was in the hospital with his wounded sister. His mother and father were dead, and the doctors had amputated his leg. His home was gone. Other than his sister, J. P. was alone in the world and with nothing left. The air attack killed at least forty Lexoviens, including his parents, and wounded many more. Cordier lived until 1992 and never forgot his experience that night. Today, he is buried with his family in the Lisieux Cemetery, along with other victims of that terrible evening.[1]

J. P. Cordier's experience was not unique; many Normans perished during the Allied assault. On D-Day Allied bombers killed almost 4,000 French civilians as they attempted to support the troops onshore and prevent German reinforcements from reaching the combat zone. For more than a week after the landings, the air assault continued, as bombers destroyed towns, bridges, and rail installations to delay the arrival of enemy armored divisions. As Operation Neptune ended with the capture of Cherbourg at the end of June, dozens of French towns lay in ruins, with between 8,000 and 11,000 Normans dead from all causes.[2] Tens of thousands of French citizens survived these bombardments but suffered physical and psychological wounds that sometimes took decades to heal. One often-overlooked aspect of air operations during Operation Neptune was the effect of Allied heavy and medium bombers on the French population.

Other authors in this collection examine the totality of the air effort during the Battle of Normandy. This chapter centers on forty-eight hours of the Allied bombardment, from just after midnight on 6 June until midnight on 7 June. This period corresponds with some of the most brutal fighting faced by the Allies along the landing beaches. By the morning of 8 June, more than 3,000 Norman civilians had perished and thousands more suffered injuries. In addition, the air attacks destroyed or damaged more than thirty cities in this small part of France.[3] Why did so many French men, women, and children become casualties of airpower during those first forty-eight hours?

One reason an accounting of the French experience during Operation Neptune is lacking is that it does not fit into a straightforward narrative of operations. Unlike the assaults on Sword or Utah Beaches, the bombardment of French territory took place over a large region. In addition, the Allies had multiple reasons for striking the same town: for example, it might have a rail yard, a bridge, or perhaps a German artillery battery. As a result, various air forces may have attacked the same town on other days for different reasons. Finally, of course, it made little difference to the civilians on the ground as to which program caused their demise. Still, it does explain the difficulty historians have had in accounting for French casualties. Yet the Allied records of bombing missions and internal communications are relatively complete and available. The documents contained in departmental archives are extensive, and French historians have done a superb job of gathering evidence about what took place in Normandy.

To summarize the effects of airpower on the French population during those first two days, we can organize the bombardment of French territory into three general categories. The first was the German defenses attacked by Allied bombers on the Normandy beaches. These targets included artillery batteries, defensive positions, radar installations, and command posts. Because French civilians often lived close to these facilities, it was logical that they might become casualties. The second type of bombardment was the programs that had been ongoing for several months and continued after the landings. These targets included airfields, bridges, and rail yards. The third kind of Allied air strikes on French towns resulted from the landings on the morning of 6 June. This group of missions, directed by the ground commanders, was the destruction of French communities to prevent German troops from passing through. No matter how one evaluates the use of airpower during Operation Neptune, it has a connection to the French people and countryside, which would never be the same again.

The German Defenses

The first category of French casualties came from the physical landings on the Calvados and La Manche beaches that morning. The unfortunate Norman civilians were in the wrong place at the wrong time. After over a year of planning, the Allied component commanders agreed on a program of air bombardment to neutralize enemy defenses during the landings. On 8 April the chiefs of staff for the ground, air, and naval components signed the Joint Fire Plan for Operation Neptune. For D-Day, which turned out to be 6 June, this document identified the targets for the heavy and medium bombers. These included ten artillery batteries that RAF Bomber Command would attack early in the morning and the defenses on the beaches that the U.S. Eighth and Ninth Air Forces needed to neutralize as the landing craft approached.[4] While the senior commanders and staff officers had reached a consensus, the Joint Fire Plan was still far from being ready. It now shifted into the domain of junior planners at various secondary levels, whose task involved distributing hundreds of targets throughout France and Belgium among more than 678 air squadrons and 12,600 aircraft. Additionally, they needed to devise flight paths that ensured aircraft would fly specific routes to avoid collisions with other units moving eastward and avoid disrupting the parachute drops.[5]

Naval officers encountered significant challenges organizing and coordinating seven battleships, two monitors, twenty-three cruisers, 108 destroyers, and numerous additional vessels within the assault zone, along the flanks, and out into the Atlantic Ocean. The complexity of their task was exacerbated by the presence of over four thousand other ships moving at night while blacked out as they transported troops and supplies to and from the landing beaches. Before any of this could happen, minesweepers, operating underneath fire from both Allied vessels and enemy shore defenses, needed to clear mines and obstacles from the designated routes to the shore.[6]

The German high command, of course, could interfere with this operation. Allied air force and naval planners were tasked with the critical analysis of each target, identifying the appropriate types of munitions and subsequently aligning these with the available ships and squadrons capable of executing the assigned missions. It was essential to prioritize and schedule these operations to ensure they were well timed. This meticulous planning was crucial to prevent any inadvertent friendly fire incidents during the landings. Ultimately, highly detailed targeting schedules were disseminated to both naval ships and air squadrons.

A key consideration in the Neptune plan was the maintenance of continuous bombardment to prevent enemy forces from regrouping or reinforcing their positions. For the aerial offensive, the Allied Expeditionary Air Force (AEAF), under the command of Air Chief Marshal Trafford Leigh-Mallory, developed a comprehensive Air Plan that specified the responsibilities assigned to each Allied air force.[7]

The aim of the Joint Fire Plan was to ensure "the maximum effort of the Navy, Air Force, and Army were to be concentrated upon drenching the defenses of this stretch of coast in a continuous rain of fire from the time the Assault Forces came within range until the time when they arrive at their objectives."[8] Army and navy planners continued to adjust their target sets right up until the day before the landings while designating the intent of air-force attacks on each of the recommended targets.[9] The navy wanted airpower to knock out the large German coastal batteries as the Allied fleet closed on the beaches. The staff supporting Admiral Bertram H. Ramsay, commander in chief of the Allied Naval Expeditionary Force, identified over forty German batteries that threatened the Allied fleet. The ten most dangerous based on location, caliber, range, and significance were made priority targets. These sites were well defended, and the planned aerial bombardment aimed to disrupt and neutralize their operations for the key hours on either side of the landings.[10]

On 14 May Lieutenant General Omar N. Bradley, whose U.S. First Army was to land on Utah and Omaha Beaches, sought a few changes to the Joint Fire Plan. His staff requested the heavy bombers to hit eleven artillery batteries as well as twenty-nine defensive localities, split equally between the two beaches. He also identified several targets that the navy requested to be bombed. For Bradley and his V and VII Corps commanders, neutralization of the enemy installations, not necessarily destruction, was the goal.[11] Two days later the British commander similarly adjusted his air support request. Lieutenant General Miles C. Dempsey, whose British Second Army was designated to land on Gold, Juno, and Sword, organized his requests by corps. For XXX Corps, landing on Gold and Juno, he sought thirteen missions. For I Corps, landing on Juno and Sword, Dempsey's staff made nineteen new requests. Some of these targets were heavy batteries previously identified by Ramsay's planners.

The army commanders who had been present at the Allied landing during Operations Torch (North Africa), Husky (Sicily), Avalanche (Salerno), and Shingle (Anzio) were under no illusions about what aerial bombardment could accomplish. They fully understood the strengths, and especially the limitations, of air support during landing operations. That being said, they welcomed any and all cooperation with the air forces.[12]

RAF Bomber Command was ordered to hit the major German artillery positions at Crisbecq, Longues-sur-Mer, and Merville-sur-Mer. These batteries were considered a major threat to the Allied fleets and needed to be neutralized as soon as possible. The attacks began just after midnight. The Germans had situated their defenses based on the best terrain available. Unfortunately for French civilians, it was often near where they lived and worked. Although Organization Todt constructed the famous artillery batteries of Pointe du Hoc and Longues on high cliffs above the coast, usually they established these massive defensive complexes ten to twenty kilometers behind the beach and often near French villages. The informal name for most of these installations took on the name of the nearby town, such as Maisy, Grandcamp, and Merville. The Joint Fire Plan directed Bomber Command to attack ten of these artillery batteries.

Air Chief Marshal Arthur T. Harris, commander of RAF Bomber Command, had argued against using his heavy bombers against these targets. While his force was relatively effective at destroying German cities, it was not so appropriate for attacking precise targets. The bomber crews' ability to find the correct target, camouflaged and not presenting much of a visual or electronic signature, was limited. If they found the right target, hitting it with any precision was almost impossible. The poststrike air photographs of these targets provide evidence of how inaccurate these missions were. In most cases the bombers did minor damage to the installations. In some cases, such as Battery Crisbecq near Utah Beach, the battery stayed in action for several days and took a toll on Allied naval ships and ground troops.[13]

General Bernard Montgomery's 21 Army Group staff took the lead in identifying the next group of targets: the enemy positions that defended the landing beaches. The plan noted, "The importance of neutralizing the beach defenses requires their engagement by air attack, though due to their nature complete destruction is only likely to be achieved in a very small proportion of cases."[14] These positions, referred to by the Germans as "resistance nests" (*widerstandsnest*), contained a company or battery that could interfere with the landing of the American, British, or Canadian infantry. Bradley and Dempsey identified these as positions they wanted "neutralized," or put out of action for an hour, so their troops could overrun them before the defenders could regain their composure and resist any ground assault. In a military context, "neutralize" means to temporarily impair the effectiveness of an enemy position. This could mean limiting the defending soldiers' ability to accurately fire at friendly troops, to maneuver or evacuate from their positions, to communicate with higher command or interlocking defensive positions, or to reinforce their own position. This was the intended outcome of the air attacks sought by the army.[15] Sometimes these positions were at a distance from French communities, such as the defenses on Utah Beach. In other cases, especially along Juno and Sword Beaches, the German army engineers integrated coastal buildings into their defensive scheme. Obviously, civilians living in the vicinity would suffer when attacked from the air and sea.[16]

The problem becomes more complicated when we consider how Lieutenant General James Doolittle's Eighth Air Force, responsible for neutralizing the defenses on Omaha, Gold, Juno, and Sword Beaches, executed its mission. Rather than approaching the coast and then turning to bomb the targets while flying over them from east to west, the bombardment groups flew toward the coastline on a perpendicular axis. That meant that any problem with identifying the target and releasing the bombs would result in ordnance hitting terrain, and possibly villages, well behind the beach. In addition, Brigadier General Orvil A. Anderson, the Eighth Air Force A-3, or operations officer, without Doolittle's knowledge changed the plan to limit friendly casualties by inserting a bombing delay into the operation schedule. Rather than release their bombs when the Pathfinder aircraft's H2X Radar operator identified the target, crews were now to delay the drop from five to thirty seconds, depending on the time of the first troops' arrival on the beach. Given the bombers' flight speed, a delay of only a few seconds could ensure the bombs fell well behind the beach and possibly on top of a French town.[17]

Once the beach bombers departed, Admiral Ramsay's two naval task forces approached the shore. While the troop-laden landing craft closed in on the coast, warships from all Allied belligerents took their assigned positions. Around 0545 hours, they began firing at enemy positions, especially the coastal-artillery fortresses at Crisbecq, Longues, Ouistreham, and Merville. Other than Longues in the center of the landing sector, all of these batteries were near civilian villages. As the troops approached the shore, especially in the Commonwealth sector, artillery on board landing craft added its gunfire to the sea bombardment. Those French living within the landing sector now were in even more danger, a peril that only increased once the troops were ashore and fighting among the individual positions.[18]

At least thirty-two towns and villages suffered casualties from the bombardment. Because the Allies required surprise, they could not warn those who lived along the coastline. The injury and destruction to their homes and farms were all part of the horror of war. This was collateral damage to the more extensive operation. In some cases, especially near the powerful

German coastal-artillery batteries such as Crisbecq, Merville, and Maisy, the cause for the damage can be directly linked to inaccurate attacks by Bomber Command. At Crisbecq, for example, the two nearby villages of St. Marcouf and Fontenay-sur-Mer reported a combined death toll of forty-five civilians dead. These included five members of the Bazin, six members of the Carre, and four members of the Tixer families. The toll might have been higher in some places, such as Fontenay, if the Germans had not moved some families away from the fortifications and, in early June, warned some to stay away from the battery area.[19]

The intensive bombing of the three-battery complex at Maisy, on the western edge of Omaha Beach, resulted in at least forty-eight dead in the villages of Grandcamp and Maisy. In other instances the proximity of the German defenses to civilian homes makes a firm determination of the cause of death more difficult. The victims in Ouistreham (ninety-eight), Courseulles-sur-Mer (fourteen), and St. Aubin-sur-Mer (twenty-five) fall into this category. But no matter the reason, several hundred French civilians were killed or wounded, primarily by Allied airpower, that morning. We should also not forget the toll the bombardment and subsequent fighting took on the coastal infrastructure. The villages of Courseulles, Port-en-Bessin, and Ouistreham, among others, were ruined. Surviving families now needed someplace to live but were restrained from leaving the area because of the ongoing fighting at the Normandy beachhead.[20]

Legacy Programs

While the landings were in process, bombers continued to strike at targets from operations that began months earlier. These included major airfields, bridges, and rail centers. Since the earliest days of the Battle of Britain, the Allies had been attacking airfields in occupied France, Belgium, and the Netherlands. Operation Neptune's planners worried that the Luftwaffe would surge aircraft into the Normandy area once they realized the amphibious assault was underway, but to make this redeployment possible, they needed large airfields. Kerlin-Bastard, Brittany's prominent fighter and bomber base outside of Lorient, was the most important of these. On 7 June, 134 B-17s went after the airfield to ensure it would not be operational. Medium bombers and fighter-bombers also struck at a wide variety of installations across northern France, including the fighter-control station at Rennes and airfields at Meuvaines near Gold Beach and Châteaudun, southwest of Paris.[21] Fortunately for the civilian population, these targets were relatively easy to find and identify. Additionally, few homes were near the hangers and runways, so it was rare for these missions to affect the civilian population.

More dangerous to the French were the Allied attacks on bridges, especially those over the Seine and Loire Rivers, that framed the Overlord area. Dropping these structures into the water was a legitimate example of interdiction, the military term for limiting the movement of enemy forces. German reinforcements would find it difficult to reach the front lines without a bridge spanning a major river. By April, AEAF planners had identified the important bridges on the two rivers. The most essential bridge-dropping operation was along the Seine, and the Ninth Air Force had essentially completed this task by the end of May. Its culmination was what the citizens of Rouen called "La Semaine Rouge" (the red week) for the resulting damage and destruction. Unlike airfields, bridges were in or near towns and thus French homes and shops. While the first waves of bombers or fighter-bombers might drop their munitions on or close to the bridge, it was generally not the case for the following aircraft groups. Smoke over the area usually affected the ability of pilots and bombardiers to find the target, and German antiaircraft systems were often engaging the attacking aircraft as well.[22]

While the main bridge-destroying operation was along the Seine, the Loire River valley was never far from planners' minds. Nantes, Angers, Tours, Blois, and Orléans possessed large rail yards and bridges spanning the wide river. Any significant movement of German reinforcements from the south of France or Italy by rail or road would have to pass through these areas. Of most concern were the 17th SS Panzer Grenadier Division (southeast of Angers) and the 2nd SS Panzer Division (near Toulouse), which could be highly effective in throwing back the Allied landing forces. Therefore, the planners identified ten bridges along their potential lines of march. The Allies, fearful that focusing attacks on the river's bridges too early would permit German intelligence analysts to bracket the targeted area, held off. Finally, on 26 May Montgomery believed it was time to take the risk and notified AEAF planners that he wanted the Loire's rail bridges and rail yards destroyed before 5 June, the anticipated date for D-Day. Most of these targets were beyond the effective range of medium bombers, so they were the responsibility of Bomber Command and the Eighth Air Force. Doolittle, however, was unable to get his heavy bombers over the bridges before D-Day.[23]

On 7 June Doolittle's Eighth Air Force sent 216 bombers against the Loire bridges and related targets at Nantes, Angers, and Tours. The attack against Tours is typical of what happened and one of the best examples of the limitations and dangers of using heavy bombers on missions against precision targets over friendly territory. None of the aircraft could find the city that day. Rather than return to England with their ordnance, many pilots scattered their bombs, more than 291 tons of them, on "other targets."[24] Did the bombardiers aim at an identified objective, or did the bombs haphazardly land in fields or, worse, on French towns and villages in the Loire Valley? Perhaps local historians have the answer. Regardless, on 8 June the Eighth Air Force sought to remedy its failure, as 227 heavy bombers struck the Tours bridges.[25] They arrived around 0800 hours, and the attack lasted almost an hour. The raid killed at least seventy civilians and wounded an equal number. Yet for this, all the bridges were missed and remained open. In a letter to her family, Jacqueline, a young survivor of the attack, described the bombs landing far from the intended target and killing her brother's friend and his parents.[26] Tours was far from the Normandy beaches, yet its inhabitants became casualties of Operation Overlord.

The most famous legacy programs were those of the so-called Transportation Plan against sixty-four French and Belgian rail yards. This list of targets—not a plan—focused on the "maximum destruction of motive power potential anywhere in France, Belgium or west Germany and the maximum dislocation of all the other elements in the rail system in the areas concerned with OVERLORD."[27] Since March, Allied bombers had sought to destroy any nodes they thought the German high command might need to deploy its strategic reserves by train from one part of Europe to the landing zone. Since most railroad workers lived near the train stations and marshaling yards, AEAF planners fully expected many civilian casualties. British prime minister Winston S. Churchill was very concerned about the number of deaths and its effect on French morale. He often asked his senior air leaders, by note and in person, "How many Frenchmen did you kill today?" This program was still underway as the Allied forces hit the Normandy beaches, and these casualties were part of the overall total. Indeed, in May the French Committee on National Liberation protested to the Allies that the preparatory bombardment was significantly affecting French morale and support.[28] Yet the issue of civilian casualties was usually in the minds of the planners. Major Robert Baker, on General Dwight D. Eisenhower's staff, noted in forwarding a list of rail targets to the command group that "from a political viewpoint, the casualties resulting from these air attacks might cause an unhealable breach between France and Great Britain/USA."[29] The final Air Ministry estimate indicated that 282,100 French citizens were at risk and as many as 8,840 would perish in the bombing attacks.[30] Harris; Lieutenant General Carl A. Spaatz, commander of the U.S. Strategic Air Forces in Europe; and Doolittle all opposed participating in the bombing of rail yards, both because it was a diversion from their strategic tasks and because of the danger the air strikes poised to French civilians.[31]

Towns

The final and most sinister way the Allied air forces killed French civilians was by purposely destroying the centers of towns and small cities. Many of these ancient communities developed along a stream, where the people installed a mill to process the grain the farmers brought in from the field. They often constructed a small dam and a bridge across the river near the mill. Local trails, ultimately small roads, converged on this crossing site that now contained the primary regional market, small shops, and homes. Nevertheless, Allied senior officers, especially Allied Supreme Commander Eisenhower and the overall ground-force commander Montgomery, lived in fear of the German panzer (armored) divisions counterattacking before their own forces were in a position to repel them. Army planners believed that German motorized troops would have to pass through these constricted areas, which they called "chokepoints," to get to the front line. If they could destroy these crossing sites, the enemy would have to travel cross-country, slowing their movement and making them targets for American and British

Photo 7-2 • The marshaling yard at Argentan, a village at the mouth of the Falaise Pocket, was completely wrecked by Allied bombing attacks during the summer of 1944. While use of the rail lines and supporting facilities were denied to the Germans, the bombing also destroyed much of the town at a great cost to the local population—sixty-two residents were killed in the first twenty-four hours of the landings, and many more deaths followed. *U.S. Air Force Photo 53625AC*

fighter-bombers, the dreaded Jabos. Obviously, if they destroyed the town center, the Allies would kill many civilians.[32]

By the end of April, planners at 21 Army Group identified twenty-six towns they wanted "heavily bombed on D-Day and D-Day plus one to create road blocks."[33] In other words, the army wanted the air forces to turn French homes to rubble to slow the German movement.[34] Neither Harris nor Spaatz wanted anything to do with this; therefore, Air Chief Marshal Arthur W. Tedder, Eisenhower's deputy supreme commander and responsible for coordinating all air operations, convened a meeting of senior aviation leaders on 3 May to consider options for using the heavy bombers. All agreed that the "bombing of the towns would not achieve the desired object of blocking roads and disrupting communications, as alternative routes would be found."[35] Tedder, in concert with Spaatz and Doolittle, believed that air attacks on road centers would be ineffective and inefficient, as they were to be based only on map surveys of the area. As such, they were likely to be wasteful of aircraft and their crews as well as cause significant civilian casualties.

Yet the fear of a German counterattack led by Field Marshal Erwin Rommel caused Montgomery to demand that the heavy bombers destroy these towns. The debate continued until he got involved and made it clear that, after the bridge bombing on the Seine and Loire, stopping the movement of panzers within the "inner zone close to the bridgehead" should be a high priority. Two days later, on 22 May, Leigh-Mallory met with the Eighth Air Force commander. Doolittle was adamant that "heavy bombers were not a tactical weapon." But Montgomery insisted, and while Tedder and Spaatz were still not convinced, there was now little they could do about it.[36]

Norman France was the home of hundreds of irreplaceable churches, abbeys, chateaux, and castles large and small. It contained the historical remains of ancient Gaul, Rome, and Viking communities. The Allied leaders now ordered their destruction with no serious discussion of the historical, environmental, or demographic consequences. Instead, they decided to drop leaflets to warn the inhabitants to leave as a sop to the expected casualties.[37] Of course, most French civilians had no ability to leave under German occupation, as roads were blocked with military traffic, they lacked the means to travel, and their young men were away and unable to help. Such movement for local residents was generally impossible and a ridiculous gesture. Over the next two days, the results on civilians were simply devastating. To the French survivors, these towns became known as the "villes martyres de Basse-Normandie," the martyred cities of lower Normandy.[38]

Lisieux, an ancient town that Julius Caesar visited during his Gallic Wars, was the home not only of the Cordier family but also of bicycle maker Paul Cornu. Cornu had experimented with vertical flight, and aviation historians credit him as one of the helicopter's early inventors, based on his 1907 experiments.[39] He lived just outside the city center. On 5 June Cornu was at home and joined by two sisters, his brother Antoine and his wife Jeanne, and their eleven children. Antoine and his family lived in the city center near the rail yard, so he thought it best to join his brother in the suburbs based on the leaflets he had seen. That night Allied bombs fell on Paul Cornu's house. Paul, the oldest at sixty-two, was killed along with nine other family members, the youngest only six months old. Ironically, Antoine's house in the city was undamaged in this attack.[40]

For this first air strike on the evening of 6 June, only twenty-five out of seventy-seven aircraft could find the city, dropping more than 73 tons of high explosives on the civilian buildings. Later that night ninety-six RAF Lancaster and Halifax bombers arrived, and bombs again rained down on the city for twenty minutes. This destroyed the western suburb Saint-Désir and punished other portions of the town center.[41] The next day, a little after 1300 hours, seventy-four Eighth Air Force B-24 bombers arrived, dropping an additional 217 tons of bombs and completing the city's destruction. These three strikes killed more than 780 of the town's inhabitants (approximately 4.5 percent of its population), wounded many more, and left thousands homeless.[42]

During the planning for Overlord, Caen was the first city that the AEAF scheduled for destruction. Planners identified four targets in this ancient home of William the Conqueror: Two were near the bridges and the rail station. One was northwest of the city near the modern university and the Jardin des Plantes. The fourth was to the northwest and near the ancient medieval Abbaye aux Hommes, begun by William in 1077. As Allied troops were landing on the beaches, Doolittle sent 163 B-24 and B-17 bombers from his 1st and 3rd Bombardment Divisions to destroy these locations as Leigh-Mallory directed. No aircraft could find the city through the thick cloud cover that day. The 3rd Division reported that 47 aircraft hit Caen, but residents had no memory of such an attack. At 1030 hours the 1st Division returned with 60 more aircraft but, again, the bomber crews could not find the city.[43]

Alarmed by the German forces moving toward the beaches, Montgomery wanted the Eighth Air Force to try again. So, on relatively short notice, it dispatched seventy-three B-24 bombers to hit the bridges near the rail station. These arrived overhead at 1330 hours, as the women and children were at the city market stocking up for the battle that they knew was on the way. Recognizing the massive Château, William's castle, bombardiers released their ordnance. Without warning, more than 155 tons of explosives hit the busy streets. None of the bombs hit the targeted bridges, but rather fell short in the residential area east of the Château or to the south near the seventh-century Church of Saint-Jean de Caen. The attack lasted less than ten minutes, but more than four hundred civilians, primarily women, children, and old men, perished. The city's center erupted with flames, and firefighters could not stop the blaze.[44]

After the heavy bombers departed, the city's civil-defense organization went about the damaged districts looking for survivors buried under the rubble. Then, around 1630 hours, while most of the population was in the streets looking for survivors, the Americans struck again. This time it was sixty-six B-26 Marauder medium bombers from the Ninth Air Force. The attack was unexpected and caught the rescue workers in the open. Again the bridges were missed, but another two hundred civilian dead were added to the day's roll of horror.[45] That night No. 5 Group from RAF Bomber Command arrived with 111 Avro Lancaster bombers and added to the destruction. With no pretense of conducting an accurate mission, this was an exercise in carpet bombing using the same methods Bomber Command used against cities in the heart of Nazi Germany. But this was occupied France. At least two hundred more corpses joined the casualty lists. Those who were able fled the city. The carnage over Caen continued for another six weeks, until the last German forces withdrew.[46]

If destruction was the goal, the air assaults were successful; a dozen villages as selected by army-group planners were turned into piles of rubble in the first two days of the operation. What residents had gone through was horrific: it was a programmed destruction of these chosen towns.[47] The remains of ancient homes, shops, archives, and churches lay in the street. While this rubble slowed the German army's movement, ultimately, most of the troops sent to the front arrived. But while the French would be able to rebuild the physical structure, they could never replace the lives lost over 6–7 June alone:

- Thury-Harcourt—33
- Pont Évêque—36
- Villers-Bocage—41

- Argentan—62
- Flers—97
- Falaise—151
- Coutances—269
- Condé-sur-Noireau—276
- Vire—341
- Saint-Lô—500
- Lisieux—781
- Caen—1,741[48]

More than 4,200 French civilians died in less than two days as a result of Allied bombing. To put these numbers in perspective, the American 1st and 29th Infantry Divisions, the two units that landed on Omaha Beach, suffered a total of 1,228 soldiers dead in the entire month of June 1944. Of course, the Germans wounded three times that number, but the same calculations apply to civilian casualties.[49] In addition, these were friendly, occupied cities and not enemy fighting positions; at the time of the bombardment, all of these locations were undefended and open. Generals Eisenhower and Montgomery chose to ignore the provisions of The Hague Convention of 1907. Article 25 notes, "The attack or bombardment, by whatever means, of towns, villages, dwellings, or buildings which are undefended is prohibited."[50]

Conclusions

From our perspective in the second decade of the twenty-first century, it may seem quaint to cite rules made almost 120 years ago and before the many evolutions of airpower. Yet the rules had a purpose that military leaders often forget: to limit the effect of war in stroking popular passions and inciting longstanding hatred. Prime Minister Churchill knew this when he wrote to General Eisenhower on 3 April 1944, cautioning him about killing too many French civilians as part of the Transportation Plan.[51] Ultimately, the French did not forget, and towns such as Saint-Lô and Rouen erected monuments to remind their citizens of who destroyed their communities.

In the summer of 2019, while the Anglo-Americans were in the middle of celebrating D-Day's seventy-fifth anniversary, a combined edition of the magazines *Normandie* and *Historia* published an edition with the cover story,

Photo 7-3 • Two French boys watch from a hilltop as convoys of Allied vehicles pass through the badly damaged city of Saint-Lô en route to the battle front on 28 July 1944. The city was subjected to numerous Allied bombing attacks immediately after D-Day and suffered additional destruction during the fighting in late July. This photo was used on the cover of the combined edition of the French magazines *Normandie* and *Historia* published on the seventy-fifth anniversary of the D-Day landings to accompany the lead story about the bloody summer of 1944, when thirty Norman towns suffered under the bombs of the Allied air forces. *U.S. National Archives C-2242*

"1944, l'été sanglant—30 VILLES NORMANDES SOUS LES BOMBES" (1944, the bloody summer—30 Norman towns under the bombs) superimposed over the classic photograph of two boys looking at a destroyed Saint-Lô. In less than a hundred illustrated pages, the issue summarizes much of the French D-Day narrative, including operations of the Resistance, those killed by German troops, and those wounded, traumatized, or slain at the hands of Allied bombers. Every other page has a small heading: "Liberté, le prix du sang" (Liberty: the price in blood). On every page testimony from survivors, photographs, or analysis reminds the reader that France, like those men who landed on the Normandy beaches, paid the price on 6 June. In the two départements where the landings took place, this journal estimated a toll of 11,000 civilians dead during the Battle of Normandy.[52] This narrative reminds us that airpower's French connection was not limited to knocking out bunkers, rail yards, or bridges but also caused much death and destruction to the French population. It is a story that remains alive in Norman France.

NOTES

1. J. P. Cordier, "Souvenirs personnels—Lisieux Bombardement de Juin 1944," 1984, Témoignages écrits, Mémorial de Caen, Caen.
2. Patrick Fissot, "Manche-Calvados: 11000 Victimes Civiles." *Normandie-Historia* (2019): 56–60.
3. Fissot, "Manche-Calvados."
4. SHAEF, "Neptune: Joint Fire Plan (8 April 1944)," Record Group 331, National Archives and Records Administration, College Park, MD [hereafter NARA].
5. Air Historical Branch, Air Ministry [hereafter AHB], *The Liberation of North West Europe* (Northolt, UK: Air Historical Branch, 1945), vol. 3, Appendix 1.
6. Christopher D. Yung, *Gators of Neptune: Naval Amphibious Planning for the Normandy Invasion* (Annapolis, MD: Naval Institute Press, 2006), 76–82; Correlli Barnett, *Engage the Enemy More Closely: The Royal Navy in the Second World War* (New York: W. W. Norton, 1991), 753–809.
7. AHB, *The Liberation of North West Europe*, 3:439–42; AEAF, "Operation Neptune, Overall Air Plan," n.d., RG 331, NARA.
8. AHB, *The Liberation of North West Europe*, 3:117.
9. AHB, *The Liberation of North West Europe*, 3:117.
10. AHB, *The Liberation of North West Europe*, 3:117–20; AEAF, "Operation OVERLORD—Preparatory Air Operations," 30 April 1944, UK National Archives, Kew [hereafter UKNA] AIR 37/519.

11. SHAEF, "Neptune: Joint Fire Plan"; AEAF, "Operation OVERLORD—Preparatory Air Operations."
12. AEAF, "Operation OVERLORD—Preparatory Air Operations."
13. AHB, *The Liberation of North West Europe*, 3:119–22.
14. SHAEF, "Neptune: Joint Fire Plan."
15. U.S. Department of War, *FM 6-20 Field Artillery Tactical Employment* (Washington, DC: Department of War, 1944), 5.
16. AEAF Joint Planning Committee, AEAF Bombing Operations Committee Meetings, 29 May–2 June 1944, UKNA AIR 37.
17. Stephen A. Bourque, *D-Day 1944: The Deadly Failure of Allied Heavy Bombing on June 6* (Oxford, UK: Osprey, 2022), 44–48.
18. Jean Quellien and Bernard Garnier, *Les victimes civiles du Calvados dans la bataille de Normandie: 1er mars 1944–31 décembre 1945* (Caen: Editions-diffusion du Lys, 1995), 37–43. Yung, *Gators of Neptune*, 177–87; Steven J. Zaloga, *D-Day Fortifications in Normandy* (Oxford, UK: Osprey, 2005).
19. Email, Magali Desquesne to author, 28 March 2022, copy in author's possession.
20. Quellien and Garnier, *Les victimes civiles du Calvados*, 449–69.
21. Eighth Air Force Headquarters, "Eighth Air Force Tactical Operations in Support of Allied Landings in Normandy, 2 June–17 June 1944," Field Order 735, 1944, Air Force Historical Research Agency, Maxwell AFB, AL [hereafter AFHRA]; IX Bomber Command Headquarters, Mission Summary, Field Order 348-S, 6 June 1944, Record Group 243, NARA; AEAF Daily INT/OPS Summary No. 133, 7 June 1944, Papers of Air Vice-Marshal E-J Kingston-McClorighry, Imperial War Museum, London.
22. AAF Evaluation Board in the European Theater of Operations, *Effectiveness of Air Attack against Rail Transportation in the Battle of France* (n.p., 1945), Iris # 00113952, AFHRA, Maxwell AFB, AL, 24–26; Stephen A. Bourque, "Rouen: La Semaine Rouge," *Journal of Military and Strategic Studies* 14, nos. 3–4 (2013), 29 January 2013, https://jmss.org/article/view/58051.
23. AHB, "*The Liberation of North West Europe* (Northolt, UK: Air Historical Branch, 1945), 1:180–81, Richard G. Davis, *Carl A. Spaatz and the Air War in Europe* (Washington, DC: Center for Air Force History, 1993), 406; Air Vice-Marshal E. J. Kingston-McCloughry, "The Transportation Plan," 1946, Imperial War Museum, London, 14–16.
24. Eighth Air Force Headquarters, *Tactical Operations in Support of Allied Landings in Normandy*.
25. Eighth Air Force Headquarters, *Tactical Operations in Support of Allied Landings in Normandy*.

26. "1944: les Bombardements sur Tours," https://web.archive.org/web/20210620191041/http://clauderioland.com/les-rioland/histoire/guerres-menu/1944-les-bombardements-sur-tours/ (accessed January 2025).
27. Kingston-McCloughry, "Transportation Plan," 10.
28. Lindsey Dodd and Andrew Knapp, "'How Many Frenchmen Did You Kill?': British Bombing Policy towards France (1940–1945)," *French Historical Studies* 22, no. 4 (Spring 2008); AHB, "RAF Narrative," 1:153–75.
29. Robert Baker, Memorandum for Chief of Staff, Subject: Bombing of Rail Targets in France, 20 April 1944, Box 66, RG 331, NARA.
30. "FCNL invites most serious attention . . . ," May 5, 1944, SHAEF SGS Files, Dwight David Eisenhower Presidential Library, Abilene, KS; Chiefs of Staff Committee, Attacks on Rail Targets in Enemy Occupied Territories, 19 March 1944, RAF Center for Air Research, Northolt, UK.
31. AHB, *The Liberation of North West Europe*, 1:145–61.
32. AHB, *The Liberation of North West Europe*, 1:181–89; AEAF, Minutes of Bombing Operations Committee Meeting, 29 May 1944, UKNA WO 184/185.
33. AHB, *The Liberation of North West Europe*, 1:181.
34. Eighth Air Force Headquarters, *Tactical Operations in Support of Allied Landings in Normandy*, introduction; AEAF, Minutes, 29 May 1944.
35. Arthur Tedder, "Alternative Plans for Employment of Strategic Bomber Forces, Meeting," 3 May 1944, UKNA AIR 37/1116.
36. AHB, *The Liberation of North West Europe*, 1:182; AEAF Joint Planning Committee, AEAF Bombing Operations Committee, 29 May–2 June 1944.
37. AHB, *The Liberation of North West Europe*, 1:184.
38. Eric Alary, Bénédicte Vergez-Chaignon, and Gilles Gauvin, *Les Français au Quotidien, 1939–1949* (Paris: Perrin, 2006), 522.
39. "Incredible Cornu, the Helicopter Cyclist from Lisieux," Normandy Then and Now, 15 November 2014, https://www.normandythenandnow.com/incredible-cornu-the-helicopter-cyclist-from-lisieux/ (accessed March 2022).
40. Email Philippe Cornu to Author, 4 July 2019, copy in author's possession.
41. Bomber Command Intelligence Narrative of Operations No. 819, 7 June 1944, AFHRA A5275; Quellien and Garnier, *Les victimes civiles du Calvados*, 54–60; Eighth Air Force Headquarters, *Tactical Operations in Support of Allied Landings in Normandy*.
42. Quellien and Garnier, *Les victimes civiles du Calvados*, 60; Bomber Command Intelligence Narrative of Operations No. 818, 6 June 1944, AFHRA A5275.
43. AHB, *The Liberation of North West Europe*, 3:207.
44. Quellien and Garnier, *Les victimes civiles du Calvados*, 37–43; Françoise Passera and Jean Quellien, *Les Civils Dans La Bataille de Normandie* (Bayeux: OREP Éditions, 2014), 22–25.

45. Quellien and Garnier, *Les victimes civiles du Calvados*, 42.
46. Quellien and Garnier, *Les victimes civiles du Calvados*, 61–66; Bomber Command Intelligence Narrative of Operations No. 819; Eddy Florentin, *Quand les Alliés bombardaient la France* (Paris: Perrin, 1997), 407–13.
47. Passera and Quellien, *Les civils dans la bataille*, 28–45.
48. Françoise Passera and Jean Quellien, *Les Normands dans la Guerre: Le temps des épreuves, 1939–1945* (Lonrai [Orne]: Tallandier, 2021), 602–6; Quellien and Garnier, *Les victimes civiles du Calvados*, 61–66; Michael Boivin and Bernard Garnier, *Les victimes civiles de la Manche dans la Bataille de Normandie: 1er avril–30 septembre 1944* (Caen: Centre de recherche d'historie quantitative, 1994), 100; Gérard Bourdin and Bernard Garnier, *Les Victimes Civiles de l'Orne dans la Bataille de Normandie: 1 avril–30 september 1944* (Caen: Éditions-Diffusion du Lys, 1994), 15–23.
49. Tradoc Historical Office, "Normandy—June and July 1944: Battle Casualties, U.S. Divisions," 1976, Historical Reference Collection, Fort McNair, DC.
50. Department of Army, *FM 27-10, The Law of Land Warfare*, Department of the Army Field Manual (Washington, DC; Department of Defense, 1956), 19.
51. Winston S Churchill, Letter to Eisenhower, re.: French Casualties, 3 April 1944, Dwight David Eisenhower Presidential Library, Abilene, KS); Alfred D. Chandler Jr. and Stephen E. Ambrose, eds., *The Papers of Dwight David Eisenhower: The War Years*, vol. 3 (Baltimore: Johns Hopkins Press, 1970), 1630.
52. Frédérick Cassegrain and Guillaume Malaurie, *1944, L'été sanglant—30 Villes Normandes sous les bombes*, special issue, *Normandie-Historia* (May–June 2019): 56–60.

8

Airpower in a Set-Piece Attack

U.S. Ninth Air Force and the Capture of Cherbourg, 22–30 June 1944

Mike Bechthold

The capture of the port of Cherbourg had loomed large for Allied planners since the Normandy coastline was chosen as an objective for the Overlord landings. Three American infantry divisions, supported by the first large-scale and closely coordinated air–ground attack since D-Day itself, were assigned to the final drive on Cherbourg. It took more than a week of intense fighting to capture the port. In the aftermath of the battle, postmortems attempted to understand the role played by the air force. The army was disappointed in the air support its troops received, having expected the large air contribution to pave the way to victory. The air force was also disappointed, as it believed the high cost in aircraft and pilots lost, not to mention ordnance expended, did not justify the results obtained. An air force report written soon after the war even went so far as to declare Cherbourg "one of the few significant misapplications of tactical air power in the entire career of the Ninth Air Force in the European Theater of Operations."[1] Yet contrary to the contemporary views of the U.S. Army and the U.S. Army Air Forces (USAAF), the application of tactical air support materially aided the ground offensive and was an early indication of the role that it would play during the Normandy Campaign.

Tactical airpower was a major factor in Allied success in the Second World War. The air forces worked closely with the armies to facilitate ground operations. Heavy bombers struck frontline targets; medium bombers interdicted the battlefield by targeting road junctions, rail yards, and bridges; and fighter-bombers attacked targets of opportunity and guarded against enemy air attacks. Ground commanders recognized the importance of these operations, but for them, the most important task was the close support of their operations. Enormous air resources were devoted on 5–6 June 1944, when 11,590 aircraft supported the Operation Overlord landings. Despite an abundance of airpower on D-Day, its success was mixed. The vast size of the Allied air fleets combined with the paucity of a Luftwaffe response meant that the air forces held uncontested mastery of the skies. This crucial support prevented most enemy raids during the highly vulnerable period of the initial landings and allowed the Allies to conduct their own air operations with minimal interference. Many successful attacks were made by Allied fighter-bombers and medium bombers that day, but the inability of the heavy bombers to accurately strike their targets along the Normandy coastline prevented the full potential of the air attacks from being felt by the ground forces.[2]

The open beaches north of Caen and Bayeux were the focal point of the Allied landings, but Utah Beach on the eastern coast of the Cotentin Peninsula was included to widen the bridgehead and ensure the quick capture of Cherbourg.[3] Logistics were central to Allied success, and planners believed that taking the port city early on was essential to facilitate the vast flow of food, fuel, ammunition, and other items needed by an industrial army engaged in high-intensity operations. The beachheads formed at Utah Beach, and the landing zones of the U.S. 82nd and 101st Airborne Divisions were meant to secure the right flank of the Allied landings before providing a start line for a northern thrust to capture Cherbourg. The Overlord plan called for the initial lodgment, including the areas of Grandcamp-Maisy, Bayeux, and Caen, to be secured on the first day. The next eight days would see its further expansion, including a western drive from Utah to secure room for the turn north toward Cherbourg. Planners expected that the port would be captured by D+14 (21 June).[4]

The success of the initial D-Day landings exceeded expectations. By the end of 6 June, the British and Canadians were solidly ashore along their assigned stretch of coastline and had successfully defeated several small German counterattacks directed primarily at Sword Beach. In the west the Americans quickly captured Utah against light resistance, and Omaha, where the situation was critical earlier in the day, was secured by nightfall. The Germans were never able to launch a major counterattack to throw the "little fish" back into the sea, but by 10 June, they were able to create a secure perimeter around the Allied lodgment.[5] Caen, a British objective on D-Day, was still in German hands and would take more than a month of hard fighting to capture. German resistance against the U.S. advance was fierce and greatly assisted by the Norman terrain. The ancient system of hedgerows surrounding farm fields, known as bocage, necessitated a slow, cautious, and costly advance by the Americans.

With the lodgment secure, Lieutenant General Omar N. Bradley, commander of the U.S. First Army, turned his attention to the capture of the Cotentin Peninsula and Cherbourg. By 18 June, Lieutenant General J. Lawton Collins, commander of U.S. VII Corps, had advanced across the neck of the peninsula, and the next day he turned northward to attack. His men made steady progress and, by the evening of 21 June, were poised to attack Cherbourg. The capture of the port gained an even greater importance when a severe and unexpected storm lashed the region from 19 to 21 June. The gale forced a pause on the delivery of supplies to Normandy and destroyed the newly constructed Mulberry harbor at Omaha Beach while severely damaging the British Mulberry at Arromanches. The loss of this logistical capacity raised serious concerns about the sustainment of the Allied armies in the field.[6]

The German hold on Cherbourg was tenuous. When the Americans cut the peninsula, they left the enemy with two options: concede the Cotentin or fight until the end. Not surprisingly, Hitler ordered the defenders of Cherbourg to hold fast. On 12 June the OKW (Oberkommando der Wehrmacht), the

German high command, directed Seventh Army that "every strong point and resistance nest surrounded by the enemy must fight to the last man and the last bullet."[7] As Collins' VII Corps tightened the noose on Cherbourg, Generalleutnant Karl-Wilhelm von Schlieben, commander of the 709th Division, issued a desperate order to his commanders on the morning of 21 June: "Withdrawal from the present positions is punishable by death. I empower all leaders of every grade to shoot on sight anyone who leaves his post because of cowardice. The hour is serious. Only willpower, readiness for fighting and heroism to the death can help."[8]

This order did not stop German soldiers from surrendering during the battle, but it made them think twice before doing so. Morale may have been low among the defenders at Cherbourg, but it would take hard fighting for the Americans to finish the job.

Air support for the American armies in Normandy was provided by the Ninth Air Force, a composite tactical air force that fielded a mix of fighters, bombers, and transport aircraft. The IX Bomber Command was formed around light- and medium-bomber units. Its heavy punch was primarily directed at airfields and towns, rail yards, bridges, and other large-scale infrastructure. The IX Fighter Command, composed of two air support commands, IX and XIX, operated fighters and fighter-bombers. The IX Air Support Command worked with the U.S. First Army, while the XIX Air Support Command was scheduled to work with the U.S. Third Army upon its activation.[9] The ongoing tension between the air and ground forces was revealed in April 1944, when the name "air support command" was replaced by "tactical air command." The USAAF was determined to "discard" terms that were "misleading with respect to the status and role of the Tactical Air Forces in relation to ground forces."[10] The change occurred primarily to expunge the notion that the air force "supported" the army and to emphasize the team concept that revolved around "cooperation."

The IX Fighter Command and IX Air Support Command were both commanded by Major General Elwood R. Quesada. An outstanding fighter pilot, Quesada had amassed a good deal of combat experience in the Tunisian, Sicilian, Corsican, and Italian Campaigns while serving in a variety of positions, including deputy commanding general of the Northwest African

Photo 8-1 • Generalleutnant Karl-Wilhelm von Schlieben (*center*), commander of the German 709th Division, threatened his men with death if they surrendered to the Americans. This was not sufficient to forestall the combined air and ground attack launched against his men on 22 June 1944. Here, Schlieben is being interviewed on 27 June by Lieutenant General J. Lawton Collins (*back to camera*), commander of U.S. VII Corps. Watching to the left is Admiral Walther Hennecke, commander of the German naval garrison at Cherbourg. *U.S. National Archives 111-SC-190787-S*

Coastal Air Force.¹¹ He was described as a "rarity" among senior USAAF and Royal Air Force (RAF) commanders due to his strong commitment to tactical air operations.¹² This attitude won him praise from both above and below. Bradley, who worked closely with Quesada through much of the Normandy Campaign, opined: "This 40-year-old airman helped more than anyone else to develop the air–ground support that was to speed us so successfully across France on the heels of the breakout. He succeeded brilliantly in a task where so many airmen before him had failed, partly because he was willing to dare anything once. Unlike most airmen who viewed ground support as a bothersome diversion to war in the sky, Quesada approached it as a vast new frontier waiting to be explored."¹³

The plan for the Cherbourg operation was developed quickly and would feature the first closely coordinated, large-scale use of tactical aviation since D-Day. On the afternoon of 17 June, U.S. First Army notified Ninth Air Force that its forces required a large-scale air operation in support of its attack on Cherbourg. Lieutenant General Lewis Brereton, commander of Ninth Air Force, and his chief intelligence officer, Colonel Melon Hall, along with Quesada, met with Lieutenant General Bradley at his headquarters at Au Gay in Normandy to discuss the plan. Bradley wanted to make "special use of air power" to support the attack. He believed it would serve the dual function of speeding up the completion of the operation and preventing unnecessary casualties.¹⁴ The air commanders supported the plan but considered it too ambitious for Ninth Air Force alone.¹⁵

Quesada flew to England the next day to confer with the air force chiefs and seek additional resources. He proposed a maximum air effort by 2,000 aircraft, which would be one of the largest air operations up to that point in the war. Not surprisingly, his plan was met with skepticism. Neither Air Chief Marshal Arthur Harris of Bomber Command nor Lieutenant General Jimmy Doolittle of Eighth Air Force was willing to divert their heavy bombers for a tactical mission in support of the army. Despite these protests, Lieutenant General Carl Spaatz, the senior American airman and commander of the U.S. Strategic Air Forces in Europe, liked Quesada's presentation and ordered Doolittle to make his 1,200 heavy bombers available to support the operation. The tactical air force commanders, Air Chief Marshal Sir

Photo 8-2 • Major General Elwood R. Quesada (*center*), commander of IX Fighter Command and IX Air Support Command, meets with Lieutenant General Lewis Brereton (*left*), commander of Ninth Air Force, in Normandy on 8 June 1944. *U.S. Air Force Photo 52443AC*

Trafford Leigh-Mallory (Allied Expeditionary Air Forces), Lieutenant General Brereton (Ninth Air Force), and Air Marshal Sir Arthur Coningham (Second Tactical Air Force) were all in favor of the plan.[16] Air Chief Marshal Sir Arthur Tedder, General Dwight D. Eisenhower's deputy supreme commander, was in favor of using heavy bombers against transportation targets to support the invasion as well as using them tactically to support the army at key points in the campaign. In his memoirs after the war, Tedder recalled a mid-June telephone conversation in which Eisenhower told General Bernard Montgomery, the overall ground forces commander: "Please do not hesitate to make the maximum demands for any air assistance that can possibly be useful to you. Wherever there is any legitimate opportunity we must blast the enemy with everything we have."[17]

On the morning of 21 June, Brereton, Quesada, and Collins met to finalize the air plan. Collins thought the use of heavy bombers was unnecessary as there was no crust of German defenses to break. Instead, he asked for an "air pulverization" of the target area aimed primarily at destroying the morale of the defenders and disrupting their communications. Collins proposed bombing the approaches to Cherbourg, "the objective being primarily to weaken the already failing morale of the defenders and possibly induce them to surrender."[18] On his recommendation, the U.S. heavies were pulled from the operation and replaced with fighters and fighter-bombers supplied by the RAF's Second Tactical Air Force.[19]

The ground attack on Cherbourg was to be made by three U.S. infantry divisions—the 4th, 9th, and 79th—in a plan described by Collins as a "double envelopment." The 79th Division (Major General Ira Wyche) was to make a holding attack in the middle to fix the enemy, while the 9th (Major General Manton Eddy) and 4th Divisions (Major General Raymond O. Barton) moved to isolate the city from the west and east respectively. Upon achieving isolation, the 79th Division would continue forward. Intelligence reports suggested the Germans were disorganized, and commanders hoped that a heavy preliminary air attack would complete the enemy's demoralization and facilitate the capture of the city.[20]

The planning for the air assault was compressed into a very short time frame. Much of the process was carried out at Hillingdon House, the headquarters of Ninth Air Force in England. Brigadier General D. M. Schlatter, assistant chief of staff, operations (A-3), and Brigadier General R. F. Stearley, director of operations, represented the USAAF, while Air Vice-Marshal Sir Victor Groom, the senior air staff officer of Second Tactical Air Force, was the RAF representative. There were no army representatives present during the planning process, but Quesada supplied the planners with the general ground-force plan for the operation along with their air support requests. It took only six hours to work out a complete plan for the participation of twelve fighter-bomber groups from IX and XIX Tactical Air Commands, eight medium bomber groups, and three light-bomber groups from IX Bomber Command. In addition, Second Tactical Air Force contributed twelve squadrons of Typhoons and Mustangs. The planning was completed in time to send operations orders to all the air units involved. But its late completion required Schlatter to fly to France in the early hours of 22 June to personally deliver and explain the air plan to the officers of VII Corps.[21]

The Cherbourg operation began at noon on 22 June when VII Corps artillery fired a counterbattery barrage at German antiaircraft positions to clear the way for the aircraft. Starting at 1240 hours, an eighty-minute air program commenced prior to the ground assault at 1400 hours. The air target area was originally planned to be two "L" shaped areas in front of each attacking division. This was changed late in the planning process to be one large area located to the south and southwest of Cherbourg in front of the positions held by 9th and 79th Divisions. There were no air attacks in front of the 4th Division. The southern edge of the target area, which corresponded to a bomb line marked by white smoke, ran roughly along the line of les Chevres–Hardinvast–Sideville–west of Flottemanville-Hague. The northern boundary of the target area ran to the south of Cherbourg. Priority targets in that area were to be marked by white smoke fired by the artillery. No attacks were to be carried out south of the bomb line.[22]

Despite the large target area, this was not a "carpet bombing" mission like those that later preceded Operations Charnwood, Goodwood, and Cobra, among others. No heavy bombers were involved and only medium and fighter-bombers were used with the main goal to break the will of the Cherbourg garrison. Their morale had been reported as low, and Allied forces

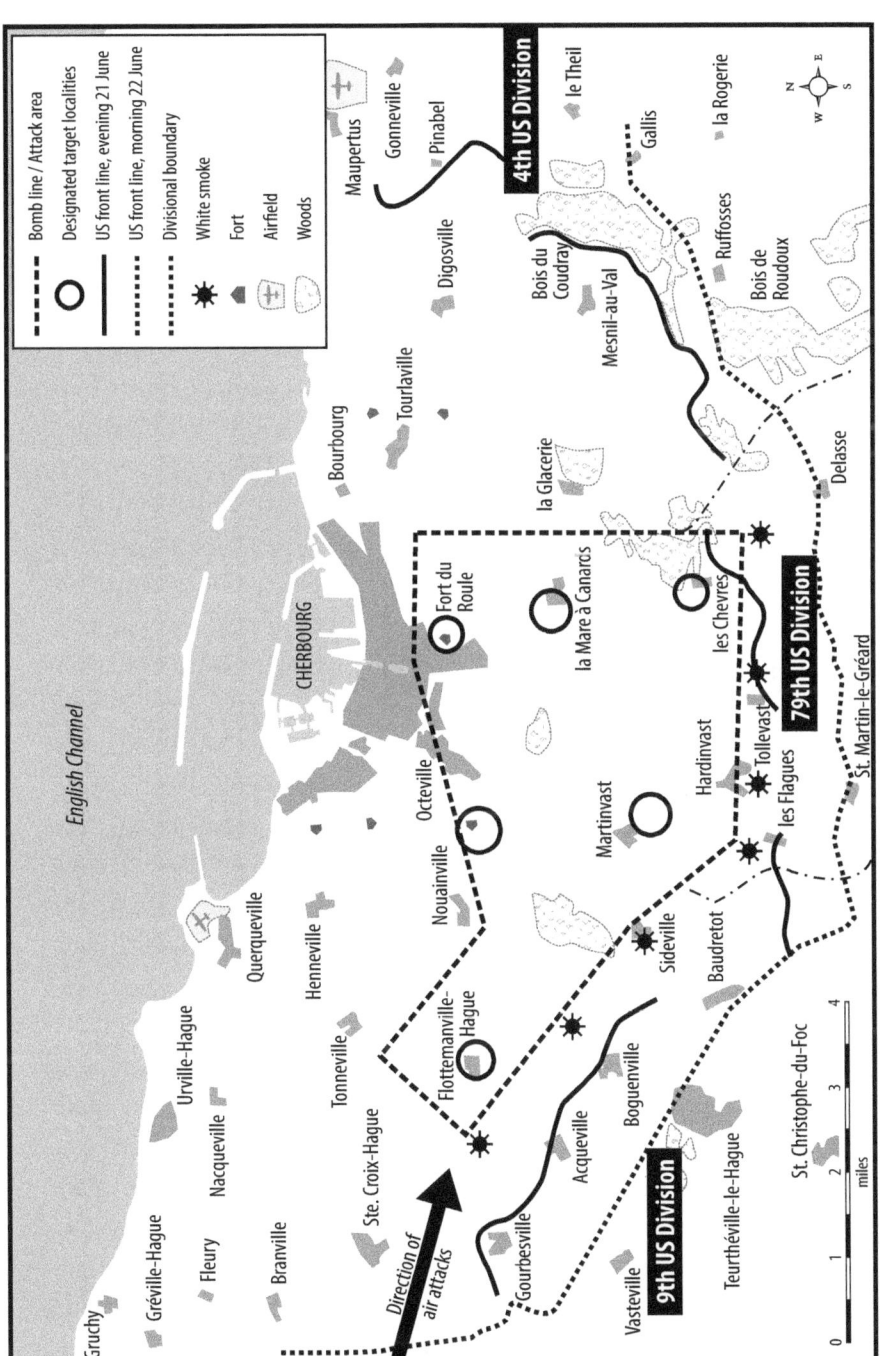

Map 8-1 • Cherbourg

made attempts to secure a surrender prior to the attack. No response to the surrender demands came from the German defenders in the Cherbourg area. The Americans would soon discover that the garrison's morale was not low enough to cause a capitulation without a fight.[23]

Airpower was a notoriously blunt and inaccurate weapon in World War II. In anticipation of the air strikes, U.S. ground forces were ordered to withdraw at least 1,200 yards from the front line to diminish the chance of friendly fire incidents. Artillery batteries targeted known and suspected German antiaircraft positions, with the goal of destroying or neutralizing as many guns as possible before the aircraft arrived. At 1240 hours four squadrons of RAF Typhoons from Nos. 198, 609, 164, and 183 Squadrons arrived and attacked from west to east. The Hawker Typhoon possessed enormous firepower, with four 20-mm cannons and carrying eight rocket projectiles. The damage caused by a full salvo of rockets was likened to a broadside from a naval cruiser; one rocket was sufficient to destroy any German tank. But the inability of Typhoon pilots to find and hit pinpoint objectives greatly impeded their chances of destroying those targets.[24]

The weather on 22 June was not ideal for aerial attacks. The sky was predicted to be completely overcast, with 10/10s clouds at a height of 1,000–2,000 feet. Fortunately as the day progressed, the ceiling had increased up to between 10,000 and 12,000 feet by the time the air strikes began. The fighter-bombers attacked under the cloud ceiling, often pressing their runs as low as 200 feet. The medium bombers delivered their payloads at a height of 11,000–13,000 feet, and many were unable to visually sight their targets. Some aircraft resorted to using Oboe, a very accurate British blind-bombing radio-beacon targeting system, to aim through the cloud cover.[25]

The Typhoon attacks lasted for ten minutes, after which six squadrons of British Mustangs entered the battle area.[26] Using only machine guns, these aircraft spent an additional ten minutes strafing German positions between the southern edge of Cherbourg and the bomb line. The operations order issued to the British squadrons gave very specific instructions aimed at preventing friendly casualties. The attack timings were very specific, and late aircraft were ordered to return to base. Pilots were given map references for the bomb line and told to look for white smoke fired by American artillery to mark it. No attacks were to be made south of the origin of this smoke. U.S. frontline positions were indicated by colored panels and yellow smoke. All fighter-bomber attacks were scheduled to conclude by H-Hour to avoid hitting the advancing American troops.[27]

A total of 118 RAF aircraft participated in the attack, losing seven aircraft and three pilots killed.[28] Squadron Leader I. J. Davies, the commanding officer of No. 198 Squadron, was one of those lost when his Typhoon was hit by flak near Cherbourg. Davies attempted to get his aircraft back to American lines but was forced to bail out when his engine quit. He jumped too low for his parachute to properly deploy and was killed.[29] Two No. 315 Polish Squadron Mustangs were also lost to flak. F/LH. Stefankiewicz was killed when his aircraft was hit by ground fire, while W/O T. Tamoweicz successfully crash-landed in a nearby marsh. The squadron commanding officer, Squadron Leader E. Horbaczewski, saw Tamoweicz's aircraft go down. He landed his Mustang at a nearby emergency landing strip, commandeered a U.S. jeep, and rescued Tamoweicz from his aircraft. He then squeezed Tamoweicz into the cockpit of his fighter and flew him back to England for medical treatment.[30] Based on known American fighter casualties (32 destroyed and 62 damaged—a 1:2 ratio), it can be assumed that an additional 12–16 RAF aircraft sustained damage but returned to base.[31]

At 1300 hours, as the last Second Tactical Air Force aircraft left the area, IX Tactical Air Command began its attacks. Over the next hour, thirty-six squadrons of fighter-bombers arrived at five-minute intervals to bomb and strafe targets in front of the American lines. The fighters were all routed to fly from west to east, parallel to the front line. They targeted enemy military installations, troops, and transportation as well as targets of opportunity within the specified area. These pilots paid particular attention to six designated localities within the general target area. Consisting of Flottemanville-Hague, Martinvast, les Chevres, la Mare à Canards, Fort du Roule, and a defended locality just west of Octeville, these contained key German strongpoints. Each P-51 Mustang and P-38 Lightning carried two 500-pound bombs, while the P-47 Thunderbolts each carried three 500-pound bombs. After dropping their ordnance, the aircraft strafed the target area. Overall, 557 fighter-bombers dropped a total of 520.5 tons of bombs.[32]

Many of the Americans expected a milk run, but that was not the case. German flak over the target area was so intense that one fighter pilot remarked it was only safe to fly at treetop level. But even that tactic did not ensure survival. Captain Jake Reed, a P-38 Lightning pilot in the 367th Fighter Group, was flying low through a ravine when the two aircraft ahead of him were shot down in flames. Reed completed his mission but learned upon returning to his English base that his group had lost seven aircraft and six pilots in the attack.[33]

The mission of the fighter-bombers was greatly impeded by conditions in the target area. German resistance and obscuring smoke and dust made it extremely difficult for pilots to identify their assigned targets. In many cases they simply attacked any target that presented itself. Not surprisingly, this led to numerous "friendly fire" incidents. Brigadier Generals Schlatter and R. E. Nugent were attacked by RAF fighters near Valognes while they made their way to the front with the air plan for Lieutenant General Collins. Attacks were made against 9th Division artillery battalions located well south of the bomb line. Nobody was immune, it seemed. While watching the attack from a hedgerow half a mile south of the front line, Collins and Major General Quesada were forced to dive for cover when they were strafed. The air forces believed that no more than ten out of seven hundred fighter-bombers mistakenly attacked outside the target area; there were no casualties and little damage reported from the friendly fire incidents, but this small number of incidents greatly affected the view of ground troops regarding the value of air support.[34]

The final stage of the aerial bombardment coincided with the launch of the ground assault. The IX Bomber Command delivered "a series of attacks designed to form an aerial barrage moving northward in anticipation of the ground forces."[35] All eleven groups of light and medium bombers from IX Bomber Command participated in attacks on eleven pinpoint localities. Three of these overlapped with fighter-bomber targets while also targeting strongpoints, artillery batteries, and other fortifications. The attacks were made from altitudes ranging from 10,000 to 13,000 feet using both visual and blind-bombing techniques.[36] Of 395 aircraft dispatched, a total of 387

Photo 8-3 • A Douglas A-20 Havoc of the Ninth Air Force attacks targets in the Cherbourg area in support of the U.S. Army ground operations, 22 June 1944. *U.S. Air Force Photo 51672AC*

completed the mission, dropping more than 590 tons of bombs. Losses to the bombers were light, with only 1 aircraft shot down and a further 91 damaged by flak but successfully returned to base. The lower casualties sustained by the bombers can be attributed to the higher altitude from which they attacked as well as their use of "Window" (chaff) to confuse German radar-directed antiaircraft guns. Aircrews found it necessary to use Oboe guidance as the raid progressed and as targets became obscured due to dust and smoke from earlier attacks. Brigadier C. C. Oxborrow, the brigadier-general staff (air) at 21 Army Group and one of the military's air support experts, believed that the U.S. B-26 Marauder medium bomber was the best of all the support aircraft due to its bombing accuracy.[37] This view was not shared by U.S. Army ground forces at Cherbourg. Lieutenant General Bradley believed that the mediums left "much to be desired in close support operations." On 22 June medium bombers twice targeted units of the 9th Division, whose men subsequently treated air support with extreme caution for the rest of the war.[38]

Despite the problems, 9th Division commanders considered the bombing satisfactory and commenced their assault on schedule. Initial progress was slow but the division's three regiments made good speed against an enemy it considered demoralized. The 79th Division found the fighting hard on its front but captured the les Chevres strongpoint, while the defended locality at la Mare à Canards stubbornly resisted. The slowest progress was made by the 4th Division to the east, which did not directly benefit from any air attacks on its immediate front. It struggled to advance on the twenty-second and had to contend with German troops infiltrating behind the lead battalions.[39]

It is difficult to assess the results of the air attacks, as there are numerous methods that can be used to evaluate the success or failure of the mission. The destruction of German targets is an obvious measure, as is the cost to the Allied air forces. The success of the ground attack must be considered as well as the opinions of those involved. It is virtually impossible to separate the effects of the various phases of the attack, but a few observations are possible. In postraid debriefing reports, fighter pilots and bomber crews claimed that their attacks were good, with definite hits on a variety of targets, including machine-gun emplacements, railway marshaling yards, rail embankments, trains, flak guns and artillery emplacements, a radio station, flak towers, and various German motor-transportation and troop concentrations. The official USAAF report provides the following summary of claims:[40]

Type	Destroyed	Probable	Damaged
gun positions	0	0	9 (neutralized)
flak towers	2	0	3
buildings	20	0	26+
radio stations	1	0	0
fuel dumps	1	1	0
trucks	2	0	2

Immediate appraisals of the effectiveness of the Cherbourg air strikes were disappointing. The slow rate of advance by the ground forces seemed to indicate the failure of the raids. Major General Quesada was dismayed by the results. He felt that the strafing operations were a "waste of bullets."[41] In terms of destroying enemy morale, the air attacks were certainly a complete failure. There was no indication of a precipitous drop in German spirits resulting in immediate surrenders, but the attacks did affect German morale in some ways. The defenders of Cherbourg continued to fight tenaciously until the very last. By the end of 23 June, only a small portion of the aerial target area had been overrun by the ground troops.[42] One postwar air-force analysis concluded that it was possible the results did not justify the losses (33 aircraft destroyed and 132 damaged) and expenditure of fuel, ammunition, and ordnance. But a report issued less than a month after the attack was more circumspect: "Results obtained in operations of this size *may not be commensurate with the numbers of aircraft lost*. . . . In this case, it is felt that the operations were justified [emphasis added]."[43]

The initial attack on Cherbourg had not achieved the immediate success expected by the Americans, but the shock effect on the defenders was substantial. By sunset on 22 June, the German commander, Generalleutnant Schlieben, realized the American offensive heralded the end of the siege. The dire situation was also realized in Berlin, prompting Hitler to exhort Schlieben to fight to the end: "Even if worst comes to worst it is your duty to defend the last bunker and leave to the enemy not a harbor but a field of ruins. . . . The German people and the whole world are watching your fight; on it depends the conduct and result of operations to smash the beachheads and the honor of the German Army and your own name."[44]

Schlieben responded with a factual, yet defeatist, dispatch. He reported that his overage, poorly trained troops lacked effective leadership, were exhausted in spirit and body, and suffered from *verbunkert* (bunker paralysis). Without additional troops, the port was sure to fall. Sending reinforcements by road was considered but ultimately dismissed. Allied pressure had effectively isolated the Cherbourg garrison, so there were only small-scale resupply efforts by sea and air. The OKW briefly contemplated sending additional troops by sea or even parachute drop, but these plans were sensibly canceled due to the destruction of the city's port facilities and the unavailability of transport aircraft. Schlieben was on his own.[45]

The evidence shows that the Allied air attacks materially sped up the advance of VII Corps. The interrogation of prisoners of war following the battle revealed that the air strikes, especially the dive bombing and strafing, seriously diminished the men's will and ability to fight. Though the defenders fought hard, they were dazed, slow to react, and resigned to the fact that defeat was inevitable. With the element of time so important in this operation, a USAAF report estimated that the air attacks hastened the capture of Cherbourg by forty-eight hours.[46]

It is clear from an examination of the relevant documents that many of the appraisals of the Allied air operation are based on a comparison between anticipated and actual results without considering how the actual results material aided the ground operations. Commanders and planners presumed the air attacks would eliminate resistance and preclude the need for heavy fighting. They also projected aircraft losses to be light. Neither of these expectations were met. Judged by these standards, one can see why the application of tactical airpower at Cherbourg was viewed as unsuccessful. At that point in the war, the Allies had not yet fully worked out how aircraft could be used to greatest effect on the battlefield. Cherbourg showed that close air support was not a battle-winning weapon on its own. But air support there did facilitate the ground action, and judged by the standards in place by the end of the summer, the attacks were very successful.

Air strikes against targets in the Cherbourg area continued following the main assault. Between 23 and 29 June, a total of eight fighter-bomber and six medium bomber missions were flown against strongpoints and gun positions. Ninth Division recorded several successful air attacks. On the evening of 23 June, "32 dive-bombers bombed emplaced guns at Querqueville with disastrous effect." Two days later the divisional air support party directed air attacks that completely destroyed the heavy-gun batteries at Gruchy and Gréville. Supermarine Spitfires of No. 63 Squadron actively directed naval-gunfire support in the Cherbourg area during this period. Air operations were severely restricted by weather 26–28 June. No aircraft from England were able to participate on these days, but some sorties were flown by fighter-bombers based on the Continent.⁴⁷ Fighting in the city effectively ended on 26 June, and the garrison formally surrendered the next morning. All organized German resistance outside of Cherbourg was over by the afternoon on 1 July. From the German perspective, the loss of the port was a major defeat that occurred much quicker than expected.⁴⁸ The application of tactical airpower played an important part in this Allied success.

Cherbourg provided an operational laboratory in the development of close air support. Mistakes were made, but lessons emerged that improved the entire system. The question of planning revealed the strengths and weaknesses of the tactical air system as it existed in June 1944. The ability to quickly plan, revise, and disseminate a large-scale, complicated effort such as the assault on Cherbourg would not have been possible earlier in the war. Major General Quesada and his planners conceived, planned, and successfully executed a complex operation involving 1,100 USAAF and RAF aircraft with only a few days' warning. Not everything went smoothly. The rushed timetable affected coordination between the air and ground forces. There were no military representatives present during the final planning stages, and the completed plan was delivered to ground commanders only hours before the air strikes. This contributed to poor coordination once the attack started. Prisoner reports clearly remarked that the air attacks initially caused significant disorganization. German officers could not keep their troops together in the face of continuous dive-bombing and strafing attacks, but this effect was short lived.⁴⁹ The 9th Division observed after the battle:

> Best results were obtained when air bombardment took place when the assaulting troops were not more than 1000 yards from the target, and when they moved in rapidly as soon as the bombardment was over. ... When such tactics were employed, success invariably followed. If, on the other hand, air bombardment took place at too great a distance from the attacking troops, it was found habitually that the defenders had an opportunity to recover and to man their positions before the attackers could arrive.⁵⁰

Problems with planning and coordination were compounded by the limits of communications. Many infantry commanders were dissatisfied with the air support they received because the targets they needed neutralized were not being hit. A related matter was the number of friendly fire incidents during the operation in which both fighter-bombers and medium bombers mistakenly targeted friendly troops. Though tactical conditions, such as smoke and dust in the target area and active enemy flak, contributed to these errors, there was no system in place to allow ground observers to talk directly to the aircraft overhead. The importance of direct contact between the frontline troops and the pilots overhead was shown on 22 June. Three infantry regiments—the 22nd, 47th, and 60th—radioed their headquarters to implore a stop to attacks by American aircraft.[51] With no direct radio link to the aircraft, it was impossible to contact the offending pilots. This coordination function could be directly fulfilled by air support parties (ASPs) without reference to a higher headquarters. Each division involved at Cherbourg had ASPs to relay requests for air support. These requests would be radioed to England, where they would be evaluated and be either rejected or sent forward to the air forces. Though the ASPs had the ability through their VHF radios to contact the pilots overhead, this action was prohibited without prior authorization. Restrictions on communications were so severe that the ASPs were not even permitted to signal aircraft that were attacking friendly troops or attacking the wrong target. This limitation was imposed by the air forces, which did not want their forward attack control to develop into target control and thus erode the centralized system of air support. Cherbourg showed the importance of terminal control and helped convince air leadership that a more decentralized system was essential for successful operations. This evolutionary change was implemented within a few weeks, thereafter becoming standard practice for the ASPs to brief by radio pilots in the air just before they reached the target area. The introduction of armored column cover by the end of July marked a complete break from the air support system in place on D-Day.[52]

A second lesson learned from observations at Cherbourg was that fighter-bomber attacks had a much greater effect on the morale of the enemy than did level bombing by medium bombers. The first strikes on 22 June were made by fighter-bombers, while the mediums attacked only as the troops began to advance. If fighter-bomber attacks had a greater effect on enemy morale, and if that effect was short-lived, then it made sense to use the medium bombers first to attack targets farthest from the bomb line and then bring in the fighter-bombers to attack close to the troops in immediate anticipation of their advance. This strategy also made sense due to the greater accuracy of fighter-bombers compared to the mediums. The air plan for Operation Cobra in late July incorporated this lesson. Fighter-bombers were assigned the target area closest to the American troops in two waves, both before and after the heavy and medium bombers arrived, to maximize the morale effect of their attacks. Hopes were that the accuracy of the fighter-bombers compared to the mediums and heavies would help limit friendly casualties.[53]

Cherbourg provided experience in other areas. The first was cooperation between the air and the artillery. Most discussions on air–artillery coordination focused on aerial spotting for the guns. Very little credit has been given to the support given by the artillery to the air. During the Cherbourg operation, this occurred in two ways. Prior to the air attack, the artillery engaged in counterbattery fire to suppress German antiaircraft defenses. The results of this kind of support are largely intangible, but aircraft losses would have been much greater without it. The second type of artillery support was the marking of the bomb line and principal targets with smoke. Though some friendly fire casualties did occur, the existence of a visible bomb line lowered the risk. There were some reports that marking targets with smoke was worthless since the markers quickly dissipated and became mixed with smoke and dust from previous attacks. If nothing else, smoke shells fired by artillery indicated the general location of a target to the attacking aircraft, which eased the task of the pilot. The effect of target marking was greatly enhanced if the air and the ground were in close contact so the pilot could be told when to expect the laying on of smoke. In this way it was much more likely that the correct target would be struck. At Cherbourg the use of smoke was rated a moderate success and demonstrated enough potential to recommend its continued use by artillery to mark targets.[54]

Cherbourg was an important milestone in the development of tactical air doctrine during the Second World War. It was the first major use of a set-piece plan involving tactical airpower following the D-Day landings. The immediate impression of the air support judged it ineffective. Both air and ground observers were disappointed that the fighters and bombers did not have a more tangible, immediate effect on the battle. Lieutenant General Collins' hope that the air attacks would destroy German morale and induce the enemy troops to surrender did not occur. American ground forces were not able to penetrate the German defenses as deeply as hoped on the first day of the assault, but several key defended areas and much of the high ground overlooking Cherbourg were captured. The disappointment of army leadership in the air support they received was more a disconnect between their unrealistic expectations of what it could do rather than any failing by the air forces.

Though there was no immediate German collapse, by the end of 22 June, it was evident to both the Americans and the Germans that it was only a matter of time until Cherbourg fell. At the time, the USAAF estimated that air operations sped the capture of the port by up to forty-eight hours. Communications between the air and ground forces needed to be improved, as did the involvement of the army in shaping the final plan. But it was impressive that such a complicated plan involving many partners could be conceived, designed, and carried out in such a short period of time. Tactical air doctrine would continue to evolve and improve during the Normandy Campaign. While airpower was not decisive in the capture of Cherbourg, it clearly was not a "significant misapplication" of the available resources.

NOTES

1. *Condensed Analysis of the Ninth Air Force in the European Theater of Operations* (1946; repr., Washington, DC: Office of Air Force History, 1984), 23.
2. Wesley Frank Craven and James Lea Cate, eds., *The Army Air Forces in World War II*, vol. 3, *Europe: Argument to V-E Day, January 1944 to May 1945* (Chicago: University of Chicago Press, 1951), 192.
3. Gordon A. Harrison, *Cross-Channel Attack* (1951; repr., Washington, DC: Center of Military History, U.S. Army, 1989), 57.
4. Harrison, *Cross-Channel Attack*, 78.
5. Just after midnight on D-Day, Standartenführer Kurt Meyer, a brigade commander in 12th SS Hitler Youth Division, was warned of the tremendous strength of the Allied invasion force. He dismissively commented: "Little fish! We'll throw them back into the sea." Quoted in Milton Shulman, *Defeat in the West* (London: Secker and Warburg, 1947), 105.

6. Harrison, *Cross-Channel Attack*, 422–26; Omar N. Bradley, *A Soldier's Story* (New York: Henry Holt, 1951), 213–14; Russell F. Weigley, *Eisenhower's Lieutenants: The Campaign of France and Germany, 1944–1945* (Bloomington: Indiana University Press, 1981), 101–3; Carlo D'Este, *Decision in Normandy* (New York: Harper Perennial, 1983), 200–201.
7. German Seventh Army, *Kriegestagebuch* [KTB] 1.1.-30.VI.44 (headquarters war diary), 12 June 1944, quoted in Harrison, *Cross-Channel Attack*, 411.
8. Quoted in William B. Breuer, *Hitler's Fortress Cherbourg: The Conquest of a Bastion* (New York: Stein and Day, 1984), 181.
9. U.S. Third Army under Lieutenant General George S. Patton was activated on 1 August 1944; XIX Air Support Command was active in Normandy before that date. Craven and Cate, *Army Air Forces in World War II*, 3:112–13.
10. AAF Evaluation Board (ETO), "Report on Tactical Air Cooperation, Organization, Methods, and Procedures with Special Emphasis on Phase III Operations," 31 July 1945, 4, U.S. Air Force Historical Research Agency [AFHRA], microfilm roll A1174. See also Alan F. Wilt, "Allied Cooperation in Sicily and Italy, 1943–1945," in *Case Studies in the Development of Close Air Support*, edited by B. F. Cooling (Washington, DC: Office of Air Force History, 1990), 198.
11. "Biographical Notes on Brigadier General E. R. Quesada," 14 November 1943, Headquarters IX Fighter Command, AFHRA, microfilm roll B5838; Craven and Cate, *Army Air Forces in World War II*, 3:112.
12. Weigley, *Eisenhower's Lieutenants*, 103–4.
13. Bradley, *Soldier's Story*, 250.
14. Col. Melon Hall, "Memo on Cherbourg," Headquarters Ninth Air Force, 19 June 1944, AFHRA, microfilm roll B5725.
15. Thomas Alexander Hughes, *Overlord: General Pete Quesada and the Triumph of Tactical Air Power in World War II* (New York: Free Press, 1995), 159.
16. Hughes, *Overlord*, 159–60.
17. Arthur Tedder, *With Prejudice: The War Memoirs of Marshal of the Royal Air Force Lord Tedder, GCB* (London: Cassell, 1966), 554–55.
18. J. Lawton Collins, *Lightning Joe: An Autobiography* (Novato, CA: Presidio, 1994), 218.
19. Craven and Cate, *Army Air Forces in World War II*, 3:199; Hughes, *Overlord*, 161.
20. J. Lawton Collins interview, 1972, interview 3, Senior Officers Oral History Program, U.S. Army Military History Institute, 21; report, "Air Force Operations in Support of Attack on Cherbourg, 22 June thru 30 June 1944," n.d., 1–2, appended to General Brereton to General Arnold, 29 July 1944, AFHRA, microfilm roll B5724.

21. Brig. Gen. R. E. Nugent, "Air Support of the Attack on Cherbourg Peninsula, June 22, 1944," HQ AEAF, 20 July 1944, Ike Skelton Combined Arms Research Library, Call no. N2086, https://cgsc.contentdm.oclc.org/digital/collection/p4013coll8/id/4921/rec/57; "Air Force Operations in Support of Attack on Cherbourg," 2–3.
22. "Air Force Operations in Support of Attack on Cherbourg," 2–3.
23. Harrison, *Cross-Channel Attack*, 428–38.
24. "The Accuracy of Attacks on Small Targets by Fighter-Bombers and R.P. Fighters," Operational Research Section [ORS] (AEAF) Report 16, 10 June 1944, UK National Archives AIR 37/497. See also Mike Bechthold, "Spitfires, Typhoons, and Mustangs: RCAF Fighters in Normandy," *Royal Canadian Air Force Journal* 8, no. 2 (2019): 48–67.
25. Nugent, "Air Support of the Attack on Cherbourg Peninsula," 1–2.
26. The RAF Mustang wings were No. 122 (Nos. 19, 65, and 122 Squadrons) and No. 133 (Nos. 306, 315, and 129 Squadrons); the Typhoon wings were No. 123 (Nos. 198 and 609 Squadrons), No. 124 (No. 181 Squadron), No. 136 (Nos. 164 and 183 Squadrons), and No. 146 (No. 164 Squadron). A British wing was equivalent to an American group. Each formation comprised three squadrons.
27. 2nd Tactical Air Force, Operation Order 188, "Support for VII United States Corps attack on Cherbourg," 0600 hours, 22 June 1944, AFHRA, microfilm roll B5725; M. S. Eddy, "Report of Operation Conducted by Ninth Infantry Division US Army, Cotentin Peninsula France 14 June–1 July 1944," 14 July 1944, 12, Ike Skelton Combined Arms Research Library Digital Library, https://cgsc.contentdm.oclc.org/.
28. Published figures range from a low of five to a high of fourteen aircraft destroyed. Norman L. R. Franks, *Royal Air Force Fighter Command Losses of the Second World War*, vol. 3, *Operational Losses: Aircraft and Crews 1944–1945* (Leicester, UK: Midland, 2000), 56; Craven and Cate, *Army Air Forces in World War II*, 3:200. The high number was probably derived from total British aircraft lost that day, not just those active at Cherbourg. The accepted figure of seven is taken from Christopher Shores and Chris Thomas, *2nd Tactical Air Force*, vol. 1, *Spartan to Normandy, June 1943 to June 1944* (Surrey, UK: Classic, 2004), 175.
29. Craven and Cate, *Army Air Forces in World War II*, 3:200; Shores and Thomas, *2nd Tactical Air Force*, 1:174.
30. Franks, *Royal Air Force Fighter Command Losses*, 3:56; Shores and Thomas, *2nd Tactical Air Force*, 1:174.
31. Nugent, "Air Support of the Attack on Cherbourg Peninsula," 6.
32. "Air Force Operations in Support of Attack on Cherbourg," 2–4; Robert H. George, *Ninth Air Force, April to November 1944*, Army Air Forces Historical Study 36, October 1945, 101–4, AFHRA, microfilm roll K1005.

33. Richard Groh, *The Dynamite Gang: The 367th Fighter Group in World War II* (Fallbrook, CA: Aero, 1983), 122–23.
34. Nugent, "Air Support of the Attack on Cherbourg Peninsula." Collins, *Lightning Joe*, 219; Eddy, "Ninth Division Report of Operation," Annex 5—Division Artillery Reports, 4; "Air Force Operations in Support of Attack on Cherbourg," 7.
35. George, *Ninth Air Force*, 103.
36. "Air Force Operations in Support of Attack on Cherbourg," 3.
37. W. A. Jacobs, "The Battle for France 1944," in Cooling, *Case Studies in the Development of Close Air Support*, 292; Charles Carrington, *Soldier at Bomber Command* (London: Leo Cooper, 1987), 154.
38. Omar Bradley, "The Effects of Strategic and Tactical Air Power on Military Operations, European Theater of Operations," 1945, AFHRA, microfilm roll B5724; Hughes, *Overlord*, 164.
39. Harrison, *Cross-Channel Attack*, 429–30; Eddy, "Ninth Division Report of Operation," 12.
40. "Air Force Operations in Support of Attack on Cherbourg," 4; Nugent, "Air Support of the Attack on Cherbourg Peninsula," 6.
41. Ninth Air Force Commanders' Meeting. 23 June 1944, AFHRA, microfilm roll B5602.
42. Craven and Cate, *Army Air Forces in World War II*, 3:200; "Air Force Operations in Support of Attack on Cherbourg," 4, 7; *Condensed Analysis of the Ninth Air Force*, 23.
43. AC/AS Intelligence, "9th Air Force Operations, 1–30 June 1944, with Special Study of Close Air Support in the Assault on Cherbourg," 27 July 1944, AFHRA, microfilm roll B5725; *Condensed Analysis of the Ninth Air*, 23.
44. German Seventh Army, KTB 1.1.-30.v1.44, 22 June 1944, quoted in Harrison, *Cross-Channel Attack*, 430.
45. Harrison, *Cross-Channel Attack*, 430.
46. "Air Force Operations in Support of Attack on Cherbourg," 6–8; Weigley, *Eisenhower's Lieutenants*, 105.
47. "Air Force Operations in Support of Attack on Cherbourg," 8–10; Headquarters, Ninth Air Force, "Summary of Operations of Ninth Tactical Air Force, June 1944," 7, AFHRA microfilm roll B5861; Eddy, "Ninth Division Report of Operation," 13–15; No. 63 Squadron RAF, Operations Record Book, June 1944, UK National Archives, AIR 27/587/17.
48. Roland G. Ruppenthal, *Utah Beach to Cherbourg* (1947; repr., Washington, DC: Center of Military History, U.S. Army, 1984), 193, 197, 199, 208.
49. "Air Force Operations in Support of Attack on Cherbourg," 5–7.
50. Eddy, "Ninth Division Report of Operation," Annex 2—Lessons Learned from Present Campaign, 1.

51. Ruppenthal, *Utah Beach to Cherbourg*, 172.
52. Headquarters 21 Army Group, "Overlord: Direct Air Support," 23 April 1944, 2, AFHRA, microfilm roll B5725; Jacobs, "Battle for France," 254. This situation would change later in the campaign. For a full discussion of the evolution in air support tactics, see Mike Bechthold, "'The Development of an Unbeatable Combination': US Close Air Support in Normandy," *Canadian Military History* 8, no. 1 (Winter 1999), 7–20.
53. AC/AS Intelligence, "9th Air Force Operations, 1–30 June 1944"; Martin Blumenson, *Breakout and Pursuit* (Washington, DC: Office of the Chief of Military History, 1961), 185–88; Weigley, *Eisenhower's Lieutenants*, 147–50; Craven and Cate, *Army Air Forces in World War II*, 3:228–30. Heavy friendly fire casualties were sustained by American forces in Operation Cobra, but these occurred for other reasons.
54. "Air Force Operations in Support of the Attack on Cherbourg," 5.

9

The Blunted Harpoon

Luftwaffe Antishipping Operations off Normandy, June–August 1944

Russell A. Hart

During the Normandy Campaign, the Luftwaffe undertook determined antishipping operations designed to interdict the Allied invasion of France. Despite its persistent efforts, the Luftwaffe neither stopped the Allied landings nor significantly slowed the subsequent buildup of troops, forces, and supplies ashore. Indeed, the German aircraft only managed to sink or damage a tiny fraction of the Allied warships and merchant vessels committed to Operation Overlord and only minimally delayed the buildup ashore.

This failure reflected the reality that the Luftwaffe was a broken war machine. Ground down by constant attrition and operating under adverse conditions—near-absolute Allied air superiority that necessitated primarily nocturnal operations—it attacked the invasion fleet in highly disadvantageous circumstances. Likewise, the Luftwaffe's specialized antishipping units represented a fraction of its limited aircraft strength, and they, too, had been attritted into ineffectiveness. Moreover, new weapon systems—glide bombs and air-launched missiles introduced in 1943—proved less effective at Normandy as the Allies developed effective countermeasures. New weapons, such as the Mistletoe composite aircraft, proved to be too little, too late. Consequently, the Luftwaffe inflicted negligible damage on the invasion fleet. Its most effective weapon proved to be air-dropped mines, which, while sinking or damaging only a few vessels, nonetheless compelled the Allies to divert considerable resources to minesweeping operations.

What follows is a brief overview of Luftwaffe antishipping operations off Normandy during summer 1944. These attacks were undertaken with five types of ordnance—conventional bombs, air-launched torpedoes, glide bombs, air-dropped mines, and Mistletoe composite glide bombers. The efficacy of each of these weapons is explored and assessed.

On 1 June 1944 Luftflotte III (Third Air Fleet) in the West disposed 815 aircraft, of which only 319 were operational.[1] This low readiness rate was the product of constant attrition while defending in multiple theaters. The "Baby Blitz," the raids on the British Isles during the spring of 1944 that cost at least 524 aircraft, accelerated this decline in operational readiness.[2] On D-Day the bombers of Luftflotte III were concentrated in two major subcommands. The IX Fliegerkorps (Ninth Flying Corps), based in northern France, Belgium, and the Netherlands, deployed one ground-attack wing (*schlachtgeschwader*) of Focke-Wulf Fw 190 fighter-bomber and ground-attack aircraft as well as two bomber wings (*kampfgeschwadern*) comprising nine bomber groups (*kampfgruppen*) and totaling sixty-seven operational Junkers Ju 88 medium bombers. The X Fliegerkorps (Tenth Flying Corps) in southern and western France had elements of three bomber wings (totaling five groups) tasked for antishipping operations in the Atlantic Ocean and Mediterranean Sea and a third wing dedicated to maritime reconnaissance. In total, the Luftwaffe's bomber force in the West comprised elements of six bomber wings (totaling eleven groups and thirty-two squadrons), three autonomous groups (with six squadrons), and four autonomous squadrons, a grand total of fourteen groups and forty-seven squadrons (see table 9-1).[3] Thus, on D-Day Luftflotte III deployed approximately 422 bombers in the West.[4]

Yet this total was misleading. Five groups were reequipping or reconstituting and were therefore only partially operational on D-Day. The Luftflotte III

Table 9-1 • Luftwaffe Bomber Forces in Western Europe, 1 June 1944

Unit	Location	Aircraft	Quantity by Type
Kampfgeschwader 6 HQ	Melsbroek	1	Ju 88 A14
1st Group (1st, 2nd, 3rd Squadrons)	Brétigny	22	Ju 188 A2
2nd Group (4th, 5th, 6th Squadrons)	Melun–Villaroche	3	Ju 88 A4
3rd Group (7th, 8th, 9th Squadrons)	Melsbroek	25	Ju 188 A2
Total (9 squadrons)	total aircraft:	51	3 x Ju 88 A4, 1 x A14; 25 x Ju 188 A2
Kampfgeschwader 26 HQ	Montpellier	0	Ju 88 A17
2nd Group (4th, 5th, 6th Squadrons)	Valence	41	Ju 88 A17
3rd Group (7th–9th Squadrons)	Montpellier	35	8 x Ju 88 A4(LT), 27 x A17
Total (6 squadrons)	total aircraft:	76	8 x Ju 88 A4(LT), 69 x A17
Kampfgeschwader 40 HQ	Bordeaux–Mérignac	0	He 177A
1st Group (1st, 2nd Squadrons)	Orléans–Bricy	43	4 x He 177 A3, 23 x A5; 7 x Fw 200 C4, 5 x C8, 1 x C6, 3 x C3
2nd Group (4th, 5th, 6th Squadrons)	Bordeaux–Mérignac	32	1 x He 177 A3, 31 x A5
3rd Group (7th, 8th, 9th Squadrons)	Cognac	29	15 x Fw 200 C4, 9 x C8, 2 x C3; 3 x C6
Total (8 squadrons)	total aircraft:	104	4 x He 177 A3, 23 x A5; 1 x Fw 200 C3, 7 x C4, 1 x C6, 5 x C8
2nd Group, KG 51 (4th, 5th, 6th Squadrons)	Gilze–Rijen	24	Me 410 A1/U2
1st Group, KG 66 (1st, 2nd Squadrons)	Avord	31	22 x Ju 188 E1, 9 Ju 88 S1w
4th Squadron/KG 66	St. André	c.5	Ju 188 E1 (4th–6th Squadrons totaled 15 aircraft)
6th Squadron/KG 66 (arrived 5 June)	Montdidier	c.5	Ju 188 E1 (4th–6th Squadrons totaled 15 aircraft)
4th & 6th Squadrons, KG 76	Istres	16	Ju 88 A4
Kampfgeschwader 77 HQ	Orange–Caritat	1	Ju 88 A17
1st Group (1st, 2nd, 3rd Squadrons)	Orange–Caritat	28	Ju 88 A17
3rd Group (7th, 8th, 9th Squadrons)	Orange–Caritat	25	Ju 88 A17
Total (6 squadrons)	total aircraft:	54	54 x Ju 88 A17
Kampfgeschwader 100 HQ	Toulouse–Francazal	4	1 x He 177 A5, 2 x Do 217 E5, 1 x K3
3rd Group (7th, 8th, 9th Squadrons)	Toulouse–Francazal	1	6 x Do 217 K2, 16 x K3, 5 x M1, 1 x E4, 3 x E5
Total (3 squadrons)	total aircraft:	35	
2nd Group, Lehrgeschwader 1 (3 Sdrns)	Villafranca	1	Ju 88 A4
Intervention Squadron KG 101	St. Dizier	0	Mistletoe composites
Grand Total: 6 wings, 14 groups, 47 squadrons			
Total bombers in France, Belgium, & the Netherlands, 6 June 1944		c.422	bombers and fast bombers

Source: Adapted from "Flugzeugbestand und Bewegungsmeldungen, 3.42–12.44," Michael Holm, *The Luftwaffe, 1933–1945*, last updated 20 March 2023, https://www.ww2.dk/oob/bestand/kampf/bkampf.htm.

Photo 9-1 • This aerial photo of the Mulberry harbor and anchorage off Omaha Beach provides an indication of the enticing targets the Allied vessels presented to the Luftwaffe. Note the airfield on shore, U.S. Emergency Landing Ground E-1/Advanced Landing Ground A-21. Construction started on 7 June while the engineers were still under fire. It became partially operational on 8 June and was fully opened by the next day. *U.S. Air Force Photo 72990AC*

official strength returns of 1 June list 469 bombers on strength, of which 224 were operational.[5] These figures overstate actual strength since various subunits allocated to Luftflotte III were reconstituting in the Reich. An analysis of bomber-unit strength returns deployed in Western Europe (see table 9-1) indicates that on D-Day, Luftflotte III possessed about 422 bombers, of which approximately 190 were operational.

Most of these available aircraft were conventional bombers with crews trained for land-based missions. The Luftwaffe's dedicated antishipping units were all based in southwestern France, where they could be committed to Mediterranean, Atlantic, or English Channel operations. The flying corps deployed in southwestern France primarily conducted antishipping operations in the Atlantic and western Mediterranean. It deployed one bomber wing (*geschwader*) and two groups (*gruppen*) that included Heinkel He 177 heavy bombers, as well as Ju 88, Junkers Ju 188, and Dornier Do 217 medium bombers. The 2. Flieger Division (2nd Flying Division), subordinated to X Fliegerkorps, operated two antishipping torpedo wings (*Torpedogeschwadern*) in southern France fielding medium bombers equipped to drop aerial torpedoes.[6] These were the backbone of German antishipping forces in the West.

While these forces were meager, the OKL (Luftwaffe high command) had developed plans to reinforce its western defenses, given an Allied invasion. During 6–10 June, ninety medium bombers transferred from Italy and the Reich, and forty-five torpedo bombers redeployed from southern to northern France.[7] Consequently, maximum bomber strength in the West was achieved on 8 June with 392 bombers. This number steadily declined as attrition outstripped replacements.[8] Indeed, the Luftwaffe's bomber forces suffered catastrophic losses in Normandy: during June, at least 313 bombers were lost, written off, or so badly damaged that they required factory overhaul.[9] This represented 80 percent of the bombers in the West on D-Day. Meanwhile, only 83 bombers arrived up to 7 July with reinforcing units (see table 9-2).[10]

So, the total number of German bombers deployed in combat units in the West during the Normandy Campaign ranged between 603 and 708 aircraft. In addition, 1,002 known replacements were received by these units between June and August 1944, though this total includes at least 389 internal transfers, as withdrawing units handed over their remaining aircraft to other squadrons.[11] Thus, at least 613 replacement bombers were dispatched to the West. Therefore, a minimum of 1,226 Luftwaffe bombers were committed to defend Western Europe during the summer of 1944.

Luftflotte III reported the operational loss of 224 bombers in June.[12] This figure significantly understated total losses because it excluded planes destroyed or written off on the ground due to strafing attacks or accidents as well as a substantial number so severely damaged that they required factory overhaul. In reality, Luftflotte III lost at least 313 bombers during June 1944

Table 9-2 • Luftwaffe Bomber Unit Reinforcements, June–August 1944

Unit	Date	From	To	Aircraft	Quantity by Type
HQ & 1st Group/KG 54	6 June	Germany	Juvincourt	14	14 Ju 88 A4 (received 25 replacements in June)
HQ & 1st–3rd Groups/KG 2	7 June	Germany	Courvon	26+	12 x Ju 188 A2, 7 x E1; 1 x Do 217 K1, 6 x M3
5th Squadron/KG 76	10 June	Italy	Montdidier	7	Ju 88 A4
HQ & 1st Group/LG 1	10 June	Italy	Le Culot	22	22 x Ju 88 A4 (received 22 replacements in July)
3rd Squadron/KG 66	26 June	Germany	Montdidier	c5	Ju 88 E1
9th Squadron/KG 3	28 June	Germany	Eindhoven	c2	1 x He 111 H6, 1 x H11
5th Squadron/KG 66	30 June	Germany	Montdidier	>16	Ju 188 E1 (includes 4th squadron already in West)
HQ & 1st Group/KG 30	10 July	Germany	Le Culot	25	25 x Ju 88 S3
3rd Group/KG 30	18 July	Germany	Couvron	3	Ju 88 S3 (received 39 replacements in July)
Einsatz Kommando Schenk	20 July	Germany	Châteaudun	9	Me 262 A2a jet fighter-bombers
HQ Kampfgeschwader 53	15 Aug.	Germany	Toul	1	He 111 H6
2nd Group/KG 53	17 Aug.	Germany	Le Bourget	30	1 x He 111 H16, 29 x H20
3rd Group/KG 53	17 Aug.	Germany	Toul	33	He 111 H16
1st Group/KG 53	21 Aug.	Germany	Nancy	25	20 x He 111 H16, 5 x H20 (plus 21 replacements)

Total: 5 wing HQs, 10 groups, 5 autonomous squadrons, totaling 35 squadrons. A total of 218–323 aircraft reinforced the West as part of redeployed whole combat units. Official figures list 173 aircraft transferred with their units, thus up to an additional 150 aircraft arrived as reinforcements.

Source: Adapted from "Flugzeugbestand und Bewegungsmeldungen, 3.42–12.44," Michael Holm, *The Luftwaffe, 1933–1945*, last updated 20 March 2023, https://www.ww2.dk/oob/bestand/kampf/bkampf.htm.

from all causes.[13] Moreover, the deteriorating combat situation in Normandy increasingly forced its bombers to support the ground battle from late July.[14] The Allied breakout in Normandy saw ground support missions predominate and antishipping strikes dwindle. In the interim the Luftwaffe's bomber arm failed abjectly to halt the invasion, to slow the Allied buildup, or to divert significant Allied resources from the ground campaign. The ensuing discussion explains the Luftwaffe's failure via an analysis of its weapon systems employed in antishipping operations.

Advanced Weapon Systems—Glide Bombs

The Luftwaffe placed high hopes on two recent advanced weapon systems—the HS 293 rocket-propelled glide bomb and the Fritz-X radar-guided glide bomb—as the mainstay of their ship-killing capabilities. These weapon systems had inflicted significant casualties, particularly during the Salerno and Anzio landings in Sicily and Italy. During 1943–44, the Luftwaffe's specialized glide-bomb unit, the 100th Bomber Wing (KG 100), averaged one hit per seven sorties, one ship damaged per nine sorties, and one ship sunk per eighteen sorties.[15] The pinnacle of this success was the sinking of the capitulating Italian battleship *Roma*, with the loss of almost 1,400 crew, on 9 September 1943 by two Fritz-X glide bombs.[16] Consequently, the Germans expected these advanced weapons to wreak havoc on the Allied invasion fleet off Normandy. But the Allies had recognized the threat these weapons posed and developed extensive countermeasures to neutralize the German glide-bomb threat in the Bay of the Seine during the summer of 1944.

Advanced Glide Bombs—HS 293

The Luftwaffe attached great faith in the HS 293's ability to cripple the Allied invasion fleet. The glide bomb could be launched from three platforms: the He 177 heavy bomber, the Focke-Wulf Fw 200 Condor long-range reconnaissance aircraft, and the Do 217 medium bomber. On D-Day elements of four Luftwaffe wings in the West possessed HS 293 launch-capable aircraft. In the 40th Bomber Wing (KG 40), the 1st and 2nd Groups (I/KG 40 and II/KG 40) deployed five squadrons with thirty-seven operational He 177s, including thirty-three upgraded A5 models that could carry three HS 293s.[17] The 3rd Group (III/KG 40) deployed HS 293–capable Fw 200s, but only one was operational. The Condors were old, complex, slow, and out of production. They were brittle and required extensive maintenance. KG 40 also continued its traditional Atlantic maritime antishipping missions in addition to Channel operations. Consequently, the group flew rare missions, with few Condors over the Channel. In addition, the 3rd Group of KG 100 (III/KG 100) deployed thirty-one HS 293–capable Do 217 medium bombers, of which thirteen were operational.[18] On D-Day KG 40 had thirty-eight He 177 heavy bombers and forty-five Fw 200 Condors, totaling eighty-three aircraft.[19] In total, the specialized antishipping units in the West on D-Day possessed 114 HS 293–capable bombers, of which 51 were operational.[20]

Reichsmarschall Hermann Göring labeled KG 40 as the "spearhead of the anti-invasion force," but the bomber wing faced great difficulties.[21] Prior to D-Day, Luftflotte III planned for nocturnal missions: its officers had concluded that daylight glide-bomb missions would be suicidal. Dusk missions, the preferred attack method, were impractical because this required a daylight approach through Allied-dominated skies. This left night attacks as the only viable option.[22] Unfortunately, the Luftwaffe had only ever flown ten previous night missions, all with disappointing results.[23] Nocturnal vectoring against blacked-out targets was problematic. Target acquisition (due to the lack of pathfinders) was difficult, and guiding the weapon after launch at night was equally challenging. Moreover, over two hundred Allied warships provided an unprecedented antiaircraft defense in depth in conjunction with layers of day and night fighters, now forward based at Normandy airfields. Thus, merely penetrating the Allied naval and aerial defensive screens was difficult for Luftwaffe bombers. In addition, the Germans met unprecedented new electronic countermeasures, including CXGE jamming, that significantly neutralized the HS 293 guidance capability.[24] Therefore, Luftwaffe antishipping units were forced to press glide-bomb attacks in the face of insurmountable odds.

KG 40 HS 293 Glide Bomber Operations in Normandy

On D-Day I/KG 40, comprising the 1st and 2nd Squadrons, was based at Orléans–Bricy under X Fliegerkorps and engaged in Atlantic and Mediterranean antishipping operations. To enhance its ability to strike shipping in the Channel, the group moved on 18 June to Toulouse–Bagnac and transferred to the dedicated antishipping IX Fliegerkorps. Here it remained until 12 July, when it was withdrawn. The II/KG 40 was based at Bordeaux–Merignac, also under X Fliegerkorps. The III/KG 40 with its Condors was based at Cognac. This group, however, was slated to return to the Reich for conversion training. The Condor's incredibly low operational readiness reflected that it was out of production, that only 276 were ever built, and that the complex aircraft were worn out by extensive long-range maritime operations. In addition, III/KG 40 operated four Condor variants.[25] Most of its Condors were fitted out for maritime reconnaissance, and only a few upgraded C4s and late production C8s had modern antiship radars (Rostock or FuW 200 Hohentwiel sets). Thus, very few of its Fw 200s were equipped for antishipping strikes with the HS 293.

Moreover, the Condor had not proven very effective when it could employ the HS 293: the Do 217 and He 177 were the preferred launch platforms. Consequently, the number of Condor sorties against the invasion fleet was limited. Even then, losses were high: during June, III/KG 40 lost eight Condors.[26] Thus, it launched few HS 293 antishipping attacks in the Channel, focusing these against Atlantic convoys in the Bay of Biscay and in the western Mediterranean.[27] Instead, it undertook mainly conventional bomb attacks against the Allied invasion and support fleet. The Condor's growing obsolescence, dwindling numbers, and appalling operational-readiness rates ensured its increasing transition to a transportation role during the summer. Moreover, the German evacuation of the western Atlantic coast in mid-August compelled III/KG 40 to abandon its base at Bordeaux, effectively ending its maritime antishipping operations. Overall, the group's contribution to the anti-invasion efforts was negligible.

HS 293 Glide Bomb Missions in Normandy

On the night of 6–7 June, twenty-six He 177s of KG 40 sortied from Orléans–Bricy and Bordeaux–Merignac and arrived at dusk over the Channel.[28] The raid was detected by radar-equipped ships, then intercepted by Mosquito night fighters, leading to what became known as the "Slaughter of the Heinkels."[29] At least six He 177s were lost.[30] Most glide bombs were jammed and no hits were achieved.[31] The following night, III/KG 40's Fw 200 Condors joined the remaining He 177.[32] Once again, night fighters pounced on the He 177 heavy bombers, and KG 40 lost an additional 2–3 aircraft that night.[33] Then early on 8 June, the destroyer USS *Meredith* was likely struck by an HS 293 glide bomb and badly damaged; taken under tow, she was sunk by conventional bombs the next day.[34] This represented the zenith of HS 293 success in Normandy. Also, on the night of 8–9 June, the Do 217s of III/KG

100 joined the attack, near missing the headquarters ship HMS *Bululo* but losing two of the nine Dorniers committed.[35]

During the night of 10–11 June, III/KG 100 attacked anew, striking shipping off Barfleur. Two Liberty ships were hit—the SS *Charles Morgan* was sunk and the SS *William N. Pendleton* damaged—for the loss of two Do 217s.[36] That same night KG 40 also attacked, losing five aircraft but so badly damaging the SS *Fort McPherson* that it required dockyard repair.[37] On the night of 12–13 June, the destroyer HMS *Boadicea* was sunk, possibly by a conventional-torpedo hit from a Ju 88 but possibly by an HS 293 from III/KG 100.[38] KG 40 lost two more aircraft that night.[39] If *Boadicea* was sunk by an HS 293, it represented the last operational success for the glide-bomb units in Normandy.

The large, slow, and cumbersome He 177 bomber proved vulnerable to Allied countermeasures, and KG 40 suffered catastrophic losses during June. I/KG 40 lost two A3 models and sixteen A5 models (50 percent and 70 percent respectively of the group's D-Day strength in these variants).[40] II/KG 40 suffered severe losses too: of its thirty-two aircraft on 1 June, no less than twenty-five were lost, so badly damaged to require factory overhaul, or were written off.[41] That represented 78 percent of the group's D-Day strength. Indeed, II/KG 40 averaged four aircraft lost in each of its six missions conducted during the month.[42] These losses were unsustainable and effectively destroyed KG 40. The meager return of shipping sunk and damaged could not justify the loss of bombers and aircrews. Consequently, in early July the shattered groups were relocated to Norway for reconstitution.[43] Never again would the He 177A be deployed against shipping in the West.

III/KG 100 likewise suffered heavy losses. Of the thirty-one Do 217s the group possessed on 1 June, twenty-three were lost, written off, or sent for factory repair during June, a 74-percent attrition rate.[44] Moreover, it had few of the HS 293–capable E5 version. Thus, the group's glide-bomb attacks dwindled as it continued to suffer heavy losses—twelve Do 217s in July (including two E5s) and fifteen in August. Sustained attrition eventually compelled the disbandment of its 9th Squadron. Consequently, only sixty-four HS 293 missions were launched in July, mostly by III/KG 100.[45] These attacks against the invasion fleet ceased in mid-August, when the group evacuated to Bavaria after its Toulouse base was threatened by the Operation Dragoon landings in southern France.

Advanced Glide Bombs—Ruhrstahl PC 1400 FX "Fritz-X"

The Luftwaffe deployed a second advanced glide bomb, the PC 1400 "Fritz-X." A modified cylindrical PC 1400 1,400-kg (3,090-pound) "Fritz" armor-piercing (AP) bomb, it was a radio-controlled glide bomb that posed a potent threat to capital ships. It was dropped close to a target from high altitude (typically 6,000 meters [20,000 feet]) and guided by radio onto the vessel. But to steer the ordnance, the launching aircraft had to fly slow, straight, and level, making it vulnerable to attack; destruction of the launch plane ended control of the bomb.[46] This glide bomb had proved its potency at Salerno, Italy, where two Fritz-X strikes sank the Italian battleship *Roma*.[47]

The number of planes capable of launching the Fritz-X in the West, however, was much more limited than for the HS 293. There was only a single dedicated Fritz-X unit: III/KG 100. It was equipped with Fritz-X launch-capable Do 217 E5s, K3s, and M11s. But the glide bomb's employment was constrained by its limited production and stockpile in France. Indeed, in November 1943 the Luftwaffe possessed only 373 Fritz-X glide bombs.[48] This limited supply ensured that III/KG 100 primarily relied upon the HS 293. Several Fritz-X-armed Do 217 K3s operated in the Bay of the Seine on 8 June, and the frigate HMS *Lawford* was possibly sunk by one.[49] In total in June the group lost fifteen Fritz-X bombers.[50]

As a consequence of dwindling planes, aircrews, fuel, and ordnance, III/KG 100 dropped only fourteen Fritz-X glide bombs during July.[51] On the night of 4–5 July, six Fritz-X carrying Do 217s sortied, scoring a near miss on the patrol boat *PC 617* but losing three aircraft.[52] Another Fritz-X mission was launched in the Channel on 7 July, but thereafter attrition and shortages forced abandonment of Channel Fritz-X attacks.[53] Nonetheless, such missions continued in the Bay of Biscay, where a freighter was struck on 11 August.[54] In early August the group was also committed to tactical air support missions and launched multiple sorties against the captured bridges at Pontabault, Avranches, and Pontorson during the U.S. breakout. These attacks were to no avail, and three Do 217s were lost.[55] The group's final missions occurred after 15 August in response to the Allied invasion of southern France. Nine Do 217s, two of which carried the Fritz-X, attacked that day.[56] Renewed strikes occurred on 17 August with five planes, several carrying the Fritz-X.[57] The group managed to sink the *LST 282*.[58] On 18 August III/KG 100 withdrew to Germany, where it was amalgamated into a single squadron.[59] This ended the Luftwaffe's glide-bomb attacks against Allied shipping.[60]

Conventional Torpedo Attacks

The Luftwaffe conducted primarily conventional torpedo attacks. It developed ten aerial torpedoes during the Second World War. Most commonly used in Normandy was the Lufttorpedo (LT) 5, which was released from fifty meters (150 feet) by an aircraft flying at 300 kmh (180 mph).[61] The primary German torpedo aircraft was the Heinkel He 111 H6, which was being phased out by June 1944, and few He 111s therefore flew over Normandy.[62] But most of those deployed against the Allied invasion fleet were either a few of the older Ju 88 A4 "Luft Torp" (LT) torpedo bombers or more of the newer A17 models, which could carry two underwing torpedoes versus the single ventral torpedo carried by the A4 and the He 111 H6. The southern France–based 2. Flieger Division undertook most torpedo attacks with the dedicated antishipping torpedo groups (II and III) of KG 26. These were reinforced by two groups of KG 77 that had converted to torpedo bombing during the spring of 1944. On 1 June the II/KG 26 and III/KG 26 numbered seventy-seven Ju 88s (eight A4s and sixty-nine A17s) while II/KG 77 and III/KG 77 had fifty-four Ju 88 A17s. Yet of these 131 aircraft, only 44 were operational.[63]

After D-Day these four torpedo-bomber groups remained in southern France so they could continue western Atlantic and western Mediterranean attack missions simultaneously. For attacks in the Channel, the groups' aircraft refueled at intermediate airfields near Chalon-sur-Saône, Dijon, and Fécamp. This made for lengthy nocturnal approach and return flights, which increased accident rates. In addition, III/KG 26 had begun transitioning to conventional bombing, but many of its aircraft remained outfitted for torpedo missions.

The groups' deployment in southern France was one major operational limitation. Others included high attrition and the concomitant inexperience of most crews. In addition, the units suffered from a significant torpedo shortage that constrained operations.[64] As the campaign progressed, mounting fuel shortages further limited missions. Thus, on average, torpedo bombers flew one sortie a week with approximately forty operational aircraft.[65]

In total the Luftwaffe flew 1,683 bomber sorties in the week following the Normandy landings.[66] These included at least four major nocturnal torpedo missions.[67] During June, KG 26 lost twelve pilots killed or missing, while KG 77 lost at least five torpedo bombers.[68] To ease attrition, II/KG 26 moved to Valence and Montpellier to more easily strike the Channel. Early on 13 June, ninety-one Ju 88 torpedo aircraft from the two wings attacked a convoy off Portland Bill. Indeed, that night the Germans flew 131 antishipping missions, and torpedo bombers likely torpedoed and sank the destroyer HMS *Boadicea*, their most significant sinking of the campaign.[69] On 18 June sixty-nine torpedo-bomber sorties were flown, and KG 26 sunk the munitions ship SS *Albert C. Field*.[70] In aggregate during June, the Luftwaffe flew 384 torpedo-bomber sorties.[71]

Both torpedo-bomber wings suffered heavily during June, losing fifty-nine aircraft, half their D-Day strength; KG 26 lost thirty-four aircraft, and KG 77 lost twenty-five.[72] German conventional torpedo-bomber strength had fallen to ninety-four aircraft by 1 July. As a result, torpedo-bombing operations waned during July as losses continued to mount and torpedo stockpiles dwindled. *Fighter Direction Tender 216* was sunk off Barfleur by an aerial torpedo on 7 July.[73]

Known July missions occurred on 17–18 July, 26–27 July, 28–29 July, and 31 July–1 August.[74] In August missions were flown on 3–4 and 6–7 August.[75] The Operation Dragoon landings on 15 August diverted KG 26 to operations in southern France, ending torpedo attacks in the English Channel. With their bases threatened, the remaining conventional torpedo-bomber units withdrew in late August to Germany for reconstitution.[76]

The losses the two wings suffered were crippling. KG 26 lost 103 percent of its D-Day strength.[77] Its two groups flew at least thirteen missions over the invasion fleet and lost at least sixty-nine pilots, an average of five pilots permission.[78] The Luftwaffe's veteran torpedo-bomber wing was decimated in Normandy and would never recover. Air-launched torpedoes had to be dropped at low speed from low altitude, which made the attacking aircraft vulnerable. Losses, even during nocturnal attacks, were high. Darkness mitigated some challenges but exacerbated the difficulties of target acquisition. Allied aerial and maritime mastery significantly diminished the efficacy of the Luftwaffe's attacks. German torpedoes lacked any homing capacity that could have allowed their blind dropping and left a highly visible wake that allowed ships to take evasive action.[79]

Specialized Torpedo-Bombing Units: Circling Torpedo-Bomber Units

An uncommon torpedo was the LTS 350 circling torpedo, which was dropped near the target, then circled to acquire it. The LTS 350 was a small, 350-kg, parachute-dropped Italian torpedo adopted after Italy's capitulation in September 1943, but it remained in extremely limited production. Its ability to circle made it easier for LTS 350–equipped units to blind drop them, which increased plane survivability and prospects of a successful strike. But it was only available in limited numbers.[80]

The Luftwaffe's sole torpedo-bomber unit that employed the LTS 350 was KG 54. It flew Ju 88A aircraft fitted with special drop racks modified to launch the LTS 350. Nominally allocated to IX Fliegerkorps, the wing was replenishing in Germany on 6 June. Immediately after D-Day, headquarters and I/KG 54 moved west. Wing headquarters moved to Eindhoven in the Netherlands and I/KG 54 redeployed to Juvincourt in northern France with at least fourteen Ju 88 A4s.[81] III/KG 54 subsequently followed to Juvincourt after reconstituting.

The wing immediately launched antishipping operations in the Channel, dropping circling torpedoes, bomb-mines (BM 1000), and 1,000-kg PC 1000 conventional bombs. During its first five days, KG 54 lost at least twenty-three aircraft.[82] This unsustainable attrition continued, and by 1 July, it had lost forty-eight aircraft.[83] During July, KG 54 lost forty-four more aircraft and an additional thirty-eight in August.[84] Shattered, the wing was withdrawn to Germany in late August.

Little information has survived about individual KG 54 missions. Given the limited supply of LTS 350 torpedoes and the wing's delivery of multiple ordnance packages, circling-torpedo attacks were uncommon. On 17 June

KG 54 torpedo bombers, each heavily laden with two BM 1000 mines and three LT 350 circling torpedoes, operated in the Bay of the Seine.[85] On 30 June–1 July, KG 54 Ju-88s, each equipped with three LT 350 circling torpedoes, again attacked shipping off Normandy but without success.[86] Moreover, the rising threat posed by Allied tactical aviation compelled the wing to move to safer bases: I/KG 54 went to Orléans–Bricy on 26 June, and then both it and III/KG 54 moved on 10 July to Eindhoven.

On the night of 3–4 August, the wing again launched bomb-mine and circling torpedoes against Channel shipping but scored no hits and lost four aircraft.[87] As the Allies broke out from Normandy, circling-torpedo missions tapered off. Moreover, it is unclear if any Allied vessels were sunk or even damaged by LTS 350s. Allied intelligence believed, however, that the circling torpedoes had damaged the cruiser HMS *Frobisher* and the repair ship HMS *Albatross* on 18 July, but these may have been launched by E-boats that deployed a naval-variant circling torpedo.[88] Two destroyers were also possibly hit by Luftwaffe air-dropped LTS 350s.[89] Flying the older, slower Ju 88 A4 and carrying very heavy combined loads of mines and circling torpedoes, KG 54 aircraft were very vulnerable to Allied countermeasures and suffered unsustainable losses. The wing lost at least 102 aircraft during the Normandy Campaign, an almost 400-percent turnover rate in three months.[90] KG 54 was destroyed as a combat-capable command. On 22 August the wing withdrew to Germany and never dropped circling torpedoes again. Thus, the Normandy Campaign proved the death knell of the Luftwaffe's specialized circling-torpedo bomber force.

Most German bombers in the West were conventional day bombers trained to attack ground targets. Naturally, this conventional bomber force primarily attacked the Allied beachhead. But they were also pressed into night-time bombing of the invasion fleet. Conventional bombing was inherently inferior to attacks with torpedoes and other advanced antishipping weapons. Moreover, bomb strikes on shipping had invariably been conducted during daylight. In Normandy the Luftwaffe undertook nocturnal raids arrayed against a massive defensive night-fighter shield and heavy fleet antiaircraft fire. In addition, the paucity of pathfinders made it difficult to locate blacked-out Allied vessels. Thus, green Luftwaffe bomber crews faced enormous obstacles carrying out a novel mission. Their best prospects of success occurred with a nocturnal approach to the target area followed by dawn attacks, but these risked daylight Allied interception and destruction on the return leg. Consequently, Luftwaffe losses in conventional-bombing attacks were high.

It is difficult to identify which bomber units participated in antishipping attacks because they were lumped together with other such raids in official reports. At best we can partially deduce the extent of antishipping strikes by conventional bombers. Ju 88s of KG 6 did sink the USS *Meredith* on 9 June. The destroyer, damaged the previous day and under tow, was nearly missed by several 1,000-kg bombs, whose concussive effects ruptured its hull and caused it to sink.[91]

Conventional bombers used an array of ordnance. The Luftwaffe fielded ten high-explosive (HE) bombs, eight AP bombs, three AP cluster bombs, and four semi-AP fragmentation bombs.[92] Additionally, it developed three specialized unguided, cylindrical, rocket-propelled AP bombs appropriate for antishipping operations. These were the PC 500Rs, the PC 1000Rs, and the PC 1800Rs, respectively with 14-kg (31-pound), 54-kg (119-pound), and 360-kg (794-pound) HE warheads.[93]

Limited stockpiles of the larger HE and AP bombs restricted conventional operations. Nonetheless, during June, Luftwaffe medium bombers flew over 3,000 sorties. Indeed, between 6 and 12 June, the Germans flew 1,683 bomber sorties, most of which were conventional bombing missions.[94] These attacks sunk or damaged several Allied ships. On 7 June the headquarters ship HMS *Bulolo* was damaged by a bomb strike, while a direct hit sank the frigate HMS *Lawford* the following day.[95] On 10 June the Liberty ship SS *Charles Morgan* was sunk by a conventional bomb just off Utah Beach.[96]

Among the reinforcements sent west were KG 30 headquarters, I/KG 30, and II/KG 30, which arrived at Le Culot and Couvron over 10–18 July with twenty-eight Ju 88 S3 aircraft.[97] This was the latest Ju 88 variant with improved speed, and they, too, were committed to nocturnal bombing attacks. The two groups lost fifty-five aircraft in July and a further forty-one bombers the following month. The decimated groups were subsequently withdrawn and returned to Germany to convert to fighters.[98] The complete destruction of a wing equipped with Germany's most-advanced Ju 88 model encapsulates the complete eclipse of the Luftwaffe bomber force in Normandy.

To augment antishipping capabilities, the Luftwaffe dispatched additional and heavier bombs to western bomber units, including the PC 1400 (1,400 kilograms) and PC 1800 (1,800 kilograms).[99] The Germans also extensively dropped the 1,000-kg bomb-mine (BM 1000), a dual-purpose weapon that doubled as a mine if it did not strike a target directly. During the last two weeks of June, the Luftwaffe dropped 971 BM 1000s against shipping in the Bay of the Seine.[100] During July, however, bombing missions tapered off significantly to 480 sorties, during which 171 torpedoes, sixty-four HS 293 glide bombs, and fourteen Fritz-X glide bombs were launched, indicating that around 200 conventional-bomb missions were flown.[101] Conventional bombs did sink the antisubmarine-warfare trawler HMS *Lord Wakefield* on 29 July off Omaha Beach.[102] Apart from that, confirmed conventional-bomb hits were meager. Ships damaged by bombs include the frigate HMCS *Matane* on 20 July and two small craft on 26 July.[103] Conventional bomber successes dwindled to next to nothing in August, and by the end of that month, the bomber units had been pulled back to the Netherlands and Germany for reconstitution.

Mine-Laying Operations

The most effective Luftwaffe antishipping weapon during the Normandy Campaign was the aerial mine. Mines sank and damaged a limited number of Allied ships, but when combined with maritime minelaying by E-boats, the threat they posed compelled substantial diversion of resources to minesweeping and other mine countermeasures. Indeed, protection of the invasion fleet consumed all Allied maritime minesweeping assets and left other sectors bereft during the summer of 1944.

The Luftwaffe had two parachute-dropped modified sea mines in its inventory, the 500-kg Landmine A (LMA) and the 1,000-kg Landmine B (LMB), which sank to the seabed and were detonated by proximity magnetic-acoustic detonators. In addition, the Luftwaffe possessed bomb-mines, airdropped without parachutes, particularly the 1,000-kg BM 1000.[104] The primary aircraft adapted to drop mines were He 111 and Ju 88 medium bombers. IX

Fliegerkorps had sixty-seven Ju 88s operational on D-Day; when they were not committed to bomb or torpedo attacks, they were used for nocturnal minelaying operations.

During the spring of 1944, Luftflotte III had begun airdrop operations to reinforce the defensive minefields in the English Channel.[105] After D-Day it resumed these minelaying missions. During June, IX Fliegerkorps aircraft flew 954 minelaying sorties and dropped 971 BM-1000 and 1,035 LMB mines in the Bay of the Seine.[106] From 6 to 15 June, mines sunk nine warships and seventeen merchant vessels and damaged others.[107] During the second half of June, an additional 971 BLM 1000 and 614 LMB were dropped.[108] In all, seventeen Allied merchant vessels totaling 80,024 gross register tonnage (GRT) were sunk in June.[109] If one includes landing craft, the Allies lost forty-three ships to mines up to 3 July.[110]

Minelaying operations were conducted in adverse circumstances: nocturnal blind dropping, while running the gauntlet of Allied fighter defenses. Aerial reconnaissance was almost nonexistent. Aircraft staged from southern France and refueled at intermediate bases in the Paris–Angers–Tours area. It is impossible to differentiate vessels sunk by air-laid mines and sea mines (laid primarily by E-boats) since both services deployed near-identical ordnance. Nonetheless, they proved the Luftwaffe's most deadly antishipping weapon. The Luftwaffe was initially slow to recognize this, as minelaying remained secondary to priority direct attacks with missiles, glide bombs, torpedoes, and conventional bombs.

As the Allies began operating day- and night-fighter squadrons from forward bases in Normandy, the obstacles facing Luftwaffe antishipping operations escalated along with losses. Thus, by early July, Luftflotte III had concluded that aerial mining represented its most efficient and economical antishipping operations, and shifted assets toward these missions.[111] The change presented several challenges to the Luftwaffe: first, relatively few aerial mines were available in the West, and these were stored at depots far away from operational airfields. This problem was alleviated when the Luftwaffe organized special trains to transport stored ordnance to the operational airfields. Second, there was a major shortage of firing triggers. The Luftwaffe addressed this problem by persuading the Kriegsmarine to release for use its newest proximity detonator. Once received, crews frantically mounted the detonator on available mines, and units used them operationally from 16 June.[112] The Luftwaffe soon after enjoyed its greatest antishipping successes with mines, among them the sinking of the troopship MV *Derrycunihy* off Sword Beach on 24 June.[113]

To address this growing threat, the Allies diverted significant resources to mine countermeasures. Indeed, they had committed 225 minesweeping vessels to the invasion, utilizing all such available assets.[114] After D-Day this force was further augmented as aerial-mining operations by IX Fliegerkorps increased. In July the Luftwaffe flew 1,837 bomber sorties over the sea, 1,357 of which laid some 2,683 mines.[115] Allied countermeasures steadily diminished the efficacy of these operations, and the constant efforts of minesweeper squadrons kept German successes comparatively low.[116] Consequently, during July, only four Allied vessels were lost to mines: the merchant ship *Empire Broadsword* on 2 July; *MTB 360* on 3 July; *MMS (Motor Minesweeper) 55* on 10 July; and *MMS 304* on 20 July.[117] Additionally, nine vessels were damaged by mines.[118] Yet the forced abandonment of forward air bases and the increasing diversion of bombers to ground support missions in August caused a significant decline in German aerial-mining operations. Consequently, Allied losses to mines dwindled to where they became little more than a nuisance. Ultimately, like all the other Luftwaffe antishipping operations, aerial mining proved mostly fruitless.

Mistletoe Attacks

The Luftwaffe employed a new, secret antishipping weapon codenamed Mistletoe (*Mistel*), which paired an obsolete unmanned bomber with a piloted fighter. The bomber was fitted with a penetrating nosecone packed with 3,500 kilograms (3.85 tons) of explosives and released as a giant glide bomb against targets.[119] But this system was still in development, with only a handful of preproduction models ready, on D-Day.[120] The Mistletoe originally was designed to hit large static targets rather than moving ships. A special-operations squadron (*Einsatzstaffel*) of II/KG 101 had experimented with a few of the preproduction composite aircraft at Dessau, Germany, during the late spring of 1944.

The first composite Mistletoe S1 aircraft were assembled from overhauled, obsolete Ju 88 bombers and new-production Messerschmitt Bf 109 fighters at the Construction Staff Schwab at the Mittelbau slave-labor construction site at Nordhausen in the Harz Mountains.[121] In the late spring, training moved to Kolberg on the Baltic Sea, where the intervention squadron was redesignated as the 2nd Squadron of KG 101 (2/KG 101).[122] After D-Day, frenetic efforts brought the squadron to operational readiness.[123] From 10 June it began assembling east of Paris at St. Dizier airfield. The squadron was allocated the entire first preproduction run of fifteen Mistletoe S1s.[124] The first of the component aircraft began arriving at St. Dizier, where the Ju 88s had their cockpits removed and their warhead nosecones mounted. They were then field mated with their manned Bf 109 fighter and immediately committed to combat on the night of 14–15 June.[125]

All five completed Mistletoes in France sortied. It was an inglorious debut: two combinations were shot down, and no ships were hit.[126] By 16 June, the Allies had identified that the Mistletoe "glide bomber" could not be controlled once released and authorized ships to undertake evasive maneuvers as the most beneficial countermeasure, recognizing its limitations as a weapon against the invasion fleet.[127] By 17 June, just two Mistletoes remained operational.[128] New components and aircraft combinations trickled in as they came off the conversion line.[129] On 24 June five Mistletoes attacked shipping in the Bay of the Seine.[130] KG 101 claimed hits by four glide bombers, while the fifth was jettisoned due to mechanical failure. But only one partial success was achieved when one hit near the frigate (and brigade-group headquarters ship) HMS *Nith* off Arromanches, so damaging the vessel that it had to undergo dry-dock repair.[131] This represented the zenith of Mistletoe accomplishment in Normandy. The price was high: one Mistletoe crashed on takeoff and a second was likely shot down.[132]

In early July four additional Mistletoe antishipping attacks were launched, but no Allied vessels were sunk.[133] Moreover, the Mistletoe base at St. Dizier came under repeated bombing.[134] On 18 July Mistletoes were ordered to attack a "French battleship" that had been identified off Normandy. Yet several grounded Gooseberry blockships composing part of the Mulberry artificial harbor were mistakenly targeted instead, and no hits were achieved.

Photo 9-2 • The *Mistel* (Mistletoe) was a German composite-aircraft configuration that used a large twin-engine bomber as an explosive-laden unmanned drone controlled by a single-engine fighter. The combination shown here, photographed after its capture by the Americans in 1945, consists of a Junkers Ju 88 carrying a Focke-Wulf Fw 190. Other configurations utilized a Messerschmitt Bf 109 as the piloted control aircraft. This weapon system achieved limited success in Normandy and is generally considered a failure. *U.S. Air Force Photo 58019AC*

Mistargeting the Gooseberries again on 25–26 July, five Mistletoes sortied and suffered grievously: four composites were lost. One composite did, however, strike one Gooseberry blockship, the old French dreadnought *Courbet*.[135] On the nights of 9–10 and 10–11 August, Mistletoes again operated over the English Channel but sunk no ships.[136] In the latter operation one pilot became disoriented and jettisoned his bomber over southern England, where it crashed landed in Hampshire.[137] On 18 August the Allies heavily bombed St. Dizier anew, damaging several Mistletoe combinations. Follow-up bombing the next day compelled withdrawal of 2/KG 101, with its few remaining Mistletoes, on 19 August back to Rhein-Main in Germany.[138] This ended Mistletoe attacks against Allied shipping in the channel.

The Mistletoe proved an abject failure. Once again it represented too little, too late: only fifteen composites were committed, and as an antishipping weapon it had profound drawbacks. The Mistletoe had a large profile, was slow, and was ponderous, thus making it very vulnerable. It was also technically complex, cumbersome, and prone to break down.[139] Most significantly, the inability to control the released bomber after launch ensured that enemy vessels usually could evade the oversized glide bomb. Consequently, Mistletoes failed to sink a single Allied ship off Normandy and only damaged one warship. As an invasion-fleet buster, the Mistletoe proved a complete bust.

Conclusion

Despite its determined efforts, the Luftwaffe failed miserably to smash the Allied invasion fleet. By June 1944, years of attrition had gutted the air service, and it was a shadow of its former self. Its small, elite antishipping force had been attritted during 1943–44. Moreover, it was further weakened by the "Baby Blitz" campaign in the spring of 1944. Thus, the Luftwaffe in the West on D-Day possessed a few hundred bombers, many nonoperational and with young inexperienced crews, allowing only one hundred average nocturnal sorties against the invasion fleet. Allied aerial mastery, forward antiaircraft defenses, Continental air bases from which defensive fighters intercepted the German bombers, and the fleet's own formidable antiaircraft defenses created the most challenging operational environment the German antishipping forces had yet encountered. Reduced to attacking at night, inevitably, antishipping strikes achieved few successes. Moreover, the bombers' bases were attacked regularly by Allied fighter-bombers, and the Allied aerial interdiction campaign significantly impeded Luftwaffe resupply efforts. Fuel, bombs, mines, and torpedoes all remained in short supply, and logistical constraints reduced operational tempo. All these obstacles seriously impeded antishipping operations.

Indeed, the inhospitable operational environment ensured staggering losses, and nocturnal missions dramatically escalated noncombat accident rates. Luftwaffe bombing strength, therefore, steadily declined, as these losses could not be made good with replacement aircraft or crew. Of the at least 1,226 bombers deployed in France during the summer of 1944, over 745 were irrecoverably lost.[140] Likewise, the Luftwaffe bomber arm hemorrhaged experienced pilots, who could only be replaced by young, newly trained men who themselves, statistically, became casualties more rapidly. The bomber units in the West, therefore, were steadily and inexorably attritted. Only by cannibalizing units and internally transferring aircraft could operational readiness be sustained. By late August, nineteen of the twenty-four bomber groups committed in France had been disbanded, amalgamated, or withdrawn to Germany for reconstitution. Consequently, German bombers proved unable to significantly damage the Allied invasion fleet, despite employing every weapon available in the Luftwaffe arsenal—heavy bombs, torpedoes, mines, glide bombs, and Mistletoe composite aircraft. The glide bombs that had been so effective the previous year were now neutralized by Allied countermeasures, particularly jamming. The new Mistletoe was deployed in far too few numbers, and being unguided, it also was an ineffective weapon system against maneuvering ships.

The Allied breakout from Normandy in late July and subsequent landings in southern France on 15 August increasingly compelled the diversion of German bomber units to participate in ground support operations. Allied advances then rapidly overran Luftwaffe operational bases, compelling the remaining bomber units to relocate back to Germany by late August. Consequently, by the time the Allies entered Paris on 25 August, antishipping attacks against the invasion fleet had all but ended. In the process the Luftwaffe's elite antishipping force was shattered and never effectively reconstituted; what remained was withdrawn to Norway to lick its wounds. Ultimately, the Luftwaffe's grandiose plan to destroy the Allied invasion fleet and scupper a successful and permanent Allied return to the shores of western Europe in Normandy proved to be a complete bust.

NOTES

1. Harold Thiele, *Luftwaffe Aerial Torpedo Aircraft in World War Two* (Crowborough, East Sussex: Hikoki, 2004), 68.
2. Horst Boog, Gerhard Krebs, and Detlaf Vogel, *Das Deutsche Reich und der Zweite Weltkrieg Band 7: Das Deutsche Reich in der Defensive: Strategischer Luftkrieg in Europa, Krieg im Westen und in Ostasien, 1943–1944/45* (Stuttgart, Ger.: Deutsche Verlags-Anstalt, 2001), 377. See also John Cohn, *The Little Blitz:*

The Luftwaffe's Last Attack on London (Oxford: Fonthill Media, 2014); and Ron Mackay, *The Last Blitz: Operation Steinbock, the Luftwaffe's Last Blitz on Britain—January to May 1944* (Stourport-on-Severn, UK: Red Kite, 2011).

3. The figures given by Alfred Price overstate German strength. Price includes five groups that were not in the West on D-Day. Several had been withdrawn in May and others arrived only as reinforcements. Alfred Price, *Luftwaffe Data Book* (London: Greenhill, 1997), 113–16; Michael Holm, *The Luftwaffe, 1933–1945*, last updated 20 March 2023, https://www.ww2.dk.

4. For two squadrons, the 4th and 6th Squadrons of KG 66, we do not know the total number of aircraft deployed. Based on the group's average squadron strength, five aircraft per squadron has been estimated. The 6th Squadron only arrived in the West on 5 June. *Bestand u. Bewegungsmeldungen* (monthly strength and movement reports) of all the Luftwaffe bomber units in France, compiled from "Flugzeugbestand und Bewegungsmeldungen, 3.42–12.44 Kampfverbände," Holm, *Luftwaffe, 1933–1945*, https://www.ww2.dk/oob/bestand/kampf/bkampf.htm.

5. Aircraft identifiable by type (not all were) under command included 221 Junkers Ju 88s, 96 Junkers Ju 188s, 39 Dornier Do 217s, 50 Heinkel He 177s, and 29 Focke-Wulf Fw 200s. Operational were 119 Ju 88s, 42 Ju 188s, 14 Do 217s, 36 He 177s, and 1 Fw 200. Price, *Luftwaffe Data Book*, 113–16.

6. KG 26 and KG 77 deployed forty-four operational torpedo bombers on 1 June. KG 26 u KG 77, Stand: 1 Juni 1944, "Flugzeugbestand und Bewegungsmeldungen," Holm, *Luftwaffe, 1933–1945*, https://www.ww2.dk/oob/bestand/kampf/bkampf.htm.

7. Thiele, *Luftwaffe Aerial Torpedo Aircraft*, 68.

8. Oberst Walter Gaul, "The G.A.F. [German Air Force (Luftwaffe)] and the Invasion of Normandy, 1944," 1946, Office of Naval Intelligence, U.S. Navy, Washington, DC, chap. 3, para. 18, https://www.history.navy.mil/research/library/online-reading-room/title-list-alphabetically/g/gaf-invasion-normandy.html [hereafter cited as Gaul, "German Air Force"].

9. "Flugzeugbestand und Bewegungsmeldungen, 3.42–12.44," Holm, *Luftwaffe, 1933–1945*, www2.dk/oob/bestand/kampf/bkampf.htm.

10. Gaul, "German Air Force," chap. 3, para. 20.

11. "Flugzeugbestand und Bewegungsmeldungen, 3.42–12.44," Holm, *Luftwaffe, 1933–1945*, https://www.ww2.dk/oob/bestand/kampf/bkampf.htm.

12. Gaul, "German Air Force," chap. 3, para. 22.

13. "Flugzeugbestand und Bewegungsmeldungen, 3.42–12.44," Holm, *Luftwaffe, 1933–1945*, https://www.ww2.dk/oob/bestand/kampf/bkampf.htm.

14. Gaul, "German Air Force," chap. 24, para. 26.

15. During World War II, glide bombs sank one battleship, two cruisers, ten destroyers, one antiaircraft vessel, ten merchant ships (76,000 GRT), and three small ships; they damaged four battleships, six cruisers, twelve destroyers, twenty-nine merchant ships (215,000 GRT), and one escort vessel. Martin J. Bollinger, *Warriors and Wizards: The Development and Defeat of Radio-Controlled Glide Bombs of the Third Reich* (Annapolis, MD: Naval Institute Press, 2020), 150.
16. Giuseppe Fioravanzo, *La Marina italiana nella seconda guerra mondiale*, vol. 15, *La Marina dall'8 settembre 1943 alla fine del conflitto* (The Italian navy in the Second World War, vol. 15, the navy from 8 September 1943 to the end of the conflict) (Rome: Italian Navy Historical Branch, 1971), 8–34.
17. Not all five squadrons were fully operational, however, as II/KG 40 was reforming. In total, the two groups possessed fifty-nine He 177s (including five older A3s and fifty-four newer A5s), of which thirty-seven were operational on 1 June. In November 1943 the Luftwaffe possessed 2,885 HS 293 glide bombs, a total that dropped to 2,741 in October 1944. I/KG 40, Stand: 1 Juni 1944, "Flugzeugbestand und Bewegungsmeldungen," Holm, *Luftwaffe, 1933–1945*, www.ww2.dk/oob/bestand/kampf/bikg40.html; III/KG 100, Stand: 1 Juni 1944, ibid., www.ww2.dk/oob/bestand/kampf/bikg100.html. See also Price, *Luftwaffe Data Book*, 113–16; Friedrich Lauck, *Der Lufttorpedo: Entwicklung und Technik in Deutschland, 1915–1945* (München, Ger.: Bernard & Graefe, 1981), 123.
18. Only the E5, K3, and M variants of the Do 217 could launch the HS-293, while only the Do-217 K3 and M11 were capable of launching the Fritz-X. Manfried Griehl, *Do-217, Do-317, Do-417: An Operational History* (Washington, DC: Smithsonian Institute, 1991), 167, 236–37.
19. Price, *Luftwaffe Data Book*, 113–16.
20. I/KG 40, Stand: 1 Juni 1944, "Flugzeugbestand und Bewegungsmeldungen," Holm, *Luftwaffe, 1933–1945*, www.ww2.dk/oob/bestand/kampf/bikg40.html; III/KG 100, Stand: 1 Juni 1944, ibid., www.ww2.dk/oob/bestand/kampf/bikg100.html.
21. Alfred Price, *The Last Year of the Luftwaffe: May 1944 to May 1945* (Mechanicsburg, PA: Stackpole Books, 1991), 58.
22. Bollinger, *Warriors and Wizards*, 149–50.
23. Bollinger, *Warriors and Wizards*, 150.
24. Bollinger, *Warriors and Wizards*, 150–51.
25. On 1 June KG 40 possessed two Fw 200 C3, fifteen C4, three C6, and nine C8 variants. III/KG 40, 1 Juni u. 1 Juli 1944, "Flugzeugbestand und Bewegungsmeldungen," Holm, *Luftwaffe, 1933–1945*, www.ww2.dk/oob/bestand/kampf/biiikg40.html.

26. III/KG 40, 1 Juni u. 1 Juli 1944.
27. For example, III/KG 40 attacked convoy USG46 off Oran during 8–16 July and USG48 off Bougie during 1–2 August. Some fifteen bombers attacked shipping off Corsica on 10–11 August, losing four aircraft. Thiele, *Luftwaffe Aerial Torpedo Aircraft*, 70.
28. Lawrence Patterson, *Eagles over the Sea, 1943–1945: A History of Luftwaffe Maritime Operations* (Barnsley, UK: Seaforth, 2020), 319.
29. Brian Cull, *Diver! Diver!* (London: Grub Street, 2008), 16.
30. Bollinger, *Warriors and Wizards*, 153.
31. David Chandler and James Lawton Collins Jr., eds., *The D-Day Encyclopedia* (New York: Simon and Schuster, 1994), 538.
32. Patterson, *Eagles over the Sea*, 319.
33. Bollinger, *Warriors and Wizards*, 153, 155.
34. Samuel Morison, *History of US Naval Operations in World War II*, vol. 11 (Edison, NJ: Castle Books, 2001), 170.
35. Ulf Balke, *Kampfgeschwader 100 "Wiking": Ein Geschichte aus Kriegestagebüchern, Dokumente, und Berichten, 1934–1945* (Stuttgart, Ger.: Motorbuch Verlag, 1981), 302.
36. Balke, 302; Lewis Andrews, *Tempest Fire & Foe: Destroyer Escorts in World War II and the Men That Manned Them* (Magnolia, TX: Narwahl, 1999), 103–4.
37. Bollinger, *Warriors and Wizards*, 155.
38. Patterson, *Eagles over the Sea*, 320–21.
39. Bollinger, *Warriors and Wizards*, 155.
40. I/KG 40, Stand: 1 Juni 1944 u 1 Juli 1944, "Flugzeugbestand und Bewegungsmeldungen," Holm, *Luftwaffe, 1933–1945*, www.ww2.dk/oob/bestand/kampf/bikg40.html.
41. II/KG 40, Stand: 1 Juni u 1 Jul 1944, "Flugzeugbestand und Bewegungsmeldungen," Holm, *Luftwaffe, 1933–1945*, www.ww2.dk/oob/bestand/kampf/biikg40.html.
42. Patterson, *Eagles over the Sea*, 319.
43. Stab, II/KG 40, 1 Juli, 1 August 1944, "Flugzeugbestand und Bewegungsmeldungen," Holm, *Luftwaffe, 1933–1945*, www.ww2.dk/oob/bestand/kampf/biikg40.html.
44. III/KG 100, 1 Juni u. 1 Juli 1944, "Flugzeugbestand und Bewegungsmeldungen," Holm, *Luftwaffe, 1933–1945*, www.ww2.dk/oob/bestand/kampf/biiikg100.html.
45. Patterson, *Eagles over the Sea*, 323.
46. Bollinger, *Warriors and Wizards*, 12.
47. Bollinger, *Warriors and Wizards*, 28–32.
48. Lauck, *Der Lufttorpedo*, 123.

49. Griehl, *Do-217*, 167.
50. Ten K3s, two E5s, and three M1s. III/KG 100, 1 Juli 1944, "Flugzeugbestand und Bewegungsmeldungen," Holm, *Luftwaffe, 1933–1945*, www.ww2.dk/oob /bestand/kampf/biiikg100.html.
51. Patterson, *Eagles over the Sea*, 323.
52. Douglas L. Roberts, *Rustbucket 7: Chronicle of the USS PC 617 during the Great War* (Newcastle, ME: Mill Pond, 1995), 112–13; Griehl, *Do-217*, 167.
53. Bollinger, *Warriors and Wizards*, 156.
54. Griehl, *Do-217*, 168.
55. Griehl, *Do-217*, 168.
56. Bollinger, *Warriors and Wizards*, 162.
57. Bollinger, *Warriors and Wizards*, 164.
58. Griehl, *Do 217*, 168–69.
59. Bollinger, *Warriors and Wizards*, 164; Griehl, *Do 217*, 169.
60. Griehl, *Do 217*, 169.
61. Wolfgang Fleischer, *Deutsche Abwurfmunition im Zweiten Weltkrieg. Basiswissen über Bomben, Behälter, Lufttorpedos, Minen, Verpackungen und Zünder* (Aachen, Ger.: Helios-Verlag, 2015); Lauck, *Der Lufttorpedo*.
62. The only He 111 H6s to see service in Normandy came as reinforcements with KG 53, which received six as replacements in August 1944. KG 53, Stand: 1 September 1944, "Flugzeugbestand und Bewegungsmeldungen," Holm, *Luftwaffe, 1933–1945*, https://www.ww2.dk/oob/bestand/kampf/bkampf.htm.
63. Thiele, *Luftwaffe Aerial Torpedo Aircraft*, 68.
64. On 11 November 1943 the Luftwaffe possessed only 1,283 LT 5Fb and 211 LT 5FW torpedoes. Thiele, *Luftwaffe Aerial Torpedo Aircraft*, 61.
65. H. L de Zeng, D. G. Stanket, and E. J. Creek, *Bomber Units of the Luftwaffe, 1933–1945: A Reference Source*, vol. 1 (Teddington, UK: Ian Allan, 2007), 86.
66. Gaul, "German Air Force," chap. 3, para. 17.
67. Kampfgeschwader 26 Pilot Casualty List for 1944, Onlineprojekt Gefallenendenkmäler, www.denkmalprojekt.org/2018/verlustliste-Kampfgeschwade -26-1944_wk2.html.
68. The 12–13 June mission alone cost III/KG 26 ten pilots killed or missing. Kampfgeschwader 26 Pilot Casualty List.
69. Thiele, *Luftwaffe Aerial Torpedo Aircraft*, 68.
70. Thiele, *Luftwaffe Aerial Torpedo Aircraft*, 68.
71. Patterson, *Eagles over the Sea*, 319.
72. Stab, II U/KG 26; Stab, II u III/KG 26, 1 Juni u 1 Juli 1944, "Flugzeugbestand und Bewegungsmeldungen," Holm, *Luftwaffe, 1933–1945*, https://www.ww2 .dk/oob/bestand/kampf/bkampf.htm.

73. Patterson, *Eagles over the Sea*, 323.
74. Thiele, *Luftwaffe Aerial Torpedo Aircraft*, 70.
75. Thiele, *Luftwaffe Aerial Torpedo Aircraft*, 70.
76. Thiele, Luftwaffe Aerial Torpedo Aircraft, 70–71.
77. Stab, II/ u III/KG 26, Juni, Juli, August 1944, "Flugzeugbestand und Bewegungsmeldungen," Holm, *Luftwaffe, 1933–1945*, https://www.ww2.dk/oob/bestand/kampf/bkampf.htm.
78. Kampfgeschwader 26 Pilot Casualty List for 1944, Onlineprojekt Gefallenendenkmäler, www.denkmalprojekt.org/2018/verlustliste-Kampfgeschwader-26-1944_wk2.html.
79. Thiele, *Luftwaffe Aerial Torpedo Aircraft*, 65.
80. Fleischer, *Deutsche Abwurfmunition im Zweiten Weltkrieg*.
81. Secondary sources identify III/KG 54 in southern France on D-Day, but it had actually been withdrawn for reconstitution in Germany in late October 1943. Stab, I u. III/KG 54, Stand: 1 Juni 1944, "Flugzeugbestand und Bewegungsmeldungen," Holm, *Luftwaffe, 1933–1945*, https://www.ww2.dk/oob/bestand/kampf/bkampf.htm.
82. De Zeng, Stanket, and Creek, *Bomber Units of the Luftwaffe*, 183–90.
83. I u. III/KG 54, Stand: 1 Juli 1944, "Flugzeugbestand und Bewegungsmeldungen," Holm, *Luftwaffe, 1933–1945*, https://www.ww2.dk/oob/bestand/kampf/bkampf.htm.
84. I u. III/KG 54, Stand: 1 August 1944 u 1 September 1944, "Flugzeugbestand und Bewegungsmeldungen," Holm, *Luftwaffe, 1933–1945*, https://www.ww2.dk/oob/bestand/kampf/bkampf.htm.
85. Thiele, *Luftwaffe Aerial Torpedo Aircraft*, 68.
86. Thiele, *Luftwaffe Aerial Torpedo Aircraft*, 69.
87. Thiele, *Luftwaffe Aerial Torpedo Aircraft*, 70.
88. The naval version of the circling torpedo was the Ge7 "Dackel." Jürgen Rohwer, *Chronology of the War at Sea, 1939–1945: The Naval History of World War Two*, 3rd rev. ed. (Annapolis, MD: Naval Institute Press, 2001), 346.
89. Samuel Morison, *History of US Naval Operations in World War II*, vol. 11, *The Invasion of France and Germany, 1944–1945* (Edison, NJ: Castle Books, 2001), 192.
90. I u. III/KG 54, Stand: 1 Juni, I Juli, 1 August u. 1 September 1944, "Flugzeugbestand und Bewegungsmeldungen," Holm, *Luftwaffe, 1933–1945*, www2.dk/oob/bestand/kampf/biikg54.html.
91. Patterson, *Eagles over the Sea*, 320.
92. Conventional bombs: SC 50, 250, 500, 1000, 1200, 1800, 2000, 2500, and SB 1000, 1800, 2500; cluster bombs: SC 10, SC 10 DW, SC 4 HL; fragmentation

bombs: SD 500 and SD 1700. *Catalog of Enemy Ordnance Material*. Office of the Chief of Ordnance, 1 August 1945, 314–18.
93. "Rocket-Propelled Bomb PC 1000 Rs," *Catalog of Enemy Ordnance Material* (Washington, DC: U.S. Office of the Chief of Ordnance, 1 August 1945), 316; U.S. Army Technical Manual TM 9-1985-2; Air Force Technical Order TO 39B-1A-9 "German Explosive Ordnance."
94. Vice-Adm. Eberhard Weichold, "The German Naval Defense against the Invasion of Normandy" (Washington, DC: U.S. Naval Intelligence Division, 1946), 19.
95. Morison, *US Naval Operations in World War II*, 11:190.
96. Morison, *US Naval Operations in World War II*, 11:171.
97. Stab, I u II/KG 30, Stand: 1 Juli 1944, "Flugzeugbestand und Bewegungsmeldungen," Holm, *Luftwaffe, 1933–1945*, https://www.ww2.dk/oob/bestand/kampf/bkampf.htm.
98. The wing received no fewer than ninety replacement Ju 88 S3 during its six weeks in Normandy. Patterson, *Eagles over the Sea*, 324.
99. Gaul, "German Air Force," chap. 3, para. 20.
100. Gaul, "German Air Force," chap. 3, para. 20.
101. Patterson, *Eagles over the Sea*, 323.
102. Patterson, *Eagles over the Sea*, 323.
103. Gaul, "German Air Force," chap. 4, para 25.
104. Fleischer, *Deutsche Abwurfmunition im Zweiten Weltkrieg*.
105. Gaul, "German Air Force," chap. 3.
106. Christopher Chant, ed., *Warfare and the Third Reich: The Rise and Fall of Hitler's Armed Forces* (New York: Salamander Books, 1996), 388; Patterson, *Eagles over the Sea*, 321.
107. Gaul, "German Air Force," apps. I, II.
108. Gaul, "German Air Force," chap. 3, para. 20.
109. Gaul, "German Air Force," chap. 3, para. 21.
110. U.S. Naval Forces Europe, "United States Naval Administrative History of World War II," vol. 5, "Operation Neptune: The Invasion of Normandy," chap. 7, sec. H, https://www.history.navy.mil/research/library/online-reading-room/title-list-alphabetically/o/operation-neptune-invasion-normandy.html. See also *HM Ships Damaged or Sunk by Enemy Action in World War Two* (London: HMSO, 1952).
111. Gaul, "German Air Force," chap 3, para. 20.
112. Gaul, "German Air Force," chap 3, para. 20.
113. Some twenty-five crew and 183 soldiers of the 43rd Wessex Reconnaissance Regiment were killed and 120 wounded in the single-worst loss of life off the Normandy beaches. Patterson, *Eagles over the Sea*, 321–22.

114. Allied minesweepers were concentrated in twelve minesweeping and thirteen motor-minesweeping flotillas along with thirty-four minesweeping motor launches. To increase this strength, one new flotilla was activated, one was reconstituted with obsolete World War I minesweepers, a third was recalled from the Mediterranean, and a fourth was transferred from convoy-escort duties. U.S. Naval Forces Europe, "United States Naval Administrative History of World War II," vol. 5, chap. 7, paras. 46–47.
115. This includes 1,644 LMB and 993 BM 1000. Gaul, "German Air Force," chap. 4, para 25.
116. Gaul, "German Air Force," chap. 4, para 25.
117. Gaul, "German Air Force," app. II.
118. Gaul, "German Air Force," app. II.
119. Three kinds of Mistletoe aircraft were developed. The S1 was a Ju 88 A4 plus a Messerschmitt Bf 109 F4. The S2 used a Ju 88 G1 plus an Fw 190 A8. Finally, the S3c married a Ju 88 G10 with an Fw 190A. Only the S1 was deployed in Normandy. Rodger Ford, *Germany's Secret Weapons in WWII* (Osceola, WI: MBI, 2000).
120. Only six or seven preproduction Mistletoes had been completed at Köthen by D-Day. Robert Forsyth, *Mistel: German Composite Aircraft and Operations, 1942–1945* (Gaithersburg, MD: Classic, 2001), 64.
121. Forsyth, *Mistel*, 64.
122. Forsyth, *Mistel*, 64.
123. Forsyth, *Mistel*, 64–65.
124. Forsyth, *Mistel*, 65.
125. Eight refurbished Ju 88 bombers arrived at St. Dizier on 12 June. Nick Beale, *Kampfflieger: Bombers of the Luftwaffe*, vol. 4, *Summer 1943 to May 1945* (Hersham, Surrey: Classic, 2005), 337.
126. Bruce Halpenny, *Fighter Pilots in World War II: True Stories of Frontline Air Combat* (Barnsley, South Yorkshire: Pen & Sword Aviation, 2004), 127–34.
127. Forsyth, *Mistel*, 68–69.
128. Forsyth, *Mistel*, 69.
129. One arrived on 18 June and another on 19 June. Forsyth, 70.
130. Forsyth, *Mistel*, 70.
131. Forsyth, *Mistel*, 74.
132. Forsyth, *Mistel*, 74.
133. Halpenny, *Fighter Pilots in World War II*, 127–34.
134. Forsyth, *Mistel*, 75–76.
135. Forsyth, *Mistel*, 75.
136. *Warship International* 35, no. 4 (1998), 423.

137. Forsyth, *Mistel*, 76–78.
138. Forsyth, *Mistel*, 79.
139. Beale, *Kampfflieger*, 4:337.
140. Incomplete records for July and August indicate that at least an additional 269 and 263 bombers were permanently written off. The actual total is appreciably higher. Stand: 1 August u 1 September 1944, "Flugzeugbestand und Bewegungsmeldungen," Holm, *Luftwaffe, 1933–1945*, https://www.ww2.dk/oob/bestand/kampf/bkampf.htm.

10

The Allied Tactical Airpower System in Normandy

Paul Johnston

How did the Allied system for tactical airpower actually work? Some controversy has attached to this question, the effectiveness of which remains one of the disputed issues of the campaign. But despite such debate about airpower in Normandy, there has been surprisingly little examination of how the system worked in practice. In fact, by D-Day, a well-articulated and flexible system that could focus airpower and call down strikes within minutes had been developed.

Allied air supremacy over Normandy has often been described as crushing, dooming the Germans. In his early classic history of the war in Europe, Chester Wilmot wrote, "The value of this air supremacy can hardly be overrated."[1] The German army expressed the same sentiment both at the time and afterward. Field Marshal Erwin Rommel famously complained in a 12 June situation report, "Our own operations are rendered extraordinarily difficult and in part impossible to carry out [owing to] the exceptionally strong and, in some respects overwhelming, superiority of the enemy air force."[2]

It is therefore striking how there is also criticism of airpower in Normandy. This began even while the battle was underway, in the form of complaints from ground officers that the air forces were stinting and inflexible, and continued in postwar commentary.[3] Such sentiment was colored by anger at the numerous fratricide incidents by the Allied air forces, which is understandable, but more fundamentally army leaders did not believe that independently commanded air forces would ever be suitably responsive.[4] For example, a 1950 article by a serving U.S. officer argued, "The existing system for close air support for ground troops on the battlefield fails to meet ground force needs for speed and simplicity."[5] Around the same time, U.S. Army brigadier general T. S. Timbernan was arguing that cooperation with the tactical air forces, rather than command over them, "can be a dangerous thing."[6] In Canada, Major General C. C. Mann, who as a brigadier had been the chief of staff at First Canadian Army Headquarters during the campaign, argued that the command system used in Normandy was "unsound" and that the army should command the associated tactical air forces.[7] Many historians have discussed the issue, generally in tones disapproving of the RAF.[8] Historian Ian Gooderson, in his analysis of Allied tactical airpower, concluded: "The British system proved very successful in processing pre-planned air support strikes, but the more difficult test was how quickly air support could be provided in response to impromptu requests from forward troops, where speed was vitally important. In this respect ... the process was simply not fast enough."[9]

Are such accusations fair, or even accurate? Any effort to wrestle with such questions must first begin with an understanding of what tactical airpower in 1944 was and how it worked.

Fundamentals: Doctrine, Parts, and Process

We begin with an overview of fundamentals—the doctrinal principles of the time, the various parts that constituted the Anglo-American system for tactical airpower, and the processes they followed. All were well developed and elaborate by D-Day.

From very early on, a coherent body of tactical-airpower theory argued for several tenets: focusing firstly upon air superiority; concentrating upon decisive points, something best facilitated by organizing it centrally under a single air commander; and finally emphasizing the attack of targets deeper in the enemy rear, rather than simply adding firepower along the front lines.[10] While those principles were all established before the war, actual working doctrine went through a painful and complex evolution but, by the Normandy Campaign, had achieved its mature form.[11] The most contentious issue in that evolution had been, as ever with airpower, command and control, in particular whether that should be centralized (more under air force authority) or decentralized (more subject to ground commanders).[12] After repeated disputes over that issue earlier in the war, by 1943, a system of joint command, focused at the army level, was settled upon.[13] As British doctrine of the time put it, "The Army Commander tells the Air Force Commander what he wants to achieve, and the Air Staff, having examined the problem, make Air plans with the Army's aim constantly in view."[14]

Tactical airpower was thus not distributed to individual army formations, as some of it had been in the First World War, but was instead grouped into air-force organizations, which the British termed "tactical air forces" and the Americans simply numbered.[15] The British organization for the Normandy Campaign was Second Tactical Air Force (2 TAF), and the Americans had the Ninth Air Force (9 AF), both commanded by air officers.[16] The major subdivision of those tactical air forces, known by the British as groups and the Americans as tactical air commands (TACs), were each paired with an army level headquarters. It was at this level, the pairing of a field army with a group or TAC, that was the focus of the system of joint command. The paired headquarters would co-locate and form what the British called a joint battle room and the Americans a combined operations center (COC), with radio communications to both the front line and the airfields. At this joint battle room, requests for air strikes were evaluated, prioritized, and assigned.[17]

In terms of the actual attack of targets, official doctrine distinguished between "indirect" and "direct" support.[18] Indirect meant "attacks on objectives which do not have immediate effect on the land battle, but nevertheless contribute to the broad plan"—typically, lines of communication and logistics targets, often struck by medium or even heavy bombers, but fighter-bombers could be used against such targets as well. Direct support, on the other hand, was defined as "attacks upon enemy forces actually engaged in the land battle." This included enemy strongpoints at the front but more typically were hostile artillery batteries, concentrations of armor, or headquarters somewhat behind the front. "Direct support" is thus broader than the modern concept of "close air support," a term that did not appear in the official doctrine of either the British or Americans in 1944, although the expression did appear in some common usage.[19]

Direct support was further categorized as "prearranged" or "impromptu" requests based on urgency. Prearranged air strikes were planned through the staff process, sometimes several days ahead of time, but routinely for the next day. Impromptu, or "immediate," requests originated in the heat of battle from leading ground elements and were sent via the special air-request radio network described below.[20] U.S. practice was essentially the same, with somewhat different terminology: prearranged missions were "planned," "pre-planned," or "request"; impromptu missions were "immediate request," "emergency call," or simply "call" missions.[21] The greatest difference between U.S. and British doctrine was the American insistence upon a strict hierarchy in targeting priorities: enemy air capabilities first, deep interdiction second, and only then air support in the vicinity of the battle lines.[22]

Table 10-1 • Categories of Air Support

	Direct	Indirect
Prearranged or Planned	Most routine requests fell into this category, as did air plans for major offensives.	Most of the deeper interdiction work by medium bombers fell into this category.
Impromptu or Call	Urgent calls from the forward elements fell into this category.	In principle there was no provision for indirect impromptu or call missions, but on a few occasions high-value targets were identified and, after a rush effort, struck by medium bombers.[a]

Notes:
[a] An example of this is the attack on Headquarters Panzer Group West on 9 June 1944. See David Kenyon, *Bletchley Park and D-Day* (New Haven, CT: Yale University Press, 2019), 219–20; and Christopher Shores and Chris Thomas, *2nd Tactical Air Force*, vol. 1, *Spartan to Normandy, June 1943 to June 1944* (Surrey, UK: Classic, 2004), 147–49.

Aircraft

The most obvious parts of the system were, of course, the aircraft. The RAF had resisted specialized ground-attack aircraft, but by 1944, they found themselves with fighter-bombers, light bombers, and medium bombers, all specially modified for the role.[23] The Americans were always more amenable to ground attack, and by 1944, both air forces had a stable of aircraft types for the role.[24]

The light and medium bombers were assigned to the tactical air forces in a supporting role, concentrated in specialized formations.[25] They operated in similar fashion to the heavier strategic bombers, and indeed, there was some overlap in types. The bombers were not generally used for direct or close support, but they carried a heavier payload than the fighter-bombers and could operate at night. They were typically used for interdiction of deeper targets, in particular line-of-communication facilities like rail yards and bridges in planned missions. This generally meant that targets would be struck the day following a request, yet in extremis, planned missions were sometimes rushed through within a single day.[26]

But the principal aircraft of the tactical air forces was the fighter-bomber, originally designed for air-to-air combat and later adapted to ground attack. First developed as an expedient in 1941–42, by 1944, fighter-bombers were in common use.[27] The venerable Spitfire, for example, was modified to carry bombs, and pilots were also trained in effective ground strafing. But the most capable British fighter-bomber was unquestionably the Typhoon, which carried either bombs or air-to-ground rockets—referred to as rocket projectiles (RPs)—specifically designed to attack hardened targets. For the Americans, the primary fighter-bomber was the P-47 Thunderbolt, a heavy aircraft that made an excellent fighter-bomber, able to carry a good load of ordnance and absorb heavy damage. The lighter, faster, and more maneuverable P-51 Mustang was also used effectively in this role.[28]

The fighter-bombers used three types of weapons to attack ground targets:

Bombs. All fighter-bombers carried bombs, usually 250- or 500-pounders, but the heavier Typhoon could also carry 1,000-pounders. Most bombing attacks by these aircraft were made in steep dives with

Table 10-2 • Light and Medium Bombers

Mosquito FB Mark 6	
Speed: Maximum: 400 mph Typical: 200 mph Combat radius: 550 miles	Armament: up to 4,000 lbs. of bombs; usually 2,000 lbs. (typically 4–8 x 500-lbs.) 4 x .303-inch machine guns 4 x 20-mm cannon could be fitted with 8 x RPs
Boston/A-20 Havoc	
Speed: Maximum: 300 mph Typical: 250–300 mph Combat radius: 450 miles	Armament: up to 4,000 lbs. of bombs 6 x fixed forward-firing .50-cal. machine guns 2 x .50 cal. machine guns in dorsal turret 1 x .50-cal. machine gun in belly
B-25 Mitchell	
Speed: Maximum: 275 mph Typical: 225 mph Combat radius: 1,250 miles	Armament: up to 6,000 lbs. bombs total 18 x .50-cal. machine guns could be fitted with 8 x HVARs

Sources: Aircraft data from Robin Higham and Carol Williams, eds., *Flying Combat Aircraft of USAAF-USAF*, vols. 1–2 (Mechanicsburg, PA: Stackpole Books, 2004); Robert Jackson, *Aircraft of World War II: Development, Weaponry, Specifications* (Edison, NJ: Chartwell Books, 2003); John Batchelor and Malcolm Lowe, *Plane Essentials: Mosquito* (Victoria, Australia: Publishing Solutions, 2008); René Francillon, *McDonnell Douglas Aircraft since 1920*, vol. 1 (London: Naval Institute Press, 1988); and Jerry Scutts, *North American B-25 Mitchell* (Ramsbury, UK: Crowood, 2001).

low-altitude release, more accurate than conventional level bombing but also riskier and still lacking pinpoint accuracy.[29]

Guns. The strafing of ground targets using machine guns or cannons was one of the original forms of air attack. By 1944, the technique was well developed, and the 20-mm cannons on many fighter-bombers allowed for successful engagement of armored vehicles. Strafing was probably the most accurate form of fighter-bomber attack of the Normandy Campaign.[30]

Table 10-3 • Fighter-Bombers

Spitfire Mark IX

Speed:
Maximum: 400 mph
Typical: 250 mph

Combat radius:
170 miles (internal fuel)
280 miles (w/drop tanks)

Armament:
4 x .303-inch or 2 x .50-cal. machine guns
2 x 20-mm cannon
up to 500 lbs. of bombs (2 x 250 lbs. or 1 x 500 lbs.)

P-47 Thunderbolt

Speed:
Maximum: 430 mph
Typical: 300 mph

Combat radius:
235 miles (internal fuel)
375 miles (w/drop tanks)

Armament:
up to 4,000 lbs. of bombs
6 x fixed forward-firing .50-cal. machine guns
2 x .50-cal. machine guns in dorsal turret
1 x .50-cal. machine gun in belly

Typhoon

Speed:
Maximum: 400 mph
Typical: 325 mph

Combat radius:
235 miles (internal fuel)
500 miles (w/drop tanks)

Armament:
up to 2,000 lbs. of bombs (typically 2 x 500 lbs.)
4 x 20-mm cannon
could be fitted with 8 x RPs

P-51 Mustang

Speed:
Maximum: 400 mph
Typical: 360 mph

Combat radius:
400 (internal fuel)
750 (w/drop tanks)

Armament:
6 x .50-cal. machine guns
up to 2,000 lbs. of bombs (typically 2 x 500 lbs.)
could be fitted with 6 x HVARs

Sources: Aircraft data from Robin Higham and Carol Williams, eds., *Flying Combat Aircraft of USAAF-USAF*, vols. 1–2 (Mechanicsburg, PA: Stackpole Books, 2004); Robert Jackson, *Aircraft of World War II: Development, Weaponry, Specifications* (Edison, NJ: Chartwell Books, 2003); Leonard Bridgman, *Jane's Fighting Aircraft of World War II* (1946—47; repr., London: Bracken Books, 1989); Alfred Price, *The Spitfire Story*, rev. ed. (Sparkford, UK: Haynes, 2010); Eric Morgan and Edward Shacklady, *Spitfire: The History* (Stamford, UK: Key Books, 2000); Warren M. Bodie, *Republic's P-47 Thunderbolt: From Seversky to Victory* (Hiawassee, GA: Widewing, 1994); Corey Graff, *P-47 Thunderbolt at War* (St. Paul, MN: Zenith, 2007); Kev Darling, *Hawker Typhoon, Tempest and Sea Fury* (Wiltshire, UK: Crowood., 2003); Richard Townshend Bickers, *Hawker Typhoon: The Combat History* (Wiltshire, UK: Crowood, 1999); Kev Darling, *P-51 Mustang* (Shrewsbury, UK: Airlife, 2002); and Malcolm Lowe, *North American P-51 Mustang* (Wiltshire, UK: Crowood, 2009).

Rockets. Unguided rockets, attached to hardpoints under a fighter-bomber's wings and one of the innovations of the campaign, were specifically intended as antiarmor weapons. British RPs had a 60-pound warhead, while the American equivalent (HVAR) had a 45-pound warhead delivered with higher velocity. Typically fired all at once in a volley, they packed a wallop capable of destroying even the heaviest tank *if* they hit their target. Rockets were also used against strongpoints and, less often, dug-in artillery batteries as well as trains and vehicle columns on roads.[31]

Aside from questions of accuracy, one of the key limitations of the aircraft was range and endurance. Air-to-air refueling had not yet been invented, and the fighter-size aircraft of the era had an effective combat radius of roughly 250 miles, with an endurance over the battle area of about an hour.[32] But the more critical limitation was accuracy. Trials by the RAF at the time concluded that achieving a 50-percent probability of a hit against an individual tank required, on average, eighteen Typhoon sorties under ideal conditions.[33] This is why rockets were generally fired salvo against a column or train, rather than against a single, isolated target. While the balance of opinion among historians is that their inaccuracy made them less effective than often thought at the time, when employed en masse, especially against columns trapped in narrow, hedge-bound roads, RPs could be devastating.[34] The consensus opinion among historians is that while often exaggerated, the overall effect of fighter-bomber weapons was considerable, especially in the suppression of German movement.[35]

The Tactical Air Forces

Another fundamental to understand is organization. Both the British-Commonwealth and American forces created not only dedicated weapons for the tactical role but also elaborate organizations for them. In the British-Commonwealth case, this was 2 TAF, which consisted of four groups, each with five to seven wings of three or four squadrons, and a reconnaissance wing of four squadrons, totaling some ninety-six squadrons with 1,700 combat aircraft. The equivalent American organization was 9 AF, consisting of four commands (the equivalent to British groups) with ninety-eight squadrons and about 1,700 combat aircraft plus some 700 transport aircraft.[36]

Attention is usually focused upon flying elements, but the tactical air forces included many ground-based elements. Most significantly, as soon as possible after the landings at Normandy, its airfields relocated from permanent bases in the United Kingdom to temporary airfields on the Continent.[37] These were primitive affairs, with airstrips plowed out of the ground by military engineers and all facilities in tents and trucks. They were thus mobile and moved forward to new hastily constructed airfields as they followed the armies' advance.[38]

Other significant ground-based organizations within the tactical air forces included the already mentioned joint battle room/COC at the headquarters level. Each fighter-bomber group/TAC had a group control center (GCC; British) or a tactical control center (TCC; American). These worked a bit like the famous control centers during the Battle of Britain, which had big table-mounted maps and unit markers pushed around by long pokers, enabling RAF commanders to direct the battle. Except in the case of tactical air forces, the GCC/TCCs were housed in tents and trucks so they could follow the advance. They were in radio communications with the aircrews themselves, as well as the other ground elements of the system, and controlled the aircraft, directing them onto targets or into patrol areas.[39] There were also mobile radars and fighter directors to provide the control for fighters in the air-defense role.[40] Finally, there were what the RAF called "servicing commandos" and Americans' "Service Command" to perform maintenance on the aircraft as well as logistics units. All told, 2 TAF numbered almost 100,000 personnel and 9 AF somewhat over 200,000.[41]

Additionally, and most crucially, specialist radio-communications units tied all this together. The creation of dedicated communications was the heart of the wartime reforms that led to developing the tactical air forces. Air Marshal Sholto Douglas quipped that all tactical airpower needed to be effective was "willingness to co-operate and good signals."[42] The British called these newly invented entities "air support signals units," which were jointly manned by the British Army and RAF and provided the communications to tie the whole operation together.[43] The Americans differed somewhat from the British in that they were all simply detachments that belonged to the 9 AF and were manned exclusively by U.S. Army Air Forces (USAAF) personnel.[44]

Another innovation was developing officers who specialized in tactical air support to staff many of the positions. The British and Commonwealth forces employed army junior officers (lieutenants or captains) drawn from the combat arms and given a short course on the principles and practice of tactical airpower. Known as air-liaison officers (ALOs), they staffed the forward-control elements and air support sections of ground-formation headquarters as well as provided contacts at the airfields who would brief pilots on the ground situation before they took off for missions.[45] The Americans used either artillery officers or tour-expired fighter-bomber pilots in this role.[46]

Forward Controllers

Perhaps the most critical part of the system, and certainly the greatest innovation, were the forward-control elements. Previous systems of air support, including the famous German blitzkrieg dive bombers, had relied upon requests up the chain of command and then planning and briefing of missions at the airfields before flying, rather than actual controllers with the forward troops.[47] For the Americans, these embedded controllers were known as air support parties (ASPs) and belonged to the TAC with which they operated.[48] The British created theirs within what they called air support signals units (ASSUs), a new type of organization, to achieve the same result. British/Commonwealth ASSUs belonged to the British Army rather than to the RAF but included air personnel in their establishment.

ASSUs consisted of mobile teams equipped with radios who went forward with the ground forces to provide advice on air support and to relay requests for air strikes back to the joint battle room. Other ASSU outstations were located at the fighter-bomber airfields. Thus, all elements of the system, from the forward requesters for air support to the joint battle room at army-headquarters level to the airfields from where the missions would be flown, were tied together on a specialized radio network. The critical feature of this system was that it did not follow the normal army chain of command—requests for air support went directly to the joint battle room, although the intervening command levels could and typically did monitor the ASSU radio net.[49]

Photo 10-1 • Taken in the fall of 1944, this photo illustrates a U.S. air support party. Major Frank Martine, a Ninth Air Force joint air–ground operations officer, guides fighter-bombers overhead to targets based on information supplied by Major Gilbert Palmer Jr., an air-ground liaison officer. If targets are not easily found by the aircraft, Major Palmer directs artillery to pinpoint the objectives with smoke shells. *U.S. Air Force Photo 55122AC*

The forward radio teams were known in the British-Commonwealth system as "tentacles," a whimsical name derived from their appearance on diagrams of the radio network.[50] It should be noted, however, that in the British and Canadian forces, there were only about a dozen tentacles per field army as compared with thirty to fifty headquarters at the corps, division, and brigade levels.[51] Thus, there were not enough tentacles to give one to every army headquarters; they had to be allocated on a priority basis, typically to the lead corps, division, or brigade headquarters for planned, "set-piece" battles. The Americans, on the other hand, with greater material resources, established an ASP as a standard part of every corps and divisional headquarters, with an additional three in every armored division.[52]

Standard Tentacles. In British practice the standard forward element of the system was not actually a controller, but a liaison-and-request element. These tentacles consisted of a single vehicle, usually a truck, with a couple of army signalers and radios and a lieutenant from the artillery who had been given a short course on tactical air support procedures. Each group would co-locate with a forward ground headquarters, usually a divisional headquarters but sometimes down to brigade level, where they would give advice on air support and pass requests directly back to the joint battle room at the army–tactical air force headquarters. It should be noted that British tentacles did not have VHF radios for communication with the aircraft themselves; any air strikes they produced were prearranged.[53]

VCPs and FCPs. An innovation introduced by the British partway through the Normandy Campaign was the visual control post (VCP). This was a forward tentacle mounted in an armored scout car, equipped with an additional VHF radio capable of voice communication with aircraft, and manned by a senior ALO from the British Army, typically a major, and an RAF pilot, usually of squadron-leader rank. As the name suggests, the original idea was that VCPs would site themselves in forward positions overlooking targets and call in air strikes, much the way an artillery observer did. In practice, such visual observation seldom proved possible, and VCPs mostly co-located with the headquarters of leading brigades in the same manner as a standard tentacle. They did, however, talk directly with aircraft overhead, describing targets and local conditions to the pilots.[54] Later in the campaign the British introduced forward control posts (FCPs). Based upon the earlier Rover David system developed in Italy, the FCP was a detachment of about a dozen personnel: an army ALO paired with an RAF fighter-bomber pilot and eight to ten army radio operators and drivers for the FCP's three or four vehicles. They would set up at corps headquarters when it was mounting a major offensive and had the radios to reach the forward tentacles, the GCC, the airfields themselves, and—most critically—the aircraft overhead. The ALO and RAF pilot would advise the corps on air support generally, and during the battle, they could assume a form of delegated control of strike aircraft directly.[55]

Photo 10-2 • A visual control post (VCP) operating from a Humber scout car in No. 83 Group's sector of operations in Normandy. Major Colin Gray, the army liaison officer (*right*), points out the coordinates for an air strike requested by the army to Squadron Leader R. A. Sutherland, who will relay the request to the army–composite group headquarters. VCPs operated as near the front line as possible, normally with an army brigade headquarters, relaying requests for air support from ground forces to the RAF group control centers and then directing aircraft onto the target by VHF radio communication. *IWM CL 565*

American ASPs. All U.S. forward controllers amounted to the equivalent of a British VCP. ASPs each included a VHF radio to communicate with aircraft as well as a tour-completed fighter-bomber pilot and an experienced ground officer (typically from the artillery). The greater U.S. capacity in forward control presumably reflects the greater resources available to the Americans.[56]

Photo 10-3 • A P-47 from the 365th Fighter Group, Ninth Air Force, flies by a column of U.S. Army Sherman tanks. Using a system known as armored column cover, a USAAF forward controller riding in a lead tank communicates with an assigned flight of aircraft to get immediate intelligence or air support. *U.S. Air Force Photo 55245AC*

Despite this technical ability, American policy initially prohibited direct communication between ASPs and aircraft overhead, a restriction that was relaxed as the Normandy Campaign progressed.[57]

Prearranged or Planned Missions

So, having examined the doctrinal principles and various parts of the system, how did it actually work? How were air strikes called down? By preference, both the British and Americans tried to plan their air support ahead of time rather than relying upon calling for air strikes during a battle. For planned major offensives, this could be done days ahead of time, and major operations such as Goodwood or Cobra included a written air plan, jointly developed by army and air planners. Such plans specified targets, timings, weapons, and desired effects, such as whether roads should be cratered.[58] In some cases key staff officers from 2 TAF or IX Tactical Air Command flew to the United Kingdom to attend planning conferences to develop such air plans.⁵⁹ Yet routinely, missions would be planned for the following day at a daily conference held at the army-headquarters level. Requests would originate from the forward army headquarters, typically a divisional or corps headquarters where there were specialists for planning air support. These requests were sent up the chain of command during the day to be considered at the daily air conference held in the evening. Requests would be prioritized and then paired with the available air resources, after which decisions would be made about what would be struck. The resulting orders for the next day's flying would then be drawn up and sent to the squadrons by teletype. The missions themselves would be planned and prepared by the flying squadrons at their airfields and briefed to the aircrews by the liaison officers at those airfields, all prior to takeoff.⁶⁰

Impromptu or Call Missions

Immediate close support in the heat of battle was provided by the impromptu system, what the Americans generally referred to as "on-call" or "call missions." The forward elements—tentacles of whatever type in the British system and ASPs in the American—generally located with leading divisional headquarters and sometimes down to brigade level, passed requests for air support through the special air support radio network directly back to group/COC–army headquarters without passing through the intermediate divisional and corps levels of command. The army–composite group staffs would then either approve or deny the request.⁶¹ The GCC/TCC, meanwhile, would also be listening in on the same net, concurrently directing the preparation of aircraft to be ready should the request be approved. Thus, immediately upon approval, aircraft could be launched. The forward tentacle or ASP that had initiated the request would be notified through the radio net that aircraft were on their way and given an estimated time of arrival. If a VCP or FCP was forward in the target area, it would establish radio communications with the strike aircraft and talk them onto target. In British and Commonwealth practice, if there was no VCP or FCP present, ground troops had to simply wait for the expected air strike—they had no means of communication with strike aircraft. American ASPs, of course, could and routinely did establish such communications with the aircraft.⁶²

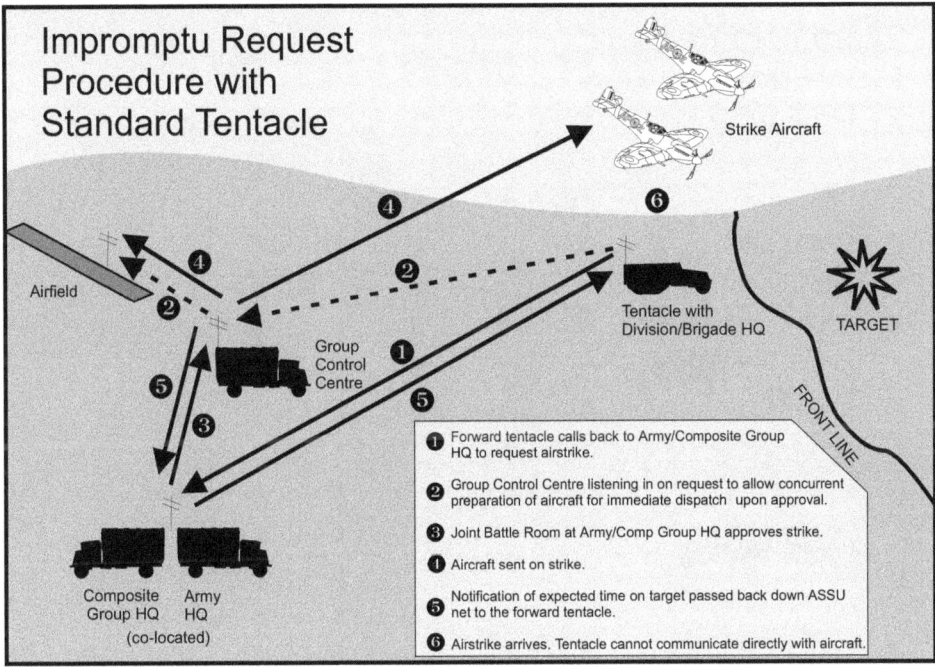

Figure 10-1 • Impromptu Request Procedure with Standard Tentacle

VCPs or FCPs co-located with a corps headquarters for major offensives would "listen in" for calls for air support from the lead tentacles. When they considered it appropriate, they would "step in" and assume control of a request. Being in communication with the GCC and even the airfields themselves, they could either direct the scrambling of aircraft or divert aircraft already in the air. The pilot on the ground with the VHF radio could describe the target and talk the aircraft onto it. This was known as delegated control by the British. It was considered responsive, but due to there being only a single FCP per field army and the drain on airpower from other areas of the front, delegated control was only employed at key points in the campaign. When and to what corps FCPs were deployed was a command decision specified in orders.[63]

Special mention should be made of the cabrank technique, or armored-column cover (ACC) as the Americans called their equivalent. This was the

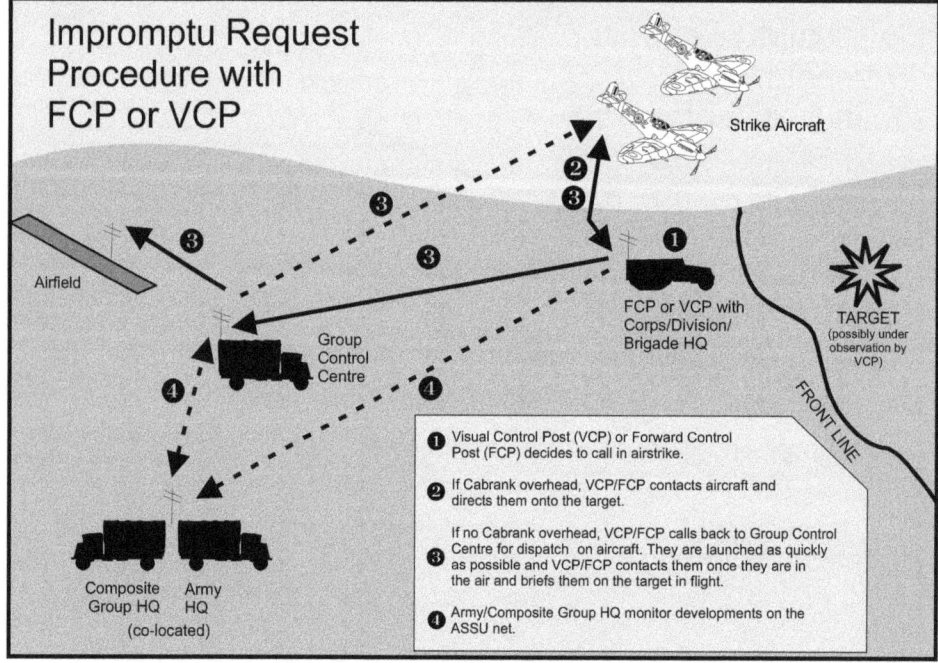

Figure 10-2 • Impromptu Request Procedure with FCP or VCP

practice of assigning a flight, typically of four aircraft but sometimes a whole squadron, either to a forward controller, a VCP or FCP, or a specific ASP with the leading units of an American armored division. Those aircraft would check in on the radio with that forward controller upon arrival in the area and then orbit just inside friendly lines, waiting for a call to strike a target. Loiter time depended upon range, aircraft configuration, fuel capacity, and sometimes weather conditions, but generally it lasted for twenty to forty-five minutes. When coming to the end of their available fuel, if they were not called down upon a target by the controller, the fighter-bombers would divert to strike a prebriefed target before returning to base. American ACC was more flexible, with the fighter-bombers ranging ahead of the tanks in the fashion of armed reconnaissance, reporting what they found deeper behind German lines, and if agreed by the controllers, striking such targets of opportunity. Cabrank or ACC bridged the divide between the prearranged/preplanned and impromptu/call categories of air support—a planned allocation of aircraft to popup targets of opportunity.⁶⁴ It was, however, used sparingly by the British in particular, as it consumed considerable resources.⁶⁵

Armed Reconnaissance

It is important to understand that the majority of tactical airpower during the Normandy Campaign was *not* delivered in the form of close support missions requested by tentacles or ASPs. The most common type of air-to-ground attack was a mission type known as "armed reconnaissance." Roughly two-thirds of sorties flown were of this sort, as opposed to either planned deliberate or immediate air strikes.⁶⁶ Armed reconnaissance was a mission type in which a group of fighter-bombers was assigned to patrol a given route or area behind German lines. While ranging over this area, they collected valuable intelligence (the reconnaissance part) and attacked any suitable targets of opportunity they found (the armed part). Interestingly, armed reconnaissance was not articulated in either British or American formal doctrine despite such deeper and more freewheeling action being the strong doctrinal preference of both air forces.⁶⁷ It was, however, clearly established practice by 1944.⁶⁸ Areas for armed reconnaissance were selected at the level of the paired army group–air force headquarters and reflected how commanders wanted the campaign shaped. Actual missions were allocated to flying squadrons within that area by the respective GCC or TCC based, in part, upon air-reconnaissance reporting of target-rich localities within the designated areas.⁶⁹ In practice, armed-reconnaissance missions were generally undertaken by a flight of approximately four aircraft, sometimes whole squadrons.⁷⁰

This was the mission type that led to so many shot-up German columns on the Normandy roads, and it came to be perhaps the most important mission category of the campaign. Indeed, more sorties were dedicated to armed reconnaissance than close support.⁷¹ Further, it has been singled out, at the time and since, as the single most effective form of air attack.⁷² Historian Ian Gooderson devoted an entire chapter to a detailed analysis of armed reconnaissance's effectiveness, coming to the conclusion that it was of "far greater value to the Allied war effort than close support," ultimately concluding that "armed reconnaissance . . . [was a] vital role for Allied air power in 1943–45."[73] Both American airpower historian Richard Hallion and RAF historian John Terraine have echoed the same theme.[74]

Consideration

So, bearing all of this in mind, how did air strikes get called in, and how long did they take to arrive? As discussed, there was a range of answers to both questions. Some air strikes were planned days ahead of time, such as for major named offensives. At the other extreme, if cabrank or ACC were laid on, strikes could be called down by controllers in direct radio communication with airborne fighter-bombers circling the battle area, generally within just a few minutes, which was faster than artillery. Of course, such response times were only possible if aircraft had been allocated ahead of time. In between those two extremes, impromptu or call missions could be laid on within an hour or two.[75] But as noted above, it should be remembered that most air attacks were delivered not through the request system, but rather by the process of armed reconnaissance for fighter-bombers or prearranged/preplanned missions for medium bombers. In fact, the stereotypical conception of an air strike, a forward controller spotting a target and calling for air attack, only accounted for a minority of tactical air missions, as most were delivered by armed reconnaissance.[76]

This was a conscious choice at the time. Armed reconnaissance was far and away the more profitable form of air attack. An operational research study in July 1944 concluded that widespread armed reconnaissance had been successful "in confusing and delaying the enemy's supplies, at the same time inflicting serious losses."[77] This emphasis upon armed reconnaissance was due to several factors. It was difficult to find suitable targets, which were not only mostly behind enemy lines but also dispersed and camouflaged.[78] The doctrinal preference was for deeper targets that were considered inherently more profitable. Finally, even when targets were known and considered an important priority, such as the columns of retreating Germans routing through the Falaise Gap, the mission type used to strike them was mostly armed reconnaissance.[79]

It is not clear that this was a poor performance, or that the more vociferous criticisms of tactical airpower's alleged slowness and unresponsiveness are fair. To return to some of the army criticisms of its responsiveness, one of the most vehement complaints had come from Major General Mann after the war. But in the heat of the campaign, he had lodged a formal complaint about the RAF's failure to service a particular air support request on 12 August. Subsequent investigation revealed that the RAF had attempted to fill the request, but a crash at the airfield had blocked the only runway, forcing cancelation of the mission.[80] That such an unfortunate incident could spark such recriminations is telling.

In fact, contrary to the army criticisms, the system of the time did have an elaborate method for providing air support, tens of thousands of sorties of it. Nor is it realistic to argue that placing those tactical air forces under the command of ground commanders could have changed anything—the same number of sorties would have been available. Even in the question of immediacy of response, it is not clear that the ground forces were ever denied air strikes because the tactical air forces were somehow holding back. Placing them under army command may have diverted sorties from armed reconnaissance to immediate support, but it is difficult to see such a change as helping the ground forces. Official army doctrine recognized the greater value of deeper targets, and operational research has corroborated the effectiveness of armed reconnaissance as the best means to strike such targets.[81] Just as army doctrine recognized the importance of concentrating artillery fire and not "penny packeting out" tanks, so it was recognized that tactical airpower should be concentrated rather than distributed along the whole front wherever it was requested.

To be fair, Normandy was a terrible fight and required hard pounding for months. There was genuine fear of stalemate and trench warfare before the breakout. The frustrations of that desperate Norman summer are the real context that should be appreciated when assessing the army criticisms of the tactical air system, for the record shows that those criticisms are unfair or at best misdirected. It is not at all clear that placing the tactical air forces under the command of the respective ground commanders could have improved responsiveness in any significant way. And there *was* a system already in place for providing immediate support, as we have seen, generally within an hour or two of request. There was even, in the form of cabrank and armored column cover, a means for providing immediate response within minutes, faster in fact than artillery could generally be brought to bear. While there was of course room for improvement, the Allied system for tactical airpower was well developed and as effective as could be expected given the technology of the time.

NOTES

1. Chester Wilmot, *The Struggle for Europe* (London: Collins, 1954), 289.
2. Quoted in Wilmot, *Struggle for Europe*, 313. It is widely repeated elsewhere. See, for example, John Terraine, *The Right of the Line* (London: Hodder and Stoughton, 1985), 637.
3. "Requests for Air Sp," 11 August 1944, file 958C009(D72), [Canadian] Directorate of History and Heritage, Ottawa [hereafter DHH]; "Air Attack requested by 4 Cdn Inf Bde 12 Aug 44," file 215C1 093(D2), vol. 10671, Record Group 27, Library and Archives Canada, Ottawa [hereafter LAC]. See also notes 5–7 below.
4. Air Chief Marshal Arthur Harris, "Report on the Bombing of Our Own Troops during Operation 'Tractable': 14 August 1944," 25 August 1944, reproduced in *Canadian Military History* 15, no. 3 (Summer–Autumn 2006), 101–12.
5. John Barnum, "The Dilemma of Close Air Support for Ground Combat," *Military Review* 30, no. 3 (June 1950), 10–26; James A. Huston, "Tactical Use of Air Power in World War II: The Army Experience," *Military Affairs* 14, no. 4 (Winter 1950), 166–85.
6. Quoted in Lee Kennett, "The US Army Air Forces and Tactical Air War in the Second World War," in *The Conduct of the Air War in the Second World War: An International Comparison*, edited by Horst Boog (Providence, RI: Berg, 1992), 462.
7. Maj. Gen. C. C. Mann, "An Analysis of the System for Direct Air Support in the Northwest Europe Campaign," 4, file 215C1.091, vol. 10671, RG 24, LAC.
8. Max Hastings, *Overlord* (London: Pan, 1984), 267, 270; Shelford Bidwell and Dominick Graham, *Fire-Power: British Army Weapons and Theories of War, 1904–1945* (London: Allen and Unwin, 1982), 250; Nigel Hamilton, *Monty*, vol. 2: *Master of the Battlefield, 1942–1944* (London: Hamish Hamilton, 1986), 620–22, 692–93. See also W. A. Jacobs, "The Battle for France, 1944," in *Case Studies in the Development of Close Air Support*, edited by B. F. Cooling (Washington, DC: Office of Air Force History, 1990), 260, 272.
9. Ian Gooderson, *Air Power at the Battlefront: Allied Close Air Support in Europe, 1943–45* (London: Frank Cass, 1998), 27.

10. These remain key tenets of air doctrine today. For an early articulation of them, see John Slessor, *Air Power and Armies* (London: Oxford University Press, 1936).
11. Matthew Powell, *The Development of British Tactical Air Power, 1940–1943: A History of Army Co-Operation Command* (London: Palgrave Macmillan, 2016); David Ian Hall, *Strategy for Victory: The Development of British Tactical Air Power, 1919–1943* (Westport, CT: Praeger, 2008); Gooderson, *Air Power at the Battlefront*; William A. Jacobs, "Air Support for the British Army, 1939–1943," *Military Affairs* 46, no. 4 (December 1982), 197–82; Paul Johnston, "The Question of British Influence on U.S. Tactical Air Power in World War II," *Air Power History* 52, no. 1 (Spring 2005), 16–33.
12. See Stephen McNamara, *Airpower's Gordian Knot: Centralized Versus Organic Control* (Maxwell AFB, AL: Air University Press, 1994), 7–36.
13. Powell, *Development of British Tactical Air Power*, 173–77; Hall, *Strategy for Victory*, 117–27.
14. Headquarters No. 84 Group, "Organization of Staffs and Operations Rooms at R.A.F. Composite Group and Army Headquarters," n.d. [circa late 1944], UK National Archives [hereafter TNA] AIR 2/7870. For the Americans, see Field Manual 100-20, *Command and Employment of Airpower* (Washington, DC: Government Printing Office, 21 July 1943) [hereafter FM 100-20]. This manual is reproduced in full in Daniel R. Mortensen, ed., *Air Power and Ground Armies: Essays on the Evolution of Anglo-American Air Doctrine, 1940–1943* (Maxwell AFB, AL: Air University Press, 1998), 167–82.
15. For an explanation of First World War command arrangements, see Alistair McCluskey, "The Battle of Amiens and the Development of British Air–Land Battle, 1918–45," in *Changing War: The British Army, the Hundred Days Campaign, and the Birth of the Royal Air Force, 1918*, edited by Gary Sheffield and Peter Gray (London: Bloomsbury, 2013), 232–47.
16. See War Office, *Army–Air Operations: Pamphlet No. 1: General Principles and Organization* (26-GS Publications-1127, 1944), 14–17 [hereafter WO, *Army–Air (1)*]; and FM 100-20, 9–14.
17. War Office, *Air Support and Air Reconnaissance: Aspects of Combined Operations in North West Europe, June 1944–May 1945*, TNA WO 233/61, chap. 3, esp. apps. A, C [hereafter WO, *Air Support and Air Recce*]; Field Manual 31-35 [FM 31-35], *Aviation in Support of Ground Forces* (Washington, DC: Government Printing Office, 1942), 5; HQ First U.S. Army G-3 (Air) [Col. E. L. Johnson] report, "Air–Ground Joint Operations," 16 July 1944, U.S. Air Force Historical Research Agency [hereafter AFHRA], microfilm B5724, 5–8 [hereafter Johnson Report].

18. For British doctrine, see WO, *Army–Air (1)*; and WO, *Army–Air Operations: Pamphlet No. 2: Direct Support* (26-GS Publications-1181, 1944) [hereafter WO, *Army–Air (2)*]. For U.S. doctrine, see FM 31-35; FM 100-20; and 9 AF, [U.S.] IX TAC, "Standard Operation Procedures for Air Support Parties," IX TAC Memo 20-2, 3 August 1944, contained in Johnson Report [hereafter IX TAC SOPs].
19. Air Historical Branch, *Air Support: The Second World War, 1939–1945*, Air Publication 3235 (London: Air Ministry, 1955), TNA AIR 10/5547 [hereafter AHB, *Air Support*]; and Johnson Report, 48.
20. WO, *Army–Air (1)*, 8; WO, *Army–Air (2)*, 12.
21. IX TAC SOPs, 47; Johnson Report, 3–4.
22. See Johnston, "Question of British Influence," 33n92.
23. Gooderson, *Air Power at the Battlefront*, 35–8; "Dive Bombers and Army Support Aircraft," March 1941–September 1943, Air Ministry file, TNA AIR 20/2970.
24. Richard P. Hallion, *Strike from the Sky: The History of Battlefield Air Attack, 1910–1945* (Tuscaloosa: University of Alabama Press, 2010), 46–54.
25. For the British, this was No. 2 Group. See Michael Bowyer, *2 Group RAF: A Complete History, 1936–1945* (London: Faber and Faber, 1974). For the Americans, it was IX Bomber Command. See W. F. Craven and J. L. Cate, eds., *The Army Air Forces in World War II*, vol. 3, *Europe: Argument to V-E Day, January 1944 to May 1945* (Chicago: University of Chicago Press, 1951), 107–227; and U.S. Army Air Forces Historical Division, *Ninth Air Force in the ETO*, Study 32 (Maxwell AFB: USAF Historical Division, 1945), 41–54.
26. On British light and medium bombers, see Bowyer, *2 Group RAF*; and Martin Bowman, *Mosquito Missions: RAF and Commonwealth de Havilland Mosquitos* (Barnsley, UK: Pen and Sword, 2012). On U.S. medium bombers, see Craven and Cate, *Army Air Forces in World War II*, 3:104–23.
27. Greg Baughen, *RAF on the Offensive: The Rebirth of Tactical Air Power, 1940–1941* (Barnsley, UK: Pen and Sword, 2018); Jacobs, "Air Support for British Army," 177.
28. For data on fighter-bomber performance, see sources for table 10-3, "Fighter-Bombers."
29. Gooderson, *Air Power at the Battlefront*, 71.
30. Gooderson, *Air Power at the Battlefront*, 77.
31. Alfred Price, "The 3-Inch Rocket: How Effective Was It against the German Tanks in Normandy," *Royal Air Force Quarterly* (Summer 1975), 127–31; Jonathan Bernstein, *P-47 Thunderbolt vs German Flak Defenses: Western Europe, 1943–45* (Oxford: Osprey, 2021), 29–31; T. W. Lee, *Military Technologies of the World*, vol. 1 (Westport, CT: Praeger, 2009), 69–70.

32. William A. Jacobs, "Tactical Air Doctrine and AAF Close Air Support in the European Theater, 1944–45," *Aerospace Historian* 27, no. 1 (March 1980), 35–49, esp. 46–47. On the notably shorter range of the Spitfire, see Gooderson, *Air Power at the Battlefront*, 64; and Jonathan Glaney, *Spitfire: The Biography* (London: Atlantic Books, 2006), 96–97, 148.
33. "Joint Report No. 3: Rocket Firing Typhoons in Close Support of Military Operations," 1945, TNA WO 291/1331, copy reproduced in Terry Copp, ed., *Montgomery's Scientists: Operational Research in Northwest Europe, the Work of No. 2 Operational Research Section with 21 Army Group June 1944 to July 1945* (Waterloo, ON: Laurier Centre for Military Strategic and Disarmament Studies, 2000), 219–39.
34. Craven and Cate, *Army Air Forces in World War II*, 3:197; Anthony Tucker-Jones, *The Normandy Air War, 1944* (Yorkshire, UK: Pen and Sword, 2019), chap. 8; "Tactics Used by 2nd TAF Squadrons during Campaign in Western Europe," RAF Headquarters 2 TAF, 1945, TNA AIR 37/871.
35. Alfred Price, "The Rocket-Firing Typhoons in Normandy: Two Major Actions," *RAF Air Power Review* 8, no. 1 (Spring 2005), 79–88; Hallion *Strike from the Sky*, 226–27; Gooderson, *Air Power at the Battlefront*, 122–23, 229–30.
36. Christopher F. Shores and Chris Thomas, *2nd Tactical Air Force*, vols. 1–4 (Classic Publications, 2004–9), esp. vol. 4; J. Davies and J. P. Kellet, *A History of the RAF Servicing Commandos* (Shrewsbury, UK: Airlife, 1989); Craven and Cate, *Army Air Forces in World War II*, 3:107–37; Rust, *Ninth Air Force*.
37. For a vivid portrayal, see Monty Berger and Brian Jeffrey Street *Invasions without Tears: The Story of Canada's Top-Scoring Spitfire Wing in Europe during the Second World War* (Toronto: Random House Canada, 1994).
38. AHB, *Air Support*, 149–50; U.S. Army Air Forces, *Condensed Analysis of the Ninth Air Force in the European Theater of Operations* (1946; repr., Washington, DC: Office of Air Force History, 1984), 79–84; "Operation NEPTUNE Allied Expeditionary Air Force, Overall Air Plan" 15 April 1944, app. F, file 200A2.016(D1), vol. 10400, RG 24, LAC; Mike Bechthold, "On the Ground: Canadian Airfields in Normandy," *Canadian Military History* 3, no. 1 (Spring 1994), 49–55.
39. WO, *Army–Air (1)*, 15–6, 30; WO, *Air Support and Air Recce*, chap. 3, app. F; Johnson Report, 43; Jacobs, "Battle for France," 260.
40. WO, *Army–Air (1)*, 16–7, 31; AAF Evaluation Board ETO, "Report of Tactical Committee on the Subject of Doctrine, Organization, Tactics and Techniques of the AAF in the ETO," 26 September 1944, AFHRA A1175, 20–31 [hereafter "AAF Evaluation Report"].

41. 2 TAF strength estimated by author from the order of battle. See L. F. Ellis, *Victory in the West*, vol. 1, *The Battle of Normandy* (London: HMSO, 1962), app. 6, 556–58; 9 AF strength from U.S. Army Air Forces, *Condensed Analysis*, 53.
42. Air Marshal Douglas quoted in "Army/Air Co-operation," C. E. Carrington Papers, Imperial War Museum, London, 81/11/6; Hall, *Strategy for Victory*, 93.
43. WO, *Air Support and Air Recce*, chap. 4.
44. "AAF Evaluation Report," 3.
45. To avoid possible confusion, note that in modern U.S. terminology, an "ALO" is an Air Force officer detached to the Army, whereas an Army officer working with the Air Force is known as a ground liaison officer (GLO). In Second World War British and Commonwealth parlance, ALOs were army officers working in air support. See WO, *Air Support and Air Recce*, chap. 5.
46. Johnson Report, 44.
47. On German air support to ground forces, see Bidwell and Graham, *Fire-Power*, 267; and James Corum and Richard Muller, *The Luftwaffe's Way of War: German Air Force Doctrine, 1911–1945* (Baltimore: Nautical and Aviation, 1998) 206–16.
48. FM 31-35, 2, 12–13, 48–49; Johnson Report, 8–10. See also Mike Bechthold, "'The Development of an Unbeatable Combination': US Close Air Support in Normandy," *Canadian Military History* 7, no. 4 (Autumn 1998), 7–20.
49. WO, *Air Support and Air Recce*, chap, 3, 8–9; 21 Army Group, *Some Notes on the Use of Air Power in Support of Land Operations and Direct Air Support* (December 1944), 17, Ike Skelton Combined Arms Research Library, Call no. N5330, https://cgsc.contentdm.oclc.org/digital/collection/p4013coll8/id/5972/.
50. Bidwell and Graham, *Fire-Power*, 265.
51. Examples of ASSU orders allocating tentacles can be seen in 1 ASSU War Diary, Military Communications and Electronics Museum, Kingston, Ont., copy.
52. That is, there was one for each Combat Command (the armored forces' brigade equivalent). Headquarters European Theater of Operations, U.S. Army, Immediate Report 1 (Combat Observations), "Close Air Support within 12th Army Group," original file 370.2 (G-3), 20 November 1944, 3, Ike Skelton Combined Arms Research Library, Call no. N9368, https://cgsc.contentdm.oclc.org/digital/collection/p4013coll8/id/4651/rec/1, pdf, 304–10; IX TAC SOPs, 44.
53. WO, *Air Support and Air Recce*, chap. 3, 8–9.
54. WO, *Army-Air (2)*, 13; AHB, *Air Support*, 153; memo, First Canadian Army, "Forward Aids to Air Support," 1 September 1944, file 215C1.093, vol. 10671, RG 24, LAC.

55. WO, *Air Support and Air Recce*, chap. 3, app. H. On its evolution from Rover David, see AHB, *Air Support*, 108-13; memo, First Canadian Army Headquarters, "Air Support in 1 Cdn Army," n.d. [probably early 1945], file 249C5(D15), vol. 10945, RG 24, LAC, 2.
56. "Close Air Support within 12th Army Group," 2-3; IX TAC SOPs, 44-46.
57. Bechthold, "Development of an Unbeatable Combination," 4, 13.
58. WO, *Air Support and Air Recce*, chap. 3, paras. 14-15; "Close Air Support within 12th Army Group," 3.
59. For example, for Totalize, Headquarters, First Canadian Army submitted a ten-page written request for air support on 4 August (file 215C1.096(D3), vol. 10671, RG 24, LAC), then the next day a conference at Main Headquarters AEAF discussed the matter (5 August 1944, TNA AIR 37/763, TLM/135/50), followed by a formal "Air Programme" on 6 August, with the operation launched late on the seventh. For the capture of Cherbourg, Brereton and some staff flew back to the United Kingdom for a hurried planning conference on 21 June, resulting in an elaborate air plan that commenced the next day. Craven and Cate, *Army Air Forces in World War II*, 3:199-201.
60. WO, *Air Support and Air Recce*, chap. 3, paras. 12-14; [U.S.] 12th Army Group, memo "Staff Action on Air Support," 29 July 1944, contained within "AAF Evaluation Report," 3.
61. WO, *Air Support and Air Recce*, chap. 3, para. 16; IX TAC SOPs, 46-47; Johnson Report, 43 diagram. See also Hallion, *Strike from the Sky*, 198 diagram.
62. Headquarters, British 51st (Highland) Division, memo, "British and American Methods of Air Support," 7 March 1945, TNA WO 205/546.
63. See note 51 above.
64. AHB, *Air Support*, 149; WO, *Air Support and Air Recce*, chap. 3, app. H, para. 5.
65. Price, "Rocket-Firing Typhoons in Normandy." On the greater U.S. employment of loitering fighter-bombers, see Bechthold, "Development of an Unbeatable Combination," 17-18.
66. "2nd TAF O.R.S. Report No. 30," July 1945, TNA WO 291/1357; "Statistical Summary of Ninth Air Force Operations: 16 Oct 1943—8 May 1945," AFHRA file 168.6006-85; and Gooderson, *Air Power at the Battlefront*, 199-201.
67. Armed reconnaissance is not specifically articulated in WO, *Army-Air (1)*; WO, *Army-Air (2)*; FM 31-35; or FM 100-20.
68. WO, *Air Support and Air Recce*, chap. 3, 10; AAF Evaluation Board Report, *The Effectiveness of Third Phase Tactical Air Operations in the European Theater, 5 May 1944-8 May 1945* ([Dayton, OH: Wright Field], 1946); Gooderson, *Air Power at the Battlefront*, 199-201.
69. WO, *Air Support and Air Recce*, chap. 3, 10.

70. Based upon review of the operations record books of squadrons, a flight of four aircraft was common, with larger groupings used only for mass efforts, such as over the Falaise Gap. See TNA AIR 27.
71. Ian Gooderson stresses this point. See *Air Power at the Battlefront*, 200.
72. Operational Research Report, "RP and F/B Effectiveness 22 Jun–7 Jul," quoted in No. 84 Group Operations Record Book, 8 July 1944, TNA AIR 25/709.
73. Gooderson, *Air Power at the Battlefront*, 245.
74. Richard P. Hallion, "Battlefield Air Support a Retrospective Assessment," *Airpower Journal* 4, no. 1 (Spring 1990), 8–28, 11; Hallion, *Strike from the Sky*; Terraine, *Right of the Line*, 658–62.
75. For the one-hour claim, see Memo, "Report on Visit to 84 Group on the 28th July, 1944," TNA AIR 2/7870; and Johnson Report, 4. Other sources suggest this was often two or even three hours. See, for example, Headquarters, British 51st (Highland) Division, memo, "British and American Methods of Air Support."
76. Gooderson, *Air Power at the Battlefront*, 200–201.
77. Operational Research Report, "RP and F/B Effectiveness."
78. "Allied Expeditionary Air Force: Operation 'Neptune': Review of Air Operations. Narrative History," 520. TNA AIR 37/1210.
79. John Golley, *The Day of the Typhoon: Flying with the RAF Tankbusters in Normandy* (Wellingborough, UK: Patrick Stephens, 1986; repr., Wrens Park, Eng.: Airlife Classics, 2000); Desmond Scott, *Typhoon Pilot* (London: Arrow, 1988); Bill Colgan, *World War II Fighter Bomber Pilot* (Blue Ridge Summit, PA: TAB Books, 1985).
80. "Requests for Air Sp," 11 August 1944, File 958C009(D72), DHH; "Air Attack Requested by 4 Cdn Inf Bde 12 Aug 44," vol. 10671, RG 27, file 215C1 093(D2), LAC.
81. On this preference for deeper targets, see note 10; FM 100-20, 12.

11

The Air Support Rollercoaster
Canadian Soldiers' Morale in Normandy

Alexander Fitzgerald-Black

The soldiers of the Highland Light Infantry of Canada had been in Normandy for a little over a month. Originally recruited and raised in Galt, Ontario, the battalion landed on Juno Beach around noon on D-Day as part of the reserve brigade of the 3rd Canadian Infantry Division. Now, on 7 July 1944, they occupied positions near les Buissons, a small French commune to the north of Buron, a larger village. Buron had changed hands multiple times in the desperate fighting of 7 June, as the Canadians attempted to expand their bridgehead while the 12th SS (Hitler Youth) Panzer Division sought to throw the Allies back into the sea. This area had been on the front line for the past month. Anglo-Canadian forces now planned to unleash a storm of steel to capture the city of Caen. The Highlanders' job would be to capture Buron the next day.

The overall offensive, codenamed Operation Charnwood, would see the heavy bombers of Royal Air Force (RAF) Bomber Command used in a close support role for the first time. While these four-engine aircraft targeted positions behind the German line, fighter-bombers of the 2nd Tactical Air Force attacked German frontline positions. Nine Hawker Typhoons of No. 439 "Sabre-Toothed Tiger" Squadron, Royal Canadian Air Force (RCAF)—affectionately known as "Bombphoons" because RCAF Typhoon squadrons were armed with bombs rather than the rocket projectiles common to most RAF Typhoon units—attacked Buron. The pilots dropped their bombs amid bursts of flak and antiaircraft tracers, then flew the six miles back to their base at Airfield B-9, near the seventeenth-century Château de Lantheuil. The squadron recorded the attack as a notable success: "Since the actual target was in close proximity to our forward troops, the terrific damage wrought by dive bombing Typhoons was easily apparent to them all. It is a terrific morale booster to our troops and a shattering blow to the enemy troops."[1]

The Highland Light Infantry witnessed the Typhoon and heavy bomber attacks. "Air activity increased during the day," their war diarist recorded. "At 2100 hours Typhoons rocket-bombed targets around Buron. At 2210 hours Lancasters swept overhead in a great stream to bomb the area Caen–St. Germain–Carpiquet. They met terrific flak but only one plane was seen to be hit and it returned over our lines safely. Estimated 500 planes employed and all agreed it was a grand show."[2]

Both the Typhoon squadron and infantry battalion accounts share an emphasis on the morale effects of close air support. The RCAF account noted that the Canadian troops had a "ringside seat" to watch the attack and implied that providing a morale boost to friendly troops was part of the job of fighter-bomber pilots. The Typhoon diarist's note that the raid was "a shattering blow to the enemy troops" was probably an exaggeration and almost certainly not based on any evidence. Perhaps the shattering blow was the five hundred heavy bombers that followed nearly an hour later. The infantry account placed more emphasis on this impressive show of airpower. These accounts and others illustrate important linkages between morale and airpower—particularly Allied—throughout the Battle of Normandy.

In the late 1990s Ian Gooderson's *Air Power at the Battlefront* argued that much of air support's benefit was psychological.[3] This is harder to measure than the number of targets destroyed by aircraft (which is also difficult to verify, even when the army later takes control of the target area). Nevertheless, the Germans feared Allied airpower and limited their daylight road movements. On 12 June 1944 Field Marshal Erwin Rommel, commander of Army Group B, complained to Field Marshal Wilhelm Keitel, chief of the Oberkommando der Wehrmacht (OKW), the high command of Nazi Germany's armed forces:

> The enemy has complete control of the air over the battle area up to a distance of about 100 km behind the front, and with powerful fighter-bomber and bomber formations, immobilizes almost all traffic by day on roads or in open country.... Movements of our troops on the battlefield by day are thus almost entirely impossible, while the enemy can operate without hindrance. In the country behind, all roads are exposed to continual attack, and it is therefore very difficult to bring up the necessary supplies of fuel and munitions.[4]

Airpower ultimately removed Rommel from command in Normandy. His replacement, Field Marshal Günther von Kluge, was also concerned about the effectiveness of unmatched Allied airpower, in this case the use of heavy bombers in direct support of the Allied armies. He wrote, "The psychological effect on the fighting forces, especially the infantry, of such a mass of bombs raining down upon them with all the force of elemental nature, is a factor which must be given serious consideration."[5]

We may know something about the psychological effect of Allied air support on the Germans, but what of its effect on Allied troops? Gooderson's work provides glimpses of this, but to be fair, the army's morale was not his focus. In more recent years, army historians have made morale their focus. Robert Engen wrote about combat motivation in the Canadian Army during and after the Battle of Normandy in his 2016 book, *Strangers in Arms*. He defined "morale" as "the willingness on the part of the infantrymen, individually and in groups, to fight and persevere in fighting; and 'high morale' ... a high willingness to participate in combat."[6] One of the primary sources for Engen's analysis was battle-experience questionnaires filled out by ninety-one junior infantry officers after their time in Normandy. Interestingly, when these men were asked which factors helped raise morale, "Allied air support" placed third, with thirty-eight officers indicating it as a factor. Only "mail and parcels" and "food and rations" (forty-eight and forty-seven officers indicating respectively) scored higher. Also of interest, eleven officers indicated the combined category of friendly fire and bombing by friendly aircraft as a morale-lowering factor.[7] This relatively low number probably reflects the fact that this was an infantry survey. Artillery and armored officers might have reported differently (as discussed below).

The data from these questionnaires suggest airpower had a significant effect on Canadian Army morale during the Battle of Normandy. But what was the nature of that effect? Jonathan Fennell's 2019 book, *Fighting the People's War*, surveys the wartime morale of the British and Commonwealth armies in World War II. He defines "morale" in similar terms to Engen, adding, "The degree of morale of an individual or group relates to the extent of their willingness or discipline to act, or their determination to see an action through."[8] Poor morale among the Canadians, Fennell contends, helps explain their failure to break out and overcome numerically inferior German defenders in Operations Totalize and Tractable. In large part he attributes low morale to friendly bombing incidents in both operations.[9]

But how did air support affect the morale of Canadian soldiers in Normandy? Too often, the air war tends to get separated from the ground war in studies and retellings of the Battle of Normandy. Furthermore, as demonstrated above, good work exists on the morale of the army, but more could be done to consider how airpower affected the troops' morale, especially given the prominence of its appearance in the infantry-officer questionnaires. Finally, airpower studies like Gooderson's typically focus on the psychological effect of airpower on the enemy, rather than on friendly troops. Allied air support in Normandy should also be noted for its significant positive and negative effects on friendly soldiers' morale on the battlefield.

Engen and Fennell have pioneered the use of innovative sources to better understand army morale. In addition to officers' battle-experience questionnaires, Engen used field-censor reports of soldiers' mail to gauge morale. Censor officers examined 15 percent of the millions of letters sent home by soldiers and used these surveys to produce reports analyzing trends and patterns in the troops' prevailing attitudes.[10] Fennell likewise used the same reports. Going back to some basic sources—mainly the Canadian Army war diaries for the Normandy Campaign—helps supplement this existing work on soldier morale and gauge airpower's influence on it.

So, what did the Canadian soldier think about the air support he received in Normandy, and what were the consequences of this for his morale? War diaries and memoirs of the fighting on the ground contain myriad compliments and criticisms about what the Allied air forces were doing during the Battle of Normandy from this Canadian perspective.

Clear skies and one-sided dogfights against numerically superior Allied aircraft gave the soldiers of the 3rd Canadian Infantry Division confidence in the battles of June 1944. Air support failures, including the friendly fire incidents of Operations Totalize and Tractable, depressed Canadian troops to the point that some considered the Allied air forces a bigger threat than the Luftwaffe. The compliments (peaks) and criticisms (valleys) present an undulating curve of Canadian soldiers' morale in Normandy—a rollercoaster.

D-Day

How did troops of the 3rd Canadian Infantry Division feel about their air support on D-Day? The assault troops experienced the weather firsthand while waiting in the English Channel for their time to land. For at least some troops, this reduced their expectations about the aerial bombardment. The war diarist of the 13th Field Regiment wrote: "It is a dull morning with low clouds and poor visibility, which makes the projected aerial bombardment out of the question. The wind has died down but the waves have not."[11]

Sentiments like this largely proved to be correct, and it was not just the air bombardment that was affected. After the Royal Winnipeg Rifles' landing west of Courseulles-sur-Mer, their diarist explained how the battalion stormed ashore: "The bombardment having failed to kill a single German or silence one weapon, these companies had to storm their positions 'cold'—and did so without hesitation."[12] On the other side of Courseulles, the Regina Rifle Regiment endured a similar experience. The next day their war diarist summarized a commanding officers' exchange on the aerial effort: "It was evident to all that, due to adverse flying conditions the air support had not been as great as been expected. Pillboxes and other emplacements were

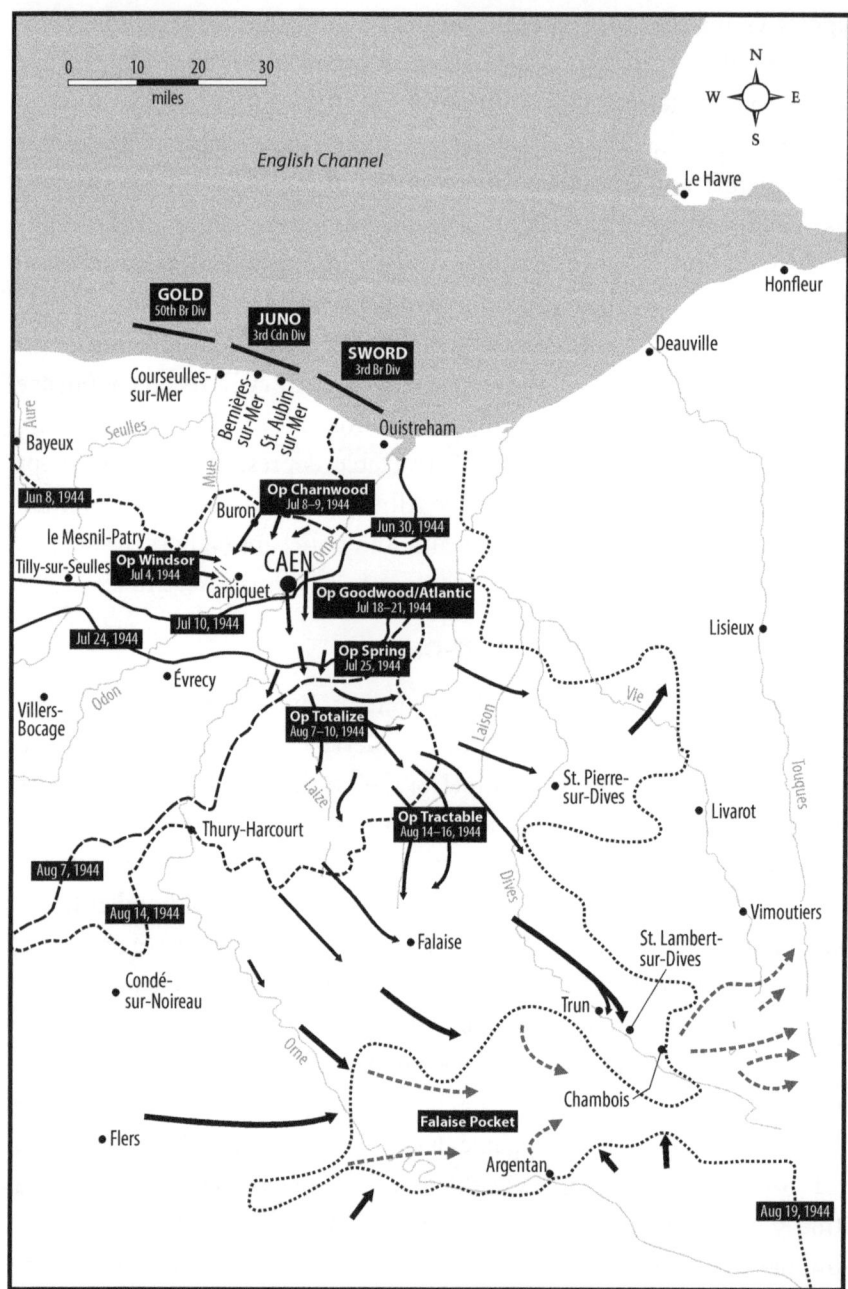

Map 11-1 • Normandy: The Canadian Sector

still open for business when our troops touched down."[13] Much of this was later confirmed by operational research, yet the psychological effect on the German defenders was also a factor.[14]

Despite the lack of physical damage, there is evidence that the Allied troops' morale was improved by the massive aerial armada deployed in support of the assault (at least when it could be seen through the overcast). This was particularly true among the reserve soldiers, who waited offshore during the assaults. Sixteen miles from the coast at 0600 hours, the Stormont, Dundas, and Glengarry Highlanders observed "large numbers of planes... passing over the clouds." They had yet to sight an enemy aircraft. Later, as the overcast cleared and the temperature rose, they saw their first German warplane. The diarist gleefully recorded that "a couple of Spitfires are hot on its tail."[15]

The troops appreciated the relative absence of the Luftwaffe and the presence of their air umbrella. When the Highland Light Infantry landed along with the rest of 9th Canadian Infantry Brigade, they were caught up in a large traffic jam on the beach and as they moved through Bernières-sur-Mer. Their diarist later recorded: "It was an awful shambles and not at all like the organized rehearsals we had had. More than one uttered a fervent prayer of thanksgiving that our air umbrella was so strong."[16]

The Bridgehead and Carpiquet

As 3rd Canadian Infantry Division settled into nearly a month of static warfare, their impressions of the work of friendly aircraft continued to develop. At times the Luftwaffe made an appearance, and the Highland Light Infantry "missed [their] fine air umbrella." The German fliers struck the lodgment nightly, but their presence during the day was more limited, or at least that was the troops' impression. On 20 June the Highlanders were buzzed by a "rare sight"—a flight of German fighters. "No one was much concerned," the diarist opined. "The vaunted *Luftwaffe* has become a thing of curiosity rather than fear. We are much more interested these days in the after supper treat the RAF brings us each evening the weather permits."[17] They would watch wave after wave of Allied aircraft bomb Caen and other nearby communication centers.

On 23 June two RAF squadron leaders visited the North Nova Scotia Highlanders. In the past weeks, Allied aircraft had moved to the Continent and were now operating from airfields only minutes away by air. The diarist noted: "The air force has done a great job to date in keeping Jerry out of the skies. Let's hope they continue to do so."[18] What really caught the attention of the troops were the occasions when RAF Spitfires tangled with German fighters. It was even more exciting when an enemy aircraft crashed in their vicinity. These positive sentiments toward the air force extended beyond the Canadians. A British censorship summary examined mail from six British divisions in the Normandy lodgment and reported that the support given by the Royal Navy and RAF had "made a deep impression" on the soldiers and had offered them a "feeling of security."[19]

In early July the Canadians fought an intense battle to capture Carpiquet airfield west of Caen. Although the battalions engaged did not record much about air support, the Canadian Scottish Regiment, operating a nearby observation post at the schoolhouse in Rots, had an excellent vantage point for Operation Windsor, as it was dubbed. They noted how the rocket-firing Typhoons helped blunt the German counterattacks on Canadian positions in the village of Carpiquet. As the battalion prepared to leave the Rots area on 7 July, they observed Bomber Command's assault on Caen. The diarist noted that the "morale of the troops is always greatly heartened by this evidence of Air Force–Army cooperation."[20]

Operation Charnwood

Bomber Command's evening attack on the northern outskirts of Caen offered a stunning spectacle for Allied troops, even if its effects on the German army were less profound. After 2000 hours on 7 July 1944, 467 Halifaxes and Lancasters dropped their payloads behind the German front line. The war diaries of the frontline Canadian infantry battalions are filled with praise for this effort. There is little doubt that the "very imposing sight" was "a great morale raiser the night before battle."[21] Lieutenant Colonel Nigel Tapp with the 3rd British Infantry Division, which had been fighting north of Caen for a month, recalled: "The psychological effect . . . was electrifying . . . the noise and sight of the bombardment was a tremendous morale boost. Officers and soldiers were jumping out of their slit trenches and cheering."[22]

The massed heavy bombers were an impressive sight, but the problem was that these bombardments came some six to eight hours before the troops advanced. An adverse weather forecast had moved up the timetable for the bombing. So even if the Anglo-Canadians' morale was high going into the battle (and the delay meant the full morale advantage had likely dissipated), the Germans had time to recover and give the Allies a tough fight for Buron, Cussy, and the Abbaye d'Ardenne. Professor Solly Zuckerman, a senior RAF operational research scientist, later concluded that "apart from the enormous lift to their morale which the appearance of the heavy bombers had given, [men of 3rd British Division believed] that the bombing had made no material difference to the whole operation."[23] In fact, it may have made the army's task more difficult.

The aerial targets the British Army had selected were behind the German strongpoints. This was done for fear of the bombers dropping their loads short onto Anglo-Canadian lines and causing casualties among the assault forces. The bombs thus largely fell behind the main German defense line and wrecked the northern part of the city of Caen, killing and wounding French civilians in the process. This made the Allied troops' job more difficult for two reasons. First, it meant the enemy fought more stubbornly, as their positions were mostly intact, while withdrawal routes were blocked. Second, it meant once in the city, the British and Canadians had to advance through cratered streets filled with rubble, preventing rapid offensive movements to pursue the retreating enemy.[24] Nevertheless, the result was that the northern half of Caen was in Allied hands.

Operation Goodwood/Atlantic and Verrières Ridge

Nine days later Second British Army launched a massive armored thrust into German lines east and south of Caen. The main attack, known as Operation Goodwood, was preceded by another carpet of bombs dropped by Allied aircraft. This time the bombardment struck the German positions squarely, helping the armor punch a hole through the first defensive line.

The II Canadian Corps' role in Goodwood, known as Operation Atlantic, also benefited from the positive morale effects of the bombardment, which this time took place immediately before the initial assaults.

The Royal Winnipeg Rifles, tasked with crossing the Orne River at Caen, received a boost from the air forces. "At first light," the war diarist recorded, "the [ground] attack was preceded by a heavy bomber attack which was observed by all ranks. It was tremendously inspiring to see this flight and to know the weight of our airpower was going in ahead of us."[25] The diarists of the Highland Light Infantry and Stormont, Dundas, and Glengarry Highlanders concurred, noting that the bombers struck their objectives across the river. Later in the day both units complained that damaged roads contributed to delays in the advance to their final objectives.[26]

The Anglo-Canadian offensive ended with mixed results. The remainder of Caen had fallen to the Allies, but the Germans maintained their positions atop Verrières and Bourguébus Ridges. In Operation Atlantic and later in Operation Spring, the 2nd Canadian Infantry Division suffered heavily in its attempts to capture the Verrières feature. During and after Operation Spring, RAF Typhoons often caught the attention of Canadian infantry. "Typhoons bearing rockets had been very successful in breaking up [a] reported gathering of enemy tanks," came one report from the Highland Light Infantry.[27] On 26 July the Canadian Scottish Regiment diarist wrote: "The Typhoons of the RAF attacked their targets with greater ferocity than ever before. Salvo after salvo of rockets were cheered on the way by our troops who were privileged to view the savage attack. The enemy in this sector had no haven until darkness fell and our planes could no longer see to attack. Soon afterwards, German planes came over but did not stay long."[28]

A largely static artillery duel soon developed on the front. The soldiers appreciated when fighter-bombers attacked German guns shelling their positions. Typhoons could be observed shooting back at enemy positions that made ground troops feel helpless. The infantry's only recourse against artillery fire was taking cover in their slit trenches and hoping the shells would miss.[29] These counterbattery air strikes improved morale.

At this point in the Canadian Army's experience in Normandy, two themes related to Allied air superiority are evident. First, Canadian units located behind the front lines, especially armored and artillery units, were often subject to night attacks by German aircraft. There was some frustration as these instances repeated themselves. George Blackburn, who served with the 2nd Canadian Infantry Division's 4th Field Regiment, noted that antiaircraft batteries were instructed to hold their fire to give friendly night fighters freedom to roam the skies."[30]

Second, Canadian soldiers were impressed with the benefits of Allied daytime air superiority, even in seemingly minute ways. At the end of July, the 3rd Canadian Infantry Division, which had been in the front line for nearly two months without rest, finally got a reprieve. They retired to a rest area northwest of Caen, situated on the very battlefield they had fought over a month earlier. The 14th Field Regiment diarist was thankful for Allied air dominance: "The Regiment reaches the 'Rest Area' without incident. Our area is part of the flat open grain country north of Villons les Buissons. There is absolutely no cover and the only protection from air attack is dispersal as wide as the area allows. It is a real attribute to our air force and also our AA defence that such an area can be used thus."[31]

Allied air superiority was an important enabler of the army's morale-raising activities in addition to directly enhancing the soldiers' morale.

Operation Totalize

It was at this point that things really started to go wrong concerning air support for the Canadian Army in Normandy. The plan for Operation Totalize included two air bombardments. Prior to the advance on the night of 7 August, RAF Bomber Command attacked German-held towns on the flanks. At noon the next day, the U.S. Eighth Air Force was to hit what Allied planners identified as a second line of defenses, some of which had already been attacked by the RAF. The British attacks were successful, but two dozen American B-17s bombed short, killing and wounding 315 Canadian and Polish soldiers (25 Canadians killed and 131 wounded) assembling to exploit the effects of this second bombardment.[32]

The North Shore (New Brunswick) Regiment suffered heavy losses of twenty-three killed and seventy-five wounded.[33] Artillery units, packed up and ready to move to new positions, were also hit in the open. The 4th

Photo 11-1 • First Canadian Army received extensive air support for Operation Totalize, 7–10 August 1944. A night attack by RAF Bomber Command on German-held villages flanking the advance was largely successful, but an attack by the U.S. Eighth Air Force the next day saw two dozen bombers miss their targets and hit friendly forces, killing or wounding 315 Canadian and Polish soldiers. This photo shows Canadian troops near the front looking back toward Caen to watch the carnage caused by the American bombs. *LAC PMR 82-060*

Medium Regiment diarist recorded, "The sound, the blast, the feeling resulting from that bombing is something we cannot describe, but nobody in the regiment will ever forget this day."[34] Understandably, this friendly fire incident loomed large for the affected units, but the news also spread quickly to those who had been spared the bombardment. The Canadian Scottish Regiment diarist recorded: "Our chief subject of conversation was the fact that Major General Keller, GOC 3rd Canadian Infantry Division had been wounded [by friendly bombs]. . . . Morale of any troops is not heightened from such news."[35] George Blackburn was spared the results of this friendly fire incident. He later wrote, "What a terribly demoralizing experience for divisions preparing to enter battle, the two armored divisions [1st Polish and 4th Canadian] for the first time!"[36]

Photo 11-2 • An ammunition truck, hit by American bombs, burns furiously during the Canadian advance on 8 August 1944. *LAC PA 131375*

Blackburn was right. Admissions to No. 1 Canadian Battle Exhaustion Unit, Royal Canadian Army Medical Corps, peaked after these troops suffered from the combination of enduring their first battle and being struck by U.S. bombs. British troops serving in the First Canadian Army were also admitted in large numbers due to the bombing.[37]

Operation Tractable

Friendly fire incidents continued to plague the First Canadian Army as they fought south to Falaise in an effort to close the pocket around German forces in Normandy. This time Bomber Command was at fault. According to Air Chief Marshal Sir Arthur Harris' report written after Operation Tractable, some 77 Lancasters and Halifaxes (out of 811 dispatched), including 44 aircraft from No. 6 Group RCAF, bombed incorrectly. Forty-nine of these aircraft hit the quarry at Hautmesnil, where Canadian troops were concentrated for the drive to Falaise.[38] In fact, Lieutenant General Guy Simonds, commander of the II Canadian Corps, was at the quarry along with Air Marshal Sir Arthur Coningham. The pair took cover in an armored car, which "rocked violently to and fro" as the bombs fell to earth.[39] Major Bob Suckling, commanding D Company, Royal Regiment of Canada, later recalled: "Even [Coningham] couldn't do anything to stop them. I'd like to know what he was thinking as he bounced around inside that armoured car for an hour and a half."[40]

When the dust settled, over 150 Allied soldiers were dead and 241 were wounded.[41] Personnel carriers, trucks, guns, and gun tractors were smashed. Perhaps more importantly, the troops' morale and their confidence in the air force was shaken if not shattered. The 3rd Medium Regiment diarist wrote: "The morale of the troops has never been so low and their disgust never so great as at this moment. This makes the second time our troops have experienced bombing by our own air forces, and faith in close support bombing at the moment is negative."[42] Not surprisingly, No. 1 Canadian Exhaustion Unit experienced another peak in battle-exhaustion casualties following the Tractable friendly fire incident.[43]

War correspondents were also witness to the devastation. Ralph Allen of the *Globe and Mail* wrote, "Even those who were still unscathed . . . were badly shaken as they emerged from reeking shell craters, dugouts and slit trenches into scenes filled with the smoke of the burning supply dumps and the noise and flame of exploding ammunition lories."[44] Lieutenant General Harry Crerar, commander of First Canadian Army, was concerned about the morale consequences of the Totalize and Tractable fratricide incidents. He was equally worried about air force–army relations and the possible effects this could have on prosecuting the remainder of the war. Crerar ordered a forty-eight-hour hold on press stories about the friendly fire incidents after Tractable. He met with the correspondents to warn about the threat to "morale and internal harmony that could be caused by wild and unconsidered stories and the effect on the Allied effort." Crerar also "asked the correspondents each be guided by his own conscience on the matter."[45] The resulting stories reported what happened but refrained from criticism of the air force. Reporters indicated that the friendly bombing had little effect on the Canadian advance since most of the subjected troops were not part of the assault's spearhead.⁴⁶ Most of the bombs (in both Totalize and Tractable) had also hit their intended targets, helping the Canadian advance.⁴⁷ This public-relations battle did not change the fact that Canadian soldiers were angry, and their morale took a significant hit at this time.

These friendly fire incidents affected how commanders managed their battles. Ian Gooderson's research indicates that the morale effects of these mistaken attacks far outweighed the actual casualties. In fact, troops exhibited a hangover of reluctance to call for support.⁴⁸ The Stormont, Dundas, and Glengarry Highlanders experienced this on 14 August, when their commanding officer asked for armored support instead of aerial support because his forward companies would have had to pull back from the front line to provide the aircraft with the margin considered necessary to prevent friendly fire casualties. Later that day the unit's diarist reported that while the heavy bombers had done some "excellent work," they had also badly hit Canadian units behind their location. "This is the second time that this regrettable incident has taken place, and the confidence of the troops in the accuracy of the RAF has been shaken."⁴⁹

The 12th Field Regiment had a particularly rough go during Tractable. The vehicles and trailers of one battery were mostly destroyed before the regiment moved forward the next day to support the advance. In the afternoon they arrived near Olendon and were greeted "by two Spitfires which attacked [their] own troops very close by and started fires. Later, several Mustangs attacked vehicles on the road near position and destroyed a [truck] of the 43rd Battery." The entry concluded, "Personnel [are] very nervous now, and dive for slit trenches at the sound of a plane—particularly if Allied."⁵⁰ The Canadian Scottish Regiment lost part of their August war diary in the 14 August attack. The diarist later wrote, "After the incident of Aug 14, we don't say 'What planes are they' but rather 'Where are they attacking?'" In fact, on 19 August he recorded a new term in the soldier's lexicon: "Companies were informed that there was a likelihood of us being RAF'ed unless forward troops displayed yellow smoke."⁵¹ Unfortunately, although the army regularly used yellow smoke to mark the location of friendly troops for the tactical air force, Bomber Command Pathfinder aircraft also used yellow indicators to guide their bombers to the target. Harris' crews had not been informed of this fact prior to Tractable and thus saw the yellow smoke as a target rather than a warning.[52]

The Falaise Pocket

The increase in friendly fighter-bomber attacks did not go unnoticed at army level. Brigadier Churchill Mann, chief of staff, First Canadian Army, wrote a report detailing the friendly fire incidents on 18 and 19 August. The report listed forty-two attacks on the eighteenth and ten more the following day. He warned: "It is considered essential that all possible steps are taken by both services on a high priority to ensure the possibility of future attacks are reduced to a minimum. If this is not effected, this powerful weapon in support of the army will constitute a deterrent to ground ops rather than the stimulant of which is it potentially capable."[53] These mistaken attacks were causing significant damage; II Canadian Corps casualties from friendly air action between 16 and 18 August were listed as 78 killed and 209 wounded, with the bulk of these coming from the Polish Armoured Division. These casualties did not include the 3rd Canadian Infantry Division. All of this occurred in the frenzy that was the Allied air effort against German forces trapped in the Falaise Pocket and escaping through the Falaise Gap.

The air force did manage to recover its image in some circles. A British reconnaissance regiment noted that "visible air support is a great morale raiser for troops who do not understand what air support is when they can't see it."[54] As the Battle of Normandy climaxed, the Allied air forces had been quite visible, often in an intensely negative way. Yet as the Falaise Pocket closed and German forces began their retreat to the Seine, Allied troops witnessed the positive effects of what tactical airpower could accomplish.

In the Canadian pursuit toward the Seine River, the soldiers passed through the "Shambles" and the "Chase," regions of the battlefield full of German corpses amid masses of abandoned and destroyed equipment. The Stormont, Dundas, and Glengarry Highlanders war diary entry on 23 August reads: "The roads are lined with wrecked enemy vehicles telling the grim story of havoc dealt to the retreating enemy by our air force. . . . We are extremely thankful for our air superiority."[55] The Regina Rifle Regiment found its passage through Vimoutiers slow due to the destruction of a German convoy: "The column was literally 'caught with their pants down' and this scene of CHAOS and destruction makes everyone really appreciate the fine work our air force is doing."[56] The distance of time seems to have allowed a more forgiving attitude to develop in some units. The 1945 history of the 5th Canadian Anti-Tank Regiment, 4th Canadian Armoured Division, notes that fighter-bombers sometimes mistook their M10 tank destroyers for escaping panzers during the Falaise Pocket battle: "The 'pigeons' popularity was low, dam' low; but their errors were forgiven later as the evidence of their effective handiwork became apparent in the roads leading out of the trap."[57]

Conclusion

Air support had significant positive and negative effects on Canadian soldiers' morale in Normandy. At first the men could only form their impressions of the air force on what they experienced (or did not experience). This narrow viewpoint was based on the limited appearances made by Allied aircraft in the frontline area and the unfortunate occasions when the troops themselves became targets. Like soldiers since the dawn of airpower, if they could not personally see the aircraft in action, the air forces obviously were not doing anything useful. It was not until the end of the campaign, as the army advanced through those distant battlefields behind the lines where the air force was active, that they first observed the visible results and full power of tactical air support.

The peaks and valleys of Canadian Army morale in Normandy corresponded with the soldiers' experiences with various forms of air support. The troops' morale in northwest Europe was never higher than it was on D-Day.[58] Like their British counterparts, the Canadians received a boost as they witnessed the overwhelming support provided by the air forces covering the landings. Having an air umbrella and the relative absence of the Luftwaffe during the long summer days provided soldiers with both real and psychological security. Airpower in the form of observed bombardments behind enemy lines and close support aircraft diving on enemy guns that infantryman in a trench could do little about also raised morale. The men appreciated as well the air bombardments that preceded their advance on

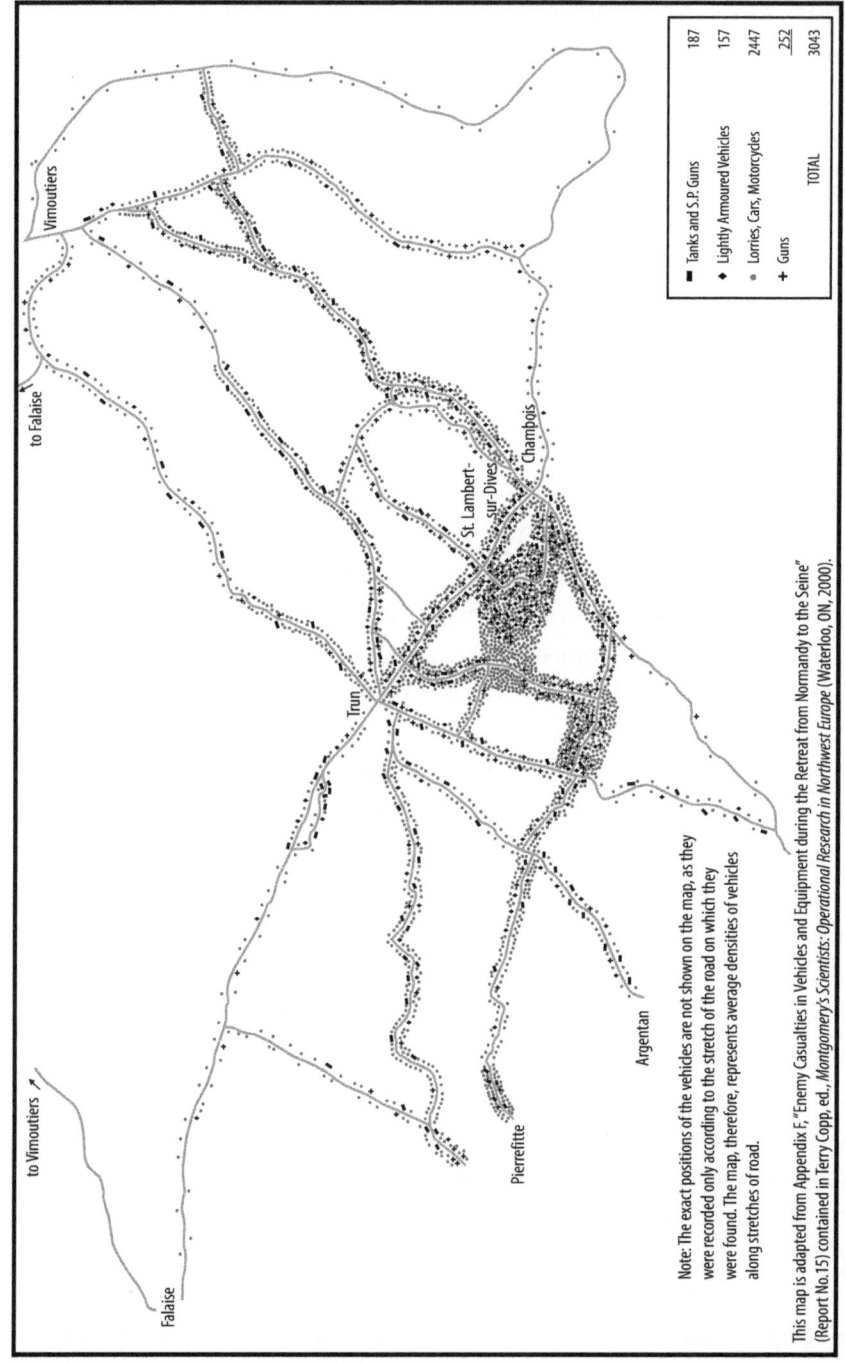

Map 11-2 The Shambles • The maps of "The Shambles" (11-1) and "The Chase" (11-3) provide an excellent visual summation of the destruction of the German army during the final stages of the Normandy Campaign. A majority of the German losses illustrated here were caused by air action, though the proportion of losses in the Shambles due to air attack was lower than in the Chase.

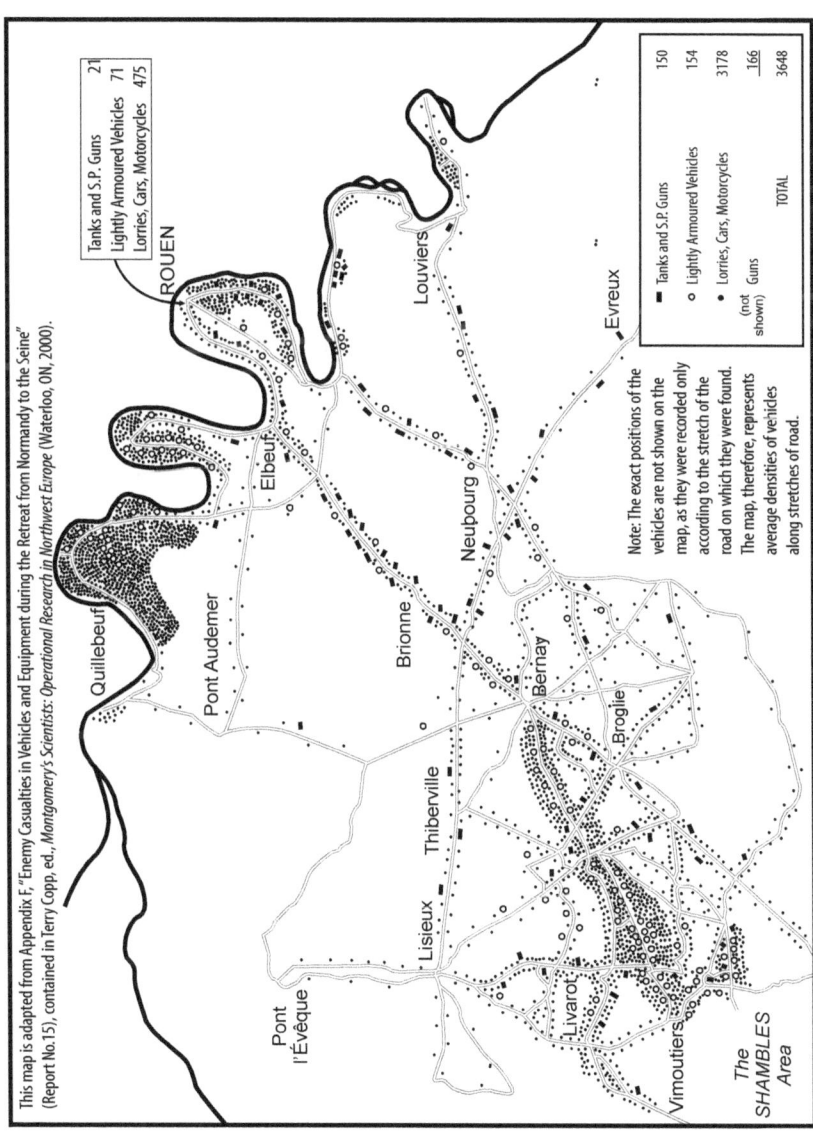

Map 11-3 The Chase • Map 11-3 best illustrates the range of reasons for the loss of German vehicles: those appearing in the lower left quadrant of the map were largely caused by air attack, while many of those shown along the Seine River resulted from the destruction of bridges at Rouen, either abandoned by the retreating German troops or destroyed to prevent their capture and use by the Allies. Not shown on either map are the estimated 10,000 draft horses killed in the Falaise Pocket.

an objective. They had good reason for this. Operational researchers later determined that not only was an air attack on the enemy lines a morale booster for friendly forces, but the attack also diminished enemy morale quicker and for a longer duration than an artillery strike. The lingering effects of an air attack would continue to affect enemy troops for ten to twenty minutes afterward compared to three minutes for artillery. If these air strikes could be followed up promptly by a successful ground assault, they also tended to yield more enemy prisoners of war.[59]

Yet by mid-August 1944, morale in First Canadian Army had suffered significantly.[60] Heavy casualties in the July battles south of Caen had a lot to do with this, but so, too, did mistakes by the Allied air forces. The frustration experienced by some units at the presence of the Luftwaffe at night likely lowered their spirits as well. More importantly, however, at times the Canadians (and their Allies) were induced to fear their own air force more than the Luftwaffe. Experiencing the mistaken bombardments firsthand or seeing friends injured or killed by friendly bombs understandably affected morale. Then as the front became unstuck and British and American fighter-bombers struck at German forces desperate to escape the Falaise Pocket, smaller-scale friendly fire incidents became more common. The Canadians, British, and Poles in First Canadian Army were understandably bitter by this point. At least some may have felt the RAF and USAAF had redeemed themselves after having observed the devastated German columns left on the roads leading to the Seine.

During the Second World War, the effect of close air support on morale (for better or worse) must be considered alongside its destruction of enemy forces. Casualty rates, time spent in heavy combat, news from home, food, and general health all determined the mental well-being of Canadian soldiers, but so, too, did airpower. This is another reason why historians must not disconnect it from the stories we tell about this epic struggle.

NOTES

1. No. 439 Squadron RCAF, Operations Record Book, 7 July 1944, RG 24-E-7, Library and Archives Canada, Ottawa [hereafter LAC], reel C-12317, image 1834.

2. Highland Light Infantry of Canada, War Diary, 7 July 1944, Vol. 15076, RG 24-C-3, LAC.
3. Ian Gooderson, *Air Power at the Battlefront: Allied Close Air Support in Europe, 1943–1945* (London: Routledge, 1998), 181.
4. Quoted in Brereton Greenhous et al., *The Crucible of War, 1939–1945: The Official History of the Royal Canadian Air Force*, vol. 3 (Toronto: University of Toronto Press, 1994), 298.
5. Quoted in John Terraine, *The Right of the Line: The Role of the RAF in World War Two* (London: Pen and Sword Books, 2010), 658.
6. Robert Engen, *Strangers in Arms: Combat Motivation in the Canadian Army, 1943–1945* (Montreal: McGill-Queen's University Press, 2016), 12.
7. Engen, *Strangers in Arms*, 238, table G.2.
8. Jonathan Fennell, *Fighting the People's War: The British and Commonwealth Armies in the Second World War* (Cambridge: Cambridge University Press, 2019), 708.
9. Fennell, *Fighting the People's War*, 543.
10. Engen, *Strangers in Arms*, 213.
11. 13th Field Regiment, RCA, War Diary, 6 June 1944, Vol. 14465, RG 24-C-3, LAC.
12. Royal Winnipeg Rifles, War Diary, 6 June 1944, Vol. 15223, RG 24-C-3, LAC.
13. Regina Rifle Regiment, War Diary, 7 June 1944, Vols. 15198–99, RG 24-C-3, LAC.
14. Gooderson, *Air Power at the Battlefront*, 136–39; Fennell, *Fighting the People's War*, 496.
15. Stormont, Dundas, and Glengarry Highlanders, War Diary, 6 June 1944, Vols. 15270–71, RG 24-C-3, LAC.
16. Highland Light Infantry of Canada, War Diary, 6 June 1944.
17. Highland Light Infantry of Canada, War Diary, 9, 20 June 1944.
18. North Nova Scotia Highlanders, War Diary, 23 June 1944, Vol. 15112, RG 24-C-3, LAC.
19. Fennell, *Fighting the People's War*, 513.
20. Canadian Scottish Regiment, War Diary, 4–7 July 1944, Vols. 15036–38, RG 24-C-3, LAC.
21. North Nova Scotia Highlanders, War Diary, 7 July 1944.
22. Quoted in Carlo D'Este, *Decision in Normandy: The Unwritten Story of Montgomery and the Allied Campaign* (New York: Pan Books, 1984), 316.
23. D'Este, *Decision in Normandy*.
24. Gooderson, *Air Power at the Battlefront*, 135–36.

25. Royal Winnipeg Rifles, War Diary, 18 July 1944.
26. Highland Light Infantry, War Diary, 18 July 1944; War Diary, Stormont, Dundas, and Glengarry Highlanders, 18 July 1944.
27. Highland Light Infantry, War Diary, 25 July 1944.
28. Canadian Scottish Regiment, War Diary, 26 July 1944.
29. Canadian Scottish Regiment, War Diary, 26 July 1944.
30. George Blackburn, *The Guns of Normandy: A Soldier's Eye View, France 1944* (Toronto: McClelland and Stewart, 1995), 149–52.
31. 14th Field Regiment, RCA, War Diary, 31 July 1944, Vols. 14471–72, RG 24-C-3, LAC.
32. G. W. L. Nicholson, *The Gunners of Canada: The History of the Royal Regiment of Canadian Artillery*, vol. 2 (Toronto: McClelland and Stewart, 1967), 318. It should be pointed out that there were 678 USAAF bombers involved in this operation, so a relatively small percentage made the mistake, although with significant consequences.
33. North Shore (New Brunswick) Regiment, War Diary, 8 August 1944, Vols. 15127–28, RG 24-C-3, LAC.
34. 4th Medium Regiment, RCA, War Diary, 8 August 1944, Vol. 14392, RG 24-C-3, LAC.
35. Canadian Scottish Regiment, War Diary, 8 August 1944.
36. Blackburn, *Guns of Normandy*, 339.
37. No. 1 Canadian Exhaustion Unit, Royal Canadian Army Medical Corps, War Diary, August 1944, app. 4, "Preliminary Report on No. 1 Cdn Exhaustion Unit RCAMC," 4, Vol. 15951, RG 24-C-3, LAC.
38. Arthur T. Harris, "Report on the Bombing of Our Own Troops during Operation 'Tractable': 14 August 1944," 25 August 1944, *Canadian Military History* 15, no. 3 (Autumn 2006): 108.
39. Blackburn, *Guns of Normandy*, 406.
40. Blackburn, *Guns of Normandy*, 416.
41. C. P. Stacey, *Official History of the Canadian Army in the Second World War*, vol. 3, *The Victory Campaign: The Operations in North-West Europe, 1944–1945* (Ottawa: Queen's Printer and Controller of Stationery, 1960), 243.
42. 3rd Medium Regiment, RCA, War Diary, 14 August 1944, Vol. 14388, RG-24-C-3, LAC.
43. No. 1 Canadian Exhaustion Unit, "Preliminary Report on No. 1 Cdn Exhaustion Unit RCAMC," 4.
44. Ralph Allen, "Canadians Bombed by 500 RAF Planes," *Globe & Mail*, 16 August 1944.

45. Quoted in Timothy Balzer, *The Information Front: The Canadian Army and News Management during the Second World War* (Vancouver: University of British Columbia Press, 2011), 164.
46. Balzer, *Information Front*, 165.
47. Indeed, Crerar took this tack when he wrote to Harris on 29 August to state that the heavy bomber support "contributed greatly to the great success" on 14 August. He continued to believe that RAF Bomber Command had an essential role to play in supporting the army on the battlefield. See Stacey, *Canadian Army in the Second World War*, 3:244–45.
48. Gooderson, *Air Power at the Battlefront*, 33.
49. Stormont, Dundas, and Glengarry Highlanders, War Diary, 14 August 1944.
50. 12th Field Regiment, RCA, War Diary, 14, 15 August 1944, Vol. 14461, RG 24-C-3, LAC.
51. Canadian Scottish Regiment, War Diary, 17, 19 August 1944.
52. See Harris, "Report on the Bombing of Our Own Troops," 107–8, 111, 112; and Stacey, *Canadian Army in the Second World War*, 3:244.
53. First Canadian Army General Staff, "Attacks by Allied Aircraft on Own Troops, 18 and 19 Aug 44," War Diary, August 1944, Vol. 13624, RG 24-C-17, LAC.
54. Quoted in Greenhous et al., *Crucible of War*, 3:307.
55. Stormont, Dundas, and Glengarry Highlanders, War Diary, 23 August 1944.
56. Regina Rifle Regiment, War Diary, 23 August 1944.
57. J. M. Savage et al., *The History of the 5th Canadian Anti-Tank Regiment: 10 September 1941–10 June 1945* (n.p., 1945), 26–27.
58. Fennell, *Fighting the People's War*, 513.
59. Gooderson, *Air Power at the Battlefront*, 181–82.
60. Gooderson, *Air Power at the Battlefront*, 514, 516.

12

Airpower Lessons Learned and Mislearned

A Comparative Analysis of Heavy Bomber Support in Operations Cobra and Queen

Christopher M. Rein

Airpower made a substantial contribution to the Allied victory in Normandy, from destroying the vaunted Luftwaffe through a sustained strategic campaign, thereby protecting the invasion convoys as they crossed the channel, to attriting German ground strength in France in a massive interdiction campaign. This success offered ample fodder for study and duplication in the campaigns that followed, though Allied ground and air planners drew some inaccurate conclusions from the overwhelming victory. While the strategic campaign and sustained interdiction of German supply lines to the front continued, the employment of heavy bombers in a tactical-support role became one of the most misunderstood aspects of the air campaign in Normandy. After Operation Cobra, the massive carpet bombing of a sector of the German front lines near Saint-Lô, facilitated the breakout of the American forces coiled within the bridgehead, ground commanders continued to request heavy bomber support in subsequent operations, although with modifications that made it less effective. As Russell Weigley has pointed out, heavy bomber support became like a drug to ground commanders, and "the American drug addicts had made it almost an article of faith that the COBRA bombing accounted for the COBRA breakout."[1] By the time much weaker U.S. forces attempted to duplicate their success in Cobra by again using heavy bombers to break cleanly through the West Wall and reach the banks of the Rhine in Operation Queen, the situation on the ground had shifted dramatically, and using heavy bombers to blast open a path for stuck ground forces no longer proved to be the panacea it once appeared to be.

As a direct result of their success, Allied air forces learned a great deal during the Normandy Campaign. The fledgling air support system had been refined over the years leading up to the invasion, and from the landings on 6 June to the breakout from the lodgment in late July, the remaining kinks were worked out. This included proving the efficacy of aircraft in the close-support role to form a truly effective air ground team, as Thomas Hughes, Ian Gooderson, and David Spires, among others, have amply documented.[2] Though some debate remains over whether these were entirely theater-derived innovations, developed under the guidance of airmen such as Brig. Gen. Elwood "Pete" Quesada, as Hughes has argued, or whether they benefited from the extensive experience gained in other theaters and in stateside training maneuvers, as others have suggested, there can be no argument that the Allied close support system was highly effective during the breakout from Normandy, in repelling the German counterattack at Mortain, and by devastating the German formations trapped in the Falaise Gap and fleeing across France for the safety of the Siegfried Line.[3]

The strategic air forces also learned a great deal during the Normandy Campaign, though much of it reinforced existing doctrine and ideas about employment. The invasion could not have occurred without the air superiority derived from the attritional campaign against the Luftwaffe, highlighted by the raids that targeted both the German aircraft industry and the large numbers of fighter aircraft charged with defending it during the "Big Week" attacks on February 1944.[4] Similarly, the interdiction campaign against French railyard, despite the enormous cost in French lives, as Stephen Bourque has so eloquently demonstrated, prevented the Germans from moving sufficient forces to Normandy and halting the Allied buildup within the beachhead, much less pushing it back into the sea.[5] But the difficulties encountered while attempting to employ heavy bombers in direct support of ground forces, attempted earlier in Operation Goodwood in the British sector and more successfully in Operation Cobra along the American front lines, seemed to confirm that this was not a proper role for the strategic forces and justified the lack of effort expended in preparing aircrews to perform this mission. The Allied "Bomber Mafia" saw tactical-support efforts as a diversion from the true role of targeting vital infrastructure deep within Germany, and they employed heavy bombers in such a role reluctantly and only under direct orders from the ground officers who commanded the theater.

But ground commanders viewed these operations, especially Cobra, in a much different light. They became convinced that using carpet bombing of the enemy's front lines to "unstick" their own ground forces was an effective, "one size fits all" solution to the problem and attempted to do so again in every subsequent major attack, including the airborne Operation Market-Garden in September, and in Operation Queen, the attempt to breach the Siegfried Line in the American sector in November. Both ground and air planners ignored specific circumstances that made Operation Cobra a success and the others failures, making additional modifications that hindered the effectiveness of heavy bombers in a ground support role. Despite these experiences, military forces continue to emphasize this mission for heavy bombers, as demonstrated by the B-52 Arc Light missions in Vietnam, the use of this same type of aircraft to attrit Iraqi forces in Operations Desert Storm and Iraqi Freedom (so much so that the authors of a volume on the latter operation titled their book *COBRA II*), and the use of B-1 bombers designed exclusively for the nuclear-delivery mission in a conventional role as JDAM-equipped "bomb trucks" during the twenty-year war in Afghanistan.[6] Thus, the employment of heavy bombers in the tactical-support role, and the lessons learned and mislearned from these efforts during the Normandy Campaign, have continuing relevance for airpower planners and practitioners today.[7]

While the Allied buildup inside the lodgment had continued unabated, Axis forces had been able to temporarily seal off the penetration. The inability to break free of these shackles gradually frustrated Allied commanders, who saw their projected phase lines, based on an expectation of linear rather than exponential progress, slipping further away. Caen, the British Second Army's D-Day objective, did not fall until over a month later, and even then German forces still held the high ground overlooking the city from the south. To break the cordon south of Caen, almost 1,600 heavy bombers from the Royal Air Force's Bomber Command blasted the German front lines at dawn on July 18. Another 1,000 U.S. Army Air Forces heavy and medium bombers followed, but the patchwork bombardment did not open a uniform pathway through the German defenses. Pockets of defenders stitched together a makeshift line strong enough to contain the British armored thrust, and by noon, the attack began to run out of steam while meeting increasingly strong German counterattacks. After pushing the lines only a few miles, British and Canadian forces began consolidating their gains, content to have drawn the Germans to their front, even if they had failed to achieve the much desired breakout.[8]

Exactly one week later, on 25 July, nearly two thousand U.S. Eighth Air Force heavy bombers carpet bombed a sector opposite the American front lines. Sadly, as smoke rose from the pulverized area and drifted over the Saint-Lô–Périers road, obscuring this important demarcation line between friendly and hostile forces, bombs began to fall among the troops poised to exploit the weakened German defenders. These killed over one hundred American soldiers, including Lieutenant General Lesley J. McNair, commander of the stateside-based Army Ground Forces, who had moved into a forward position to observe the attack. By the end of the day, the attackers had likewise achieved only modest gains, and the operation, codenamed Cobra, also appeared to be a failure.[9]

The next day, playing a hunch, the VII Corps commander, Lieutenant General J. Lawton "Lightning Joe" Collins, elected to commit two heavy armored divisions poised to exploit the breakthrough, even though his infantry divisions were still working to clear a path through the decimated defenders. Collins' instincts were correct, and by the next day, both armored divisions were rampaging through the French countryside. Within a week, the American attack unhinged the entire German defensive position, and within a month the Allies had liberated almost all of France, including the capital, Paris. Based on this success, ground commanders began to ask for

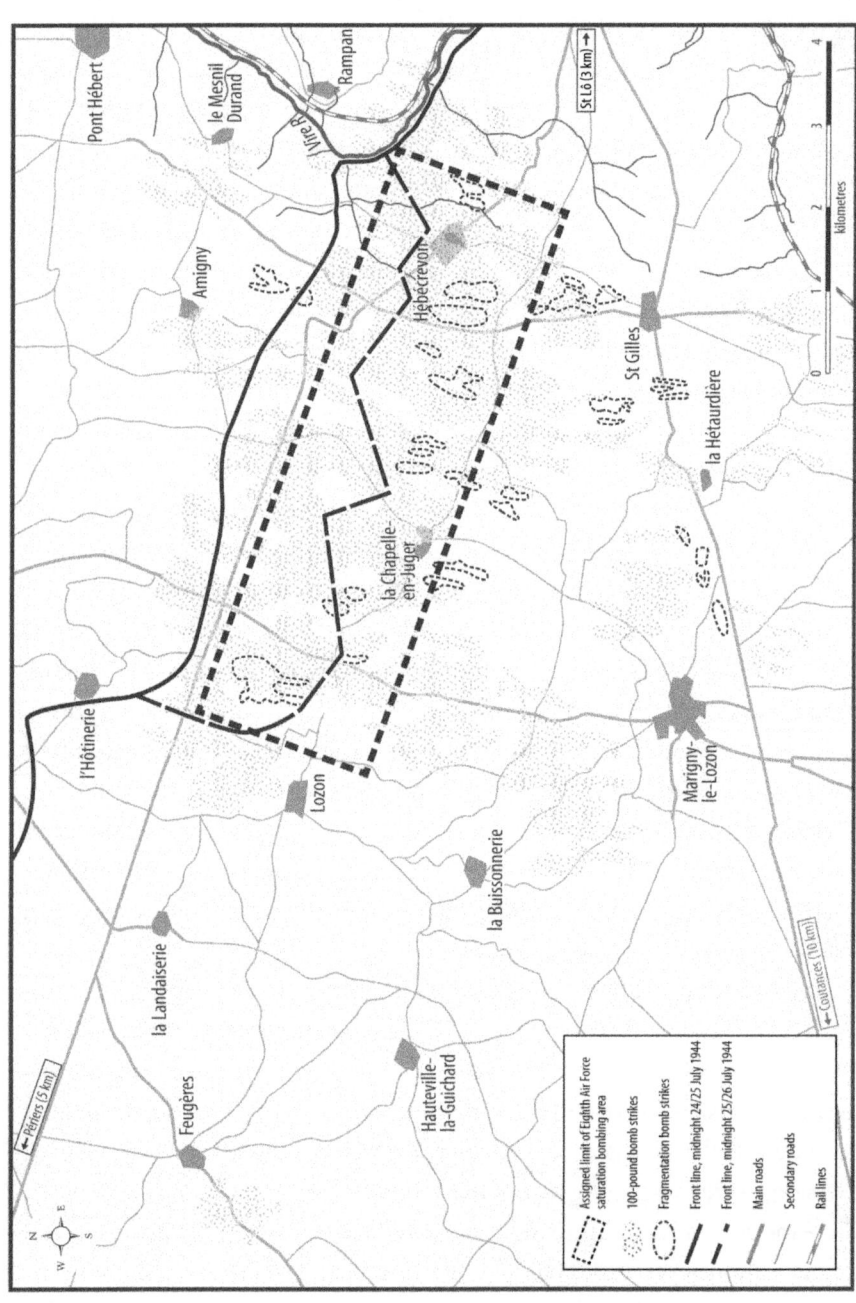

Map 12-1 • Bomb Plot, Operation Cobra, 25 July 1944

Photo 12-1 • Soldiers of the U.S. 30th Infantry Division work to dig out their fellow soldiers after they were mistakenly bombed by the Eighth Air Force during Operation Cobra, 25 July 1944. *U.S. Army photo; supplied by editor*

and receive heavy bomber support in subsequent operations, having gained a strong appetite for the instantaneous application of massive firepower in a ground offensive.[10]

Less than two months after the success of Cobra, ground forces again placed levies on the strategic air force's heavy bombers, this time in support of Field Marshal Bernard Montgomery's Operation Market-Garden, the attempt to use airborne forces to seize a string of bridges that would allow armored forces to cross the Rhine River delta and break out into the North German Plain. On September 17 and 18, almost one thousand heavy bombers flew support missions, mostly to neutralize flak batteries in an attempt to minimize casualties among the arriving airborne troops. Strong German counterattacks stalled the advance, recapturing the vital bridge at Arnhem, leaving no opportunity for the heavy bombers to improve the situation.

But ground commanders remained wedded to heavy bomber support as an essential ingredient in any offensive plan.¹¹

In arguably the most important phase of Allied operations in the autumn of 1944—the attempt to breach the Siegfried Line and debouch into northern Germany and hopefully "Win the War in '44"—ground commanders again requested support from strategic bombers that were otherwise engaged in crippling the German transportation network, industrial sites, and urban areas. Following the unsuccessful conclusion of Operation Market-Garden in September, planners orchestrated what became the primary American effort, Operation Queen. The main locus of advance occurred east of Aachen, in the only sector where Allied forces had already penetrated the German West Wall. It hoped to break through the German defenses, vault the Roer River between the towns of Julich and Duren, and reach the banks of the Rhine near Cologne. From there a joint Anglo-American offensive would be in position to encircle the vital Ruhr River industrial region, rip the heart out of the German economy, and join the Soviets for a final advance on Berlin.¹²

Unfortunately, the effort largely failed, as the American First and Ninth Armies did not achieve a clean breakthrough, and it took almost a month for them just to reach the Roer. As the exhausted troops of the divisions reached the river, they realized they could not cross as long as the Germans still held vital dams farther upstream in the Hürtgen Forest, which had already wrecked several U.S. divisions attempting to break through its incredibly difficult terrain. As the Americans plotted their next move, all the timetables for an advance were upset by the massive German counterattack just to the south in the Ardennes. The month-long battle to contain and eliminate the breakthrough postponed any American attempts to cross the Roer until February 1945, sentencing the troops to another vicious winter of war and delaying the eventual Allied victory.¹³

Juxtaposed against one another, Operations Cobra and Queen offer a stark contrast. In one case, heavy bombers effectively opened a door for the ground forces; in the other, they abjectly failed to facilitate the sort of breakthrough that might have restored mobility to a campaign bogging down on the borders of the Reich. Why did one succeed and the other fail? Was it due to errors of planning and execution? Were external factors instead more important? A postwar assessment by a high-ranking German general found "the efficacy of bombing on a par with the strength of the defenders and the initiative of the ground attackers in listing the factors which produce, or fail to produce a breakthrough in close support operations."[14] A thorough analysis of both operations reveals that, despite clear errors in both planning and execution on the part of both the ground and air forces, the answer lies in the significantly different situations on the ground, especially the conditions of both the friendly and opposing forces and the widely differing terrain and weather conditions prevailing for both operations, that affected the "efficacy" of both the ground and air attacks. Using heavy bombers in support of ground forces, while potentially decisive, depends heavily on factors that are often beyond air force control.

Employing a mnemonic device in wide use in the U.S. Army for issuing concise orders provides a framework for exploring the operations. The acronym METT-T (Mission, Enemy, Terrain and weather, Troops, and Time) offers leaders a concise guide for issuing clear orders for attaining any objective. By outlining the *mission*, the commander conveys his intent. Using intelligence to describe the expected *enemy* enables the subordinate to prepare the size and composition of his own attacking force. Providing an overview of the *terrain* gives vital information on expected cover, concealment, and obstacles; key features and avenues of approach; and both terrain and weather effects on time-distance relationships. Discussion of friendly *troops* provides quantity, condition, and capabilities of forces available to attain the objective. The final factor, *time*, provides any chronological limitations or conditions for the attack.[15]

The mission in both attacks has already been outlined. Since landing in France on 6 June 1944, Allied forces had been engaged in an attritional battle with the German defenders. Both sides rushed reinforcements into the battle area, but Allied combat power, logistical superiority, and control of the skies gradually gave them the upper hand. All that remained was to achieve a penetration somewhere along the line, forcing the Germans to retreat. Allied forces had arrived on the German frontier in late September 1944 but, in the ensuing two months, clawed desperately at the enemy's defensive belt while building up sufficient reserves to achieve a clear penetration and breakthrough into Germany. Heavy bombers played a significant role in both efforts.

As in any military operation, the enemy gets a vote, but the effectiveness of his ballot largely depends on the strength of the forces available to him. By the advent of Cobra in late July 1944, the German defenders in Normandy had been battered by increasingly stronger Allied forces. Two months of sustained heavy combat at the end of tenuous logistic lines had eroded German combat strength to the point where it was becoming incapable of absorbing the frequent blows in both the British and American sectors. In short, the German divisions were brittle, fragile, and susceptible to cracking. The effectiveness of one sharp blow was magnified by this condition.

In contrast, German forces opposing Operation Queen were in a much better condition, perhaps better than at any time since the Allied landings in June.[16] Despite the enemy's heavy materiel losses in the retreat across France, the Allies had been unable to prevent many skilled combat leaders from reaching the German frontier. In places such as the Falaise Gap and along the Seine, far too many German officers and experienced noncommissioned officers escaped the Allies' clutches. Once ensconced in formidable defensive positions and rebuilt with levies of new men and supplies from the still-functioning German war economy, brought forward on shorter and superior supply lines, many shattered divisions regained some of their former stature. Some of these divisions, including those opposing Operation Queen, were redesignated *Volksgrenadier* divisions, demonstrating both their wider composition and reinforcing the imperative necessity of defending German territory. These commands were not necessarily capable of the slashing offensives seen in the earlier blitzkrieg, but they were more than capable of trading space for time and, under skilled leadership, inflicting heavy casualties in the process.[17]

The terrain and weather conditions varied greatly between the sunny summer of 1944 in the mostly open, rolling hills south of Caen (though the dense hedgerows of the Bocage did present significant obstacles) and the misty rains of the fog-shrouded valleys, heavily forested hills, and densely packed towns and villages of the German Eifel and Roer River plain in late autumn. Both terrain and weather played a significant role in the effectiveness of the

Allies' ground and air forces. In July 1944 Allied forces profited from the generally favorable weather of summertime in northern European latitudes. Air forces enjoyed mostly clear and longer days while ground forces had few, if any, weather-related casualties. By November, things had changed significantly. The much shorter days were generally foggy or rainy, often precluding flight operations. Queen itself was delayed six days awaiting clear weather, and when finally executed, the majority of the aircrews had to use nonvisual means to bomb, significantly degrading accuracy. In addition, ground combat in the Hürtgen Forest and surrounding areas took a heavy toll on army formations. The steep valleys and ridges were covered with tall trees, increasing the effectiveness of German artillery, giving them a practical equivalent to the American proximity fuse. Rounds detonated after striking tree trunks and branches, greatly increasing both the quantity of projectiles (through fragmentation) and their effective range. Rounds that would have burrowed into the ground and directed their force vertically now detonated just over the heads of advancing infantrymen with deadly effect.[18]

In addition, the wet forests and falling temperatures dramatically increased the number of trench-foot casualties. U.S. First Army alone suffered thousands of nonbattle casualties during the month of November. The wet, rainy conditions sapped energy and morale, and logistics difficulties prevented adequate quantities of cold- and wet-weather gear from reaching the front lines. Ground units found it increasingly difficult to sustain their momentum as they were slowed by difficult terrain; robbed of supporting arms, especially armor; and weakened by high casualties, many induced by the wet weather.

The American troops employed in both operations differed qualitatively as well. While the majority of the infantrymen who crossed the beaches in early June were green, by late July most of the divisions involved in Cobra had been in combat for a month or more, long enough to acquire combat experience but not so long as to suffer high turnover from debilitating casualty rates.[19] By contrast, the units involved in Queen had either been in combat for months without relief, with the attendant turnover rates, or were, as in the case of the 104th Infantry Division, in whose sector the majority of the Allied bombs fell, a new division with little combat experience.[20] Whether inexperienced or fatigued, the friendly forces suffered from crippling logistics shortfalls, especially in artillery ammunition, brought on by the lengthy drive across France and the inability to open ports closer to the front lines. These shortages likely played a role in General Omar Bradley's insistence on heavy bomber support for his offensive and his willingness to wait almost a week for it when bad weather precluded its participation.[21]

A final factor, time, was also working for the Allies in Normandy and against them in Germany. The Allies had essentially unlimited time to build up and break out from their beachhead in Normandy. With each passing day, German forces grew weaker while the Allied density of both men and supplies within the lodgment grew stronger. Along the West Wall, a far different situation prevailed. Although the Allies were unaware then, they were working on a restricted timetable from the moment the offensive jumped off. From November 16, the day the Queen bombs crashed down on German positions, to December 16, the first day of the German counteroffensive now known as the Battle of the Bulge, the Allies had exactly thirty days to achieve their breakthrough and disrupt the German attack. In fact, had the Allies broken through, Hitler likely would have been forced to call off the offensive and use the forces assembled to attempt to seal off the penetration. This explains much of the German tenacity in defending against Queen and their willingness to employ resources, even those destined for the Ardennes, to ensure the lines only bent but did not break. Given the preponderance of German forces assembled just to the south of the Queen area, perhaps it is best that the Allies did not break through, as they then would have found themselves in the position of defending an exposed salient rather than containing one.

While the varying conditions of friendly and enemy troops and the disparate weather and terrain facing both attacks go a long way toward explaining their relative success and failure, it is worth considering whether other factors within the U.S. Army Air Forces' control might have influenced its success. Among these are its overall commitment to providing this type of heavy bomber support, heightened concerns about the possibility of injuring friendly forces with inaccurate drops, and the relative accuracy of both strikes with respect to the enemy forces targeted.

There is little doubt that the Army Air Forces viewed the use of strategic bombers in a tactical role as a misallocation of resources. In October 1944

Lieutenant General Ira Eaker, commander of the Mediterranean Allied Air forces, received a pointed rebuke from General Henry H. "Hap" Arnold for using the heavies of Fifteenth Air Force, based in Italy, to support an attack on Florence. In an assessment of Eighth Air Force's support of tactical operations, completed in April 1945, the Eighth Air Force's commander, Lieutenant General James H. "Jimmy" Doolittle, wrote: "Close-in cooperation missions for heavy bombers are, in general, a highly inefficient use of their effort on most targets, and more profitable expenditure of their firepower can be found so long as the enemy possesses a war industry capable of supporting his military forces. . . . Bombing of dug-in troops is a very inefficient use of the firepower of a fleet of heavy bomber formations."[22]

Lieutenant General Carl "Tooey" Spaatz, commander of the U.S. Strategic Air Forces in Europe, which included both Doolittle's Eighth and Eaker's Fifteenth, echoed Doolittle's sentiments in a message he released to his units the day after the Queen attack: "In view of excellent bombing under most difficult conditions of assigned target areas the commitment of Strategic Air Forces in close support of operation Q[ueen] is considered completed."[23] The statement is surprising given the Army Air Forces' awareness of the importance of persistence in achieving any objective with airpower. For example, Eighth Air Force attacked the synthetic-oil-production facility at Leuna–Merseburg no less than five times during the month of November—on the second, eighth, twenty-first, twenty-fifth, and thirtieth—during which the command suffered 77 percent of its monthly losses. Yet it was willing to abandon its support of Operation Queen, or at least turn it over to the less-capable fighter-bombers and medium bombers of Ninth Air Force, after a single day, even though the battle ground on for another month.[24]

The institutional "lack of interest" in supporting this type of mission undoubtedly affected its success. Crews had not been trained in the employment of heavy bombers in close proximity to friendly forces, a fact highlighted by the significant safety measures implemented in the Queen operation. The operational order for the mission specified elaborate criteria to prevent accidental release, including the opening of bomb-bay doors while still over the Channel and a restriction against arming bombs until over enemy lines. To help define the front lines, the order specified "a line of red Anti-aircraft

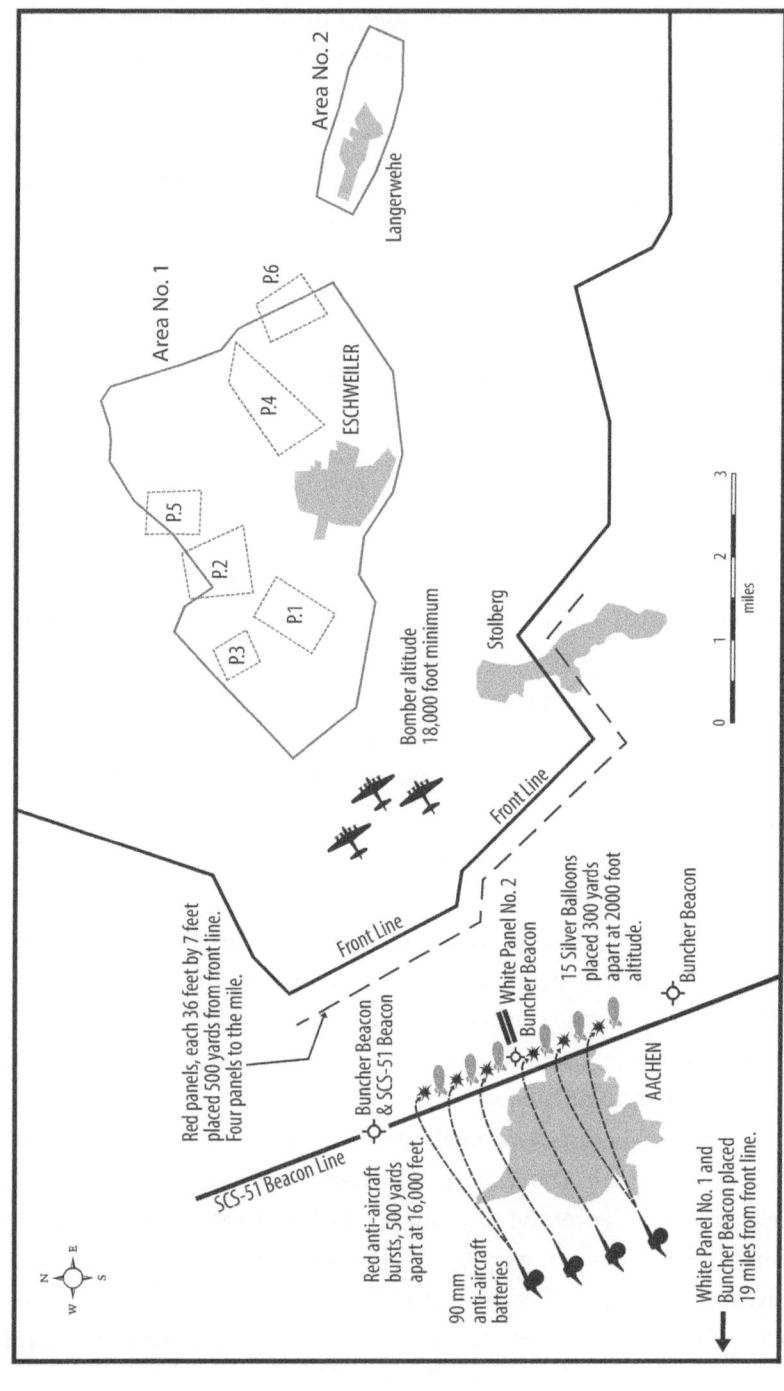

Map 12-2 • Marking Devices, Operation Queen

Photo 12-2 • Aerial recognition panels deployed by the U.S. Ninth Army to mark their front lines during Operation Queen, 16 November 1944. *U.S. Army photo; supplied by author*

flak bursts spaced 500 yards apart" several thousand feet below the attacking formations, a "line of 15 silver barrage balloons flying at 2,000 ft.," large white panels laid along the approach of the bombers, and "red and/or orange panels 36 ft. by 7 ft. laid out on the ground (4 panels per mile) 500 yards in the rear of and parallel to our front lines."[25]

In addition to the visual aids, electronic aids included a marker beacon that would cause receiving instrumentation in each aircraft to change color as they crossed a certain axis, and the by-this-time standard Gee and H2X electronic targeting aids, though Eighth Air Force still referred to this as "blind bombing" due to the aids' inaccuracy. While Gee was a significant improvement over H2X in terms of accuracy, it was also unreliable, forcing the operational order to specify, "If any formation is forced to bomb on H2X for any reason including failure of Micro-H or Gee-H equipment, this formation will continue on bomb run for 30 seconds past computed bomb release point before actually releasing bombs." At a speed of 250 mph, the additional thirty seconds translated into a distance of over two miles on the ground, a figure far in excess of the average daily advance for many units involved in Operation Queen.[26]

Concerns about "friendly fire" also affected the planning process. Rather than target the frontline positions directly opposing the American troops, as had occurred in Cobra, the Queen targets were much farther behind the lines. In fact, the strike was too far to the rear to be of immediate use, as a poststrike assessment found: "For 12 hours enemy ground troops were actually affected by the bombardment, according to PWs [prisoners of war] taken during the ground operations. However, our troops were unable to close up the 4,000 yards between our lines and the enemy positions before the effects of this stunning wore off."[27] A 12th Army Group report prepared before the conclusion of the war found, "With the satisfactory safety and accuracy aids devised, the heavy bombing effort could have been placed much closer to the front line, thus permitting the infantry to press home the advantage of the shock effect."[28]

Even with this safety cushion, crews were still unable to place their bombs on the identified enemy positions. Despite Spaatz's assertion of "excellent bombing under most difficult conditions," poststrike assessments found that the percentage of bombs that actually fell within the assigned areas ranged from a low of zero hits for target P-4 to a high of 16 percent for target P-6. The average for all targets was just over 8 percent.[29] These numbers are borne out by casualty estimates compiled by intelligence personnel based on prisoner of war interrogations. Within the 47th Volksgrenadier Division, estimates ranged from 3 percent to 4 percent, "of which a very low number were fatal." In the 275th Division rates were as high as 10 percent, "of which approximately 3 in 20 were fatal." In the 12th Volksgrenadier Division, casualties again ranged from 1 percent to 3 percent. In short, the divisions opposing the Allied advance were either not seriously affected by the bombing or had sufficient time to recover before they were actually engaged by ground troops.[30]

The exception to this came just to the north of the 104th Infantry Division, across the corps boundary in XIX Corps, Ninth Army's sector. There the 30th Infantry Division watched as some bombs fell on the towns of St. Jöris

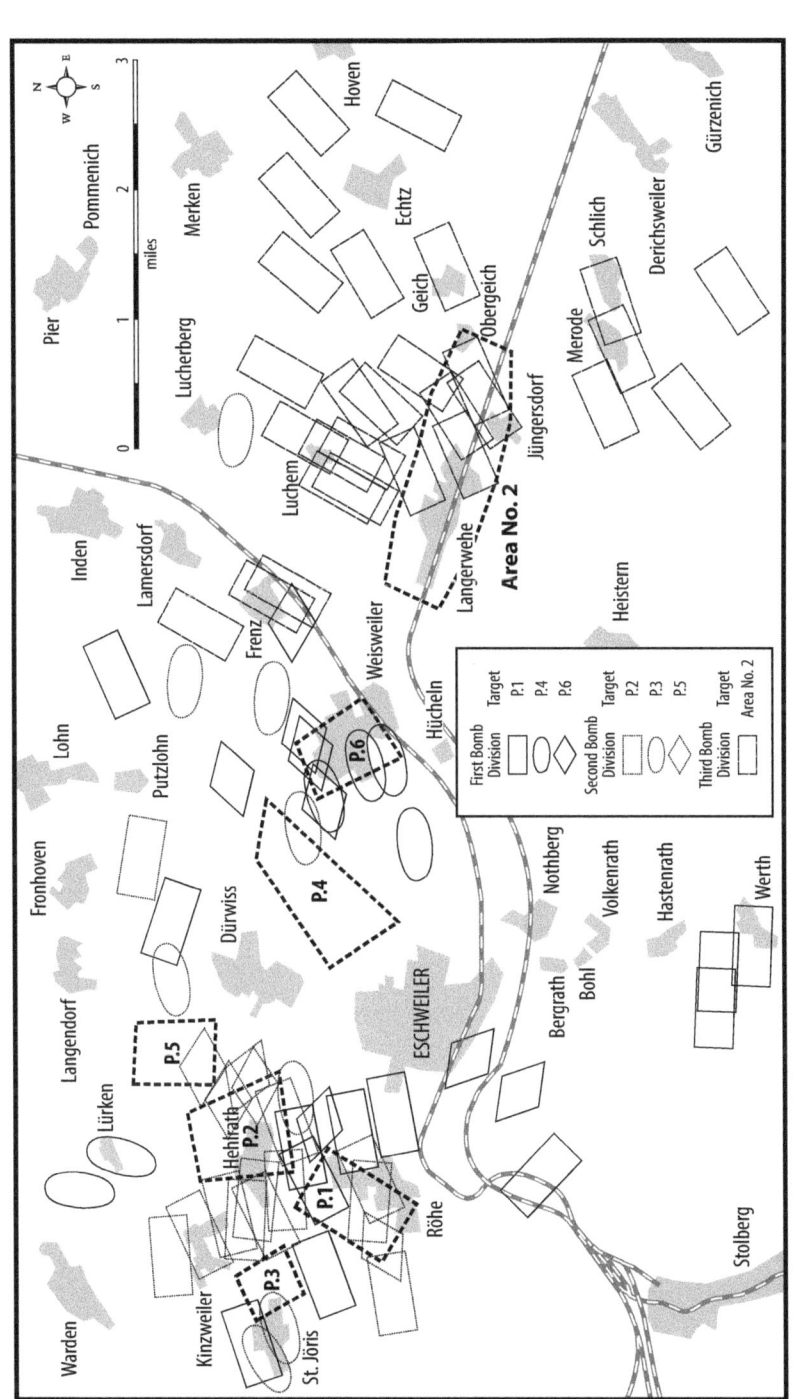

Map 12-3 • Bomb Plots, Operation Queen, Eschweiler

Photo 12-3 • A Ninth Air Force B-26 Marauder leaves the target area as fire and smoke erupt from the town of Weisweiler, Germany, during Operation Queen, 16 November 1944. *U.S. Air Force Photo 55100AC*

and Kinzweiler, just over two miles from the 117th Infantry Regiment's sector of the 30th's front line, an area already clear of the West Wall defenses that retarded the advance elsewhere in the division's sector. The 117th, attacking southeast toward the corps boundary, seized the towns while suffering light casualties on the morning of 19 November, albeit with the support of a heavy artillery barrage. The U.S. Army's official history notes, "The 30th Division's advance was one of the better gains made anywhere during the early days of the November offensive."[31]

In between the 104th and 1st Divisions, one combat command of the 3rd Armored Division had the task of seizing four small villages before being pinched out in the concentric advance. By accidental good fortune, all three squadrons of the 91st Bomb Group placed their bombs on the first of these villages, the tiny town of Werth, several miles south of its assigned target.

In its attack Combat Command B of the 3rd Armored "had little difficulty. In about two hours Werth and Koettenich were in hand."[32] Unfortunately, German forces on hillsides flanking the towns that had escaped bombing prevented any further advance.

Within the 104th Infantry Division's sector, stubborn resistance on Hill 287, at the division's junction with the 1st Infantry Division, held up the 104th's advance for three days. Not until 20 November did the division's lead elements reach the edge of the carpet-bombed area west of Eschweiler, far too slow to achieve a clean breakthrough. Still, the large urban area fell in less than two days, with only moderate casualties for even the inexperienced 104th Division. The U.S. Army's official history notes, "The 104th Division's ... attack had carried almost four times as far as had the 1st Division's in the VII Corps main effort, despite the urban nature of the battlefield."[33] While this attests to the difficulty of the forested terrain in the Big Red One's sector, it also demonstrates that the bombing had a beneficial effect in the 104th's area. The division's advance, coupled with that of the 30th Division to the north and Combat Command B, 3rd Armored to the south, proves that heavy bombers can and did have a beneficial effect on the advance of the ground forces. Unfortunately, the area where most of the bombs fell was designated a flank or secondary effort for both corps, depriving the main effort of each of any substantial support. Air planners likely would have had a greater effect on the battle had they placed their bombs in front of the 29th Division, XIX Corps' main effort, just to the north of the 30th, or directly in front of the 1st Infantry Division, just to the south of the 104th.

Comparisons of the Queen bomb plots with those from Cobra are striking. The vast majority of the Cobra bombs fell within the assigned target area (see map 12-1). The commander of the most heavily affected unit, Generalleutnant Fritz Bayerlein of the Panzer Lehr Division, later described his positions after the attack as a *mondlandschaft* (moonscape), with casualties as high as 70 percent in the frontline positions. The thirty to forty tanks in his frontline positions were all knocked out, "some turned over on their backs and some unable to climb out of craters."[34] General Bradley and the 12th Army Group staff later assessed the bombing efforts of the two operations: "Pattern bombing of a large area by the bombers was effective at ST LO where the air attack was exploited quickly by the ground forces. Pattern bombing of selected smaller areas within a larger area as in the QUEEN operation, while effective to a degree, was too far forward for maximum exploitation by the assaulting troops, and hence had little direct effect in reducing the resistance offered."[35]

All of which begs the question, if the Allied attacks of 16 November had been better planned and better executed, could they have led to the same breakthrough as achieved in Normandy in June?

Undoubtedly, the answer remains "no." Even a more rapid advance to the Roer would have left the dams upstream in enemy hands, preventing any crossing due to the fear that the Germans would open the floodgates and unleash a torrent that would wash out any bridges and isolate the troops that had managed to gain the far shore. Even with the dams in Allied hands, the penetration likely would have been subjected to the counterattack previously described, an Ardennes offensive oriented to the north instead of to the west. And there still remained the formidable obstacle of the Rhine between the Allies and the Ruhr, which the ground forces did not cross until March 1945 and then only after a significant depletion of German combat strength by the Western Allies in the Bulge and the Soviets in Poland. In hindsight perhaps Doolittle was correct, and in this particular case, the heavy bombers might best have been used in yet another attack on Leuna-Merseburg, a mission for which their aircrews were specially trained and certainly committed.[36]

Does this make operations like Cobra and Queen irrelevant? Hardly. The potential for devastating attacks on ground forces by "strategic" assets of the air forces remains. Among German commanders interviewed after the war, "there was unanimity in regarding this type of close support as our most effective use of the air."[37] In Vietnam, American ground forces in danger of being overrun came to depend on B-52 Arc Light missions, which pummeled North Vietnamese attackers. In Operation Desert Storm the same nuclear-capable U.S. B-52's inflicted debilitating casualties on Iraqi ground troops, greatly facilitating the advance of the coalition ground forces. But the B-52s were available for this mission only because of the shortage of strategic targets in the theater and the availability of stealthier assets to penetrate more heavily defended areas. Evidence suggests that the U.S. Air Force retains its strong preference for strategic attack, even at the expense of support for ground forces. In a wargame exercise for students at the Air Command and Staff College in 2001, allocating assets to both strategic attack and support for ground forces enabled the player to "win" the game in six turns. But ignoring ground forces and dedicating the entire arsenal to strategic attack resulted in a victory in only two turns.[38]

Successful integration of tactical airpower with the ground plan of attack requires both close coordination and a willingness to conduct this type of mission, even with assets not specifically designed or designated for that role. But to do so successfully, the air commander must work with the ground commander to set the proper conditions for the attack to succeed, taking into account the condition of friendly and enemy troops and the prevailing terrain and weather. And ground commanders must not expect air support to be a panacea, capable of rescuing any situation. Instead, both air and ground must have a clear appreciation of the other's capabilities and limitations, carefully planning the employment of each accordingly. Only then can they have any expectation of success.

NOTES

1. Russell Weigley, *Eisenhower's Lieutenants: The Campaign of France and Germany, 1944–1945* (Bloomington: Indiana University Press, 1981), 381.
2. Thomas Hughes, *Overlord: General Pete Quesada and the Triumph of Tactical Air Power in World War II* (New York: Free Press, 1995); Ian Gooderson, *Air Power at the Battlefront: Allied Close Air Support in Europe, 1943–45* (New York: Frank Cass, 1998); David Spires, *Air Power for Patton's Army: The XIX Tactical Air Command in the Second World War* (Washington, DC: Air Force History and Museums Program, 2002).
3. Christopher M. Rein, *Forging the Ninth Army–XXIX TAC Team: The Development, Training, and Application of American Air-Ground Doctrine in World War II* (Fort Leavenworth, KS: Army University Press, 2019); John Golley, *The Day of the Typhoon: Flying with the RAF Tank-busters in Normandy* (Ramsbury, UK: Crowood, 2000); Mark Reardon, *Victory at Mortain: Stopping Hitler's Panzer Offensive* (Lawrence: University Press of Kansas, 2002); Daniel Mortensen, ed., *Airpower and Ground Armies: Essays on the Evolution of Anglo-American Air Doctrine, 1940–43* (Maxwell AFB, AL: Air University Press, 1998); David Ian Hall, *Strategy for Victory: The Development of British Tactical Air Power, 1919–1943* (Westport, CT: Praeger, 2008); Mike Bechthold, *Flying to Victory: Raymond Collishaw and the Western Desert Campaign,*

1940–1941 (Norman: University of Oklahoma Press, 2017); Paul Johnston, "Tactical Airpower Controversies in Normandy: A Question of Doctrine," *Canadian Military History* 9, no. 2 (Spring 2000), 59–71.

4. Donald Miller, *Masters of the Air: America's Bomber Boys Who Fought the Air War against Nazi Germany* (New York: Simon and Schuster, 2006); Stephen McFarland and Wesley Newton, *To Command the Sky: The Battle for Air Superiority over Germany, 1942–1944* (Washington, DC: Smithsonian Institution Press, 1991).
5. Stephen A. Bourque, *Beyond the Beach: The Allied War against France* (Annapolis, MD: U.S. Naval Institute Press, 2018).
6. Michael Gordon and Bernard Trainor, *COBRA II: The Inside Story of the Invasion and Occupation of Iraq* (New York: Pantheon, 2006).
7. See Gordon R. Sullivan, "From Cobra to Anaconda: Some Thoughts on Air-Ground Cooperation," *AUSA: Army Magazine* (April 2003).
8. C. P. Stacey, *Official History of the Canadian Army in the Second World War*, vol. 3, *The Victory Campaign: The Operations in Northwest Europe, 1944–45* (Ottawa: Queen's Printer and Controller of Stationery, 1960), 155–80.
9. For an excellent description of Operation Cobra, see Hughes, *Overlord*, 197–217.
10. Hughes, *Overlord*, 218–21, 226.
11. "Eighth Air Force Report: Close-in Air Cooperation by Heavy Bombers with Ground Forces," Air Force Historical Research Agency, Maxwell AFB, AL [hereafter AFHRA] 520.4501A; Stacey, *Canadian Army in the Second World War*, 3:338–39.
12. Weigley, *Eisenhower's Lieutenants*, 380–81.
13. See Robert Rush, *Hell in Hürtgen Forest: The Ordeal & Triumph of an American Infantry Regiment* (Lawrence: University Press of Kansas, 2001), 63.
14. Gerd von Rundstedt quoted in Omar Bradley, *Effect of Air Power on Military Operations, Western Europe* (n.p.: Air Effects Committee, 12th Army Group, n.d.), 183.
15. The above is largely drawn from U.S. Army Field Manual 6-0, *Commander and Staff Organization and Operations*, May 5, 2014, table 10-1. Reflecting an increased concern for counterinsurgency, the U.S. Army has updated the acronym to "METT-TC," with the "C" standing for "civil considerations."
16. Robert Rush provides an excellent visual depiction of the strength of German infantry units. Using the flow of losses and replacements to a notional German rifle company, he shows a peak in combat effectiveness at the exact time of Operation Queen. See Rush, *Hell in Hürtgen Forest*, 63.
17. Rush, *Hell in Hürtgen Forest*, 114–19.

18. Charles B. McDonald, *The Siegfried Line Campaign* (Washington, DC: U.S. Army Chief of Military History, 1963).
19. The three infantry divisions taking part in Cobra had only been in combat since the second week of June. The 4th Division landed on Utah Beach on D-Day, while elements of the 9th and 30th Infantry Divisions entered the fray less than a week later.
20. According to the 104th Division's history, the unit had seen less than two weeks of combat prior to being committed to Queen: "Most of the divisions that were in the line had been in combat since D-Day; all were battle-weary and footsore." Leo Hoegh and Howard J. Doyle, *Timberwolf Tracks: The History of the 104th Infantry Division, 1942–1945* (Washington, DC: Infantry Journal Press, 1946), 113.
21. Rush, *Hell in Hürtgen Forest*; McDonald, *Siegfried Line Campaign*.
22. "Eighth Air Force Report," 150–51.
23. USSTAF A263, 17 November 1944, Folder 3, Box 4, McDonald Papers (MS 16), Special Collections, McDermott Library, USAF Academy, CO.
24. Wesley Craven and James Cate, *The Army Air Forces in World War II*, vol. 3, *Europe: Argument to V-E Day, January 1944 to May 1945* (Chicago: University of Chicago Press, 1951), 644.
25. Eighth Air Force Field Order 1314, 15 November 1944, AFHRA 520.4501A.
26. Eighth Air Force Field Order 1314.
27. Memo, "Operation QUEEN, 8 December 1944," 9th Air Force Encounter Reports, March–December 1944, AFHRA 533.3811.
28. Bradley, *Effect of Air Power on Military Operations*, 108.
29. "Eighth Air Force Report," 84.
30. HQ, IX TAC, A-2 Periodic Report 124, "The Enemy's View of our Air Support on 16 November," 24 November 1944, AFHRA 520.4501A.
31. McDonald, *Siegfried Line Campaign*, 502–3.
32. McDonald, *Siegfried Line Campaign*, 422.
33. McDonald, *Siegfried Line Campaign*, 507.
34. HQ, Air P/W Interrogation Detachment 63, "A Crack German Panzer Division and What Allied Air Power Did to It between D-Day and V-Day," 29 May 1945, Folder 10, Box 12, McDonald Papers (MS 16).
35. Bradley, *Effect of Air Power on Military Operations*, 108.
36. Craven and Cate, *Army Air Forces in World War II*, 3:640–46.
37. Quoted in Bradley, *Effect of Air Power on Military Operations*, 185.
38. Author's experience.

13

One Nation, Many Headlines
The Royal Australian Air Force Contribution to the Normandy Campaign as Portrayed by Contemporary Print Media

Adam Lunney

The authors of *The Oxford Companion to Australian Military History* have judged the Empire Air Training Scheme (EATS) to have been detrimental to the defense of Australia during the Second World War, describing it as having the intent of being "most productive" yet concluding it was "wasteful and inefficient."[1]

While the actual (and perceived) threat of invasion by Japanese forces dwindled with each Allied advance in the Pacific, Australian aircrews in Europe, including many graduates of the EATS, continued to make daily contributions to the defeat of Germany. The mood of some—particularly those sent to Europe, is perhaps best summed up by Colin "Rusty" Leith, a Spitfire pilot in No. 453 (RAAF) Squadron, who wrote home in January 1943: "The reasons for our wanting to stay are numerous. . . . [N]ow I am over here I would like to be in for the kill or the big push if and when it comes."[2] General Dwight D. Eisenhower, the supreme Allied commander, and his British deputy General Bernard L. Montgomery commanded the headlines in Australian newspapers, but reporters also wrote about uniquely Australian efforts and the experiences of those Australians mixed in with other nationalities in the Royal Air Force (RAF).

Unlike the Canadians, who were more concentrated in groups and squadrons than their Commonwealth counterparts, Royal Australian Air Force (RAAF) aircrews were scattered throughout the various commands of the RAF, sometimes together in squadrons but more often not. Australians could be found as aircrews in Spitfires, Typhoons, Lancasters, Ansons, Stirlings, Mosquitos, Beaufighters, Sunderlands, and other aircraft. Their roles covered the full range of operations, from maritime patrols to fighter sweeps, photoreconnaissance, and bombing, both strategic and tactical. More than one newspaper article even suggested that the RAF be renamed the "Royal Imperial Air Force" due to the large number of participants from outside Great Britain—and to remove the misconception that only those from England, Scotland, Wales, and Ireland were doing the fighting.[3]

The contributions of RAAF aircrews and ground crews during the Battle of Normandy were portrayed in period newspapers. A review of those articles allows us to analyze the accuracy of those reports and how well they reflected the reality of Australian aircrews in operations over Europe, clarifying the propaganda angle of some of the articles, what was overstated, what was understated, and what was left unsaid. Some things were deliberately left unsaid, of course, such as squadron numbers and specific locations, due to security concerns. But with the passage of time and additional research, these details of Australian air service over continental Europe can be properly identified.

April 1944

The month started with positive news for Australians serving in the United Kingdom. An article titled "Australians Score in Night Defence," published in the *Army News* of Darwin on 2 April, told of their success against Luftwaffe night raiders, with Wing Commander Keith Hampshire of Perth, Western Australia, singled out for his successful mission involving two claimed kills in a single night.[4] While this was not linked at the time to the coming Normandy

Campaign, the work of these night fighters was essential for the defense of the fleet and forces training and assembling for the cross-Channel landings. Had the article linked these operations to the coming landings in a more obvious way, an additional level of depth could have been achieved by the writer, with the Australian contribution to the overall effort maintained in the mind of the public. But reporting essentials and specific items of interest limited the ability of the media to make those connections, given the censorship and confidentiality rules of the time. The successes of Flight Lieutenant Charles Scherf, who had recently been awarded the Distinguished Flying Cross and had destroyed several Luftwaffe aircraft on the ground and in the air flying his Mosquito over France, were discussed in an article titled "Australian's Victory" in the *West Australian* newspaper on Saturday, 8 April 1944.[5]

Two days later an article in the *Kalgoorlie Miner* described how one RAAF Short Sunderland, while patrolling the Bay of Biscay for U-boats, fought off ten Junkers Ju 88s before crash-landing in the sea, where the surviving crew members floated in dinghies for forty-nine hours. An important connection for the people at home was the naming of certain crewmen and their hometowns. Though the action had occurred in March, and official notifications should have been able to be made by the time of publication, the article did not mention that only seven of the twelve crewmen survived.[6]

The *Sydney Morning Herald* featured a photograph of the Duke of Gloucester visiting Australian Spitfire pilots on 15 April, but it had actually taken place on 9 March. Though not named, Squadron Leader Don Andrews' face can clearly be made out in the image; he is shown not wearing his officer's cap, as he had judged that it was not sufficiently presentable for the duke's visit.[7]

The success of the recently promoted Squadron Leader Scherf continued in the article "Glen Innes Airman Has Top Score" on 18 April, when the *Glen Innes Examiner* sang his praises for shooting down an additional five Luftwaffe aircraft in early April, bringing his total to 12½ kills. Scherf expressed his desire to return home to his wife and two children in Australia and resume his work as a sheep farmer, stating, "Every time I see a jerry aircraft go up in smoke I figure I am that much closer to getting home."[8]

Though sometimes shying away from discussing crew losses in detail, the death of Pilot Officer Robert "Bob" Yarra in his Spitfire while dive-bombing

Photo 13-1 • The Duke of Gloucester, attended by Group Captain Lord Willoughby de Broke, visited No. 453 Squadron RAAF at RAF Station Ford Sussex, England, on 9 March 1944. A story and photograph of this visit was featured on the front page of the *Sydney Morning Herald* on 15 April. *AWM SUK11956*

with No. 453 Squadron on 14 April made his hometown paper four days later. The *Daily Examiner* of Grafton published "Grafton Spitfire Pilot Missing, Believed Killed," which outlined the general circumstances of Yarra's loss and reminded their readership that he was the second of two sons of his family to become a casualty—his brother, Flight Lieutenant John "Jack" Yarra, was lost in action with the same squadron in December 1942.[9]

May 1944

The *Newcastle Morning Herald and Miners' Advocate* ran a very short article on 1 May about an incident that occurred a few days prior when Wing Commander Hampshire (from No. 456 Squadron, though it was not identified in the story) and his navigator shot down a Dornier Do 217 bomber during a German night raid on Britain. This article provided a taste of the action that took place each day and night in Europe and continued the trend of naming aircrews and their hometowns.[10] The bigger picture was covered in "Many Australian Airmen Will Support Invasion" on the front page of Melbourne's *The Herald* on 2 May. This article was closely linked with another one discussing a face-to-face meeting between Prime Ministers Winston Churchill (Great Britain), William Lyon Mackenzie King (Canada), John Curtin (Australia), Peter Fraser (New Zealand), and Jan Smuts (South Africa).[11] At both ends of the scale, Australian participation in the war effort was there for all to read. Though the Normandy landings were still a month away, Australian involvement in these lead-in operations was well covered.

The next few days saw numerous articles in papers around the nation covering the change-of-command ceremony for "an Australian Spitfire fighter-bomber squadron," as No. 453 Squadron was regularly described, when Squadron Leader Don Smith took over from Squadron Leader Don Andrews.[12] Both were hailed as heroes (and their war records speak for themselves), with Andrews' 320 operational hours (fighter pilots were supposed to be rested after 200) and Smith's record flying from Malta and his recently awarded Russian Medal of Valor regularly referenced.[13] At the same time, a photograph of Wing Commander Robert "Bob" Iredale of Heidelberg, Victoria, and his ground crew standing under the nose of a Mosquito also made the rounds, with Iredale described as "the C.O. [commanding officer] of an Australian Mosquito Squadron in Britain."[14] Though unnamed in the article, this was No. 464 Squadron.[15]

In early May 1944, four war correspondents arrived at No. 453 Squadron: Flight Lieutenant Bruce Andrew from RAAF Overseas Headquarters (London), H. I. Williams, F. C. Folkard, and a man named Smith.[16] These reporters wrote frequently about the Australian contribution to the Normandy Campaign (and beyond). Their articles were repeated across many city and regional newspapers (many no longer in print), sometimes one or many days apart, bringing news about RAAF participation in the Normandy Campaign to the Australian public. These regional newspapers proudly recounted the tales of the heroism exhibited by the men from their locales.

Publishing the names and stories of Australians fighting in Europe brought a local connection to the significant world events taking place far from the country. These articles sat alongside the larger headline-grabbing items that continually speculated about the meanings hidden in the quotes from Eisenhower and Montgomery and when the Allies would return to northwest Europe (often described as an "invasion").

One such article by Folkard, titled "Smaller Planes Flown by Australians Helping to Soften Up Europe," was published in the *Telegraph* on 11 May in Brisbane. A slightly shorter version was published the next day in Adelaide in the *News* as "Australians Play Big Part in Air Invasion." Folkard recounted some activities of an "Australian Spitfire Squadron" both in training and in operations over France. He contrasted the relative danger faced by fighter and bomber crews with the safety of their various base facilities. The positive tone of the articles highlighted the push to victory.[17]

This positivity was also in evidence the previous week when the *West Australian* carried an article about a successful RAF Bomber Command raid: "Germany's Tanks—Destruction at Mailly." The attack was described in general terms, and while the presence of Luftwaffe night fighters was mentioned, the losses incurred were not. RAAF Lancaster "S for Sugar" of No. 467 Squadron was on its ninety-seventh operational sortie and was featured in the article, as was its pilot, Pilot Officer Thomas Scholefield, who was quoted as saying: "The Mailly depot looked like an inferno. I saw my stick of bombs land on the target. I have never seen what my bombs hit so clearly before, even on practice bombing."[18] But the raid, despite heavy German casualties, was costly for Bomber Command. Out of the 362 aircraft dispatched to the target on the night of 3–4 May, forty-two Lancasters were shot down, an unsustainable 11.6 percent of the total force.[19] RAAF participation in the raid was high, with seventeen Lancasters from No. 460 Squadron, ten from 467 Squadron, and eleven from No. 463 Squadron.

Mailly-le-Camp was a known military concentration located about eighty-five miles east of Paris and was easily identified from the air. The No. 463 Squadron Operations Record Book notes, "Our Squadron went into the attack with zeal, knowing they were going to kill a few thousand German soldiers."[20] While the first few bombers made it through without much trouble, communication between aircraft was poor, with one crew complaining they could only get American news on their radio. Other crews stated that they received no instructions from the MC (Master of Ceremonies—the Pathfinder Force bomb leader). Afterward, No. 12 Squadron described the raid as a "hornet's nest."[21] Attacking a few minutes after No. 460 Squadron, No. 463 Squadron approached from similar altitudes and with similar loads. Contrary to Scholefield's earlier observation, many crews reported the target being obscured by smoke and dust, and visual bombing assessments could not be made with any certainty.[22]

Australian crews witnessed at least one bomber go down in flames after being attacked by a night fighter. In total, six RAAF Lancasters failed to return (five from No. 460 Squadron and one from No. 463 Squadron) as well as thirty-six others.[23] To publish the names of all the lost aircrews would have been a demoralizing blow for the Australian public; a better tactic was to release a single name from time to time, which caused less of a shock. It was only later in the month, in a *Herald* article titled "Deadly RAAF Night Raids," that heavy casualties were admitted, though the exact target was not named.[24] It could only have been the Mailly-le-Camp mission. Although the article focused on the success of the RAAF bomber squadrons operating from Great Britain, its title certainly carried a double meaning for those paying close attention.

Controversy arose during a meeting between RAAF aircrews and Prime Minister Curtin when he visited No. 460 Squadron in May. The men asked Curtin why they were being called "Jap-dodgers" by some Australians at home. The prime minister replied: "That is untrue. I've never heard of it."[25] This incident was reported nationwide in both city and rural areas across numerous papers. The story persisted in the press for about a week until it appears to have died a natural death in late May. But another version of the event, which appeared in the *Daily Telegraph*, also included a story about a member of a UK based bomber squadron receiving a white feather, a common reference to cowardice.[26] All the articles supported the servicemen and clearly stated that the war had many aspects, with service in one location contributing to victory in others. Ridicule fell upon the person or people accusing RAAF members of being Jap-dodgers or cowards by the sending of white feathers. The prime minister was quoted as calling any such perpetrator an "idiot," with one journalist referring to anyone doing that as a "certifiable lunatic."

Another article included excerpts from a letter written by an airman to his wife in response to allegations of Jap-dodging as a way to describe the reality of the servicemen's experiences.[27] Though the RAAF personnel who served in Europe were well supported by the majority of Australians, the slanderous name-calling and accusations of cowardice caused a longstanding offense that was carried by some for many decades after the war.[28]

A much more positive and uplifting article came out around the same time. In the *Argus* Geoffrey Hutton described in detail what the RAAF was doing in Europe.[29] He presented a wide-ranging look at the various roles and aircraft flown by the Australians based in the United Kingdom. It reminded the reader that for every man in an RAAF squadron there were three in non-RAAF squadrons. "This intermixture means that Australian history is being made over the skies of Fascist-occupied Europe, and it is difficult, almost impossible, to record it as the story of the Anzacs [of World War I] was recorded."[30] Practicalities and politics aside, the lack of a concentrated Australian force (in the style of the Canadians) has been a significant obstacle to building a simple and clear picture for the Australian public about RAAF operations in Europe during the Second World War.

At the end of May, the *Brisbane Courier-Mail* profiled an Australian squadron in Coastal Command. The Beaufighters of No. 455 (RAAF) Squadron were specifically linked to the Normandy Campaign in an appropriately patriotic and enthusiastic article titled "Australian Beaufighters Cripple Nazi Shipping." It described the general method of attack, the fearlessness required to drive it home, and the effects that the Coastal Command successes were having upon the German navy.[31]

June 1944

Reporters attached to No. 453 Squadron had immediate access to stories about that unit's operations over France.[32] The result was articles such as "Australians Smash Nazi Radar," published in the *Newcastle Sun*. The same piece was carried in the *Telegraph* as "Small Planes Smash Nazi Radar Stations."[33] More coverage of 2nd Tactical Air Force was published in the *Sun* on 3 June under the headline "Australian Chateau Shatterers," which claimed (not for the last time) that RAAF airmen had nearly killed the Desert Fox,

Field Marshal Erwin Rommel, who arrived at the site of an attack shortly after it had been completed.[34]

Australians arrived in France just a few days after the landings in Normandy took place. Among the articles featuring Eisenhower and Montgomery printed on 6 June before news of the invasion was available, the *Barrier Miner* of Broken Hill, New South Wales, carried on page two an item about the "Australian Spitfire squadron" and its readiness to move to France "within a few hours of the order being given." Written by Fred Folkard, it also stated, "They will act—as they are doing in Italy—as a 'cab rank' callable by radio to dive bomb resisting enemy positions or destroy counter attack concentrations."[35] While this type of loitering direct support mission for the army was more often flown by Typhoons, No. 453 Squadron flew one such sortie on 28 June (from Airfield B.11 Longues-sur-Mer), but no attacks were made as the prearranged red-smoke signal was not given by the ground troops.[36]

The *Australian Worker* shouted "Allied Armies Invade France!" on page seven of its 7 June issue, quoting Deputy Prime Minister and Minister for the Army Frank Forde as stating: "Many of our own Australian airmen will be participating in the new operations in air squadrons of the R.A.A.F. and the R.A.F. They will play their part in the same gallant way that the Australian fighting forces have played their part in operations in almost every theatre of war."[37] This was reinforced the next day in "R.A.A.F. Plays Big Part" in the *Advertiser* of Adelaide. This article opened with "Australia's Lancaster, Halifax, Mosquito, Spitfire, Sunderland and Beaufighter squadrons have all been directly or indirectly throwing their maximum weight into the breaching of the Atlantic Wall."[38] From an informational and educational viewpoint, this was exactly what the public needed to hear to help them understand the many ways that Australians were contributing to the Normandy Campaign.

Coverage of operations involving Australians was very heavy over the following week, with on 9 June alone articles such as "Australians Get 4 Enemy Planes" (*Advocate*—Tasmania); "Australians in Thick of Air Battles over France" (*Mercury*—Hobart); "Nazi Supply Lines Strafed" (*Argus*—Melbourne); "Pilots' Stories: Contrasts, Packed Sky, Funny War" (*Morning Bulletin*—Rockhampton); and "Spitfire Pilots Eager: Nothing to Shoot At" (*Sydney Morning Herald*). Many of these pieces featured No. 453 Squadron, with the keyword "Spitfire" used as a natural and exciting hook to get readers interested. And, while the Spitfire pilots complained about a lack of opposition, other articles covered the successes of RAAF Mosquito night fighters in defending the Allied fleet from Luftwaffe night raiders in articles such as "First Good Luftwaffe Kill to Australians" and "Beachhead Kill to Aust Pilot."[39]

The message continued to be reinforced in Perth on 10 June, when the *West Australian* article "Australia There" opened with "In every air operation on the opening day of the invasion Australia was represented either by formations from Australian fighter, fighter-bomber or bomber squadrons or by one or more of the hundreds of RAAF men who fly with RAF squadrons."[40] A version of this same article appeared in Melbourne's *Argus* under the title "Our Airmen Prominent in Invasion."[41]

Warrant Officer Keith Daff of No. 453 Squadron was profiled on 13 June after an engine failure caused him to set down in Normandy. He was hailed as "the first member of the Australian armed forces to land in France this war." The article was accompanied by a studio photograph of Daff and a summary of his service history to date.[42] The *Mercury* carried a photograph of No. 453 Squadron's Flight Sergeant John Oxley Waugh Olsson on the same day, noting that he had been reported missing in action.[43]

Photographs of Australian aircrews who were participating in Normandy operations continued over the next few days, including those showing Squadron Leader Colin Milson, Warrant Officer Michael Frederick Carew Jackson, and Flying Officer William Morgan Barbour of No. 455 shown in conversation in front of a Beaufighter; Flying Officer L. J. Hansell of No. 453 Squadron in flying kit; the very young twenty-two-year-old Wing Commander John Douglas; and the often-mentioned Mosquito pilot Wing Commander Hampshire, who had shot down yet another Luftwaffe raider.[44]

On 14 June the *Sun* printed an informative article by Tom Gurr about the role photoreconnaissance played in the lead-up to the landings. In the closing paragraph he revealed that Australians were also participating in these operations, reinforcing the significance of the RAAF contribution to the Normandy Campaign from beginning to anticipated end.[45]

But the newspapers did not always get things right. On 19 June the *Daily Telegraph* published an article with the headline "Aust. Pilots get 2 Nazi

Planes." One Messerschmitt was claimed to have been shot down by Warrant Officer A. C. Wright, but there was no pilot by that name on the squadron roster—it was actually Warrant Officer C. A. Rice. The article also claimed that these German fighters, destroyed on 16 June, were the "first enemy aircraft shot down by the squadron since it was formed." Putting aside the first formation of No. 453 Squadron in 1941, the squadron already had shot down several enemy aircraft since it was reformed in Scotland in June 1942.[46]

Mosquitos were back in the news on 22 June, when the *Kalgoorlie Miner* published "Daylight Intruder Squadrons." This article highlighted the work of the Australians flying Mosquitos on intruder missions, their role being to intercept enemy aircraft in the vicinity of their airfields at night to disrupt their operations, while also mentioning Wing Commander Hampshire's nighttime success.[47] These intruder missions were escorted by Typhoons, often flown by RAAF pilots.[48]

The newspapers also profiled the role of Australians in destroying the V-1 rockets being directed against targets in the United Kingdom. "Daredevil Pilots Blast Robots from 100 Yards" was the story in the *Sun* on 22 June, sharing the exploits of RAF and Royal New Zealand Air Force Hawker Tempest squadrons and their successes against the unmanned rockets. Flight Sergeant Donald John Mackerras, named in the article, was one of the Australians involved in these operations. Another version of this story appeared in the *Kalgoorlie Miner* and profiled Mackerras as well as several other Australians, once again showing the wide range of operations in which RAAF members were participating.[49]

On 24 June the *Australasian* ran a pictorial of the RAAF in Europe. The article heavily featured No. 453 Squadron and included photos of a Mosquito, a Lancaster, and a Halifax as well as a number of aircrew. It opened with a powerful statement: "Greatest number of Australians represented in the historic invasion operations has come from the RAAF."[50]

A reference to white feathers popped up again on 25 June in the *Sunday Mail*. An anonymous mother of an Australian serving in the United Kingdom remarked, "If the censor, instead of snooping round personal mail, collected a few of these white feathers, it would prevent our boys being so cruelly villified [sic]."[51] A short article referencing white feathers also appeared at the end of June in the *Guinea Gold*, titled "Idiots Still Sending White Feathers."[52]

On 25 June the arrival of Australian Spitfires (No. 453 Squadron) in Normandy was reported in several newspapers a few days after they first landed on the Continent. One paper reported on "RAAF Planes at New Base in Normandy," another "Australian Spitfires on the Job in Normandy," and a third "Australian Spitfires Now Based in Normandy." Two of the three papers identified the unit's commanding officer, Squadron Leader Don Smith.[53]

July 1944

The *Sydney Morning Herald* opened July with an upbeat and heartening article titled "Luftwaffe Absent in Normandy," which gave a positive overview of the situation on land and in the air.[54] Positive messages were reinforced at the personal level with the story of Joe Boulton (No. 453 Squadron) being kissed by French locals. When he explained he was an Australian, a toast was made "to airmen who have come such a long way to fight for us."[55]

But it was back to kicking the Luftwaffe while it was down on 3 July, with an article by Folkard on 3 July in the *Sun* called "Nazi Pilots Won't Fight Allied Spitfires." It contained a number of theories about this proposed by members of No. 453 Squadron, including "the Germans are only interested in shooting down bombers," with the interesting but unsubstantiated detail that "Luftwaffe pilots claim four kills if they shoot down a four-engined bomber."[56] The message was reinforced on 4 July in "Enemy Avoids Air Combat" in the *Sydney Morning Herald*.[57] Two days later the *Age* carried a short but exciting article, "A 50-Mile Air Chase." It related the story of Flying Officer Jack Olver (No. 453 Squadron) shooting down an Fw 190, which displayed the tenacity of Allied pilots to ensure victory over the Luftwaffe. Kicking the Luftwaffe once again, the article noted that it was "one of the rare occasions when German pilots have turned to try to fight it out."[58]

Once again striking back at the claims of shirking a real war, on 7 July the *Daily Examiner* of Grafton printed an account by Flight Sergeant Jack Southgate of No. 467 Squadron. In a letter home he described his experience on the morning of 6 June, concluding with: "I guess I have whinged plenty about being over here, and wanting to get back. I am glad now that I am here, for I would have hated to miss this show."[59] Without the ground crews, however, no plane would be fit to fly, and their contribution was not forgotten, with some of their work and interactions with French locals being told in "Digger Hat Welcomed to Normandy" in the *Argus*.[60]

The activities of Bomber Command were described in an article titled "Bomber Command: Fine Work in Normandy," published in the *Northern Miner* of Queensland on 12 July. Squadron Leader Don Smith of No. 453 Squadron described the achievements of the heavy bombers in the lead-up to the Normandy landings and their activities against the Atlantic Wall, specifically the successful attack of a coastal battery between Isigny and Trévières. He described the bombers as having "wiped them out."[61] Several German fortifications and batteries in the area were described, but exactly which one Smith is supposed to have visited is not known, as this battery was well within the American zone, and No. 453 Squadron was based within walking distance of the Longues-sur-Mer battery. Perhaps the two were blended to make the article.

The impressive success of No. 453 Squadron against a formation of Luftwaffe fighters on 9 July excited the papers for days. The *Newcastle Sun* cover story on 11 July crowed, "RAAF Downs Germans Ten to Nil," while the *News* of Adelaide declared, "Australians in Thrilling Dogfight." The *Sydney Morning Herald* also discussed the incident on 15 July.[62] It was true enough; the Australians had claimed four enemy aircraft destroyed and six damaged (out of a formation of up to fifty) for no loss—an excellent result for just eight Spitfires that lacked both the element of surprise and an altitude advantage.[63] The *Sunshine Advocate* also described this action and took specific pride in Warrant Officer Jack Steward, a local who participated in the fighting and claimed one Fw 190 destroyed.[64]

The *Advertiser* of Adelaide ran a small cover story on 13 July about the record-breaking 1,100 operational hours flown by No. 10 Squadron RAAF Sunderlands on anti-U-boat patrols.[65] While this was a significant feat, the article missed an opportunity to trumpet the success of this squadron and others (such as No. 461 Squadron) in preventing U-boat attacks on the thousands of vessels that crossed the English Channel on the night of 5–6 June and during the many subsequent crossings.

But with success comes sacrifice, and Australian losses also received coverage. Squadron Leader William Blessing, a Mosquito pilot with No. 105

Photo 13-2 • French children show lively interest in a No. 453 Squadron RAAF Spitfire at Advanced Landing Ground B.11 as RAF and RAAF ground crews tell them all about their aircraft, July 1944. On 10 August this photo graced the front page of the *Brisbane Courier-Mail*. AWM UK1527

Squadron, Pathfinder Force, was killed on operations on 7 July.[66] His aircraft was hit by a Luftwaffe fighter and though he and his navigator escaped, their Mosquito was too badly damaged to make it back to the United Kingdom, so Blessing headed for the cluster of Allied airfields in the Normandy bridgehead. Minutes before landing, the aircraft went into a spin, and he told his navigator to jump, which saved his life. Blessing did not survive the crash.[67] The *Sydney Morning Herald* described him as "One of the Best."[68]

The Allied bombing of south of Caen, in association with Operation Goodwood (unnamed in the article), was described as a "Terrific Air Blow" in the *Cairns Post* on 20 July. Most importantly for Australian audiences, the RAAF participation was acknowledged, both in the Lancaster, Halifax, and Spitfire squadrons that participated and the "hundreds of members of the R.A.A.F. in British crews."[69] A slightly more accurate version of this article appeared in the *Examiner* on the same day.[70]

The ongoing success of Australian Mosquito night fighters (No. 456 Squadron) was reported in the *Dungog Chronicle* on 25 July. Three kills were credited to Australians, each of whom was named, his hometown provided, and the type of aircraft he shot down.[71] A night attack against German trains in France by another Australian Mosquito squadron (No. 464 Squadron) also rated a mention on the same front page. In addition, the article noted the recent appointment of Wing Commander Peter Panitz as their new commander.[72]

On 27 July the *Tweed Daily* announced, "Eisenhower Visits Normandy," which was seen as only slightly more important than its subheading, which declared, "Australians in Air Escort." The article described the general's seven-hour visit to Normandy and named two Australian Spitfire pilots, including Flight Lieutenant James Edward Schofield from No. 127 Squadron.[73] Here was yet another example of the scattered nature of Australians in the RAF and the wide range of their involvement in the Normandy Campaign.

On 28 July the *Guinea Gold* claimed, "Australian Spitfire Pilots Nearly Bagged Hitler." The article claimed that Hitler and three of his deputies (Luftwaffe chief Reichsmarschall Hermann Göring, SS leader Heinrich Himmler, and army commander Field Marshal Erwin Rommel) were inspecting "German installations" near Arromanches just before an attack by the Australian Spitfires. Such an attack did occur on 30 May 1944, when No. 453 Squadron bombed a radar station east of Arromanches, but at the time Hitler was hundreds of miles away.[74] It was a rather fanciful story of the time, and luckily one that has not persisted.

An article published in the *North Western Courier* on 31 July provided a useful overview of the RAAF in Europe. It noted the contributions of Sunderland, Beaufighter, Mosquito, and Lancaster squadrons, providing examples of their actions and the experiences of some Australians in non-RAAF squadrons, naming several of them.[75]

August 1944

A rather more focused article, titled "Australians' Big Role in Normandy," was on the front page of the *Newcastle Sun* on 1 August, written by Folkard from the front. This was yet another item about No. 453 Squadron and its operations, and no doubt the coverage given the squadron at the time was due to Folkard being based with them, providing ready access to daily events and stories from its pilots.[76]

The role of No. 455 Squadron's Beaufighters was linked with the Normandy landings in the *Goulburn Evening Post* on 2 August, with a short history of the squadron provided alongside, naming squadron members, their ages, and their hometowns.[77] The squadron made it to the papers again the following week when they attacked German R-boats and a minesweeper off Le Havre.[78]

The German counterattack at Mortain and the role of the RAF in stopping the panzers was an important story at the time and has only grown since. Folkard jumped on the Typhoon bandwagon by recounting the actions of Pilot Officer Jock Steel, a Queenslander flying with No. 174 Squadron, who parachuted into American lines after his fighter-bomber was hit by flak while attacking German armor near the town. The Americans were so happy with the air support provided by the Typhoons that they gave Steel a bottle of scotch and a jeep to return to his airfield. Folkard praised the fighter-bomber, noting that the attack "definitely established the Typhoon as the air war's most spectacular weapon."[79] Sam White continued that theme in his article for the *Argus*, "Typhoons Find Tanks Easy Game," which included accounts from the Australian pilots involved.[80]

Stories about reconnaissance pilots did not contain the same drama as attacking Nazi tanks, but their role was highlighted in the *News* of Adelaide on 11 August. The article, "Germans Make Tanks Look like Orchards," focused on the accounts of Australian Mustang pilots in Normandy. It included personal accounts describing the difficulty of detecting camouflaged German vehicles, even when flying as low as one hundred feet above the battlefield.[81]

Adding yet more variety to the coverage of Australian participation in the Normandy campaign, "Normandy—In a Hurry" told the story of a number of Australian aircrews in Transport Command flying Dakotas into Normandy with all manner of supplies. It noted, "Spare parts for tanks, propeller shafts for damaged landing craft, huge bundles of magazines and newspaper, and even motor cars are among the assortment of goods that are being ferried into Normandy every hour of the day." The *Herald* article also covered the need for blood plasma and white bread as well as the participation of Women's

Auxiliary Air Force nurses, who looked after injured troops as they were taken back to the United Kingdom on each return flight. The article also profiled Flying Officer Keith Dober, who dropped paratroopers in the first wave of the Normandy landings, and the Australian Halifax bomber crews who towed gliders across the Channel.[82]

Though the campaign was ending with the Battle of Mortain and the closing of the Falaise Gap, daily events continued to be reported, and the propaganda element continued. The *Guinea Gold* shouted, "Rocket-Firing Typhoons Doing Man-Sized Job!" on 15 August and embedded yet more Spitfire snobbery of the sort that continues to this day. "Not since the Spitfire saved Britain and the world," it started, then later continued with "It is not suggested that [the Typhoon's] contribution to the war is as vital as the Spitfire."[83] While whole books could be written in rebuttal, it was important to keep reinforcing the positive and relatively simplistic messages about the Spitfire's superiority that were easily repeated and just as easily digested. The statements were true to a degree, but during wartime, a simple and easy-to-remember message was the most effective; the nuances could be left to the historians. Propaganda was not just for the enemy but was often also a message for the masses.

It was the turn of Lancasters and Mosquitos to be given credit in "With the RAAF Overseas: Tough Australians," which appeared in the *Eastern Recorder* on 18 August, again reinforcing the range of activities undertaken by Australians in Europe.[84] But the articles during this month included more than just text and photos, with some even presented in comic-strip form, such as "One of the First Mosquito Pilots" in the *Argus* of 19 August. In a series of illustrations and captions, the story of Squadron Leader Peter Swan was told from his birth in the United Kingdom, moving to Australia, enlisting in the militia, and then joining the RAAF, flying Blenheims, Mosquitos, and Lancasters. The strip ended with the last panel briefly describing his participation supporting the Normandy landings, recent promotion, award of the Distinguished Flying Cross, and selection for Pathfinder duties.[85]

Though not as exciting or glamorous as the combat aircraft and their squadrons, the essential work of the transport crews continued. "German Wounded Flown from Normandy" was a small article in the *Geraldton*

Guardian and Express. It related the stories of some of the German prisoners taken back to the United Kingdom from Normandy and concluded by observing that one "seemed glad to be out of the war and quite happy to be a prisoner."[86]

The campaign for Normandy did not end neatly on 31 August. As the front line moved farther into France and away from the beaches, so, too, did the coverage of the RAAF. There were other operations to write about, other experiences to relate, and new stories to tell. Clearly, a great many articles were published about the experiences and contributions of the RAAF in Normandy, often picked up and reproduced in numerous papers across Australia. With ground crews and aircrews spread across so many squadrons, their contribution is difficult to express in a simple set of statistics.

While the focus of the Australian public over the past forty years has primarily swung between Kokoda and Tobruk (at least for matters involving World War II), it can be clearly seen that the Australian contribution to the Normandy air campaign did not go unnoticed or unreported at the time. Perhaps a little more effort is required to bring those Normandy days to the fore again.

NOTES

1. Peter Dennis, Jeffrey Grey, Ewan Morris, Robin Prior, and Jean Bou, *The Oxford Companion to Australian Military History* (1995; repr., Victoria, Australia: Oxford University Press, 2008), 197–98.
2. Colin Leith letters, K series, National Archives of Australia [hereafter NAA].
3. "Renaming of RAF Suggested," *Argus* (Melbourne); and *Daily Telegraph*, 15 May 1944.
4. *Army News*, 2 April 1944.
5. "Australian's Victory," *West Australian*, 8 April 1944.
6. "Air Combat," *Kalgoorlie Miner*, 10 April 1944; No. 461 Squadron Operations Record Book [ORB], NAA A9186/148.
7. "Duke Meets RAAF Pilots," *Sydney Morning Herald*, 15 April 1944; Adam Lunney, *Ready to Strike: The Spitfires and Australians of 453 (RAAF) Squadron over Normandy* (Woodend, Australia: Echo Books, 2018), 148–50.
8. *Glen Innes Examiner*, 18 April 1944.
9. *Daily Examiner*, 18 April 1944; Lunney, *Ready to Strike*, 97, 190–91.
10. *Newcastle Herald*, 1 May 1944.

11. *Herald* (Melbourne), 2 May 1944, 1.
12. Quote from *Morning Bulletin* (Rockhampton), 4 May 1944.
13. *Adelaide Advertiser*, 4 May 1944; *Guinea Gold*, 5 May 1944; *Central Queensland Herald*, 11 May 1944; and others.
14. *Border Morning Mail* (Albury), 4 May 1944.
15. Robert Wilson Iredale personnel file, NAA A9300.
16. No. 453 Squadron ORB, 5 May 1944, NAA A9186/139.
17. *Brisbane Telegraph*, 11 May 1944; *Adelaide News*, 12 May 1944.
18. *West Australian*, 6 May 1944; No. 463 Squadron ORB, NAA A9186/150.
19. Martin Middlebrook and Chris Everitt, *The Bomber Command War Diaries: An Operational Reference Book* (New York: Viking Penguin, 1985), 505–6.
20. No. 463 Squadron History, NAA 9186/150; quotation from No. 463 Squadron ORB, ibid.
21. No. 12 Squadron ORB, NAA A9186/33.
22. No. 463 Squadron History, NAA 9186/150.
23. No. 460 Squadron Unit History, January 1944–October 1945, NAA 9186/147; Middlebrook and Everitt, *Bomber Command War Diaries*, 505–6.
24. *Herald* (Melbourne), 23 May 1944.
25. *Truth* (Sydney), 21 May 1944.
26. "Suddenly You Realise What It All Means," *Daily Telegraph*, 23 May 1944.
27. *Daily News*, 24 May 1944.
28. "RAAF Blunt to Curtin," *Truth* (Sydney), 21 May 1944; John Culbert interview, 5 June 2003, no. 401, Australians at War Film Archive, UNSW Canberra, https://australiansatwarfilmarchive.unsw.edu.au/archive/401; Kenneth Gaulton interview, 3 February 2004, no. 1276, ibid., https://australiansatwarfilmarchive.unsw.edu.au/archive/1276; Norman Goldsborough (Goldie) interview, 20 August 2003, no. 627, ibid., https://australiansatwarfilmarchive.unsw.edu.au/archive/627; John Boland (Happy) interview, 19 January 2004, no. 1382, ibid., https://australiansatwarfilmarchive.unsw.edu.au/archive/1382; Keith Prowd (Keith or Skip) interview, 17 November 2003, no. 1049, ibid., https://australiansatwarfilmarchive.unsw.edu.au/archive/1049; Lawrence Woods (Laurie) interview, 12 August 2003, no. 688, ibid., https://australiansatwarfilmarchive.unsw.edu.au/archive/688. For other World War II veteran interviews that discuss this, see search results for "dodger," ibid., https://australiansatwarfilmarchive.unsw.edu.au/search/?searchFor=dodgers; and for "white feather," ibid., https://australiansatwarfilmarchive.unsw.edu.au/search/?searchFor=white+feather.
29. Geoffrey Hutton, "Australians' Role in Second Front—What RAAF Men Are Doing," *Argus* (Melbourne), 24 May 1944.

30. Hutton, "Australians' Role in Second Front."
31. "Australian Beaufighters Cripple Nazi Shipping," *Brisbane Courier-Mail*, 30 May 1944.
32. This access occurred long before reporters were "embedded" with units during the Gulf War (1990–91) and the term joined the popular lexicon.
33. "Australians Smash Nazi Radar," *Newcastle Sun*, 1 June 1944; "Small Planes Smash Nazi Radar Stations," *Telegraph*, 1 June 1944.
34. *Sydney Sun*, 3 June 1944.
35. "Australians Are Ready for Continent," *Barrier Miner*, 6 June 1944.
36. No. 453 Squadron ORB, NAA A9186/139, 139.
37. *Australian Worker*, 7 June 1944; Neil Lloyd and Malcolm Saunders, "Francis Michael (Frank) Forde (1890–1983)," *Australian Dictionary of Biography*, 2007, https://adb.anu.edu.au/biography/forde-francis-michael-frank-12504.
38. *Advertiser*, 8 June 1944.
39. "First Good Luftwaffe Kill to Australians," *Army News*, 12 June 1944, 3; "Beachhead Kill to Aust Pilot," *Courier-Mail*, 12 June 1944, 3.
40. "Australia There," *West Australian*, 10 June 1944.
41. "Our Airmen Prominent in Invasion," *Argus*, 10 June 1944, 4.
42. "Australian Pilot Who Landed in France," *Argus*, 13 June 1944, 5; Keith Daff personnel file, NAA A9300.
43. Olsson's aircraft had crashed on 21 May, but his status as a prisoner was not received by the squadron until June. "Spitfire Pilot," *Mercury*, 13 June 1944, 3; Lunney, *Ready to Strike*, 210–11.
44. "Australian Beaufighter Squadron Overseas," *Townsville Daily Bulletin*, 14 June 1944, 2; "Australians Support Troops," *Age* (Melbourne), 13 June 1944, 2; "Youngest Australian to Command Bomber Squadron," *Argus*, 14 June 1944, 5; "Hampshire Again," *West Australian*, 14 June 1944, 2.
45. Tom Gurr, "British Sky Spies See Invasion Wall Secrets: Camera Vital Weapon," *Sun*, 14 June 1944, 2.
46. *Daily Telegraph*, 19 June 1944; Lunney, *Ready to Strike*, 242–43.
47. John Herington, *Air Power over Europe, 1944–1945*, vol. 4, *Australia in the War of 1939–1945* (Canberra: Australian War Memorial, 1963), 23.
48. *Kalgoorlie Miner*, 22 June 1944, 3.
49. *Sun*, 22 June 1944; *Kalgoorlie Miner*, 22 June 1944, 3.
50. *Australasian*, 24 June 1944, 7.
51. "Told to Do Fighting, *Sunday Mail*," 25 June 1944, 4.
52. "Idiots Still Sending White Feathers," 29 June 1944, 6.
53. Sam White, "RAAF Planes at New Base in Normandy," *Argus*, 29 June 1944, 2; "Australian Spitfires on the Job in Normandy," *Morning Bulletin*, 29 June

1944, 3; "Australian Spitfires Now Based in Normandy," *Queensland Times*, 29 June 1944, 3.
54. H. I. Williams, "Luftwaffe Absent in Normandy," *Sydney Morning Herald*, 1 July 1944, 3.
55. "French Kiss Aust. Airman by Mistake," *Daily Telegraph*, 1 July 1944, 2.
56. F. C. Folkard, "Nazi Pilots Won't Fight Allied Spitfires," *Sun*, 3 July 1944, 2.
57. H. I. Williams, "Enemy Avoids Air Combat," *Sydney Morning Herald*, 4 July 1944, 3.
58. "A 50-Mile Air Chase," *Age*, 6 July 1944, 1.
59. "Grafton Airman Participates in Normandy Invasion," *Daily Examiner*, 7 July 1944, 4; Jack Southgate personnel file, NAA A9300.
60. Sam White, "Digger Hat Welcomed to Normandy," *Argus*, 7 July 1944, 16.
61. "Bomber Command: Fine Work in Normandy," *Northern Miner*, 12 July 1944, 7.
62. F. C. Folkard, "RAAF Downs Germans Ten to Nil," *Newcastle Sun*, 11 July 1944, 1; F. C. Folkard, "Australians in Thrilling Dogfight," *News*, 12 July 1944, 2; H. I. Williams, "R.A.A.F. Tackles Mantoni," *Sydney Morning Herald*, 15 July 1944, 3.
63. Lunney, *Ready to Strike*, 288–91.
64. "Local Spitfire Pilot," *Sunshine Advocate*, 14 July 1944, 1; Lunney, *Ready to Strike*, 289–90.
65. *Advertiser* (Adelaide), 13 July 1944.
66. "Braidwood Hero," *Goulburn Evening Post*, 13 July 1944, 1.
67. UK National Archives [hereafter TNA], AIR 27/927/37.
68. "One of the Best Killed," *Sydney Morning Herald*, 13 July 1944, 3.
69. Australian Associated Press, "Terrific Air Blow," *Cairns Post*, 20 July 1944, 5.
70. Air Chief Marshal Trafford Sir Leigh-Mallory was incorrectly identified as "Arthur" (likely mixed up with Air Chief Marshal Sir Arthur Tedder) in the earlier article. "The Normandy Smash," *Examiner*, 20 July 1944, 5.
71. "Four Enemy Planes in Night," *Dungog Chronicle*, 25 July 1944, 1.
72. "Ace Train-Buster Reopens Account," *Dungog Chronicle*, 25 July 1944, 1.
73. Some articles claim three Australians among the four escorts, but one of the pilots may have been from New Zealand. *Tweed Daily*, 27 July 1944; James Edward Schofield personnel file, NAA A9300; No. 127 Squadron ORB, TNA AIR 27/929; *Sun*, 26 July 1944.
74. Lunney, *Ready to Strike*, 217; Ian Kershaw, *Hitler, 1936–1945: Nemesis*, vol. 2 (New York: W. W. Norton, 2000), 635–38.
75. "RAAF over Europe," *NW Courier*, 31 July 1944, 3.
76. *Newcastle Sun*, 1 August 1944.
77. "R.A.A.F. Beaufighter's Forays," *Goulburn Evening Post*, 2 August 1944, 2.

78. "Beaufighter Boys Have a Field Day," *Telegraph* (Brisbane edition), 8 August 1944, 4.
79. F. C. Folkard, "'Scotch' Gift for Aussie Typhoon Flier," *News*, 10 August 1944, 2.
80. Sam White, "Typhoons Find Tanks Easy Game," *Argus*, 10 August 1944, 16.
81. *Adelaide News*, 11 August 1944, 2.
82. "Normandy—In a Hurry," *Herald*, 11 August 1944, 4.
83. *Guinea Gold*, 15 August 1944, 5.
84. "With the RAAF Overseas: Tough Australians," *Eastern Recorder*, 18 August 1944, 4.
85. "One of the First Mosquito Pilots," *Argus*, 19 August 1944, 5; P. H. Swan personnel file, NAA, A9300.
86. "German Wounded Flown from Normandy," *Geraldton Guardian and Express*, 30 August 1944, 3.

CONCLUDING THOUGHTS

Mike Bechthold

The ceremonies to mark the eightieth anniversary of the D-Day landings showed just how much work remains to ensure airpower is a key element of the story of the Normandy Campaign. Not surprisingly, a survey of the main political speeches delivered on 6 June 2024 demonstrates a focus on the land and sea elements of Operation Overlord. U.S. president Joe Biden mentioned the heroic acts of several D-Day veterans: Kenneth Blaine Smith, a U.S. Navy radar operator who was on the first ship to arrive off the Normandy coast; Bob Gibson, a U.S. Army antiaircraft gunner who landed on Utah Beach; and Ben Miller, an 82nd Airborne Division medic who saved lives while the battle raged around him.[1] He did not spotlight an Army Air Forces veteran. The focus of his comments was on the land battle, and airpower received only a token mention when he thanked "every aviator who destroyed German-controlled air fields, bridges, and railroads."[2]

The comments by British prime minister Rishi Sunak and Canadian prime minister Justin Trudeau similarly focused on the landings. Sunak made passing references to the air war while mentioning by name three men who took part in the landings: Ken Cooke of the Green Howards, Royal Navy veteran Stan Ford, and Royal Marine Dennis Donovan.³ Trudeau honored the "359 Canadians [who] lost their lives on the day of the landing," but it is telling that his figure only included the men who landed on Juno Beach or dropped in with 1st Canadian Parachute Battalion. His statistic does not include the twenty-two Canadian airmen killed in action on D-Day. Trudeau singled out "Honorary Lieutenant General Richard Rohmer, who turned 100 this year. He is also with us today, [and] is one of Canada's most decorated veterans. Over the decades, he's participated in and organized many commemoration events. In his words, the costly D-Day success at Juno Beach laid the unforeseeable foundation for the betterment of mankind. It is important for him that we never forget."⁴ These are noble words, but few listening would have known that on D-Day Rohmer was flying reconnaissance missions above the beaches in a North American Mustang as a member of No. 430 Squadron, Royal Canadian Air Force.

Each of these leaders recognized that the air forces were a part of the D-Day story, but one that lay in the shadows, seemingly undeserving of recognition as a leading component of the victory.

French president Emmanuel Macron took a different tone than his English-speaking colleagues. While he also focused on the spirit of sacrifice, he did not avoid the ugly realities of the war. Delivering his address in Saint-Lô on 5 June 2024, he referred to the town as the "capital of ruins" and paid tribute to the civilian victims of the Allied bombings.⁵ It was a fitting location for such a discussion. The town was considered an important communications hub by the Allies, who scheduled it for destruction to stop or delay the movement of German reinforcements toward the invasion zone. An attack on the morning of 6 June was scrubbed when Eighth Air Force bombers could not find the town through heavy clouds. They returned that afternoon. Thirty-six B-24s were still unable to locate Saint-Lô, but an equal number found their target and smothered the urban area with 128 tons of bombs, using the city

Photo 14-1 • This aerial photograph captures a bombing raid in progress on the town of Saint-Lô, likely on 7 June 1944. The intent of the attack was to block the converging roads in the town center to slow the movement of German reinforcements to the front, but hundreds of innocent French civilians were killed in the process. *U.S. Air Force photo 52676AC*

center as their aiming point. RAF Bomber Command added to the death and destruction later that night when 110 Lancasters and Halifaxes hit the city with as much as 700 tons of high explosives. Locals called it "la nuit du grand cauchemar"—the night of the great nightmare. Estimates of the dead ranged from a low of 300 to over 3,000.[6] Macron referred to "these dead" as the "victims of our fight for freedom and the homeland."[7] He discussed how Saint-Lô was 90-percent destroyed during the war, mostly by aerial bombardment, and held it up as a symbol of all the cities martyred from the air—Caen, Lisieux, Flers, and Le Havre, among others. It is significant that between 50,000 and 70,000 civilians were killed by Allied air attacks in France, including 10,000 in Normandy during the summer of 1944.[8] This is an aspect of airpower that cannot be ignored, but it is only one facet of an elaborate campaign.

Photo 14-2 • Bulldozers work to clear the roads through Saint-Lô in late July. The combination of Allied bombing and the later shelling by U.S. and German forces during the fighting in late July completely devastated the town. *U.S. National Archives 111-SC-192065*

Of course, our knowledge of the past would be sadly lacking or even skewed if we relied on politicians to teach us history, but their comments are indicative of a wider lack of awareness regarding airpower issues in the Normandy Campaign. This collection has demonstrated that there remains much to be learned.

Telling the story of airpower and the Normandy Campaign is not a straightforward task. To properly cover the topic requires a solid understanding of the ground and naval campaigns. It is a multinational narrative that encompasses political, strategic, operational, and tactical realms. Spatially, it covers thousands of square miles, from London to Amsterdam to Brussels to Berlin to Paris to Nantes, and includes vast swaths of the Atlantic Ocean,

English Channel, and the North Sea. Temporally, the air campaign started months before D-Day and involved issues of personnel, morale, leadership, technology, logistics, tactics, media, and much more. The diverse perspectives of the contributors whose work make up this book demonstrate the disparate nature of the topic.

This collection covers many important topics related to airpower in Normandy. The first section examines the preparations for the upcoming landings. Mike Pavelec sets the stage by examining the strategic background to the use of airpower in Normandy. Stephen Moore and Seb Cox examine the operational effects and political intrigue behind the Transportation Plan. Heather Venable provides an innovative look at questions of motivation and battle fatigue among U.S. bomber crews and fighter pilots, while Matt Bone discusses how the Allies attempted to knock out German radar sites before D-Day.

The second section focuses on the application of airpower from a variety of perspectives. Christopher Finn and Russell Hart look at the intersections of navies with airpower, from both an Allied and a German perspective respectively. Stephen Bourque considers the difficult story of how French civilians were affected by Allied bombings. Mike Bechthold and Christopher Rein look at the tactical application of airpower on the battlefield by analyzing the use of fighter-bombers and medium bombers at Cherbourg and by comparing the set-piece heavy bombing attacks that accompanied Operations Cobra and Queen. Paul Johnston explores the details of how the Allied air support system worked, Alex Fitzgerald-Black looks at how tactical air support was viewed by Canadian ground troops, and Adam Lunney considers the air war from an Australian perspective by examining how it was reported in newspapers back home.

Taken together, these thirteen chapters provide new insights and a better understanding of the nature and complexity of the air campaign. Yet they only scratch the surface. There is much still to be learned, understood, and appreciated. Many aspects of the air campaign in Normandy would benefit from this type of study—aerial reconnaissance, transport and supply operations, airfield construction and logistics, aeromedical evacuations, medium bomber operations, Coastal Command missions, and, especially, a detailed look at what the Luftwaffe accomplished—to name just a few. Some of these topics have not yet received a detailed academic treatment, while others have been only partially examined in the past. It is time to revisit and update our understanding of the air war over Western Europe based on the wide range of sources available to the modern researcher.

Our hope is that the chapters in this collection have clarified and informed readers about the role of airpower in Normandy as well as inspired further research and writing on this important topic.

NOTES

1. Pres. Joseph Biden, "Remarks by President Biden Commemorating the 80th Anniversary of D-Day, Collevile-sur-Mer [sic], France," 6 June 2024, https://www.whitehouse.gov/briefing-room/speeches-remarks/2024/06/06/remarks-by-president-biden-commemorating-the-80th-anniversary-of-d-day-collevile-sur-mer-france.
2. Biden, "Remarks."
3. Prime Minister Rishi Sunak, "Prime Minister's Remarks for the 80th Anniversary of D-Day," 6 June 2024, https://www.gov.uk/government/speeches/prime-ministers-remarks-for-the-80th-anniversary-of-d-day.
4. Prime Minister of Canada Justin Trudeau, "Transcript—Remarks Commemorating the 80th Anniversary of D-Day and the Battle of Normandy," 6 June 2024, https://www.pm.gc.ca/en/videos/2024/06/06/remarks-commemorating-80th-anniversary-d-day-and-battle-normandy.
5. Francesco Fontemaggi, "Macron loue 'l'esprit de sacrifice' en lançant les commémorations," *La Presse*, 5 June 2024, https://www.lapresse.ca/international/europe/2024-06-05/80e-anniversaire-du-debarquement/macron-loue-l-esprit-de-sacrifice-en-lancant-les-commemorations.php.
6. Stephen Alan Bourque, *Beyond the Beach: The Allied War against France* (Annapolis, MD: Naval Institute Press, 2018), 238–43.
7. Fontemaggi, "Macron loue 'l'esprit de sacrifice.'" The quote is a translation of "Ces morts furent les victimes de notre combat pour la liberté et la patrie."
8. Fontemaggi, "Macron loue 'l'esprit de sacrifice.'"

CONTRIBUTORS

Mike Bechthold holds a PhD in history from the University of New South Wales, Canberra, Australia, and an MA from Wilfrid Laurier University, Waterloo, Ontario, Canada. He is the author or editor of twelve books, including his most recent monograph, *Flying to Victory: Raymond Collishaw and the Western Desert Campaign* (2017); *100 Objects for 100 Years: A History for the Royal Canadian Air Force Centennial* (2024); and a series of battlefield guidebooks on Canada and the Second World War. He teaches history at Wilfrid Laurier University and is a fellow of the Royal Historical Society in the United Kingdom.

Matthew Bone is a business analyst by trade and hosts and produces the aviation-history podcast *The Damcasters*. A chance encounter with a Hawker Typhoon led to a fascination with tactical airpower, with a particular focus on the efforts of the British Second Tactical Air Force throughout the Second

World War. He is the author of the forthcoming *Hawker Typhoon vs. German Flak Defences: Western Europe, 1943–45* (2026).

Stephen A. Bourque is professor emeritus at the U.S. Army Command and General Staff College. He retired from the U.S. Army in 1992 after twenty years of enlisted and commissioned service, with duty stations in the United States, Germany, and the Middle East. After earning a PhD at Georgia State University, he has taught American and European history as well as tactics and operational art at several military colleges and universities. His books include *Jayhawk!: The VII Corps in the 1991 Persian Gulf War* (2002), *The Road to Safwan* (2007), and *Beyond the Beach: The Allied War against France* (2018), the French translation of which won the 2020 Grand Prize for (aviation) literature from l'Aeroclub de France. His most recent book, *"Tubby": Raymond O. Barton and the US Army, 1889–1963*, was published in the fall of 2024. Bourque has led more than twenty-eight tours and staff rides in the United States, France, and Germany.

Sebastian Cox is the former head of the Air Historical Branch, RAF, in the UK Ministry of Defence and one of the three codirectors of the Royal Air Force Centre for Air Power Studies. A graduate of Warwick University and Kings College London, he served two terms as an elected trustee of the Society for Military History and is a fellow of the Royal Historical Society, a member of the British Commission for Military History, chair of the Research Board of the Royal Air Force Museum, and ex-officio member of the Committee of the Royal Air Force Historical Society. In addition, he is a member of the Editorial Board of the Royal Air Force's *Air and Space Power Review* and the Editorial Advisory Board of the *British Journal for Military History*. He served as historical advisor to the Bomber Command Memorial Trust, responsible for the Bomber Command Memorial, opened by Her Majesty Queen Elizabeth II in London in 2012. Cox has written widely on the history of the RAF and airpower, editing two book series related to the field, and has lectured on airpower and related topics to military and civilian audiences on four continents, including military colleges in the United Kingdom, United States, Canada, Australia, France, Germany, Norway, and Kuwait.

Christopher Finn, a freelance battlefield guide, lecturer, and writer, as well as a volunteer guide at the Battle of Britain Memorial Flight, joined the RAF in 1972 as a navigator. He then flew predominantly the Buccaneer as an electronic warfare, weapons, and tactics specialist and was twice awarded the Queen's Commendation for Valuable Service in the Air. As wing commander he was the British laser-guided bomb specialist and targetter in the Coalition Air Headquarter for the 1991 Gulf War. His final flying tour was as the officer commanding the Navigator and Airman Aircrew School. A graduate of the Joint Services' Defence College, Finn gained an M.Phil. in international relations at Cambridge University in 1999 and later became the director of Defence Studies, RAF. From his retirement in 2005 to 2015, he was a senior lecturer in Air Power Studies with King's College London at RAF College Cranwell.

Alexander Fitzgerald-Black is the executive director at the Juno Beach Centre Association, the charity that owns and operates Canada's Second World War Museum on the D-Day landing beaches in Normandy, France. He holds an MA in military history (University of New Brunswick) and an MA in public history (Western University), is the author of *Eagles over Husky: The Allied Air Forces in the Sicilian Campaign, 14 May to 17 August 1943* (2018), and has cowritten multiple exhibitions at the Juno Beach Centre, including From Dieppe to Juno: The 80th Anniversary of the Dieppe Raid and Rising to the Challenge: The RCAF in the Second World War. His research interests include airpower in the Second World War, with a particular focus on the Mediterranean and Normandy, and Canadian military history.

Russell A. Hart is professor of history and director of the Diplomacy and Military Studies Program at Hawai'i Pacific University in Honolulu, Hawai'i. He holds an MA and PhD in military history from Ohio State University. He is the author of *Clash of Arms: How the Allies Won in Normandy* (2001) and *Guderian: Panzer Pioneer or Mythmaker?* (2006). Hart has coauthored ten additional books, including *The Second World War, pt. 6, Northwest Europe, 1944–1945* (2002), and *The Second World War: A World in Flames* (2004);

published numerous articles; and participated as a consultant in a variety of historical documentaries. He lives in Kailua, Oahu, Hawai'i.

Paul Johnston is a Royal Canadian Air Force officer employed at the RCAF Aerospace Warfare Centre in the History & Heritage Office. He is a longtime scholar of air force history, having published numerous articles and book chapters in the field. He holds a PhD in history from Queen's University, Kingston, Canada, and is preparing a book based upon his doctoral dissertation on the evolution of NATO tactical airpower during the Cold War.

Adam Lunney has had a lifelong interest in military history and has read widely on the subject for more than thirty years. He holds an MA in military history from UNSW College at the Australian Defence Force Academy. His first book, *Ready to Strike: The Spitfires and Australians of 453 (RAAF) Squadron over Normandy* (2018), was awarded a "Highly Commended" honor in the 2018 RAAF Heritage Awards. His second book, *We Together: 451 and 453 Squadrons at War* (2020), was approved to carry the badge of the RAAF on the cover. In 2022 Lunney was made honorary historian of 453 Squadron.

Stephen Moore is a latecomer to historical research, earning an MA and PhD in European history from Newcastle University after twenty-five years in the pharmaceutical industry. His thesis, "After the Blitz: Luftwaffe Operations over the United Kingdom and the Development of the Defence Systems: May 1941 to December 1943," was completed in 2019 and is being revised for publication by the University Press of Kentucky. Working outside of academia, Moore is researching a new history of the Battle of Britain that will draw on different perspectives to present a familiar story in a distinctive way.

S. Mike Pavelec is the program director for U.S. Space Force Education (ILE PME) embedded at Johns Hopkins University–SAIS, Washington, DC. Since receiving his PhD in history from the Ohio State University in 2004, he has taught at both military and civilian schools, including Hawaii Pacific University, the U.S. Naval War College, National Defense University's Joint

Advanced Warfighting School, and the Air University. Pavelec has seven books in print, along with numerous articles and book chapters, and he has made TV appearances.

Christopher M. Rein is the senior historian at Headquarters, U.S. Air Forces Europe/Air Forces Africa at Ramstein Air Base, Germany. He earned his MA in history from LSU in 2001 and a PhD in history from the University of Kansas in 2011. He is the author or editor of seven books, including *The North African Air Campaign: The U.S. Army Air Forces from El Alamein to Salerno* (2012) and *Forging the Ninth Army–XXIX TAC Team: The Development, Training, and Application of American Air-Ground Doctrine In World War II* (2019). A retired USAF lieutenant colonel, he has previously served as an associate professor of history at the U.S. Air Force Academy in Colorado Springs; an associate professor and the airpower studies course director at the Air Command and Staff College at Maxwell Air Force Base, Alabama; a research historian for the U.S. Army at the Combat Studies Institute, Fort Leavenworth, Kansas; and the managing editor of Air University Press.

Heather Venable is director of research and an associatet professor of military and security studies in the Department of Airpower at the U.S. Air Force's Air Command and Staff College. As a visiting professor at the U.S. Naval Academy, she taught naval and Marine Corps history. She received her PhD in military history from Duke University.

INDEX

A-20 Havoc/Boston bombers, 191, 239
Adam, Ken, 120
aerial mines and minelaying operations, 10, 204, 219–21, 225, 231n113, 232n115
Afghanistan and Afghanistan War, 6, 286
Air Corps Tactical School, 22, 34n6, 98
Air Defence of Great Britain (Fighter Command): aircrew and aircraft losses, 4; Leigh-Mallory command of, 40; radar site attacks by, 114; renaming Fighter Command as, 128n12; sorties flown by, 3, 4
Air Force, U.S. Eighth: aircraft industry bombing by, 26, 28; aircrew and aircraft losses, 4, 93, 94; bombing German defenses on Normandy beaches by, 159–64; French town bombing operations of, 167–74, 329–31; oil and rubber industry bombing by, 29; operational priorities of and the Transportation Plan, 40, 53, 57; sorties flown by, 3, 4; tactical-support role of heavy bombers in, 295; targets hit and tons of bombs dropped under Transportation Plan, 50, 51–53; Totalize Operation friendly-fire incident, 271–73, 282n32; Tours and Tours bridges attack by, 166; Transportation Plan bombing operations of, 38, 44, 45, 47–50, 51, 52, 57; Transportation Plan targets for, 42; VIII Bomber Command, 3; VIII Fighter Command, 3

Air Force, U.S. Fifteenth, 28, 29, 295
Air Force, U.S. Fifth, 5
Air Force, U.S. Ninth: aircraft and aircrew losses at Cherbourg, 190–91, 193; aircrew and aircraft losses, 4; bombing operations in France by, 159, 165, 171; bridge-dropping operations of, 165; Cherbourg operations and air support from, 181, 186, 189–92; French town bombing operations of, 171; Leigh-Mallory command of fighters and light bombers in, 40; organization of for Normandy, 236, 241–43, 244; sorties flown by, 3, 4
Air Force, U.S. Twelfth, 96
Air Force/Army Air Force, U.S. (USAF): air support command renaming as tactical air command, 181; airpower theory and doctrine application by, 22–25; close air support and battlefield interdiction mission of, 5–7, 13nn13–14; nuclear mission of, 5–6; offensive defense airpower theory of, 21–22; tension between air and ground perspectives on air support, 3, 5–7, 181, 198, 235, 252–54
Air Power at the Battlefront (Gooderson), 262–63
air superiority: air supremacy of Allied forces in Normandy and for rest of the war, 30, 44, 179, 234–35; attainment of before D-Day, 65–68; importance of in

341

Normandy, 2, 234–35, 285–86, 331–33; morale and, 82, 85, 270–71; morale of the enemy and, 263

air support parties (ASPs), 194, 196, 243–44, 246–47, 248, 250, 251, 258n52

air support signals units (ASSUs), 142–43, 146, 147, 152, 242–44, 249, 250, 258n51

air support/close air support: accuracy of hitting targets, 241; air support command renaming as tactical air command, 181; air support rollercoaster, 11, 277, 280; aircraft for, 238–41, 256n26; British system for, 235, 236–37; Cherbourg operations, 178–79, 181, 183–98; communications with pilots and evolution of communication practices for, 196, 202n52; D-Day air support and the morale of Canadian troops, 265–67, 277; direct support, 236–37; doctrine, parts, and process for, 235–37, 255n10; forward-control elements for, 243–47, 252, 258nn51–52; friendly-fire incidents and criticism about, 235; friendly-fire incidents and reluctance to call for, 275; impromptu/call requests for, 235, 237, 248–51, 252–54, 260n75; indirect support, 236–37; lessons learned from Cherbourg operations, 195–98; mechanisms for requests for, 10; morale effects of, 11, 261–65, 277, 280; performance and effectiveness of, 252–54, 260n75, 274–75, 280; prearranged/planned requests for, 235, 237, 247–48, 252, 259n59; range of aircraft and, 240, 241, 257n32; relevance of, 5–6; response times of aircraft, 235, 252–54, 260n75; soldiers' opinion about air support without aircraft operating overhead, 3, 6–7, 277, 280; system in Normandy, 10, 234–35, 236–37; tactical air forces for, 236, 241–43, 257n37; tension between air and ground perspectives on, 3, 5–7, 181, 198, 235, 252–54, 274–75, 277, 280; U.S. system for, 236–37; USAF mission of, 5–7, 13nn13–14; weapons for ground targets, 238–41

aircraft: aircrew and aircraft losses against Berlin, 41; aircrew and aircraft losses at Cherbourg, 178, 189, 190–91, 193, 200n28; aircrew and aircraft losses in Normandy, 4, 5, 126, 129n41; aircrew and aircraft losses in Radar War, 105–6, 124, 125, 126, 127; losses from enemy antiaircraft fire, 151; Luftwaffe aircraft and aircrew losses in Normandy, 207–8, 211–12, 215–16, 217–18, 224–25, 233n140; number of Allied aircraft in support of invasion, 1, 30; types available for Normandy, 26–27, 30

aircrews: aircraft and aircrew losses against Berlin, 41; aircraft and aircrew losses at Cherbourg, 178, 189, 190–91, 193, 200n28; aircraft and aircrew losses in Normandy, 4, 5, 125, 129n41; aircraft and aircrew losses in Radar War, 105–6, 124, 125, 126, 127; feelings about Germans, 89–90; landing in neutral countries to escape the war and morale of, 94, 97; Luftwaffe aircraft and aircrew losses in Normandy, 207–8, 211–12, 215–16, 217–18, 224–25, 233n140; masters of the air name for, 82. *See also* morale and motivation

airfields: French civilian casualties from bombing, 159, 164–67, 174; plans for bombing, 66

AirLand Battle concept, 6

air-liaison officers (ALOs), 243, 245, 258n45

airpower: central role in victory in Normandy, 1–3, 11–12, 284, 331–33; criticism of value of in Normandy, 2–3, 12n5; D-Day landings success and, 31–32, 179; differing views of Allied commanders on best application of, 25–27; morale effects of, 11, 261–65; offensive defense theory of in U.S., 21–22; studies and writings about, 5–6, 7–8, 13–14nn20–24; tension between air and ground perspectives on, 3, 5–7, 181, 198, 235, 252–54; theories and doctrine for application of, 19–22, 25, 33, 35n17; unification of tactical and strategic under Spaatz, 97–98; value of and central role in Normandy Campaign, 1–5, 11–12, 31–32, 284, 331–33; victory and correct use of, 33. *See also* air support/close air support

air-sea rescue (ASR) operations, 120, 125, 140, 146, 147, 148, 153

Allen, Ralph, 274

Allied commanders/commanding officers: differing views on best application of airpower for victory in Germany, 25–27; Overlord Operation planning and selection of, 38–39; personal relations and creation of tactical-airpower system to support ground troops, 12; struggle over Transportation Plan implementation

or strategic air campaign by, 9, 40–42, 44–46, 57, 62–79, 80n39, 167
Allied Expeditionary Air Force (AEAF): Bombing Committee of, 39–40, 63–65; bombing German defenses on Normandy beaches by, 160; effectiveness of, 39; formation of, 138; interdiction operations of, 38, 52–53; Leigh-Mallory command of, 27, 39, 138; photo of meeting of Supreme Command, 64; resources of to support invasion, 39–40; struggle within Allied high command over strategic bombing offensive or Transportation Plan, 9, 27–29, 40–42, 44–46, 57, 62–79, 80n39, 167; targets hit and tons of bombs dropped under Transportation Plan, 50–53
Anderson, Frederick, 70, 72, 78, 94–95, 97, 98
Anson aircraft, 307
antishipping operations of Luftwaffe: aerial mines and minelaying operations, 10, 204, 219–21, 225, 231n113, 232n115; air superiority of Allies and, 10, 204–5; aircraft and aircrew losses, 211–12, 215–16, 217–18, 224–25, 233n140; circling torpedo-bomber units, 216–17, 230n81, 230n88; conventional bombs and bombing attacks, 204, 216–19, 230–31n92; conventional torpedo attacks, 204, 214–16, 225, 229n62; effectiveness of aerial mines, 219–21; focus and purpose of, 10, 203; glide bomb attacks, 203–4, 209–14, 219, 225, 227n15, 227nn17–18; limitations of, 10, 204–5; Mistletoe attacks, 204, 221–24, 225, 232nn119–120; outcome/failure of, 10, 203, 208, 224–25; units and aircraft for, 203–8, 224–25, 226n3–6; weapons/ordnance for, 203–4, 225
Anzio (Operation Shingle), 161
Argument, Operation (Big Week), 28, 44, 67, 285
armed-reconnaissance missions, 251–52, 253, 259n67, 260n70, 260n81
armored column cover (ACC, cabrank technique), 196, 247, 249–51, 252, 253–54
Army, U.S.: bombing German defenses on Normandy beaches by, 160–61; Cherbourg operations of and air support for, 180–81, 183, 185–92, 194–98; Cobra Operation role of, 293, 305n19; METT-T/METT-TC framework for operations, 291, 304n15; Queen Operation role of, 293–94, 305n20; tension between air and ground perspectives on air support, 3, 5–7, 181, 198, 235, 252–54; Third Army activation, 181, 199n9; trench-foot and nonbattle casualties in, 293
army forces: central role in victory in Normandy, 3; number of troops landed in Normandy, 32; opinion about air support without aircraft operating overhead, 3, 6–7, 277, 280; tactical-airpower system creation to effectively support, 11–12
Arnold, Henry H. "Hap," 22, 29, 32, 67, 91, 93–94, 95–96, 96–97, 295
Arromanches-les-Bains, 107, 117, 180, 222, 320
Atlantic, Operation (Operation Goodwood), 266, 269–71
Aulnoye railway center, 43, 46
Australia: Japanese invasion threat to and Jap-dodger accusations against RAAF, 11, 306, 311–12, 317–18. *See also* newspapers/Australian newspapers; Royal Australian Air Force (RAAF)
Avalanche, Operation (Salerno), 161

B-17 Flying Fortress bombers, 24, 111, 164–65, 170
B-24 Liberator bombers, 24, 49, 170, 329–30
B-25 Mitchell bombers, 239
B-26 Marauder bombers, 31, 111, 171, 191–92
Baker, Reg, 125
Baker, Robert, 167
Baldoli, Claudia, 38
Baldwin, "Johnny," 114–15, 128n14
Barfleur-le-Vicel radar site, 123
Battleaxe, Operation, 3
battlefield air interdiction, 7
Beaufighter aircraft and squadrons, 307, 314, 315, 321
Belgium: alliance with Free French and not bombing targets in, 29; Ostend radar site attack, 114–16, 122. *See also* rail yards and rail infrastructure
Berlin: crew members' feeling about bombing, 85–86, 88–89, 91; RAF bombing of, 22–23, 25, 35n17, 40–41
Bernstein, Jonathan, 128n23
Beyond the Beach (Bourque), 10
Biden, Joe, 328
Big Week (Operation Argument), 28, 32, 44, 67, 285
Biting, Operation, 106
Blackburn, George, 271, 272–73

Blainville-sur-l'Eau rail yard, 42, 47–48
Bomber Barons (strategic bomber forces commanders) and strategic bombing operations, 9, 27–29, 40–42, 44–46, 57, 62–79, 80n39, 167
bombers, heavy: accuracy of hitting targets, 41, 46–47, 50–51, 61n79, 111; availability for Normandy, 26; Berlin bombing by, 41; carpet-bombing missions of, 186, 269–70, 286, 287; Charnwood Operation attacks with and morale of Canadian troops, 268–69; Cherbourg operations use of, 185; Cobra Operation use in support of ground forces, 10–11, 284–85, 286–89, 290–94, 304n9; D-Day sorties flown by, 30, 179; priorities for use of, 64–65, 66–67; Queen Operation use in support of ground forces, 10–11, 285, 286, 290–94, 295, 304n16; radar station bombing with and probability of site destruction, 111; support for Overlord Operation with, 63–65; tactical role of in Transportation Plan, 8; tactical-support role of and conditions for success of, 284–86, 294, 302–3; tactical-support role of as misallocation of resources, 294–95; Transportation Plan bombing operations of, 72–73; Transportation Plan bombing operations with, 38, 51; U.S. war plans for bombing Germany, 24
bombers, light and medium: accuracy of hitting targets, 111; air support role of, 238–39, 240, 256n26; availability for Normandy, 26; Cherbourg operations of, 186, 188, 190–92; D-Day sorties flown by, 30, 31, 179; interdiction operations with, 238; morale of the enemy and attacks by, 196–97; radar station bombing with and probability of site destruction, 111; Transportation Plan bombing sorties with, 29–30
bombers, long-range, heavy-lift commercial platforms redesigned as, 22
bombs and bombing operations: air support missions using bombs, 238–39, 240; bomb load for attacks on radar sites and number dropped in Radar War, 111, 112, 113, 126, 127; carpet-bombing missions, 186, 269–70, 284–85, 286, 287; Circular Error of Probability (CEP) and accuracy of attacks, 119; Oboe bombing aid, 41, 45, 46–47, 50–51, 57, 61n79, 110, 111, 188; Pathfinder targeting technique, 41, 275–76; pattern bombing, 301–2; target-marking and bombing techniques, 41, 44, 46–47, 50–51, 57, 61n79, 295–98; targets hit and tons of bombs dropped under Transportation Plan, 51–53
Boston/A-20 Havoc bombers, 191, 239
Bottomley, Norman, 72–74, 75, 77–78
Bourque, Stephen A., 7, 10, 32, 38, 54, 58n6, 285
Bradley, Omar, 6, 64, 161, 180, 183, 191–92, 301–2
Brant, E. D., 39, 63, 69
Brereton, Lewis, 183, 185, 259n59
bridges: bombing and destruction of, 27, 29–30; French civilian casualties from bombing, 159, 164–67, 174; Market-Garden Operation and seizure of, 289–90; priority of attacks on, 53, 70–71
Britain, Battle of, 22, 39, 164
Brooke, Alan, 77
Brooker, Peter, 120, 123–24
Bufton, Sidney, 69–70, 72, 73–74, 75, 77–78
Bulge, Battle of the, 294
Buron, 261–62, 266, 268–69

C-47 Skytrain/Dakota, 26, 30, 321–22
cabrank technique (armored column cover, ACC), 196, 247, 249–51, 252, 253–54
Caen, 39, 54, 170–72, 179–80, 266, 267–68, 269, 270, 280, 287, 330
Canadian Armed Forces: air-land integration in, 6; names of, 13n18; organization of groups and squadrons of, 307; South Saskatchewan Regiment Dieppe Raid role, 123–24. *See also* Royal Canadian Air Forces (RCAF)
Canadian Army: air support on D-Day and morale of, 265–67, 277; Allied air superiority and morale of, 270–71; Carpiquet and Caen operations and moral of, 266, 267–68, 280; Charnwood Operation and morale of, 261–62, 268–69; D-Day operations and losses, 329; Falaise Pocket friendly-fire incident and morale of, 276–77; friendly-fire incidents and morale of, 11, 264, 265, 280; Goodwood/Atlantic Operation and morale of, 269–71; map of operations, 266; morale effects of air support, 11, 261–65, 277, 280; Totalize Operation friendly-fire incident and morale of, 11, 264, 265, 271–73, 274–75, 280, 282n32; Tractable Operation friendly-fire

Index   345

incident and morale of, 11, 264, 265, 273–76, 280
Cap d'Antifer radar station, 110, 117, 119–20, 125
Cap de la Hague radar sites, 117, 118–19, 122, 125
Cap de la Hève radar site, 117, 121–22, 126
Casablanca Conference, 24
Chain Home radar system, 106, 136–37, 138
Châlons-sur-Marne rail yard, 42, 47–48, 49
Charnwood, Operation, 186, 261–62, 266, 268–69
Chase region, 276–77, 278–79
Chattanooga Day, 30
Cherbourg: air plan and plans for capture of, 179–80, 183, 185–86, 259n59; aircraft and aircrew losses at, 178, 189, 190–91, 193, 200n28; capture of and end of Neptune operations, 158; friendly-fire incidents during operations at, 190, 196; German army defense of, 180–81; importance of capture of, 179–80; operations to capture, 10, 178–79, 186–92; outcome of and analysis of ground and air operations, 192–94, 195–98; surrender of German garrison at, 195; tactical airpower misapplication at, 10, 178–79, 194, 198
Cherbourg–la Brasserie radar station, 109, 117
Cheshire, Leonard, 47
Chimney (Wasserman radar), 108, 109, 112, 114, 116, 117, 126–27
Churchill, Winston: directive to Eisenhower for Normandy, 26–27; French civilian casualties concerns of and Transportation Plan approval by, 48, 50, 54, 166–67, 172; French civilian casualties estimate from, 32; masters of the air name given to bomber crews by, 82; newspaper article about meeting with, 310; opposition to bombing targets in France, 29; Overlord command arrangements recommendation of, 69; planning at Quadrant Conference by, 25
circling torpedo-bomber units, 216–17, 230n81, 230n88
Circular Error of Probability (CEP), 119
civilian populations: casualties from bombing and resentment toward Americans for high-altitude attacks, 54; crew members' feeling about bombing, 85–86, 88–89, 91; de-housing campaign against German cities, 22–23, 25–26, 27–28, 35n20, 62;

effects of Allied bombing on the French population, 10, 158–74; evolution of airpower theory for bombing, 21, 34n8; French casualties during first two days after landings, 10, 156–58, 174; French casualties from bombing airfields, bridges, and rail centers, 159, 164–67, 168, 174, 285; French casualties from bombing German defenses on Normandy beaches, 159–64; French casualties from bombing towns and small cities, 159, 167–74, 329–31; French casualties from Transportation Plan bombing, 32, 38, 46–48, 50, 54, 56, 57, 166–67, 172; *Normandie* and *Historia* articles about Normandy casualties and destruction, 172–74
Clausewitz, Carl von, 33
close air support. *See* air support/close air support
Cobra, Operation: accuracy of hitting targets during, 301–2; air plan for and fighter-bombers use during, 197, 247; carpet-bombing missions for, 186, 287; damage from bombing attacks during, 12n5; friendly-fire incidents during, 197, 202n53, 287, 289, 298; heavy bomber operations during, 10–11, 284–85, 286–89, 290–94, 304n9; success of, 289, 387
Collins, J. Lawton "Lightning Joe," 180, 181, 182, 185, 190, 198, 287
Combined Bomber Offensive (CBO): American bombing crew resilience during, 83–84; effectiveness of, 25; implementation of, 24–25; morality of targeting cities and morale of crews, 83–84, 88–89; official histories about, 37–38, 58n3; plan for, 24; Spaatz's support for and plan for completion of, 28–29, 74
command and control (C2) of airpower: D-Day operations, 138–39, 148–49, 155n45; Dieppe raid and joint amphibious operations, 133, 134–37; disputes about centralized or decentralized, 236; fighter direction tenders (FDTs), 134, 138, 139, 143–53, 215; headquarters (HQ) ships, 134–38, 139, 141–43, 146–48, 150–51, 152–53; Mediterranean theater operations, 133, 137–38; Overlord operations, 138–43, 148–53; sea-based network for Neptune operation, 10, 133–34, 138–43, 148–53; system for Overlord operation, 10, 133–34

Command of the Air (Douhet), 20–21, 34n6, 35n20
Coningham, Arthur, 143–44, 185, 274
Cooke, Ken, 329
Cooling, Benjamin Franklin, 7
Copp, Terry, 3
Cordier, J. P., 156–57
Corkscrew, Operation, 137
Cornu, Paul, 169–70
Courage in Air Warfare (Wells), 83–84
Crerar, Harry, 274–75, 283n47
Curtin, John, 310, 312

Darlow, Stephen, 38
D-Day/D-Day landings: air activities/missions to support, 1, 30; air support on D-Day and morale of Canadian troops, 265–67, 277; airpower and success of, 31–32, 179; anniversary ceremonies and focus on land battle over airpower, 328–31; diversion to disguise location of, 39, 51; number of Allied aircraft in support of, 1, 30; number of Allied ships and aircraft in support of, 148–49, 155n42; number of sorties flown on, 30; number of troops landed during, 32; seventy-fifth anniversary celebration of, 172, 174; success of, 180
de Havilland Mosquitos. *See* Mosquito fighter-bombers
Dempsey, Miles C., 161, 162
Devers, Jacob L., 92
Dieppe Caude Côte radar site, 117, 123–24
Dieppe raid (Operation Jubilee), 117, 123–24, 133, 134–37
dive-bombers and dive-bombing techniques, 47, 110, 112, 113, 194–95, 308–9
Donovan, Dennis, 329
Doolittle, James H., 92, 95–96, 163, 166, 167, 169, 183, 295, 302
Douhet, Giulio, 20–21, 25, 33, 34n6, 35n17, 35n20
Dye, Peter, 34n6

Eaker, Ira, 23, 25, 92, 96–97, 295
Ehlers, Robert S., Jr., 7
Eisenhower, Dwight D. "Ike": aircraft available for Normandy, 26–27, 30; Australian newspaper coverage of, 306–7, 311, 320, 326n73; Cherbourg air operations support by, 185; decision about air campaign by, 19, 29; directive from Roosevelt and Churchill for Normandy, 26–27; Hague Convention on bombing towns and bombing operations under, 172; Overlord command arrangements recommendation to, 69; photo of meeting of Supreme Command, 64; supreme commander role of, 38–39; Transportation Plan planning and decisionmaking by, 8–9, 26–29, 31–32, 45, 57, 63, 78–79; Transportation Plan target decisions by, 48, 50
Empire Air Training Scheme (EATS), 306
Engen, Robert, 263–64

Falaise Pocket and the Falaise Gap, 16, 168, 172, 252, 260n70, 266, 273, 276–77, 285, 292, 322
Fennell, Jonathan, 264–65
Ferguson, James, 5, 13n14
fighter direction tenders (FDTs), 134, 138, 139, 143–53, 215
fighter-bombers: accuracy of hitting targets, 241; air support role of, 238–41; Cherbourg operations of, 186, 188–92; D-Day sorties flown by, 30, 179; development and capabilities of, 110–12, 238; morale of the enemy and attacks by, 196–97; radar site attacks by, 9, 105–6, 110–27, 128n11; range of, 240, 241, 257n32; Transportation Plan bombing sorties with, 29–30
fighters: D-Day sorties flown by, 30, 179; interdiction operations of AEAF fighters on rail centers, 52–53, 285–86; long-range drop tanks and range of escort fighters, 28, 44
Fighting the People's War (Fennell), 264
Finlayson, Stuart, 122
Fitzgerald-Black, Alexander, 7
Ford, Stan, 329
Fortitude operation, 39
forward control posts (FCPs), 245–47, 248–50
France: alliance with Free French and not bombing targets in, 29; bombing campaign effects on civilian population in, 10, 158–74; casualties and damage from Allied bombing in, 38, 158, 172–74, 329–31; civilian casualties from bombing airfields, bridges, and rail centers, 159, 164–67, 168, 174, 285; civilian casualties from bombing German defenses on Normandy beaches, 159–64; civilian casualties from bombing towns and small cities, 159, 167–74, 329–31;

civilian casualties from first two days after landings, 10, 156–58, 174; civilian casualties from Transportation Plan bombing, 32, 38, 46–48, 50, 54, 56, 57, 166–67, 172; damage from Allied bombing on D-Day and next two days, 156–58, 174; Dragoon operation and landings in southern France, 152, 213; infrastructure damage from bombing campaign in, 10, 159, 164–67, 329–31; liberation of and Allies entry into Paris, 225, 287; *Normandie* and *Historia* articles about Normandy destruction, 172–74. *See also* rail yards and rail infrastructure

Frankland, Noble, 38, 58n3, 61n79

Freeman, Hal, 122–23

Freya radar systems, 106–8, 110, 112, 113, 116, 118, 120, 122, 123–25, 126

friendly-fire incidents: battle management and reluctance to call for air support after, 275; Cherbourg operations, 190, 196; close air support criticism and, 235; Cobra Operation, 197, 202n53, 287, 289, 298; Falaise Pocket battle, 276; FDTs' role in IFF information, 150–51; Totalize Operation, 11, 264, 265, 271–73, 274–75, 280, 282n32; Tractable Operation, 11, 264, 265, 273–76, 280

FuMG 39E/FuSE 65 radars. *See* Würzburg/ Giant Würzburg radar systems

German army: air superiority and morale of, 263; air support for, 243, 258n47; bombing German defenses on Normandy beaches, 159–64; Cherbourg defense operations of, 180–81; damage to from bombing attacks, 2, 12n5; little fishes thrown back into the sea by, 180, 198n5; morale of at Cherbourg, 186, 188, 193–94, 198; surrender of and threats from Schlieben against surrender, 181, 182, 185, 188, 193–94, 195, 198; troop travel by train and effects of rail network bombings, 29, 30, 50, 52–54, 57, 65, 70–71, 75–77, 285–86

German industry: aircraft industry bombing by U.S. (Pointblank Operation), 24–25, 26, 27–28, 38, 44, 56, 63, 65–68, 285; attacks on by RAF and Allied forces, 22–29, 32, 52; attacks on during Great War, 20; effectiveness of bombing of, 25; evolution of airpower theory for bombing, 21, 34n8; oil industry and production as bombing target, 27–29, 32, 44, 52, 74–78, 295; rubber industry as bombing target, 28–29; strategic bombing to disrupt production in, 22; U.S. war plans for bombing, 24

Germany: aircrews' feelings about Germans, 89–90; bombing cities in by RAF and Allied forces, 22–28, 32, 35n20; effectiveness of bombing of, 25; reaction to Transportation Plan bombing and civilian casualties, 53–56; surrender of, 32

Gibson, Bob, 328

Giles, Barney M., 85, 96–97

glide bombs and antishipping operations, 203–4, 209–14, 219, 225, 227n15, 227nn17–18, 227n25; HS 295 glide bombs, 209–13, 219; PC 1400 FX "Fritz-X" glide bombs, 209, 213–14, 219

gliders, 26, 30, 124, 140, 322

Glimmer, Operation, 123

Gold Beach, 139, 141, 149, 161, 163–64, 165, 266

Goldwater-Nichols Act, 6

Gooderson, Ian, 7, 235, 251–52, 262–63, 264, 275, 285

Goodwood, Operation, 12n5, 186, 247, 266, 269–71, 319, 326n70

Gooseberry blockships, 222–23

Göring, Hermann, 210, 320

Graf Spee (German), 108

Grant, George, 76–77

Gray, Colin, 246

Great War (World War I), 19–21, 34n6, 236, 255n15

ground-controlled interception (GCI) sites, 138, 140, 143, 144, 145, 146–47, 149–50, 151–52, 153

Guernsey radar stations, 105, 124–25

Hague Convention, 172

Halifax bombers and squadrons, 41, 46, 170, 268, 273, 314, 316, 319, 322, 330

Hall, Melon, 183

Hall, R. Cargill, 7

Hallion, Richard, 252

Hansbury, Thomas, 87

Harris, Arthur: Berlin bombing focus of, 25, 35n17, 40–41; bombing German defenses on Normandy beaches under, 162; Cherbourg air operations opposition by, 183; de-housing campaign against German cities under, 22–23, 25–26, 27–28, 32, 33, 34n14, 35n20, 62; French town bombing operations opposition by, 168–69; photo

of, 23; RAF Bomber Command role of, 22, 25; support for Transportation Plan by, 44; Tractable Operation friendly-fire incident report by, 273; Transportation Plan opposition by and bombing operations under, 40–42, 44–46, 57, 62–63, 65, 66, 69, 167
Hastings, Max, 2, 12n5
Hawker Typhoons. *See* Typhoon Mk Ib/Typhoon fighter-bombers
headquarters (HQ) ships, 134–38, 139, 141–43, 146–48, 150–51, 152–53
Hennecke, Walther, 182
Historia article about Normandy destruction, 172–74
Hitler, Adolf, 180, 193, 294, 320
Hoarding (Mammut radar), 108, 112, 116, 117, 126–27
Holland, Frank "Dutch," 123
Hopwood, Lloyd P., 96
Horsa gliders, 30
Hughes, Richard, 65, 70
Hughes, Thomas A., 2, 7, 285
Hurricane, Operation, 98
Husky, Operation (Sicily), 137–38, 161

Identification Friend or Foe (IFF) signals, 106, 144, 150–51
industry. *See* German industry
Infatuate, Operation, 152
Inglis, Francis F., 78
Iraq and Iraq operations, 6, 286, 302
Italy: casualties and damage from Allied bombing in, 38; rail traffic disruption campaign in, 39, 40, 66, 72

Japan, 11, 89, 92, 306
Joint Fire Plan, 142, 159–64
Jones, Donald E., 90
Jones, Francis, 110
Jones, R. V., 106, 114, 115–16, 118, 123, 127
Jubilee, Operation (Dieppe raid), 117, 123–24, 133, 134–37
Juno Beach, 139, 141, 161, 162–63, 261, 266, 329

Kennedy, John, 78
Kentucky Windage, 119, 128n23
Kingston-McCloughry, E. J., 63
Kite, Ben, 7
Knapp, Andrew, 38
Korea and Korean War, 5, 6, 128n14
Kuter, Lawrence, 98

Lacey-Johnson, Lionel, 38
Lallemant, Raymond, 114–15
Lancaster bombers: Australian aircrews in, 307, 311–12, 314, 316, 319, 322; bombing German cities with, 41; French town bombing operations with, 170, 171, 330; radar station bombing with and probability of site destruction, 111
Landing Ship Tanks (LSTs), 138, 145, 214
Laon railway center, 42, 43, 46
Lawrence, Oliver, 70, 71, 74, 76–77, 78
Leigh-Mallory, Trafford: AEAF command by, 27, 39, 138; Cherbourg air operations support by, 185; control of air operations for Dieppe raid by, 134, 135–36, 137; death of, 127; French town bombing operations under, 170; opinions about and decisions of, 39, 40, 66–67, 69–70, 127; opposition to Transportation Plan by, 40; photo of meeting of Supreme Command, 64; plan for air activities to support Normandy Campaign, 27–28; Radar War review by, 125–26, 127; tactical forces under with no command over strategic forces, 39–40, 65, 66–67, 69; Transportation Plan command role of, 45, 50; Transportation Plan planning meeting called by, 69–72, 80nn27–28; Transportation Plan planning role of, 62–63, 65–68, 76–77, 78; Transportation Plan target selection by, 41; Victoria Cross endorsement by, 123
Leith, Colin "Rusty," 306
Lindemann, Frederick, 79
Lisieux, France, 156–57, 169–70
Lockheed P-38 Lightnings, 111–12, 148, 189–90
Luftwaffe: air support for ground forces by, 243, 258n47; aircraft and aircrew losses in Normandy, 207–8, 211–12, 215–16, 217–18, 224–25, 233n140; Allied air superiority and destruction of, 2; Allied air superiority and effectiveness of, 203–4; Argument Operation and crippling of, 28, 32, 44, 67; force strength for D-Day and Normandy, 203–8, 224–25, 226n3–6; missions to degrade ability to detect and react to invasion, 1; night missions of, 151, 153, 210, 216, 217–18, 224–25; sorties in defense against D-Day attacks, 30, 179. *See also* antishipping operations of Luftwaffe
Lukasik, Sebastian H., 5–6, 13nn13–14
Lynn, John, 86–87

Macron, Emmanuel, 329–30
Mailly-le-Camp mission, 311–12
Mammut radar (Hoarding), 108, 112, 116, 117, 126–27
Mandrel, Operation, 123
Mann, Churchill C., 235, 253, 276
Market-Garden, Operation, 286, 289–90
Mason, Donald, 115
McMullen, Donald, 76, 77
McNair, Lesley J., 287
Mediterranean theater: command and control of airpower in, 133, 137–38; Dragoon operation and landings in southern France, 152, 213; Eisenhower, Tedder, and Spaatz service in, 39
METT-T (Mission, Enemy, Terrain and weather, Troops, and Time), 291, 304n15
Miller, Ben, 328
mines and mining operations: aerial mines and minelaying operations of Luftwaffe, 10, 204, 219–21, 225, 231n113, 232n115; effectiveness of aerial mines, 219–21; minesweeping operations of Allies, 204, 219, 221, 232n114
Mistletoe composite aircraft, 204, 221–24, 225, 232nn119–120
Mitchell, Billy, 20, 21–22
Montgomery, Bernard: Australian newspaper coverage of, 307, 311; bombing German defenses on Normandy beaches under, 162; Cherbourg air operations support for, 185; French town bombing operations under, 167–69, 170–71; Hague Convention on bombing towns and bombing operations under, 172; Market-Garden Operation under, 289–90; photo of meeting of Supreme Command, 64; rail yards and rail bridges bombing under, 165–66
morale and motivation: air superiority and, 82, 85, 270–71; air superiority and morale of the enemy, 263; air support and morale of Canadian troops, 11, 261–65, 277, 280; air support on D-Day and morale of Canadian troops, 265–67, 277; Carpiquet and Caen operations and moral of Canadian troops, 266, 267–68, 280; Charnwood Operation and morale of Canadian troops, 261–62, 268–69; civilian population targeting and, 85–86, 88–89, 91; cognitive dissonance of leaders and, 85–86, 91–98, 102n44; combat motivation, 9, 88–92, 95–96; comparison between bomber and fighter pilots, 84–85, 87–88; depictions and stories about strength of, 82–84; effects of airpower/air support on, 11, 261–65; Falaise Pocket battle and morale of Canadian troops, 276–77; fear, fatigue, and stress experienced by bomber crews, 82–86, 92, 99n2, 99n8; fighter-bomber attacks and morale of the enemy, 196–97; friendly-fire incidents and morale of Canadian troops, 11, 264, 265, 271–76, 280, 282n32; goals and purpose of mission and, 90–92, 95, 101n38, 101nn40–41, 103n69; Goodwood/Atlantic Operation and morale of Canadian troops, 269–71; grounding and reassignment wishes of bomber crews, 82, 84–85, 92, 96–97; initial motivation, 87, 99; landing in neutral countries to escape the war and, 94, 97; pace of operations and, 85, 92; promotion of wing commanders and, 94, 97; psychological toll of combat and, 92, 94–99; stage of motivation, 86–91; survey of by medical officers, 84, 89; sustaining motivation, 87–88, 95–96, 99; views of commanders on levels of morale of crews, 9, 83, 85–86
morale of civilians: de-housing campaign against Germany and, 22–23, 33; strategic bombing effects on, 21, 22–23, 33, 34n8, 34n14
Mosquito fighter-bombers: air support role of, 239; Australian aircrews in, 307, 308, 314, 315, 316, 320, 322; capabilities of, 111–12; D-Day landings support from, 148–49; Radar War role of, 105, 111; specifications for, 239; target-marking role of, 47
Mulberry harbors, 107, 180, 206, 222–23
Mustang fighters. *See* P-51 Mustangs

Napier, Charles, 70, 71, 80n28
Navy, U.S.: bombing German defenses on Normandy beaches by, 160–61; ships and aircraft in support of D-Day landings, 148–49, 155n42, 328. *See also* Neptune, Operation
Neptune, Operation: bombing German defenses on Normandy beaches in support of, 159–64; Cherbourg capture and end of, 158; French civilian casualties and experiences during, 158–59; French civilian casualties from bombing airfields,

bridges, and rail centers, 159, 164–67, 168, 174; French civilian casualties from bombing towns and small cities, 159, 167–74, 329–31; radar site attacks and success of, 118, 125–26; sea-based C2 network for, 10, 133–34, 138–43, 148–53; sorties flown in support of, 140; Transportation Plan role in, 37

newspapers/Australian newspapers: accomplishments and coverage of operations in Normandy, 313–17, 320–23; aircraft and aircrew losses in articles in, 308–9, 312, 318–19; Australian home front view of RAAF's participation in Normandy, 11, 307; change-of-command coverage in, 310; coverage of operations leading up to D-Day landings, 307–13, 318; Eisenhower coverage in, 306–7, 311, 320, 326n73; Hitler attack, article about in, 320; Montgomery coverage in, 307, 311; positive news and local connections in, 307–8, 309–12, 317–18, 319–20, 326n70, 326n73; propaganda angle of articles in, 11, 307; renaming RAF as Royal Imperial Air Force, suggestion in, 307; reporters attached to squadrons and access of news about operations, 313, 325n32; white feathers sent to aircrew, coverage about, 311–12, 316

Niblett, John, 115, 122, 124

night missions: de-housing campaign against German cities, 22, 25–26, 35n20; limitations and dangers of, 22, 26, 41; Luftwaffe missions, 151, 153, 210, 216, 217–18, 224–25; Mitchell's offensive against Germany, 20; RAF missions under CBO plan, 24–25; target-marking technique and night precision bombing by Bomber Command, 47, 50–51, 57, 61n79

Nissenthal, Jack, 123

Noball operations, 105, 118, 120, 123

Noisy-Le-Sec, 54, 56

Norden bombsights, 24

Normandie article about Normandy destruction, 172–74

Normandy, map of, 16

Normandy Campaign/Operation Overlord: air activities/missions to support, 27, 29–30; aircraft available for, 26–27, 30; aircrew and aircraft losses, 4, 5; British official history of, 3–4; fighter patrol areas, 139; focus and purpose of, 94; little fishes thrown back into the sea by Germans, 180, 198n5; logistics and success of, 179–80; planning at Quadrant Conference for, 25; planning for, 38–39; recommendations for further studies about, 332–33; spatial settings and scope of, 331–32; strategic bombardment campaign instead of, 9, 28–29, 40, 83, 92, 93–94; value and central role of airpower in, 1–5, 11–12, 31–32, 284, 331–33. *See also* D-Day/D-Day landings

North Africa operations (Operation Torch), 92, 161

North American P-51 Mustangs. *See* P-51 Mustangs

Oboe bombing aid, 41, 45, 46–47, 50–51, 57, 61n79, 110, 111, 188

oil industry and production as bombing target, 27–29, 32, 44, 52, 74–78, 295

Olsson, John Oxley Waugh, 315, 325n43

Omaha Beach, 32, 139, 141, 149, 161, 163–64, 172, 180, 206, 219

Overlord, Operation. *See* Normandy Campaign/Operation Overlord

P-38, 155n42

P-38 Lightnings, 111–12, 148, 189–90

P-47 Thunderbolts, 28, 111–12, 189, 238, 240

P-51 Mustangs: air support role of, 238; Australian aircrews in, 321; Cherbourg operations of, 186, 188–89, 200n26; escort role for bombers destroying aircraft industry, 28; external fuel tanks and range of, 44; Radar War role of, 123; range of, 240; *Saving Private Ryan* role of, 11–12; specifications for, 240

paratroopers, 30, 88, 322

Pas de Calais, 39, 51, 117, 118–19, 137, 138

Pathfinder targeting technique, 41, 275–76

Patton, George S., 199n9

Pavelec, Mike, 57–58n1

Pointblank, Operation (aircraft industry bombing), 26, 27–28, 38, 44, 56, 63, 65–68, 285

Portal, Charles: chief of Air Staff role of, 42; target clearance by War Cabinet, role in, 45–46; Transportation Plan bombing operations under, 42, 45–46, 47; Transportation Plan planning and decisionmaking by, 62, 63, 64–65, 67–69, 72, 75–79

Price, Alfred, 108

Quadrant Conference, 25
Queen, Operation: accuracy of hitting targets during, 298–302; failure of, 290; focus and purpose of, 290; heavy bomber operations during, 10–11, 285, 286, 290–94, 295, 304n16; safety measures to protect friendly forces and target-marking aids for, 295–98
Quesada, Elwood "Pete": Cherbourg operations under, 181, 183–86, 190, 193, 195; combat experience of, 181, 183; effectiveness of close air support operations under, 285; Normandy role of, 6; support for tactical air operations by, 183; on value of airpower, 2

radar systems and sites: accuracy of hitting targets by aircraft type, 111, 113; attacks on to blind German forces (Radar War), 9, 105–6, 114–27; bomb load for attacks on, 111, 112, 113; characteristics and deployment of systems, 106–8; defenses around and hardness of targets, 9, 105–6, 108, 112, 116, 118; fighter-bomber attacks on, 9, 105–6, 110–27, 128n11; importance of destruction of, 105–6; jamming network with ghost fleet in English Channel, 123; limitations of aircraft for attacks on, 9, 110–13; losses and cost of Radar War, 105–6; order of attack on sites, 118–19; outcome and success of, 125–27; report on how to attack and probability of destruction of, 108, 110–13, 116, 118; rockets for attacks on, 112, 113, 114–27; sorties needed for successful attacks on and number during Radar War, 111, 112, 113, 118–19, 126; target list and map of, 105, 116, 117, 118–19
rail yards and rail infrastructure: bombing of French and Belgian networks, 29–30, 50, 52–53, 285–86; French civilian casualties from bombing, 159, 164–67, 168, 174; German troop use of, 29, 30, 50, 52–54, 57, 65, 70–71, 75–77, 285–86; interdiction operations of AEAF fighters on, 52–53, 285–86; map of attacks on, 54, 55; priority of attacks on, 53; rail traffic disruption campaign in Italy, 39, 40, 66, 72. *See also* Transportation Plan
Ramsay, Bertram, 64, 160–61, 163
Rankin, Operation, 77
Reeves, Alec, 110
Rein, Christopher M., 7

Republic P-47 Thunderbolts, 28, 111–12, 189, 238, 240
Retchin, Norman, 89–90
Robb, James, 58n3
rocket projectiles/air-to-ground rockets: air support missions using, 241; bomber specifications, 239; Circular Error of Probability (CEP) and accuracy of attacks with, 119; design and capabilities of, 238, 241; fighter-bomber specifications, 112, 240; HVAR, 239, 240, 241; Kentucky Windage and aiming to correct for the wind, 119, 128n23; radar site attacks with, 112, 113, 114–27; Semi-Armor Piercing (SAP) RP-3 rockets, 112, 113, 118, 119, 126–27; Typhoon operations with, 238, 241
Rohmer, Richard, 329
Rommel, Erwin, 169, 234–35, 263, 314, 320
Roosevelt, Franklin, 25, 26, 32
Ross, David, 125
Rouen, 42, 43, 117, 165, 172–74, 279
Royal Air Force (RAF): airpower theory and doctrine application by, 22–25, 34n14; evolution of airpower theory and acquisition in, 21, 34n8; renaming as Royal Imperial Air Force, 307
Royal Air Force (RAF) Air Historical Branch, 38
Royal Air Force (RAF) Bomber Command: aircraft industry bombing by, 28; aircrew and aircraft losses, 4, 41; area-bombing, de-housing campaign against German cities, 22–23, 25–26, 27–28, 32, 33, 34n14, 35n20, 62; Berlin bombing by, 40–41; bombing German defenses on Normandy beaches by, 159–64; Bombphoons squadrons, 262; French town bombing operations of, 171, 329–31; Harris command of, 22, 25; No. 5 Group low-level marking technique, 41, 44, 46–47, 50–51, 57, 61n79; operational priorities of and the Transportation Plan, 40, 42, 57; sorties flown by, 3, 4; targets hit and tons of bombs dropped under Transportation Plan, 50–53, 61n79; Tractable Operation friendly-fire incident, 273–76, 283n47; Transportation Plan bombing operations of, 38, 40–42, 44–48, 57, 72–73; Transportation Plan targets for, 42
Royal Air Force (RAF) Coastal Command, 3, 4

Royal Air Force (RAF) Fighter Command, 128n12. *See also* Air Defence of Great Britain (Fighter Command)

Royal Air Force (RAF) Second Tactical Air Force (2 TAF): aircraft and aircrew losses at Cherbourg, 189, 200n26; aircrew and aircraft losses, 4, 126, 129n41; aircrew and aircraft losses in Radar War, 105–6, 124, 125, 126, 127; Cherbourg operations of, 186, 188–89, 194–95, 200n26; direct support for ground forces by, 125; Leigh-Mallory command of, 40; organization of for Normandy, 236, 241–43; radar site attacks by, 105–6, 114–27, 128n14; sorties flown by, 3, 4, 126

Royal Australian Air Force (RAAF): accomplishments and coverage of operations in Normandy, 313–17, 320–23; aircraft and aircrew losses, 308–9, 312, 318–19; aircrew assignments in RAF commands, 307; awards and medals earned by aircrews, 308, 310, 322; change-of-command ceremony in, 310; contributions of to war and Normandy operations, 11, 306–7; Duke of Gloucester visit to Spitfire squadron, 308, 309; Goodwood Operation role of, 319, 326n70; Jap-dodger accusations against and claims of shirking real war by, 11, 306, 311–12, 317–18; Mailly-le-Camp mission, 311–12; newspaper coverage and portrayal of contributions of, 11, 306–7; operations leading up to D-Day landings, 307–13, 318; positive news and local connections in articles about, 307–8, 309–12, 317–18, 319–20, 326n70, 326n73; prisoner status of pilot from, 315, 325n43; transport operations of, 321–23; white feathers sent to, 311–12, 316

Royal Canadian Air Forces (RCAF): D-Day operations and losses, 329; name of, 13n18; organization of groups and squadrons of, 307; Radar War role of, 120, 122, 123, 124–25

Saint-Lô, 16, 117, 172–74, 284–85, 287, 301–2, 329–31
Saint-Mihiel offensive, 20
Saville, John, 125
Saving Private Ryan, 11–12
Schlieben, Karl-Wilhelm von, 181, 182, 193–94
Schoenberger, Nicholas D., 90

Scott, Desmond, 106, 122–23
Sea Lion, Operation, 2–3
Seetakt ship-watching radar, 106, 108, 116, 117, 123
Semi-Armor Piercing (SAP) RP-3 rockets, 113, 118, 119, 126–27
Shambles region, 276–77, 278–79
Sherrington, Charles, 63, 69, 76
Shingle, Operation (Anzio), 161
Sicily (Operation Husky), 137–38, 161
Siegfried Line, 285, 286, 290
Simonds, Guy, 273–74
Smith, Kenneth Blaine, 328
Smith, Walter Bedell, 64
Soesman, Pierre Léopold, 120
sorties: aircrew and aircraft losses in Normandy, 4, 5; number flown by Allied air forces, 3, 3–4, 29–30; number flown in support of Neptune, 140; number flown on D-Day, 30; number needed for radar site destruction and number during Radar War, 111, 112, 113, 118–19, 126; spatial settings for, 1
Soviet Union, 24, 26–27
Spaatz, Carl: aircraft industry bombing priority of (Pointblank Operation), 26, 27–28, 38, 44, 56, 63, 65–68; airpower to win war, views about, 98; Argument Operation and crippling Luftwaffe by, 28, 32, 44, 67; articles in service magazines written by, 91, 102n44; CBO implementation under and plan for completion of, 25, 28–29, 74; Cherbourg air operations support by, 183; cognitive dissonance of about morale and motivation of crews, 85, 91–98; French town bombing operations opposition by, 168–69; German industry bombing under, 26, 27–29, 32, 44; morale of crews, acceptance of views of commanders by, 9, 83, 85; opinion about Leigh-Mallory, 66–67; Strategic Air Forces command by, 26, 39; strategic bombardment support by and view of Normandy as unnecessary, 9, 28–29, 40, 83, 92, 93–94; support for Mitchell by, 22; on tactical-support role of heavy bombers, 295; target selection by to provoke German fighters, 91; Transportation Plan opposition by, 40, 44, 53, 57, 62–63, 65–69, 77, 78, 167; unification of tactical and strategic airpower under, 97–98

Spires, David, 7, 13n13, 285
Spitfire LF Mk V/LF Mk IX fighter-bombers: air support role of, 238, 240; Australian aircrews in, 307, 308–9, 311, 314, 315, 317, 319, 320, 322; capabilities of, 110–12; Cherbourg operations of, 194–95; D-Day landings support from, 155n42; Radar War role of, 105, 110–11, 126; range of, 240, 257n32; specifications for, 240; weapons carried by, 238
Spring, Operation, 266, 270
Stirling bombers and squadrons, 41, 111, 307
Strangers in Arms (Engen), 263–64
Strategic Air Forces, U.S. (USSTAF): integration into command chain, 45; Spaatz command of, 26, 39; Transportation Plan bombing operations of, 50, 53
strategic air/bombing campaign: effectiveness of, 25; industrial web theory of, 22; morale effects of, 21, 22–23, 33, 34n8, 34n14; RAF airpower theory for use of, 21, 34n8; Spaatz's focus on, 9, 28–29, 83, 91–98; struggle within Allied high command over Transportation Plan implementation or, 9, 27–29, 40–42, 44–46, 57, 62–79, 80n39, 167; unification of tactical and strategic airpower under Spaatz, 97–98; victory against Germany with, 8, 9, 284; victory as result of, 33
Suckling, Bob, 274
Sunak, Rishi, 329
Sunderland aircraft and squadrons, 307, 308, 314
Supermarine Spitfires. *See* Spitfire LF Mk V/LF Mk IX fighter-bombers
Supreme Headquarters Allied Expeditionary Force (SHAEF): command of strategic bombing forces by, 47; struggle within Allied high command over strategic bombing offensive or Transportation Plan, 9, 40–42, 44–46, 57, 62–79, 80n39
Sutherland, R. A., 246
Sword Beach, 139, 141, 158, 161, 162–63, 180, 221, 266

tactical air forces: forward-control elements, 243–47, 252, 258nn51–52; ground-based elements and organizations within, 242–43, 257n37; organization of for Normandy, 236, 241–43; radio-communication units, 242–47, 258nn51–52. *See also* Air Force, U.S. Ninth (9 AF); Royal Air Force (RAF) Second Tactical Air Force (2 TAF)
tactical airpower and air support: air support command renaming as tactical air command, 181; armed-reconnaissance missions, 251–52, 253, 259n67, 260n70, 260n81; Cherbourg air operations as misapplication of, 10, 178–79, 194, 198; complexity of and creation of system to support ground troops, 11–12; D-Day landings support with, 179; doctrine, parts, and process for, 235–37, 255n10; doctrine development from Cherbourg operations, 10, 195–98; Falaise Pocket battle and positive effects of, 276–77; importance of in Allied success in war, 179; targets and striking deeper targets, 253, 260n81; unification of tactical and strategic airpower under Spaatz, 97–98; victory against Germany with, 8. *See also* command and control (C2) of airpower
Tapp, Nigel, 268–69
Taxable, Operation, 123
Tedder, Arthur: Cherbourg air operations support by, 185; damage to German fuel capabilities, concern about, 44; deputy supreme commander role of, 38–39, 63; French civilian casualties concerns of, 48, 50, 53, 54; French town bombing operations opposition by, 168–69; Overlord command arrangements recommendation to, 69; photo of meeting of Supreme Command, 64; Transportation Plan air operations under, 45, 47, 48; Transportation Plan development and planning role of, 39, 63, 65–69, 73, 75–78; on value of airpower, 2
Terraine, John, 2, 252, 254n2
Thompson, George, 70, 72
Torch, Operation (North Africa operations), 92, 161
torpedo attacks: circling torpedo–bomber units, 216–17, 230n81, 230n88; conventional torpedo attacks, 204, 214–16, 225, 229n62
Totalize, Operation: air plan and air support request for, 259n59; friendly-fire incidents, 11, 264, 265, 271–73, 274–75, 280, 282n32; map of, 266
Tours, raids on, 42, 43, 46–47, 165, 166
Tractable, Operation, 11, 264, 265, 266, 273–76, 280
transport aircraft, 26, 30, 321–23

Transportation Plan: code name for, 38, 53, 56, 58n6; conference presentation about, 57–58n1, 58n6; criticism of and opposition from commanders, 8, 27–29, 40–42, 44–46, 53, 57, 62–79, 167; dates of bombing operations, 41–42, 57, 57–58n1; development of, 39–40, 45, 62–79, 79n8; Eisenhower's decision in favor of, 8–9, 26–29, 31–32, 45, 57, 78–79; focus and purpose of, 8, 27, 32, 38, 39, 56–57; French civilian casualties from bombing, 32, 38, 46–48, 50, 54, 56, 57, 166–67, 172; German reaction to bombing and civilian casualties from, 53–56; history, analysis, and understand of, 37–38, 44, 56–57, 57–58n1, 58n6; implementation of, 9, 29–30, 57; importance of execution of, 2, 32, 53; map of attacks, 54, 55; number of raids and sorties, 46, 60n54; outcome and results of, 31–32, 42, 43, 46, 50–57; planning meeting called by Leigh-Mallory, 69–72, 80nn27–28; political challenges and opposition from politicians, 9, 46–48, 57, 79; struggle within Allied high command over strategic bombing offensive instead of, 9, 27–29, 40–42, 44–46, 57, 62–79, 80n39, 167; target clearance by War Cabinet for, 45–48, 57, 79; target selection and list and map of targets, 39, 41–48, 50, 74–79; targets hit and tons of bombs dropped, 50, 51–53, 61n79

Trappes railway center, 42, 43, 46, 50, 50–53, 56, 72–73, 77–78, 78

Trenchard, Hugh, 20, 21, 34n8, 35n17

Trudeau, Justin, 329

Typhoon Mk Ib/Typhoon fighter-bombers: air support role of, 238, 240, 241; Australian aircrews in, 307, 321, 322; Bombphoons, 262; Cherbourg operations of, 186, 188–89, 200n26; Circular Error of Probability (CEP) and accuracy of attacks with, 119; design, modifications to, and capabilities of, 111–12, 121–22; flying flak cover for other aircraft, 112, 114–15, 122; maintenance of, 120–21; Radar War role of, 105, 111, 112, 113, 114–27, 128n11, 128n14; range of, 240; specifications for, 240; weapons carried by, 238

Utah Beach, 139, 141, 158, 161, 162, 179–80, 218, 305n19, 328

V-1 flying-bombs and launch sites, 105, 118, 316
Vallely, Edward, 122
Verrières Ridge, 270
Vietnam and Vietnam War, 6, 33, 286, 302
visual control posts (VCPs), 245–47, 248–50

Wasserman radar (Chimney), 108, 109, 112, 114, 116, 117, 126–27
weapons: air support missions, types for, 238–41; Circular Error of Probability (CEP) and accuracy of attacks with, 119; evolution of aerial weapons, 19; ground attacks with cannons and machine guns, 239; Kentucky Windage and aiming to correct for the wind, 119, 128n23; radar site attacks with cannon and machine-gun fire, 112, 127; strategic bombing to destroy and disrupt production, 22
Webster, Charles, 38, 58n3
Wells, Johnny, 120
Wells, Mark, 83–84
white feathers, 311–12, 316
Wigglesworth, Philip, 75, 80n39
Wigglesworth, W. S., 70, 71–72, 74, 80n39
Wilcox, Vanda, 86
Williams, Jack, 114–15
Williamson, Earl, Jr., 87
Windsor, Operation, 266, 267–68
Wood, Robert, 120
World War I (Great War), 19–21, 34n6, 236, 255n15
Würzburg/Giant Würzburg radar systems, 106, 107–8, 110, 112, 113, 116, 117, 120, 124, 126

Zeigler, Frank, 120
Zuckerman, Solly: on Charnwood Operation and morale of Canadian troops, 269; French civilian casualties estimate from, 54; Italian rail traffic disruption plan of, 39, 66, 72; Transportation Plan development role of, 39–40, 63–64, 66, 71, 75, 76

The Naval Institute Press is the book-publishing arm of the U.S. Naval Institute, a private, nonprofit, membership society for sea service professionals and others who share an interest in naval and maritime affairs. Established in 1873 at the U.S. Naval Academy in Annapolis, Maryland, where its offices remain today, the Naval Institute has members worldwide.

Members of the Naval Institute support the education programs of the society and receive the influential monthly magazine *Proceedings* or the colorful bimonthly magazine *Naval History* and discounts on fine nautical prints and on ship and aircraft photos. They also have access to the transcripts of the Institute's Oral History Program and get discounted admission to any of the Institute-sponsored seminars offered around the country.

The Naval Institute's book-publishing program, begun in 1898 with basic guides to naval practices, has broadened its scope to include books of more general interest. Now the Naval Institute Press publishes about seventy titles each year, ranging from how-to books on boating and navigation to battle histories, biographies, ship and aircraft guides, and novels. Institute members receive significant discounts on the Press' more than eight hundred books in print.

Full-time students are eligible for special half-price membership rates. Life memberships are also available.

For more information about Naval Institute Press books that are currently available, visit www.usni.org/press/books. To learn about joining the U.S. Naval Institute, please write to:

Member Services
U.S. Naval Institute
291 Wood Road
Annapolis, MD 21402-5034
Telephone: (800) 233-8764
Fax: (410) 571-1703
Web address: www.usni.org

www.ingramcontent.com/pod-product-compliance
Ingram Content Group UK Ltd.
Pitfield, Milton Keynes, MK11 3LW, UK
UKHW010918091025
463679UK00032B/7